This volume deals with the monetary history of Italy from its independence in 1861 to 1991 It provides the first complete analysis of a country which has experienced diverse and often dramatic monetary conditions.

Unlike the tradition of economic history in Italy where history is 'told' without reference to a specific interpretative framework and emphasises 'real' aspects in preference to nominal and monetary aspects, the authors adopt the opposite extreme of interpreting Italian monetary history through the looking glass of an economic model. Their interpretation is not entirely monetarist in flavour, but at the same time it is not wedded to a single model.

A key theme is that public finance is at the root of the (relatively) high Italian inflation rates of recent history. Professors Fratianni and Spinelli argue that the relationship between the government budget deficit and the monetary policy has been both strong and clear. They show that the monetary authorities have been dependent on government to assert an autonomous policy; more often than not they have accommodated the objective of government of financing large budget deficits at low rates of interest by excessive monetary base creation. A relentless growth of government spending, rather than sluggish tax revenues, has therefore been responsible for the budget deficits.

The book contains long time series of money aggregates that will prove useful to economic historians in general and monetary economists in particular. It combines economic theory, statistical data, analysis and history in an accessible way which covers the entire period. It contributes in a novel way not only to the monetary debate but also to fiscal and institutional questions.

A monetary history of Italy

A monetary history of Italy

Michele Fratianni and Franco Spinelli

Published by the Press Syndicate of the University of Cambridge
The Pitt Building, Trumpington Street, Cambridge CB2 1RP
40 West 20th Street, New York, NY 10011-4211, USA
10 Stamford Road, Oakleigh, Melbourne 3166, Australia

First published 1997

Printed in Great Britain at the University Press, Cambridge

A catalogue record for this book is available from the British Library

Library of Congress cataloguing in publication data

Fratianni, Michele.
    A monetary history of Italy / Michele Fratianni and Franco
Spinelli.
        p.   cm.
    Rev. ed. of: Storia monetaria d'Italia / Franco Spinelli e Michele
Fratianni. 1991.
    Includes bibliographical references.
    ISBN 0-521-44315-6
    1. Monetary policy – Italy – History.   2. Banks and banking,
Central – Italy – History.   3. Banca d'Italia – History.   I. Fratianni,
Michele.   II. Spinelli, Franco, 1949–   Storia monetaria
d'Italia.   III. Title.
HG1029.F69   1996   96-9736
                                                              CIP

ISBN 0 521 44315 6 hardback

Contents

Figures

Tables

Foreword

ANNA J. SCHWARTZ

A history of Italian monetary policy from 1861 to 1991 is a history of the Bank of Italy, the country's central bank, and its relations with the government and with other banks that serve the public. Readers of this volume will find a narrative and analytical study of the internal and external events that shaped that history. Rather than summarise what the authors have themselves done so well, let me comment on how the Bank of Italy compares with other central banks.

No two central banks are alike in structure and culture. Each bears the impress of its history. In some respects the Bank of Italy's history makes it unique. A law of 1894 required it to have a branch in each of the country's 95 provinces with a total of 99 which included two branches in Rome and Milan and one in Naples. The branches, however, are organised in 14 regional groupings, which are comparable with the 12 Federal Reserve districts, with which they share similar responsibilities for supervision of local banks, and the provision of currency and cheque clearing. Like the Federal Reserve Banks the Bank of Italy is not owned by the government. Its shareholders are banks and insurance companies.

The Bank of Italy High Council, comparable with the Federal Reserve's Open Market Committee, determines policy. It chooses the Governor subject to government approval. He can hold the office for long periods since there is no prescribed term. The Council includes the governor, who is chairman, and 13 members with no active political ties whom the shareholder banks choose to represent the regions. They serve for three years. At monthly Council meetings, a representative of the Treasury is present but does not vote.

In comparison with other western European central banks, the Bank of Italy, which did not gain a monopoly of currency issue until 1926, was a late-comer. Late as that earmark was, however, the distinguishing feature of independence from political authorities that central banks covet was not won by the Bank of Italy until even later, in the 1980s. It remains to be seen whether the bank is secure from the influence of public finances on monetary policy. As this book makes clear, monetary policy in Italy has been subservient to fiscal policy during much of the country's history. Italian governments monetised a large proportion of their chronic budget deficits and in so doing collected a substantial inflation tax.

What has helped the Bank of Italy acquire autonomy in the past few years has been the weakness of a succession of coalition governments, enabling the bank to set the discount rate most of the time. That authority was legalised in January 1992. This historic development reversed legislation of 1 May 1866, that required banks of issue – there were more than one until 1926 – to obtain government authorisation to alter the discount rate. That legislation also established the Treasury's right to bank of issue loans to maintain its current account. Since 1990 the Bank of Italy has been freed of the obligation to finance the Treasury's budget deficits, *de jure* since November 1993. It was then also authorised to set minimum reserve requirements for commercial banks. This action in Italy departs from procedures at the other central banks, notably the British, Canadian and New Zealand, which no longer rely on formal reserve requirements for monetary policy purposes.

Mention must also be made of the contributions of the European Monetary System, which Italy joined under special conditions, and the Maastricht Treaty of 1991 in support of the Bank of Italy's struggle to gain 'a degree of independence it never had in her history', to quote the authors. Reading their work will shed light on not only the economic and political forces at play but also on the role of the men who advanced or impeded that struggle.

Anna J. Schwartz

Preface

This book has been in the making for well over a decade, with each one of us interspersing monetary history with other subjects. An Italian version was published in 1991 by Mondadori. The English version is considerably shorter but has a longer horizon in that it covers the eighties up to the September 1992 currency crisis.

We owe our gratitude to many people who have read parts of our work throughout the years. The ones we cannot fail to mention are: Beniamino Andreatta, Michael Bordo, Karl Brunner, Filippo Cesarano, Paul de Grauwe, Renato de Mattia, Enzo Grilli, Gualberto Gualerni, David Laidler, Thomas Mayer, Allan Meltzer, Stefano Micossi, Manfred J.M. Neumann, Fabrizio Onida, Luigi Pasinetti, Mario Sarcinelli, Paolo Savona, Anna Schwartz, Luigi Spaventa, Richard Sylla, Paolo Sylos Labini, Vito Tanzi, Jürgen von Hagen, and Elmus Wicker. We thank Ralph Vonghia for competent translation.

Parts of the book were presented at Indiana University, University of Brescia, Catholic University of Louvain, the London School of Economics, University of Western Ontario, Board of Governors of the Federal Reserve System, Banca d'Italia, International Monetary Fund, Konstanz Seminar on Monetary Theory and Policy, University of Cagliari, University of Venice, Bocconi University, University of Rome- Tor Vergata, the NBER Money Workshop, University of Trento, and ISPE.

We are grateful for financial support received from the Banca Credito Agrario Bresciano; and the juries of the Scanno Prize (1991) and the St. Vincent Prize (1992) for having deemed us worthy of their first prizes for the Italian volume.

1 Structure, main themes and data of the monetary history

This study deals with the monetary history of Italy from 1861 to 1991, a span of 131 years. An earlier version of the *History* was published in 1991 in Italian by Mondadori. This version differs from the Italian version in two respects: it is temporally longer in that we treat the 1980s, whereas the Italian version stops in 1980; and it is more compact, having eliminated many historical details that we judged to be of lesser interest to an English-speaking audience.

Several reasons inspired us to write this *History*. First, traditionally the economic history of Italy is 'told' without reference to a specific interpretative framework. When a framework is used, the preference is for microeconomics rather than macroeconomics. That is, Italian economic history emphasises 'real' aspects in preference to nominal and monetary aspects, which are the proper domain of macroeconomics. Hence, we felt that this book would fill a vacuum. We did not want to fill this vacuum by going to the opposite extreme of interpreting the Italian monetary history through the looking glass of a single model. While our interpretation is monetarist on balance, we are not wedded to a single model. Our purpose is to interpret monetary history with reference to alternative economic models.

The second reason involves the quality of the monetary debate and the state of monetary policy in Italy. After the 'high' point of the 1950s, the following years were marked by deterioration both in debate and policy. From a theoretical viewpoint, the concept of money lost its importance and was substituted by the fuzzier concept of domestic credit. Credit, in practice, provided the technical backdrop for a monetary policy that progressively became subservient to the financing requirements of the public sector. The nadir of monetary permissiveness occurred in the 1970s, when the Italian monetary authority was no more than an extension of the Treasury and inflation reached its highest level in post-war times. At the end of the seventies, an intellectual and institutional turnaround began that, over a period of several years, would lead to a more independent (from the Treasury) central bank, and progressively tighter control of the money stock yielded a greater degree of monetary stability. The critical moments were the decision to join the European Monetary System (EMS) in 1979 and the so-called 'divorce' in 1981 of the Banca d'Italia (BI) from the Italian Treasury, which would free the central bank from being a residual buyer of government securities at the auctions.

Predecessors

This is not the first systematic monetary history of Italy since political unification, although the others have had a much more limited temporal horizon than ours. Among those histories, the most notable are those by Supino (1895, 1929), Alberti and Cornaro (1931), Corbino (1931 and 1938) and Di Nardi (1953). Supino relies on an informal structure – a methodology that well suits the times – and few statistics. The data he uses pertain to bank currency, loans (*anticipazioni*), the exchange rate and the government budget. Information on prices is scanty.

Alberti and Cornaro put more emphasis on the role of the government budget deficit and the relationship between Italy and the rest of the world. Interpretation of the events is mostly institutional. The five volumes published by Epicarmo Corbino are much more analytical and detailed than the other studies. The author provides a wealth of institutional and statistical information to buttress his arguments. Di Nardi analyses the banks of issue since 1893 and makes better use of theory than Alberti and Cornaro. The dominant theme of the study is the interaction between banks of issue and the political authority. The latter facilitates the creation and development of these banks but also uses them for political ends.

Organisation of the book

The book consists of two parts. The first part, which includes chapters 1 and 2, has the dual objective of discussing the data bank we have constructed and presenting the main topics of the monetary history. Chapter 1 is a general theme chapter. Chapter 2 looks at the central theme of our subject, that is, money growth and its determinants over the 131-year history. The long time series are displayed either graphically or in tabular form. The actual monetary statistics have been placed in an appendix to chapter 2 and are intended for those interested readers who would like to duplicate our results or go beyond them.[1]

The second part of the book, consisting of chapters 3 through 10, provides the actual account and interpretation of the main events according to a seven-period classification: from political unification to 1913 (chapter 3), the First World War (chapter 4), the inter-war period (chapter 5), the

Second World War and the stabilisation of 1947 (chapter 6), the fifties and sixties (chapter 7), the seventies (chapter 8) and the eighties (chapter 9). Conclusions are drawn in chapter 10.

Space limitations prevented us from including a third part, which would have been dedicated to a critical assessment of the thinking of the four Governors – Donato Menichella, Guido Carli, Paolo Baffi and Carlo Azeglio Ciampi – who have led BI since the Second World War. We refer interested readers with a knowledge of Italian to consult Spinelli and Fratianni (1991, chapters 11, 12 and 13), where the philosophy of the first three governors is dissected through the looking glass of Banca d'Italia's Annual Reports.

In light of the substantial amount of new data we had to collect for the *History*, we begin with a detailed account of definitions, methods and sources of our monetary statistics, followed by other statistics. We then present the stylised facts of the *History*, starting with an international comparison, then a consideration of the behaviour of the four variables that enter into the exchange equation and end with a discussion of Italian public finance.

The monetary statistics of the history

The construction of long time series across a variety of 'regimes' and with a financial system in continuous evolution is bound to pose conceptual and statistical difficulties. Over the 131-year history under consideration Italy has swung from the gold standard to an inconvertible fiat money; alternated periods of fixed exchange rates with periods of flexible rates; and experimented alternatively with interest-rate, domestic-credit and monetary-base targeting. To complicate matters, form and substance at times have been at odds; witness times (such as in the early part of the twentieth century) when the regime was one of inconvertible paper money *de jure* but gold standard *de facto* (Fratianni and Spinelli 1984). Last but not least, Italy had several financial institutions acting as banks of issue until 1926, each one in competition with the other (Fratianni and Spinelli 1985). Only in 1926 did BI emerge as the issue monopolist.[2] The competitive nature of 'central banking' and the overlap between central banking and ordinary banking further complicate matters.

Banks also evolved over the 131-year history. At first, non-issue banks wrote deposit notes against specie and extended loans over a very restricted geographical area. The local or provincial character of these banks can be inferred from their charter labels: 'popular' banks, 'rural' banks, 'pawn' banks and so on. To be sure, there were banks whose activities extended over the city, the province, or even the region; but these tended to be issue

banks rather than ordinary depository institutions. As the economic integration of the country deepened, banks acquired an increasingly national
character. Today, the banking system is dominated by a few institutions
with branches over a large part of the nation. Indeed, the large banks –
Banca Commerciale Italiana, Credito Italiano, Banco di Roma and Banca
Nazionale del Lavoro among others – are present virtually everywhere in
the country.

The economic crisis of the 1930s provided the impetus for a great deal of
government intervention in the financial system. Government went into
banking in a big way. Besides acquiring the largest depository banks – those
mentioned above – government prescribed what activities banks could do,
following the pattern of the United States and other countries. Depository
banks were disallowed to own equities of private corporations but were
allowed to employ their funds in either government or quasi-government
paper or in loans to the private sector with a maturity of less than eighteen
months.[3] For longer maturities the legislator created a new class of financial
institutions, so-called special credit institutions (*istituti di credito speciale*),
which were prohibited, however, from tapping the money market.

In essence, the Banking Law of 1936, which still regulates most financial
transactions in modern Italy, aimed at separating the money market from
the bond market. One class of institutions, the so-called ordinary credit institutions (*aziende di credito ordinario*) could issue liabilities in the form of sight
and term deposits at regulated maximum rates of interest to finance the
private sector on a short-term basis. The second class of institutions, the
most representative being the Istituto Mobiliare Italiano, could venture into
long-term commitments but were impeded from issuing deposit liabilities.
The formal overlap between the two classes of financial institutions resided
in their unrestricted ability to buy government and quasi-government paper,
regardless of maturity. The actual overlap stemmed from the practical
impossibility of distinguishing between short and long-term loans, given the
widespread banking practice of rolling over loans at maturity.

The basic distinction between ordinary credit institutions and special
credit institutions does not lie on the assets side but on the liability side of
the balance sheets; the former have deposit-type liabilities, the latter bond-
type liabilities. It is on the basis of this distinction that our study includes the
ordinary credit institutions but not the special credit institutions.

The monetary base

The monetary base consists of a collection of ultimate medium-of-exchange
assets. The monetary base can be thought of as the apex of an inverted
pyramid containing assets with different degrees of moneyness, wherein the

distance away from the apex measures the loss of moneyness relative to the monetary base. All assets can be exchanged into monetary base but at a variable price. Monetary-base assets give the holder an information and transaction advantage for which one bears an opportunity cost expressed in terms of foregone interest. This definition is broad enough to accommodate commodity as well as fiduciary standards and, among fiduciary standards, institutional arrangements with a single monetary authority, with several but cooperating monetary authorities – as is true in modern Italy – or competing central banks – as was true until 1926.

For purposes of presentation, we find it useful to discuss the process generating the monetary base by starting with modern Italy, that is, the period after the Second World War. Four institutions act as monetary authorities in modern Italy: BI, the Ufficio Italiano dei Cambi (UIC or Italian Exchange Office), the Treasury, and the Cassa Depositi e Prestiti (hereafter Cassa DD.PP). BI was created in 1893 as a result of the merger of Banca Nazionale nel Regno d'Italia with Banca Nazionale Toscana and Banca Toscana di Credito per le Industrie e il Commercio d'Italia. BI acquired the liabilities of the failed Banca Romana and competed with Banco di Sicilia and Banco di Napoli as a bank of issue until 1926. In that year it became the monopolist of issue. UIC was created in 1945 with complete authority to regulate the foreign exchange markets and manage the country's foreign reserves and exchange rates.[4] Although there is a formal separation between BI and UIC, in practice UIC is best described as part of BI. The Governor of BI is the ex-officio President of UIC; the Bank provides, in addition, the bureaucratic apparatus for UIC to execute interventions in the foreign exchange markets. So integrated are the activities of these two authorities that their balance sheets are often shown on a consolidated basis.

The Cassa DD.PP is an independent unit of the Treasury that grants loans to local governments and obtains funds by accepting postal deposits. As in the case of UIC, the independence of the Cassa DD.PP is merely formal; in fact, the minister of the Treasury is the ex-officio chairman of the Board of Directors of the Cassa. The Treasury is clearly primus inter pares within the set of institutions that we call monetary authorities. The activity of BI falls under the direct jurisdiction of the Treasury minister who also presides over the Interministerial Committee for Credit and Saving (CICR), the highest decision-making body in matters of saving, credit and foreign exchange in Italy. Both law and custom, however, give the Governor of BI a degree of policy freedom. The policy freedom or independence of BI is not comparable to that of the Bundesbank (Alesina and Summers 1993; Fratianni and Huang 1995).

Table 1.1 summarises the essential information on the sources and uses of the monetary base, MB, at the end of 1968. The table is the consolidation of

Table 1.1 *The monetary base at the end of 1968 (billions of lire)*

A1:	sum of all previous budget deficits	14,640	L1:	coins and currency held by the public	5,260
	bonds owned by public	−2,684	L2:	deposits of the public with Treasury, Cassa DD.PP.	
	bonds owned by banks	−2,997			
A2:	loans and advances to banks	1,828		BI-UIC plus Treasury bills	41
A3:	other assets minus other liabilities	−426	L3:	postal deposits of the public	5,266
A4:	net foreign assets of BI-UIC	3,770	L4:	coins and currency held by banks	323
A5:	convertible foreign exchange of banks	266	L5:	deposits of banks with BI	140
			L6:	deposits of banks with Treasury and Cassa DD.PP	178
			L7:	banks' credit line with BI	511
			L8:	banks' convertible foreign exchange	266
			L9:	banks' deposits with BI to meet reserve requirements	2,412
Sum sources		14,397	Sum uses		14,397

Note: Consolidation of tables 2 and 3 of the appendix.
Source: See appendix.

an idealised balance sheet of the Treasury, Cassa DD.PP and government corporations and the consolidated balance sheet of BI and UIC, in essence the consolidation of the activities of the four Italian agencies acting as monetary authorities. The separate accounts and a detailed description of the institutional process underlying them can be found in the appendix to this chapter.

The left-hand side of table 1.1 shows the sources of the monetary base, identified as 'As'; the right-hand side the uses, identified as 'Ls'. Statistically, the construction of the monetary base from the uses side is considerably easier than from the sources side. This is the approach we have followed ourselves. Items L1 through L9 are available on a monthly basis for most of the period after the Second World War. Before the war the statistical endowment is much narrower; institutions change and, hence, the monetary base cannot be reconstructed with the details shown in the table.

Furthermore, L1 is not based on an independent observation but is

calculated as the difference between total coins and currency outstanding
and L4. On the sources side, items A2, A4 and A5 are also available for most
of the period following the Second World War; A1 and A3 are not. We have
actually collected A4 and A5, which we label the foreign source component,
and then obtained A1+A2+A3, the domestic source component, by subtracting the foreign source component from MB.

It is useful for analytical purposes to group items on the uses side of table
1.1. The monetary base held by the public, BP, is the sum of L1 through L3

$$BP=L1+L2+L3, \tag{1.1}$$

where L1 is total currency outstanding minus L4.
The sum of L4 through L8 represents what is known in the American literature as excess reserves, BE

$$BE=L4+L5+L6+L7+L8, \tag{1.2}$$

whereas item L9 is required reserves, BR

$$BR=L9. \tag{1.3}$$

Using (1.1), (1.2) and (1.3) we obtain the monetary base

$$MB=BP+BE+BR. \tag{1.4}$$

Recalling our discussion of the sources side of table 1.1 and denoting the
domestic and foreign source components by BD and BF, respectively, we
write two additional identities

$$BF=A4+A5 \tag{1.5}$$

$$BD=MB-BF, \tag{1.6}$$

where (1.6) is written so as to emphasise that the domestic source component is calculated as a residual and not through independent observations.
The domestic component of the monetary base can be sub-divided into
lending by the monetary authority to the Treasury, $MBTR$ and lending to
banks and other non-government entities, $MBOT$

$$BD=MBTR+MBOT. \tag{1.7}$$

$MBTR$ was quantified as the non-interest-bearing component of the
national debt

$$DEBT=S+MBTR, \tag{1.8}$$

where $DEBT$ equals the stock of national debt created by the central government and S is interest-bearing debt held by the private sector. $MBTR$
consists of paper notes and coins issued by the Treasury; loans made by the

monetary authorities to the Treasury; loans made by the Cassa DD.PP, banks of public law (*di diritto pubblico*), such as Banco di Napoli and Banco di Sicilia, and the national insurance fund; and the stock of postal deposits held by the public which are direct liabilities of the Treasury. The non-Treasury component of the domestic monetary base, *MBOT*, was calculated with the aid of identity (1.7).

The money stock

The money stock is defined as the sum of the monetary base held by the public plus all bank deposits (D), regardless of whether they are on demand or at term. We consider the distinction between demand and term accounts somewhat artificial in Italy because the checking account did not develop into an important medium of exchange. More importantly, we are unable to identify over the entire period the relative costs of holding sight versus term deposits to such a degree as to test for differences in behaviour.

$$M = BP + D. \tag{1.9a}$$

In the inclusive definition of the monetary base, postal deposits are part of *BP*. In the exclusive definition, postal deposits (D^{pos}) are part of the money stock but not of the monetary base (BP^{ex})

$$M = BP^{ex} + D^{pos} + D. \tag{1.9b}$$

Sources and statistical issues

De Mattia (1969, 1977), using original documents of the banks of issue and of BI, has constructed the balance sheets of the banks of issue. These balance sheets are crucial for our calculation of the monetary base and the money stock. De Mattia's work, unfortunately, stops in 1936. Beyond this date we relied on the annual reports and *Bollettino Statistico* of BI and/or on ISTAT (1976). In several instances we had to decide among alternative series collected with different criteria or to interpolate when no observations were found. We tried to preserve the integrity of the time series over the 131-year history but not to the point of writing a number even when we thought it nonsensical.

Certain series dry up as one goes back in time because the concept no longer applies. This is the case with required reserves before 1946. Indeed, for most of the *History* we cannot distinguish between BE and BR; the series becomes simply bank-held monetary base. Up until 1936, the latter consists only of coins and paper currency. We could not construct a series of deposits kept by ordinary banks with banks of issue. The entire amount of deposit liabilities *vis-à-vis* the private sector of the banks of issue was attributed to the public until 1945. Hence, for the period 1861–1945, L2, which is supposed to quantify deposits that the public kept with the monetary authorities, overstates the true but unknown L2 to the extent that banks' deposits with banks of issue are included in the measured L2. By implication, L5, which is supposed to quantify banks' deposits with banks of issue, understates the true but unknown L5. Note that this measurement error affects the distribution of the monetary base between the public and the banks, not its total size. The effect of the measurement error on the money multiplier is ambiguous: the fact that the measured public-held monetary base is higher than the true value will tend to lower the money multiplier, but the understatement of the measured bank-held monetary base will tend to raise the money multiplier.

The definition of the monetary base used in the *History* is consistent with that employed by BI for the period after the Second World War. Our presentation has deliberately maintained this conformity. Postal deposits are part of the monetary base (cf. Fratianni 1972). However, in the 1980s, the Bank preferred to downplay the monetary base inclusive of postal deposits up to the point that in the latest Annual Reports the inclusive definition has disappeared altogether. While we maintain that postal deposits ought to be included in the monetary base, we will employ the exclusive definition as well.[5]

The stock of international reserves is equal to the foreign source component of the monetary base for the entire period under consideration, except in the modern period when BI–UIC determine how much of the banks' foreign exchange is eligible for lire conversion. More to the point, the stock of international reserves, IR, is

$$IR = A4 + A5 + \text{banks' foreign exchange not eligible}$$
$$\text{for lire conversion.} \tag{1.10}$$

The ratio of BF to IR is less than or equal to one. When $BF = IR$, the entire amount of banks' foreign exchange is eligible for an immediate cash in; when BF is less than IR only part of this foreign exchange can be cashed in at the Bank.

Other statistics

The behaviour of the public sector is central in the *History*. As a tax collector, purchaser of goods and services and dispenser of subsidies and transfer payments, the government influences the economy in many different ways. Over the period under consideration, government has grown both in absolute size and in relation to the private economy (Fratianni and Spinelli

1982). Another aspect of government, which is of direct interest to us, concerns its influence over the financial markets, that is, the markets for money and bonds. When government expenditures exceed tax revenues, government incurs a debt which can take the form of interest-bearing claims (e.g., bonds) and non-interest-bearing ones (e.g., currency). The markets for bonds and money are affected by the financing of the budget deficit.

As in the case of the monetary statistics, the data pertaining to the public finances of the nation were not ready made for analysis. A substantial amount of resources and time was invested in the collection of relevant information. In some instances we relied on primary sources; in other cases we employed data elaborated upon by scholars who, having acquired a high degree of specialisation in public-sector accounting, corrected the published data to eliminate known omissions.

Public-sector accounting makes the distinction between accrual and cash budgets: the first refers to legislated expenditures and expected tax revenues, the latter to expenditures actually incurred and taxes actually collected. Whether one type of budget is preferable to the other depends on the objective of the research. Given the emphasis of the *History* on financial markets, the cash budget was the obvious choice.

Another distinction made by public-sector accounting involves the current and capital accounts. In the former, one records transactions of the nature of current consumption (e.g., pay for the army), while, in the latter, one records transactions which generate benefits accruing over a period of several years (e.g., roads). The distinction is useful to quantify the investment components of government expenditures. However, this accounting separation has greatly reduced any intended benefits. Subsidies to firms on the brink of bankruptcy are classified as capital expenditures, whereas they are little more than transfer payments designed to maintain the level of current consumption of individuals owning and working for the firms. Partly because of this dubious practice and partly because of the financial emphasis of the *History*, we decided to ignore the distinction between current and capital accounts.

A final distinction made by public-sector accounting concerns the levels of government. The public sector is the broadest category of what is conveniently referred to as government, including the State, regions, provinces, cities and government corporations. The length of our sample period made it impossible to collect statistics on the inclusive definition of the public sector. The dictated choice fell on the narrow definition of central government.

Time series on total cash expenditures, G, and tax revenues, T, of the central government were compiled using the data in Repaci (1962) for the period 1861–1959, ISTAT's *Annuario Statistico Italiano* and BI's *Relazioni Annuali* (RA) or Annual Reports for the remaining years.[6] All observations refer to calendar year.[7] Current expenditures and taxes are on an accrual basis from 1861 to 1931, capital expenditures and taxes from 1861 to 1914; otherwise on a cash basis.

The sum of all government deficits is theoretically equal to the national debt created by the central government. According to (1.8) above, government debt is equal to the sum of privately held debt (S) and debt held by the central bank. S, in turn, is measured as

$$S = S(d) + eS(f), \tag{1.11}$$

where $S(d)$ is interest-bearing debt held domestically, $S(f)$ is interest-bearing debt denominated in foreign currency and e is the exchange rate expressed as the domestic price of foreign currency.

The variable $S(d)$ consists of consols (*consolidati*), bonds with a fixed maturity (*redimibili*), multi-year Treasury notes (*Buoni del Tesoro Poliennali*) and short-term Treasury bills (*Buoni del Tesoro Ordinari*) net of the stock held by the monetary authorities. The sources are ISTAT's *Annuario Statistico Italiano* (various issues) and BI's *Bollettino Statistico*.[8]

Foreign debt, $eS(f)$, consists of bank loans and bonds in foreign currency contracted by central government and para-governmental units like the Italian Railroads, Cassa del Mezzogiorno, Istituto Mobiliare Italiano and Consorzio di Credito per le Opere Pubbliche. The obligations of these institutions are included because they are backed by the central government. While the sources of $eS(f)$ are the same as for the domestically held debt, the quality of the data is inferior and, hence, the unknown errors of measurement are presumed to be higher.[9]

Theoretically, the change in debt is equal to the government deficit. In practice, it is not likely to be. Several factors account for the discrepancy: (i) some expenditure categories are off-budget; (ii) prices of Treasury bonds can be below or above par, whereas the stock of government debt is valued at par; (iii) exchange-rate changes can raise or lower the domestic-currency value of foreign debt in relation to the value when debt was initially incurred; and (iv) budget accounting methods may not be compatible with debt methods.

In our estimation, the four factors are in decreasing order of importance. Item (i) works in the direction of making the difference between G and T understate the true budget deficit. The bias introduced by item (ii) is ambiguous. If debt is issued primarily below par, the first difference of *DEBT*, *dDEBT*, overstates the true deficit; the opposite is true if debt is issued above par. Items (iii) and (iv) may have introduced temporary distortive effects, especially when Italy was a heavy foreign borrower. Our judgement is that the first item dominates and accounts for the fact that the average sample value of government deficits, measured by *dDEBT*, is higher than $(G - T)$. We opted to measure government deficit by *dDEBT*.

Italy's income, denoted by Y, is the net national income (ISTAT 1976; ISCO, *Quadri della contabilità nazionale* 1960–80) up to 1980 and the gross domestic product (BI R.A. 1991) for the remainder. The price level, P, is the net national income deflator up to 1980 and the gross domestic product deflator for the remainder. Real income is Y/P. Real income of the rest of the world is equal to the UK real income from 1861 to 1945 and the US real income for the remainder. UK real income is measured by an index of industrial production from 1861 to 1868 (Mitchell 1962) and by the real income variable used by Friedman and Schwartz (1982) for the years 1869–1945. For US real income the source is again Friedman and Schwartz (1982) for the period up to 1975; real net national product from 1976 to 1980 (ISCO, *Quadri della contabilità nazionale*), and by real gross domestic product for the remainder (Economic Report of the President 1992).

The price level of the rest of the world, P^*, is the French wholesale price level from 1861 to 1913 (Mitchell 1978), the UK income deflator for the years 1914–45 (Friedman and Schwartz 1982), the US income deflator (Friedman and Schwartz 1982) from 1946 to 1975, the net national product deflator from 1976 to 1980 (ISCO, *Quadri della contabilità nazionale*), and the gross domestic product deflator for the remainder (Economic Report of the President 1992).

The Italian market rate of interest, i, is the average annual yield of the *Rendita Italiana* from 1861 to 1913 (De Mattia 1978), and the average yield of the *Buoni del Tesoro poliennali* for the remainder (BI, *Bollettino Statistico*). So, the Italian interest rate is a long-term government bond yield. The market rate of interest of the rest of the world, i^*, is the long-term French interest rate (De Mattia 1978) from 1861 to 1913, the yield on high-grade corporate bonds from 1914 to 1975 (Friedman and Schwartz 1982), and the yield on US Aaa corporate bonds for the remainder (Economic Report of the President 1992). Thus, the foreign interest rate includes a small default risk, whereas the Italian rate does not.

The same periodisation of foreign prices and interest rates was employed to calculate the exchange rate, e, measured as the lira price of foreign currency: i.e., the lira/French franc rate from 1861 to 1913 (Spinelli and Fratianni 1991; Borgatta 1933; ISTAT, *Annuario Statistico Italiano* 1955), the lira/pound rate from 1914 to 1945 (ISTAT, *Annuario Statistico Italiano* 1955) and the lira/dollar for the remainder (IMF, *International Financial Statistics*).

The periods

We have partitioned the 131 years of the *History* into seven distinct sub-periods, which are discussed in seven separate chapters (chapters 3 through 9): 1861–1913, 1914–20, 1921–37, 1938–49, 1950–69, 1970–80, and 1981–91. The first sub-period, 1861–1913, approximately coincides with what is known in the literature as the international gold standard regime. For convenience, we will adopt this label, although Italy spent more time off than on the gold standard. The peculiarity of the Italian 'gold standard' period is the competitive nature of several banks of issue. BI emerged in 1893 when three banks of issue, including the Piedmontese Banca Nazionale, merged to take over the assets and liabilities of the failed Banca Romana. For 33 additional years, that is, until 1926, BI had to share the right to issue currency with Banco di Napoli and Banco di Sicilia.

The sub-periods 1914–20 and 1938–49 deal with the monetary and fiscal consequences of two world wars. As one would expect, at these times the economy was subject to large shocks, real as well as nominal. The inter-war years of 1921–37 were rich in policy and institutional innovations. The Fascist regime implemented a strong stabilisation programme to squelch the inflation legacy left by the First World War. The aim of policy was to return Italy to the gold standard and to restructure industry. In addition, the legislation of 1926 and the Bank Act of 1936 fundamentally redesigned the banking regulatory framework. Similar activity went on in other countries as regulators tried to respond to the economic and financial crises of the thirties.

The period 1950–69 coincided approximately with the Bretton Woods regime. This was a relatively prosperous phase of Italian monetary history, although in the latter half of the sixties BI began to pursue objectives that were inconsistent with price stability and fell prey to 'stop-and-go' policies. The seventies stand out in the *History* because they combined negative supply shocks (the two oil price increases), a high inflationary process and a fortress disposition on the part of the monetary authorities. The latter issued a spate of administrative directives that placed a straight jacket on the banking system and isolated Italian financial markets from those abroad. The exogenous force was the rapidly rising government debt; Italian monetary authorities accommodated fiscal profligacy by pursuing a ·policy of 'cheap' interest rates.

In the eighties the monetary authorities made a turnaround, by acquiring an increasing degree of monetary-policy independence from the fiscal authorities. In that they were aided by the external constraint of the European Monetary System and an enlightened Treasury Minister.

In addition, we also consider two broader sub-periods: the years when several banks of issue co-existed and competed with one another (1861–1925) and the monopoly-of-issue years (1926–91).

International comparisons

It is now time to outline the basic quantitative story of the *Monetary History* in an international perspective. To that end we have prepared table 1.2 wherein key Italian macroeconomic variables are compared with those of the Rest of the World (ROW). In creating ROW time series we had the option of either isolating an important country which would act as a 'representative' rest of the world or go for aggregation that would include a group of foreign countries. While a broader aggregate would have been preferable to the representative country, data availability would have severely limited the usefulness of this approach. We decided to give precedence to the 'cleaner' data of a representative foreign country rather than the 'dirtier' data of a larger set of countries.

Our representative countries are France, the United Kingdom and the United States. Each one, in different historical phases, fulfills the role of 'representative' ROW country. More specifically, ROW real income is the UK real income from 1861 to 1945 and the US real income from 1946 to 1991. For ROW price levels, market interest rates and the exchange rate, France is the representative country from 1861 to 1913, the UK from 1914 to 1945 and the US from 1946 to 1991.

Italian output growth is, on average, not different from the ROW output growth during the 131-year history. Italy grows less rapidly than the ROW in the nineteenth century and more rapidly in the twentieth century. The positive growth differential is particularly high during the First World War and the Bretton Woods period 1950–69. On the other hand, economic growth is more volatile in Italy than in the ROW, except in the two periods of higher average growth. It turned out that the Bretton Woods period was a particularly felicitous one, combining relatively high growth and low variability.

A different story emerges for inflation: the average annual Italian inflation rate exceeds the ROW's by 5 percentage points. The positive inflation differential was contained to 1 percentage point in the gold standard and the Bretton Woods years. The twentieth century displays more relative inflation than the nineteenth century, with the seventies recording the highest average inflation differential in peacetime. Also, average inflation was almost three times as high after BI became the issue monopolist than before.[10] Average and variability of inflation tend to be positively correlated, a rather common finding.

The depreciation of the lira in the exchange markets falls somewhat short of the inflation differential: the exchange rate accommodates about 80 per cent of the differences in the rates of inflation. Thus, on average, the lira tends to appreciate in real terms. The most acute phases of real lira appreciation occurred in the 1970s and the 1980s.

Table 1.2 International comparisons (annual percentage changes)

Periods	Real income			Prices			Nominal ex. rate	Nominal interest rates			Real interest rates			Real ex. rate
	Italy	ROW	diff.	Italy	ROW	diff.		Italy	ROW	diff.	Italy	ROW	diff.	
1862–1991														
Mean	2.16	2.18	−0.02	6.90	1.99	4.91	4.06	6.46	4.63	1.83	0.52	2.81	−2.28	−0.85
Standard dev.	6.54	3.64	7.52	14.38	5.58	12.77	17.29	2.92	2.31	1.34	11.35	5.33	9.70	12.32
1862–1913														
Mean	1.26	2.25	−0.99	0.65	−0.39	1.04	0.02	5.13	3.64	1.50	4.64	4.11	0.53	−1.01
St. dev.	3.94	3.00	4.84	5.63	4.15	5.34	2.54	1.60	0.70	1.17	5.83	4.32	5.42	5.06
1914–20														
Mean	0.00	−1.67	1.67	21.10	14.01	7.09	15.77	4.88	4.26	0.61	−13.78	−8.66	−5.12	8.68
St. dev.	4.30	6.27	7.79	12.68	7.40	6.13	21.15	0.83	0.57	0.35	10.20	6.17	4.90	18.11
1921–37														
Mean	2.21	2.03	0.18	0.06	−2.84	2.91	1.13	5.74	3.99	1.75	5.96	7.02	−1.05	−1.78
St. dev.	4.29	4.89	6.04	7.84	5.18	8.76	14.04	0.61	0.67	0.49	8.12	5.92	9.21	10.24
1938–49														
Mean	0.57	1.28	−0.71	32.75	4.69	28.06	26.88	5.98	2.98	3.00	−20.21	−1.53	−18.68	−1.18
St. dev.	18.63	4.30	20.75	29.67	4.21	30.41	43.40	0.71	0.36	0.84	20.92	3.92	21.40	32.19
1950–69														
Mean	5.59	3.93	1.67	3.62	2.5	1.12	0.3	5.74	3.92	1.82	2.20	1.46	0.74	−0.83
St. dev.	1.44	2.66	2.75	2.02	1.36	12.28	1.27	0.56	1.01	1.37	2.05	1.40	2.40	2.42

Table 1.2 (cont.)

Periods	Real income			Prices			Nominal ex. rate	Nominal interest rates			Real interest rates			Real ex. rate
	Italy	ROW	diff.	Italy	ROW	diff.		Italy	ROW	diff.	Italy	ROW	diff.	
1970–80														
Mean	3.23	2.26	0.97	12.95	6.72	6.23	2.83	10.04	8.01	2.03	-2.06	1.51	-3.57	-3.40
St. dev	3.15	2.52	3.11	4.66	1.25	4.05	8.49	2.93	1.30	2.07	2.37	0.81	2.27	6.54
1981–91														
Mean	2.12	2.21	-0.09	9.72	4.51	5.22	3.37	13.11	10.30	2.80	3.89	5.91	-2.01	-1.85
St. dev.	1.19	2.35	1.91	4.2	1.87	2.99	15.58	3.20	1.81	1.61	0.88	1.3	1.4	14.04
1862–1925														
Mean	1.32	1.80	-0.48	3.25	0.63	2.62	2.44	5.16	3.77	1.39	2.33	3.38	-1.04	-0.18
St. dev.	3.97	3.88	5.24	9.23	6.98	6.44	8.91	1.49	0.72	1.10	8.58	6.81	6.43	8.14
1926–91														
Mean	2.97	2.54	0.43	10.44	3.32	7.12	5.63	7.72	5.47	2.24	-1.23	2.26	-3.49	-1.50
St. dev.	8.26	3.39	9.23	17.38	3.32	16.54	22.62	3.39	2.93	1.42	13.34	3.29	11.99	15.37

Notes:

ROW indicates rest of the world, computed as follows. For real income the UK real income from 1861 to 1945 and then US real income.

For prices, French wholesale prices from 1861 to 1913, UK price deflator from 1914 to 1945 and US price deflator for the remainder.

For nominal interest rates, French, UK and US long-term interest rates using the same periodization utilized for prices.

Real interest rates were calculated subtracting the growth of prices from nominal interest rates in the same time period.

The nominal exchange rate was computed using the lira/French franc, lira/pound and lira/dollar exchange rates with the same periodization applied to prices. The percentage change in the real exchange rate is equal to the percentage change of the nominal exchange rate plus ROW inflation rate minus Italian inflation rate.

Market interest rates in Italy tend to be higher than in the ROW, but not sufficiently high to fully compensate for the inflation differential. On average, real interest rates were 2.3 percentage points lower in Italy than in the ROW. The largest negative differentials were recorded during the two world wars and the 1970s and 1980s, that is, when the country tried to isolate its financial markets from those abroad. On the other hand, during the gold standard and Bretton Woods years, the differential was positive.

In sum, exchange-rate regimes affect the relative performance in Italy. During the years of the gold standard and Bretton Woods, nominal variables behave roughly in line with those of the ROW. An Italian diversity or peculiarity emerges in the inter-war years and more so in the 1970s and the 1980s when domestic inflation was markedly higher, domestic real interest markedly lower and the lira appreciated in real terms.[11] The 1970s, more than any other historical phase, fit the characterisation of a 'national preference' for (relatively) high inflation, low interest rates and financial market segmentation.

The variables of the exchange equation

The four variables that enter into the exchange equation – money, velocity, price level and output – are critical macroeconomic variables of a monetary history (cf. Friedman and Schwartz 1963). We shall refer to them throughout our work and address the important issue of what causes what. Here we simply want to offer the reader the broadest patterns of the variables (table 1.3).

Velocity has a negative trend, or, more precisely, an average annual growth of –1.4 per cent. As figure 1.1 indicates, the decline in velocity is particularly sharp in the nineteenth century. In 1861 velocity was 6.23 and equal to 8.3 weeks of national income. By 1889 it had dropped to 1.88, or 27.6 weeks of national income. Over this period deposits were growing more rapidly than currency, reflecting the fact that Italians banked more. After 1889, velocity continued to decline until 1978 when it reached its lowest value (0.8). The persistent fall in velocity is consistent with the hypothesis of money being a luxury good, a finding of the empirical literature on the demand for money (Spinelli 1980; Calliari, Spinelli and Verga 1984). This phenomenon is not unique to Italy; in fact, in their *A Monetary History of the United States* Milton Friedman and Anna Schwartz (1963) obtain a similar result.

Table 1.3 suggests that velocity growth tends to correlate positively with inflation. In fact, velocity growth slows down when the inflation rate rises and/or people perceive accelerating future prices. During the Second World War period, velocity actually took an upward jump as inflation reached

Table 1.3 *The exchange equation (annual percentage changes)*

Periods	Money	Velocity	Prices	Real income
1862–1991				
Mean	10.49	−1.42	6.90	2.16
St. dev.	10.48	9.44	14.38	6.54
1862–1913				
Mean	4.44	−2.53	0.65	1.26
St. dev.	5.41	7.58	5.63	3.94
1914–20				
Mean	22.72	−1.62	21.10	0.00
St. dev.	9.91	12.32	12.68	4.30
1921–37				
Mean	3.27	−1.00	0.06	2.21
St. dev.	5.13	9.64	7.84	4.29
1938–49				
Mean	30.42	2.89	32.75	0.57
St. dev.	12.49	21.51	29.67	18.63
1950–69				
Mean	12.36	−3.15	3.62	5.59
St. dev.	2.19	2.78	2.02	1.44
1970–80				
Mean	17.39	−1.21	12.95	3.23
St. dev.	3.23	6.32	4.66	3.15
1981–91				
Mean	10.35	1.5	9.72	2.12
St. dev.	2.61	2.97	4.20	1.19
1862–1925				
M.S.	6.57	−2.00	3.25	1.32
Dev. St.	8.30	8.31	9.23	3.97
1926–91				
M.S.	14.28	−0.86	10.44	2.97
Dev. St.	10.68	10.46	17.38	8.26

Notes:
Money is defined as the sum of notes, coins, demand and time bank deposits and postal deposits. Prices are measured by the real income deflator. Real income is obtained by the ratio of nominal income to the price deflator. Nominal income is net national income up to 1980 and gross domestic product for the remainder. Velocity of circulation is the ratio of nominal income to the money stock. Annual percentage changes are calculated as first differences of natural logarithms.

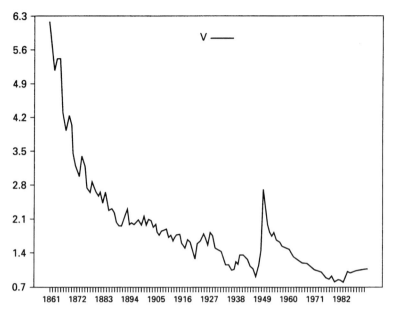

Figure 1.1 Velocity of circulation, 1861–1991

almost 100 per cent per annum (figure 1.2). The eighties appear to be an exception to the positive correlation: velocity in this period rises relative to the seventies while inflation declines. We use the word 'appear' because the eighties were years of financial innovation and liberalisation. Italy gradually eliminated controls on capital movements and exchange rates, allowing domestic interest rates to align themselves to those prevailing abroad. So while inflation declined, Italian interest rates rose relative to the underlying inflation. In sum, our data are consistent with the hypothesis that the demand for money adjusts inversely to the level of market interest rates.

Annual money growth, on average, exceeds output growth by more than 8 percentage points; and average inflation is about 7 per cent. As we have already indicated, inflation is mostly a twentieth-century phenomenon; from 1861 to 1913 the price level fluctuated virtually around the zero growth line. The two world wars stand out, not surprisingly, as high inflation periods; the inter-war years as overall price stability, encompassing, however, a phase of actual deflation; and the post-Second World War era, but especially the seventies, as of (relatively) high peace-time inflation years.

It is widely accepted that average inflation is positively correlated with its variability. This is so within a given regime, but not across regimes. In fact, inflation was more variable during the gold standard years, when the average was close to zero, than in the inflationary seventies and eighties. A

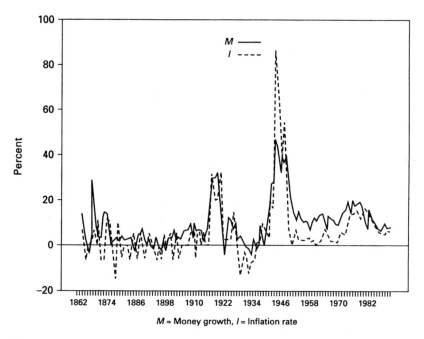

Figure 1.2 Money growth and inflation, 1862–1991

similar story holds for money growth. Figure 1.2 highlights the spike-like behaviour of these two series in the gold standard relative to later periods. For example, the price level rose by 11 per cent in 1872, declined by 16 per cent in 1875 and rose again by 11 per cent in 1877.[12] The same figure shows a tight co-movement between money growth and inflation. Given the noted higher variability of the two variables in the gold standard, the co-movement tends to be tighter after 1913. In general, the inflation amplitudes exceed those of money growth.

Economic growth was higher in the twentieth century than in the nineteenth century. In addition, it was more volatile in the gold standard and inter-war years than after the Second World War. The largest output drop took place during the Second World War (figure 1.3). There were no comparable spikes in the First World War. Of particular interest is the relationship between output growth and inflation, which is shown in figure 1.3. Post-Second World War theories, such as the one underlying the Phillips Curve, have emphasised a trade-off between output growth (or unemployment) and inflation, implying that inflation and economic growth would be positively related unless the economic system were disturbed by negative supply shocks. The Italian data exclude any systematic positive association between output growth and inflation.

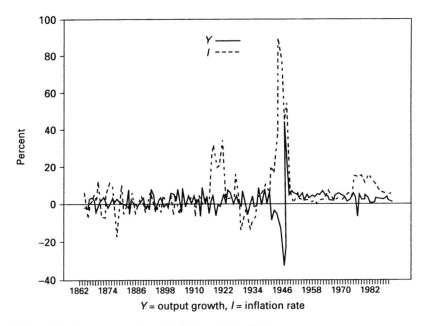

Figure 1.3 Output growth and inflation, 1862–1991

There are two ways of looking at the long record. First, one can consider the sub-periods' averages and see if increases in inflation are matched by rises in output growth. From the gold standard years to the eighties, there are five instances when the two variables move opposite to each other and only one instance when they move in the same direction (from the seventies to the eighties). That is, the raw data give no hope to the hypothesis of inflation being an engine of growth. A more formal evidence comes from the cross correlation coefficient of the unlagged yearly data. This coefficient is –0.25 for the whole period, –0.07 during the gold standard years, 0.28 from 1914 to 1920, 0.37 from 1921 to 1937, –0.43 from 1938 to 1949, –0.28 in the Bretton Woods era, –0.12 in the seventies and –0.83 in the eighties. The low cross correlation coefficient during the gold standard is consistent with the high variability of these two variables (figure 1.3). In contrast, output growth and inflation are more serially correlated in the twentieth century, especially after the Second World War. During the eighties, for example, inflation was above the period average during the first half of the decade when output growth was below average; then inflation fell below average in the second half of the decade as output rose above average (figure 1.3). Without such persistence, it would have been difficult to achieve such a high negative cross correlation coefficient. A strong negative correlation also occurred during the Second World War, whereas the stagflation years of the seventies show a surprisingly low negative correlation. Negative supply shocks were prevalent both in the Second World War and in the seventies. Many other industrialised countries suffered from the same shocks in the seventies (Bruno and Sachs 1985), but Italy was unique among them in responding with high inflation.

In sum, there is no evidence of systematically exploitable trade-offs between inflation and output growth. This is not to deny the existence of Phillips-curve effects. Indeed, our *History* will isolate a few instances where policymakers were able to rely on inflation to stimulate growth. These stimulative actions, however, had temporary effects and could not be reproduced year after year.

Public finance

A key theme of our *History* is that public finance is at the root of the (relatively) high Italian inflation. More precisely, there is a tight link between the government budget deficit and monetary policy. The monetary authorities are too dependent on government to assert an autonomous policy; more often than not they accommodate the objective of government of financing large budget deficits at low rates of interest, that is, by excessive monetary base creation. A relentless growth of government spending, rather than sluggish tax revenues, are responsible for the budget deficits. Transfer payments tend to be the least controllable expenditure category, especially after the Second World War.

Table 1.4 contains the essential information on Italian public finance. Government spending as a proportion of national income displays a very sharp upward trend: it goes from 13 in the gold standard years to almost 59 in the eighties. Also tax revenues, as a proportion of national income, have a sharp positive trend, but systematically fall short of spending; hence Italy suffers from endemic budget deficits. These tend to be much smaller in the gold standard years than in later periods and twice as large after BI became the monopolist of issue.

Abstracting from the two world wars, the seventies and the eighties were periods of high budgetary financing. In the eighties the average budget deficit reached 20 per cent of national income, against the historical average of 8 per cent.

On average, Italian monetary authorities monetised half of the budget deficits. This exceptionally high monetisation ratio is an indicator of the lack of independence of the monetary authorities from government as well as a measure of the tight link between public finance and monetary policy. One remarkable exception is the inter-war years, when the indebtedness of government *vis-à-vis* the central bank actually fell. This was also a period

Table 1.4 *Government budget and its financing (per cent)*

Periods	(G/Y)	(T/Y)	(DEF/Y)	$(dMBTR/DEF)$
1862–1991				
Mean	25.54	18.44	7.96	50.08
St. dev.	14.98	8.85	10.47	355.99
1862–1913				
Mean	13.45	12.34	2.86	82.05
St. dev.	1.87	2.04	4.11	533.54
1914–20				
Mean	44.07	14.40	29.30	38.17
St. dev.	13.94	1.10	17.62	24.70
1921–37				
Mean	23.99	17.86	2.73	−42.60
St. dev.	6.94	3.08	6.48	311.96
1938–49				
Mean	33.34	15.31	20.09	56.56
St. dev.	11.48	4.65	11.51	21.84
1950–69				
Mean	22.75	20.70	2.83	62.40
St. dev.	2.10	1.65	1.22	41.38
1970–80				
Mean	36.59	26.36	11.11	51.94
St. dev.	8.57	4.56	5.51	39.96
1981–91				
Mean	58.74	42.11	19.49	18.5
St. dev.	3.53	3.23	3.00	8.42
1862–1925				
M.S.	17.67	12.90	5.73	64.41
Dev. St.	11.12	2.29	10.82	483.49
1926–91				
M.S.	33.16	23.80	10.12	36.20
Dev. St.	14.31	9.54	9.72	156.65

Notes:
G=total spending of the central government; T=total tax revenues of the central government; DEF=first difference of central government's gross debt; Y=nominal national income; $dMBTR$=flows of monetary base created through the Treasury.

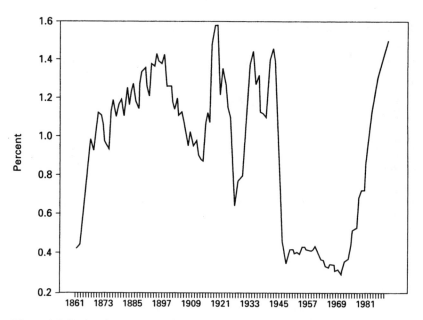

Figure 1.4 Ratio of government debt to national income, 1861–1991

when budget deficits reached an historical low. The monetisation ratios during the world wars were high, as one would expect. After the Second World War the ratios remained well above 50 per cent through the seventies. At the beginning of the eighties, the Treasury released BI from the obligation of purchasing government bonds at the auctions. Gradually the central bank, constrained by the operation of the European Monetary System, gained independence from government. The monetisation ratios fell drastically, bringing about the lowest figures of the entire period.

Figure 1.4 shows the ratio of government debt to national income. The ratio rose from approximately 0.4 when Italy was unified to 1.4 in the second half of the 1890s. Debt was accumulated to a large extent to finance the infrastructure and the basic public goods the young nation needed (Fratianni and Spinelli 1982). Subsequently, the ratio fell continuously until the start of the First World War. The war and its aftermath propelled the debt–income ratio to 1.6. The tight fiscal policy of the Fascist regime was responsible for the ratio falling to 0.6 in the twenties, but the regime's expansionist ambitions in Africa fuelled another sharp increase in the ratio. It was not until the end of the forties that debt fell below 0.4 per cent of national income, that is, to the 1861 value. The latest explosion of the debt–income ratio occurred in the early seventies when Italy, together with other industrial countries, embarked on a vast expansion of the welfare state. Transfer

Table 1A *The account of the Treasury, Cassa DD.PP and Government Corporations for 1968 (data in billions of lire)*

Government deficit	2,062	Net sales of long-term government bonds to public and banks	1,093
		Net sales of Treasury bills and postal deposits to public and banks	422
		Net sales of long-term government bonds to BI	219
		Net sales of Treasury bills, postal notes to BI, other accounts with BI	281
		Decrease in governmental liabilities *vis-à-vis* foreigners	–2
		Increase in other domestic sight government liabilities	36
		Net issue of government coins and currency	13
	2,062		2,062

payments skyrocketed; deficits contributed to new debt and old and new debt contributed to larger deficits through interest payments.

Appendix: The construction of the monetary base

Treasury, Cassa DD.PP and Government Corporations

Unlike the United States, where there is a bookkeeping separation between the fiscal and monetary operations of the Treasury, no such separation exists in Italy. The annual reports of the Bank of Italy publish the consolidated account of the Treasury, Cassa DD.PP and government corporations. We have simplified the schema of this account for 1968 in table 1A so as to emphasise the various methods used by the Italian government to finance budget deficits.

From the above account (a flow concept) one can reconstruct a balance sheet of the Treasury (a stock concept) by aggregating over all past governmental deficits. The aggregation over time is feasible because the quantities relative to all the elements on the right-hand side of table 1A are available also as a stock; the summation of all previous budget deficits can thus be computed as a residual. This is done in table 2A which describes an idealised, and thus non-existent, balance sheet of the Treasury at the end of 1968.

Table 2A *Construction of a balance sheet for the Treasury, Cassa DD.PP and Government Corporations (data in billions of lire as of 31 December 1968)*

Summation over time of all budget deficits		Treasury bills and government bonds held by BI and UIC	1,335
Minus stock of government bonds held by the public	2,684	Owed to BI-UIC	1,684
		(i) advances from BI	
		(ii) compulsory agricultural stockpiling bills	
		(iii) Treasury's account with stock of government bonds BI	
held by banks	2,997	(iv) other debit accounts with BI-UC	
		Minus:	
		(v) Treasury's holdings of coins and currency	
		Postal deposits held by the public and banks	5,249
		Treasury bills held by the public and banks	2,171
		Outstanding stock of Treasury's coins and currency	190
		Other liabilities such as deposits of the public with the Treasury	40

The items listed on the right-hand side of the balance sheet represent alternative ways to monetise the government budget deficit; simply put, different ways to create monetary base. Concerning the first item, there are no legal restrictions on the amount of government bonds BI–UIC can purchase. This item has grown since the Second World War, reflecting in large part the fact that the Bank was until the 1980s a residual buyer of government securities at Treasury auctions and, to a lesser extent, the increasing use of open market operations as an instrument of monetary policy. Before the Second World War open market operations were minimal and vitually non-existent during the period of competitive central banking. As noted, BI acts as the agent of the Treasury (Bank for International Settlements 1963, p. 199). The services performed by BI on behalf of the Treasury include payment orders by various government departments, collection of taxes due to the state, and the sale and redemption of government bills and bonds. These transactions are recorded in the 'conto corrente per il servizio di tesoreria', which is conceptually equivalent to 'deposit due to US Treasury' in the balance sheet of the Federal Reserve System (Friedman and Schwartz 1963, p. 797). Depending on whether the balance of the Treasury account is negative or positive it appears as a net liability or a net asset of the Treasury, respectively (in table 2A it is shown as a net liability). By law, the Treasury's negative balance cannot exceed 14 per cent of the estimated government expenditures for the current fiscal year.

The Treasury is also constrained by law as to how much it can borrow directly from the Bank. Compulsory agricultural stock-piling bills are Treasury liabilities which arose when the government had a policy to regulate the retail price of basic staples such as wheat and rice. The difference between the cost of production and market price is borne by the Treasury which, unable at times to meet the expense with revenues, issues notes having legal tender properties to producers who cash them in at banks; banks, in turn, treat them as reserves. This item grew enormously after the Second World War to a point where it accounted for 10 per cent of total budget expenditures. The agricultural support programme was discontinued in 1964 and the stock of these bills, consequently, has been petering out.

The largest single way for the Treasury to monetise the deficit, that is to create monetary base, is through the postal deposit system. It is somewhat controversial whether postal deposits are part of the monetary base. At issue here is the relative substitutability of postal deposits for government securities as opposed to other monetary-base assets. In this presentation we take the view that postal deposits are more closely substitutable for other monetary-base assets than for government securities.

Government agencies hold coins and currency issued by BI and the Treasury. These holdings can be thought of either as an asset of the Treasury or as a subtraction from the Treasury's liabilities. Next, we come to Treasury bills with maturity of less than a year. These are treated as a monetary-base asset during periods when interest rates were pegged by the monetary authorities. Up to April 1969 Treasury bills were issued according to a fully elastic supply schedule with a predetermined rate of return of 3.75 per cent per annum. The certainty of buying and selling this type of government paper at a known price is critical in making these assets monetary base. Again, what is at stake here is the relative substitutability of Treasury bills for other monetary-base assets as opposed to bonds. The assumption underlying the construction of table 2A is that the former is higher than the latter; note higher and not infinite. It is just as unlikely that the public treat currency and Treasury bills as perfect substitutes during a complete price-support programme as it is that banks treat vault cash and bookkeeping entries with the central banks as perfectly substitutable across 'regimes'. The issue at stake is again relative substitutability. Treasury bills reacquire the traditional role of bond financing during periods in which the authorities do not peg interest rates.

The Bank of Italy and the Italian Exchange Office

Table 3A shows the balance sheet of the second group of monetary authorities, the consolidated statement of the Bank of Italy and the Italian Exchange Office. The reader will notice that the first two items on the left-hand side of table 3A are identical to the first two groups of items on the right-hand side of the consolidated statement of the Treasury, Cassa DD.PP and Government Corporations (table 2A). Advances and rediscounts to banks historically have been a very important part of central banking; in modern Italy, as is true in the United States and other European countries, that relative quantitative significance has been diminishing over the years. The sum of the third and fourth items on the asset side of the balance sheet constitutes BI–UIC claims on the rest of the world. The reader may be puzzled as to why convertible currencies of the banks show up in the BI–UIC balance sheet. The reason is that the Italian Exchange Office has legal exclusivity on foreign exchange transactions. Technically, banks can hold foreign exchange only temporarily and must stand ready to surrender it to UIC on demand. As a result, banks treat foreign exchange as reserves denominated in lire at the prevailing exchange rate, while BI and UIC acquire a claim *vis-à-vis* the rest of the world equal to the banks' convertible currencies and a liability towards the banks for an equivalent amount. To further complicate matters, not all foreign exchange is classified as 'convertible', that is eligible to be cashed in on demand. A portion is not eligible. The criteria for eligibility are set by the Italian Exchange Office. In sum, the unconventional accounting procedure to classify a portion of the banks' foreign exchange as part of the BI–UIC claims on the rest of the world is based on the legal exclusivity that UIC has in foreign exchange matters and the policy decision of BI and UIC to treat a portion of the banks' foreign reserves as bank reserves.

The final asset item is of small importance for it includes advances to either the private sector or to the 'istituti di credito speciale'. Students of the US monetary system probably will be wary of our generic classification 'other assets' and 'other liabilities' because complicated transactions can be tucked under this innocent label; e.g., currency swap operations.

On the liabilities side of table 3A we begin with outstanding currency which includes BI-printed paper held by the domestic private sector, banks

Table 3A *Consolidated balance sheet of the Bank of Italy and the Italian Exchange Office (data in billions of lire as of 31 December 1968)*

Assets		Liabilities	
Treasury bills and government bonds	1,335	Outstanding currency	5,393
		Deposits of commercial banks	2,553
Credit *vis-à-vis* the Treasury	1,684	Banks' line of credit	511
Advances and rediscounts to banks	1,828	Other liabilities	1,149
		(i) deposits of special credit institutions	
International reserves plus net short-, medium-, and long-term foreign assets	3,770	(ii) foreign deposits	
		(iii) public's deposits	
Convertible currencies held by banks	266	(iv) other Treasury credits	
		(v) net worth	
Other assets such as advances to special credit institutions and public	723		
	9,606		9,606

and the rest of the world, if any. We recall that in modern Italy the Treasury issues coins and paper money of denominations less than 1,000 lire (cf. table 2A). Deposits of commercial banks are bookkeeping entries that make up the bulk of bank reserves. Then there is the unusual entry 'line of credit of banks' which stands for a promise by the central bank to lend to banks, should the need arise. It is treated as an actual liability even though it may not materialise. Banks include – with the permission of the central bank – this credit line as part of their reserves. The offset of this liability was placed under 'other assets' to distinguish it from actual advances and rediscounts to banks. The practice of treating a credit line with the central bank as actual bank reserves may be debatable from a theoretical viewpoint but it is an institutional fact of the Italian monetary system.

The monetary base

The consolidation of tables 2A and 3A yields table 1.1 of the text.

2 Money growth and its determinants

Introduction

In the first chapter we compared Italy with a representative rest of the world and found that she stood out because of her higher and persistent inflation rate.[1] In the present chapter we examine money growth and its determinants, that is the forces underlying the Italian inflation rate. We begin by decomposing the growth of the money stock in terms of its 'proximate' determinants and quantifying how much each of these determinants has contributed to money growth. Then we relax the assumption that the monetary base is independent of the money multiplier and explore the extent to which these two variables affect each other. Subsequently we tackle the issue of the determination of the monetary base under a regime of fixed or managed exchange rates. A major finding of our *History* is that, throughout the 131 years under consideration, Italian monetary policy has tended to accommodate fiscal policy actions. This dependence of the monetary authorities has implied that governments have monetised a very sizable proportion of their budget deficits and have collected a significant inflation tax. We explore also how entrenched fiscal dominance is in Italian history.

Decomposition of the money stock

We express the money stock as the monetary base times the money multiplier which depends inversely on the three standard ratios (Brunner and Meltzer 1964; Friedman and Schwartz 1963; Cagan 1965)

$$M_t = m_t MB_t, \tag{2.1}$$

$$m_t = (1 + k_t)/(k_t + rr_t + re_t), \tag{2.1a}$$

$$k_t = BP_t/D_t, \tag{2.1b}$$

$$rr_t = BR_t/D_t, \tag{2.1c}$$

$$re_t = BE_t/D_t. \tag{2.1d}$$

The growth rate of M can then be decomposed into the growth of the multiplier and the growth of the monetary base. In turn, these can be expressed in terms of the contribution of k, rr, re, $MBTR$, $MBOT$ and BF and their interactions; that is

$$
\begin{aligned}
&\ln m_t - \ln m_{t-1} = c(k) + c(rr) + c(re) + c(com1), \\
&c(k) = \ln(1+k_t) - \ln(1+k_{t-1}) - \ln(k_t + rr_{t-1} + re_{t-1}) + \ln(k_{t-1} + rr_{t-1} + re_{t-1}) \\
&c(rr) = -\ln(k_{t-1} + rr_t + re_{t-1}) + \ln(k_{t-1} + rr_{t-1} + re_{t-1}) \\
&c(re) = -\ln(k_{t-1} + rr_{t-1} + re_t) + \ln(k_{t-1} + rr_{t-1} + re_{t-1}) \\
&c(com1) = \ln m_{t-1} - \ln m_{t-1} - [c(k) + c(rr) + c(re)].
\end{aligned}
\tag{2.2}
$$

$$
\begin{aligned}
&\ln MB_t - \ln MB_{t-1} = c(MBTR) + c(MBOT) + c(BF) + c(com2), \\
&c(MBTR) = \ln(MBTR_t + MBOT_{t-1} + BF_{t-1}) - \ln(MBTR_{t-1} + MBOT_{t-1} BF_{t-1}) \\
&c(MBOT) = \ln(MBTR_{t-1} + MBOT_t + BF_{t-1}) - \ln(MBTR_{t-1} + MBOT_{t-1} + BF_{t-1}) \\
&c(BF) = \ln(MBTR_{t-1} + MBOT_{t-1} + BF_t) - \ln(MBTR_{t-1} + MBOT_{t-1} + BF_{t-1}) \\
&c(com2) = \ln MB_t - \ln MB_{t-1} - [c(MBTR) + c(MBOT) + c(BF)].
\end{aligned}
\tag{2.3}
$$

The notation $c(x)$ denotes the contribution of $x=k$, rr, re, $MBTR$, $MBOT$, BF to the growth of the money stock. In addition, given that changes in the variables are discrete, two interaction terms arise: $com1$ capturing the interactions of the multiplier's determinants, and $com2$ the interaction of the monetary base's determinants. For the exclusive definition of the monetary base, there are two k's instead of one: $K_1 = BP^{ex}/D$ and $k_2 = D^{pos}/D$. The decomposition procedure in this case becomes only slightly more complicated.

Table 2.1 (inclusive definition) and table 2.2 (exclusive definition) present the results of the decomposition of money growth measured in terms of the averages of the entire period and sub-periods. Consider the broad movements of the growth of money, the monetary base and the money multiplier. Figure 2.1 plots money growth and multiplier growth; figure 2.2 the growth of the monetary base and its 'Treasury' component. The annual growth rate of money over the 131-year history averages to 10.5 per cent. Growth rates are much higher during war than in peace time, and almost three times as high in the post-monopolist period than in the pre-monopolist period. Not surprisingly, money growth is very contained during the gold standard; but it is even lower in the inter-war period. As we have indicated in chapter 1, the lower money growth of 1921–37 compared with 1862–1913 came with a lower inflation rate (0.06 per cent vs. 0.65 per cent) and higher output growth. In fact, output in the inter-war period grew almost a percentage point more than during the gold standard (2.21 per cent versus 1.26 per cent). Money growth was historically high during the Bretton Woods years and was associated with an average inflation rate of 3.6 per cent and average output growth of 5.6 per cent. Money growth rose considerably during the

Table 2.1 *Money decomposition (monetary base inclusive of postal deposits)*

	1862–1991	1862–1913	1914–20	1921–37	1938–49	1950–69	1970–80	1981–91	1862–1925	1926–91
Money growth per cent p.a.	10.50	4.40	22.70	3.3	30.4	12.40	17.40	10.30	6.60	14.30
c(k)	0.73	1.18	-1.49	0.53	-0.61	1.66	1.43	-0.63	1.15	0.32
c(rr)	-0.12	–	–	–	-1.14	0.32	0.05	-0.79	–	-0.23
c(re)	0.11	0.009	-0.19	0.18	-0.82	0.82	0.3	0.26	-0.008	0.23
c(com1)	-0.005	-0.002	-0.009	0.02	-0.12	0.03	-0.01	0.01	0.005	-0.01
c(MBTR)	7.40	2.07	26.88	0.14	27.01	4.02	12.66	11.30	4.33	10.45
c(MBOT)	0.20	-0.68	-6.40	-1.09	5.09	3.45	1.05	-1.58	-0.88	1.24
c(BF)	1.15	0.84	0.58	0.13	2.43	2.23	1.13	1.25	0.75	1.55
c(com2)	0.98	1.02	3.36	3.37	-1.42	-0.17	0.77	0.51	1.23	0.74

Note:
The notation $c(x)$ denotes the contribution of x to the growth of the money stock. Refer to equations (2.2) and (2.3) in the text for the decomposition algorithm.

Table 2.2 *Money decomposition (monetary base exclusive of postal deposits)*

	1862–1991	1862–1913	1914–20	1921–37	1938–49	1950–69	1970–80	1981–91	1862–1925	1926–91
Money growth per cent p.a.	10.5	4.40	22.70	3.3	30.40	12.36	17.4	10.30	6.6	14.30
$c(k_1)$	0.98	1.79	-3.86	2.72	-4.13	2.29	1.71	0.02	1.61	0.37
$c(k_2)$	0.08	0.27	-0.54	0.87	-0.51	-0.43	-0.23	0.34	0.14	0.04
$c(rr)$	-0.14	–	–	–	-1.39	0.47	0.09	-1.13	–	-0.28
$c(re)$	0.18	0.008	-0.29	0.29	-0.97	1.16	0.45	0.39	-0.01	0.38
$c(com1)$	-0.01	-0.001	0.003	-0.002	-0.13	-0.04	-0.02	-0.006	–	0.02
$c(MBTR)$	5.64	1.02	30.50	-7.93	29.51	0.96	10.55	10.25	3.51	7.71
$c(MBOT)$	-0.20	-0.83	-10.00	-4.44	7.00	4.74	1.12	-2.60	-1.28	0.84
$c(BF)$	1.43	1.05	0.76	-0.57	2.94	3.11	1.56	1.85	0.93	1.90
$c(com2)$	2.52	1.14	6.20	12.34	-1.90	0.04	2.17	1.23	1.67	3.33

Note:

The notation $c(x)$ denotes the contribution of x to the growth of the money stock. Refer to equations (2.2) and (2.3) in the text for the decomposition algorithm. In this table there are two k ratios: $k_1 = BP^{ex}/D$ and $k_2 = D^{pos}/D$, BP^{ex}=monetary base held by the public excluding postal deposits, D^{pos}=postal deposits, D=bank deposits. The decomposition of the money multiplier is slightly more complicated than shown by equation (2.2).

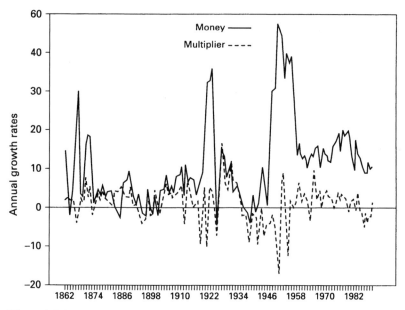

Figure 2.1 Money and the multiplier

1970s as did inflation (12.9 per cent); output growth, instead, fell to 3.2 per cent. In the last sub-period, one which roughly coincides with the operation of the European Monetary System, money growth slowed down considerably and so did inflation (9.7 per cent) and output growth (2.1 per cent).[2]

Some basic patterns can be inferred from tables 2.1 and 2.2. First, the monetary base represents the dominant factor underlying the growth of M. On average, the inclusive monetary-base growth accounts for 93 per cent of money growth over the 131 years; the exclusive definition slightly less, 90 per cent. Variability is larger for the exclusive than the inclusive definition of MB. In general, during the low money growth gold standard and inter-war periods the monetary base represented a much smaller share of money growth than during conflicts and the 1980s.[3]

Second, the Treasury component of the monetary base, MBTR, exerts an overall dominant influence on the growth of MB (figure 2.2) and on the growth of M (tables 2.1 and 2.2 and figure 2.3). The other component of the domestic monetary base, MBOT, tends to offset the effects of MBTR on money growth during the gold standard, the inter-war era and the 1980s, but reinforces them from the mid 1930s to 1980.[4] The foreign component BF – which, unlike BD, alternates periods of positive growth and periods of negative growth – contributes positively to money growth. In relative terms, its impact is largest during the gold standard and the Bretton Woods

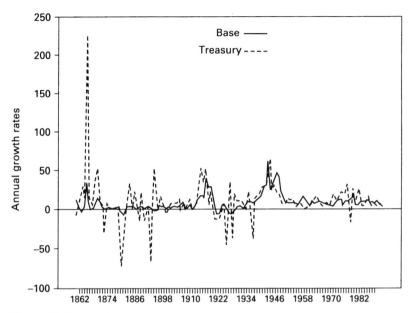

Figure 2.2 Base and treasury component

periods, that is when exchange rates are more or less fixed and reserve flows play a significant role in adjusting external imbalances.

Third, of the ratios that enter the money multiplier, k (k_1 in the exclusive definition) by far exerts the largest impact on money growth. This ratio, which is portrayed in figure 2.4, follows a sharply declining trend; this trend, in turn, reflects the wider and deeper role played by banks in the economy and the attendant decline in the net cost of holding bank deposits relative to cash and postal deposits. Given the inverse relationship between k and the multiplier, the behaviour of k has added significantly to money growth, especially in the nineteenth century when the declines in k were most dramatic. Rising uncertainty, on the other hand, induces people to switch on the margin from bank deposits to currency, thus depressing money growth. This was true during the two world wars and the financial crisis of the early 1890s.

The other two ratios, re and rr, have been of secondary importance in influencing the long-run growth of M. The excess reserve ratio (figure 2.5) has a slight negative trend from 1865 to 1939, rises sharply in anticipation of Einaudi's 1947 stabilisation programme (see chapter 6), and then follows a negative trend up to present times. Required reserves were introduced in Italy in 1947, in connection with the aforementioned post-war stabilisation programme. This fact explains the negative contribution of rr during the 1938–49 years. The required ratio rose again in the 1980s (figure 2.5).

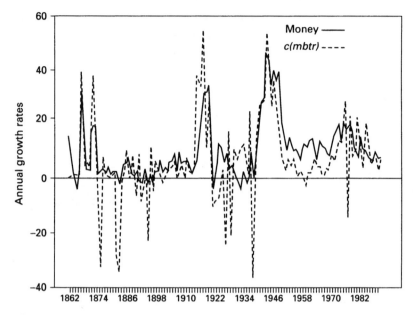

Figure 2.3 Treasury's contribution to money

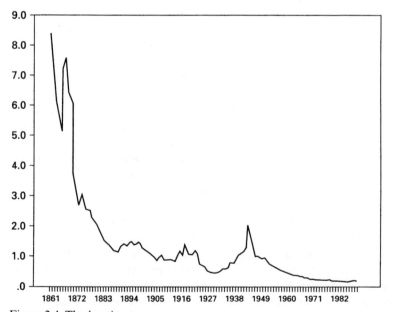

Figure 2.4 The k-ratio

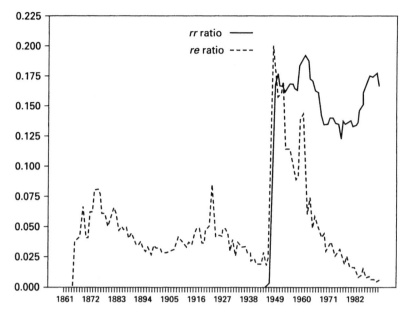

Figure 2.5 The *rr* and *re* ratios

In sum, the bulk of the long-run growth of M results from actions taken by the monetary authorities, in particular, actions connected with the financing of government deficits. The growth of central bank lending to banks and of foreign reserves plays a smaller role. The long-run growth of the money multiplier contributes but a small fraction to money growth. The sustained substitution of bank deposits for monetary base on the part of the public is the only significant force underlying the growth of the multiplier. These results are not sensitive to whether the monetary base includes postal deposits.

Interaction between the multiplier and the monetary base

In the previous section we decomposed the growth of M in terms of its five determinants. The approach was similar to growth accounting, and assumed that the money multiplier was independent of the monetary base. We now relax the independence assumption and investigate the extent to which the money multiplier responds to changes in the monetary base, and vice versa.

The theoretical underpinning of the interaction between the money multiplier and the monetary base can be found in Brunner and Meltzer (1968, 1989), Burger (1971), and Fratianni (1976). Essentially, the link between m

and MB goes through the rates of interest. Increases in the monetary base lower the rates of interest on bonds and capital, instigating marginal substitutions of money for bonds and capital. Furthermore, the public reallocates a given money demand in favour of non-interest-bearing base money (a higher k ratio). This substitution of base money for deposits is deeper the more interest rates on bank deposits adjust to prevailing market conditions. Banks also respond to lower market rates of interest by raising, on the margin, the ratio of excess reserves to deposits.

We can state the inverse relationship between the money multiplier and the monetary base by considering the value of the elasticity of the money stock with respect to the monetary base

$$\varepsilon(M,MB)=\varepsilon(m,MB)+1,$$
$$\varepsilon(m,MB)=\varepsilon(m,i)\varepsilon(i,MB)+\varepsilon(m,P)\varepsilon(P,MB), \tag{2.4}$$

where $\varepsilon(x,y)$ denotes the elasticity of x with respect to y. The monetary base influences the multiplier through the market rate of interest, i, and the price of capital, P. In the Brunner–Meltzer model (1989) $\varepsilon(m,i)$, $\varepsilon(P,MB)>0$; $\varepsilon(i,MB)$, $\varepsilon(m,P)<0$. Since increases in k and re lower the money multiplier, equation (2.4) implies that the two ratios respond positively to short-run changes in the monetary base, whereas the money multiplier responds inversely to the monetary base.[5] In Italy, bank deposits have had a relatively low transaction value and have paid relatively high explicit rates of interest. Consequently, the impact of the monetary base on the multiplier is expected to be stronger than, say, in the United States, where bank deposits have had a relatively high transaction value and have paid small or no explicit rates of interest.

Using the sample period 1862–1980, Fratianni (1988) estimates transfer functions of the multiplier, k, with the monetary base as the only input.[6] From these estimates he finds that the short-run value of $\varepsilon(m,MB)$ equals 0.5. A visual inspection of the raw data of the growth of the money multiplier and the growth of the monetary base (figure 2.6) confirms the negative correlation between the two series. Over the long run the negative correlation between the money multiplier and the monetary base disappears as $\varepsilon(i,MB)$ switches from negative to positive values.

The assumption that the monetary base is exogenous is critical in the above argument. There are two objections to treating MB independently of the multiplier. The first objection arises from exchange-rate considerations. Under fixed rates the authorities control the domestic component of the monetary base, and not the total base. BF responds to policy actions and to money demand variables (see subsequent section). Furthermore, even during flexible exchange rates, the monetary base may not act independently of the evolution of the money multiplier, if the monetary authorities

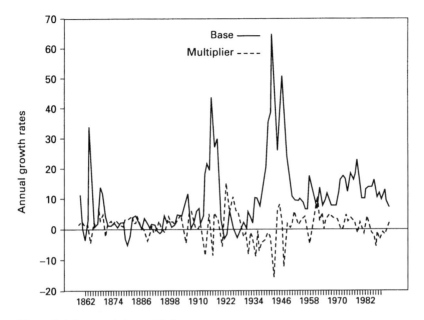

Figure 2.6 Base and the multiplier

peg or target interest rates. Shocks to the money multiplier that tend to raise the rate of interest will elicit an offsetting behaviour on the part of the authorities. For example, should k rise unexpectedly and thus raise the rate of interest, an interest-rate-pegging regime will dictate an increase in the monetary base. Hence movements in k influence the monetary base in the same direction, whereas m influences MB in the opposite direction. In sum, m and MB interact.

Fixed (or managed) exchange rates and interest-rate targeting were prevalent throughout the *History*, at times taking place simultaneously. In light of these considerations, it is not surprising that the direction of the Granger causality runs from the money multiplier to the monetary base, and not vice versa (Fratianni 1988).

In the following section we analyse to what extent the monetary base is endogenously determined by the authorities' desire to maintain stable exchange rates.

The monetary base under fixed exchange rates

In a regime of fixed or managed exchange rates the monetary authorities may not control the total monetary base: the central bank controls the domestic component, BD, but not the foreign component, BF. According to the strong version of the monetary theory of the balance of payments, changes in *BD* are fully compensated by changes in *BF*; hence *MB* cannot be altered.[7] Monetary policy is at the complete mercy of the rules governing the regime of fixed exchange rates. These results stem from the assumption that domestic and foreign assets are perfect substitutes. Under the less restrictive condition of imperfect asset substitutability, the relation between changes in *BF* and changes in *BD* can be stated as follows (Dornbush 1980, chapter 10)

$$\Delta BF_t = a_0 - (1 - a_1)\Delta BD_t + a_2\Delta Y_t - a_3\Delta i_t^* \qquad (2.5)$$

where *Y*, national nominal income, and *i**, the foreign rate of interest, are demand-for-money variables; Δ is the first-difference operator and a_2 and a_3 are positive parameters. The coefficient a_1 is minus the ratio of the slope of the demand for base money with respect to the domestic rate of interest to the slope of the demand for domestic bonds with respect to the same interest rate. The range of a_1 is from zero to one: it is zero when domestic and foreign assets are perfect substitutes; otherwise it is positive, and closer to one the weaker asset substitutability.

Equation (2.5), however, is an incomplete statement of the interaction process between ΔBF and ΔBD. Monetary authorities do not alter *BD* in a vacuum; their actions are guided by history, domestic factors and external factors. There is evidence that monetary authorities in the gold standard did not follow the rule of the game, but sterilised reserve flows to insulate, either fully or partially, the monetary base from external imbalances (Nurske 1944; Bloomfield 1959; Michaely 1968). Our reading of Italian monetary history confirms the propensity to violate the rules of the game. Concerning the reaction of the authorities to domestic factors, a major finding of our *History* is that fiscal and monetary policies have been closely intertwined. Before 1926 Italian banks of issue were willing to lend to government at an interest rate that would endanger capital outflows. After 1926 BI continued the practice and its dependence on government grew until modern times. These considerations lead us to postulate the following reactions function of the monetary authorities

$$\Delta BD_t = b_0 + b_1\Delta BD_{t-1} + b_2\Delta BF_t + b_3 DEF_t, \qquad (2.6)$$

where the lagged value of BD represents the history, BF the external objective and DEF is the government budget deficit. Parameter b_3 captures the behaviour of the monetary authorities in accommodating fiscal deficits; this parameter is expected to be positive in Italy. b_2 is the sterilisation coefficient which is negative when the authorities desire to achieve domestic objectives. In the limiting case of $b_2 = -1$, the authorities fully sterilise reserve flows. On the other hand, if the authorities intend to facilitate the balance-of-payments adjustment process, b_2 can be zero or even positive.

There are 56 years of fixed or managed exchange rates from 1862 to 1991: 1862–5, 1884–91, 1904–14, 1951–70 and 1979–91. During these years ΔY, Δi^*, DEF, and BD_{t-1} are exogenous and determine the two endogenous variables ΔBF and ΔBD. Equations (2.5) and (2.6) were estimated with an instrumental variable technique.[8] These are the estimates

$$
\begin{array}{rclc}
a_0 & = & 2875 & (1.45) \\
-(1-a_1) & = & -0.5 & (2.25) \\
a_2 & = & 0.28 & (5.19) \\
a_3 & = & -392 & (1.39) \qquad \text{(2.5 est)}
\end{array}
$$

$\bar{R}^2=0.65$, SEE$=2557.3$, LM test for residual autocorrelation $\chi^2(4)=11.6$ (p$=0.02$).

$$
\begin{array}{rclc}
b_0 & = & 471 & (3.47) \\
b_1 & = & -0.002 & (0.02) \\
b_2 & = & -0.80 & (3.69) \\
b_3 & = & 0.19 & (7.97) \qquad \text{(2.6 est)}
\end{array}
$$

$\bar{R}^2=0.93$, SEE$=2286$, $\chi^2(4)=5.49$ (p$=0.2$).

The value -0.5 of the offset coefficient $-(1-a_1)$ suggests an imperfect degree of substitutability between Italian and foreign assets, a finding that agrees with our examination of the historical episodes. On average, the monetary authorities sterilised 80 per cent of the reserve flows, in turn suggesting that domestic objectives dominated external objectives. This finding as well accords with our historical discussion. The monetary authorities often postponed taking corrective actions to redress an external imbalance. When the adjustment could no longer be delayed, the correction would be drastic. Last but not least, there is a tight link between fiscal and monetary policies, the subject of the next section.

To better appreciate the determinants of the monetary base under fixed exchange rates, we compute the reduced-form equations using the estimated coefficients (the lagged value of BD is dropped because of its insignificance)

$$\Delta BF = 4398 + 0.466\Delta Y - 653\Delta i^* - 0.16DEF$$
$$\Delta BD = -3048 + 0.32DEF - 0.37\Delta Y + 523\Delta i^*$$

Changes in nominal income raise the foreign component more than they lower the domestic component of the monetary base; hence the total monetary base rises. A Lit 1 billion government deficit causes a contraction of Lit 160 million in BF but induces the monetary authorities to expand BD by 320 million, leading to a Lit 160 million increase in MB. Increases in the foreign interest rate have a depressing effect on BF and MB.

Seigniorage and the inflation tax

In chapter 1 we saw that deficits of the Italian central government were on average 8 per cent of national income from 1861 to 1991. Apart from the two world conflicts, the highest budget deficits were recorded in the 1970s (11 per cent of national income) and in the 1980s (19.5 per cent of national income). Furthermore and more importantly for the topic of this chapter, 35 per cent of those deficits, or 2.8 per cent of national income, was monetised on average. Naturally, there were wide disparities around this long-run average. The lowest monetisation ratios occurred in the first two years of the 1880s (-7 to -8 per cent of national income) and in 1937 (-10.4 per cent of national income). The highest monetisation ratios, quite naturally, coincided with the two world wars. The global peak of 32 per cent of national income was recorded in 1944. If one excludes the two world wars, the 1970s and 1980s provide examples of least monetary discipline or of maximum monetary accommodation. In the wake of the first oil crisis and at the height of fiscal dominance, the monetisation ratios shot up to 11.9 per cent of national income in 1976, the highest value recorded during peace time. In 1981, the year when BI was freed from the obligation of being a residual buyer of government securities at the Treasury auctions, monetisation was 9 per cent of national income.

With this background let us define the budget deficit as

$$DEF^P/Y + i(S/Y) = (\Delta MBTR/Y) + (\Delta S/Y), \tag{2.7}$$

where DEF^P=primary deficit. We can solve (2.7) for the steady-state value of S/Y

$$\frac{DEF^P/Y - (\Delta MBTR/Y)}{(\Delta Y/Y) - i} \tag{2.8}$$

The second term in the numerator of (2.8) is our measure of seigniorage, which is quantified in the third column of table 2.3.[9] The extraction of seigniorage helps the authorities in reducing the long-run value of the debt-to-income ratio. In fact, for a positive value of the denominator of (2.8) – that is, stability conditions are satisfied – and a given primary deficit, the higher the seigniorage the lower the steady-state S/Y. When the denominator is negative – that is, stability conditions are not met – the government can stabilise the debt-to-income ratio by extracting more seigniorage and running a lower primary surplus. Table 2.3 shows that stability conditions were satisfied in most cases. When they were not satisfied, as in the gold standard and inter-war years, the country was running primary surpluses.

The inflation tax, while related to seigniorage, is not exactly the same. To

Table 2.3 *Seigniorage and inflation tax*

Periods	Primary deficit		Stability condition	Inflation tax
	Income	Seigniorage		
1862–1991				
Mean	5.10	3.65	2.48	2.51
St. Dev.	13.34	7.81	13.95	15.31
1862–1913				
Mean	−1.69	0.63	−2.84	−4.00
St. Dev.	4.56	3.06	6.72	6.92
1914–20				
Mean	33.16	11.80	17.39	24.75
St. Dev.	23.37	7.85	14.49	16.87
1921–37				
Mean	−1.84	0.40	−2.83	−4.15
St. Dev.	6.46	5.37	10.67	8.74
1938–49				
Mean	25.15	17.13	27.40	28.86
St. Dev.	16.68	15.83	27.50	29.60
1950–69				
Mean	1.65	1.65	2.11	0.79
St. Dev.	1.27	1.03	2.39	1.25
1970–80				
Mean	9.29	6.05	2.08	5.43
St. Dev.	4.99	5.14	4.44	2.37
1981–91				
Mean	10.23	4.27	0.13	0.89
St. Dev.	5.99	2.77	2.74	4.32
1862–1925				
Mean	2.12	1.70	−0.01	−0.40
St. Dev.	13.93	5.17	10.15	12.23
1926–91				
Mean	7.99	5.54	4.87	5.33
St. Dev.	12.17	9.37	16.57	17.42

Note:
Primary deficit is equal to total deficit minus interest payments; seigniorage is the percentage change of the Treasury component of the monetary base multiplied by the ratio of the Treasury component of the monetary base to nominal national income; stability condition is the difference between the growth rate of nominal national income and the average interest rate paid by government on his debt; the inflation tax is the inflation rate multiplied by the sum of the real value of interest-bearing debt and the monetary base minus the real value of payments on debt, expressed as a percentage of real national income.

see this point, let us rewrite (2.7) by deflating all variables by the price level, P, instead of income, and rearrange suitably

$$DEF^p/P-(\Delta MBTR/P)-(\Delta S/P)=(MBTR/P+S/P)\pi-(S/P)i. \quad (2.9)$$

The interpretation of (2.9) is straightforward. Whenever the real primary deficit exceeds the sum of the real flow of the Treasury monetary base (i.e., direct lending of the central bank to government) and the real flow of new government debt sold to the private sector, the government extracts an inflation tax. The right-hand side of (2.9) tells us that this tax is positively related to the rate of inflation, π, and the stock of debt which has a fixed nominal denomination, and inversely related to the interest flow the government pays on its debt, $(S/P)i$.

Figure 2.7 shows both seigniorage and the inflation tax, both measured as a per cent of real national income.[10] The two series are positively but not perfectly correlated. For example, from 1929 to 1934 seigniorage averaged approximately 3 per cent of real national income, whereas the inflation tax averaged −11 per cent of real national income. From 1986 to 1991 seigniorage was again approximately 3 per cent of real national income, but the inflation tax had dropped to close to −2 per cent of real national income. In both episodes, real rates of interest were at historically high values (more so in the 1930s than in the 1980s), forcing government to transfer large real net funds to holders of government securities.

Not surprisingly, the inflation tax was highest during wars (table 2.3). In 1917 it reached 42 per cent of real national income; in 1944 92 per cent. Both theory and practice would suggest that inflation is better suited than higher tax rates to pay for a large but temporary surge in government expenditures (Barro 1989, chapter 14). What is surprising, instead, is the extent to which seigniorage and the inflation tax became embedded in the Italian economy after BI was granted the monopoly of issue. Before 1926 seigniorage represented 1.7 per cent of income; after 1926 seigniorage rose to 5.5 per cent of income. Before 1926 the inflation tax was −0.4 per cent of income; after 1926 it jumped to 5.3 per cent (table 2.3). These statistics confirm once more that if there is a distinctive characteristic of the Italian economy it has to do with its relatively (in relation to the representative foreign economy of chapter 1) high inflation rate, which in turn finds its roots in a very accommodating monetary authority. Italian seigniorage is a proxy of fiscal dominance; and seigniorage and inflation are strongly correlated (see figure 2.8).

Fiscal dominance

Both the quantitative results and the historical analysis corroborate the hypothesis that much of Italian monetary policy has been shaped by fiscal

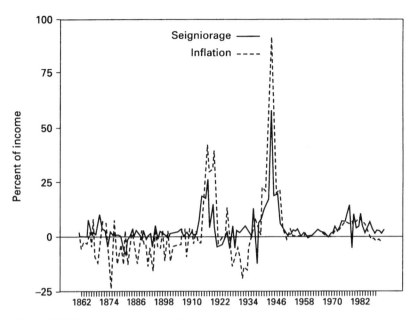

Figure 2.7 Seigniorage and the inflation tax

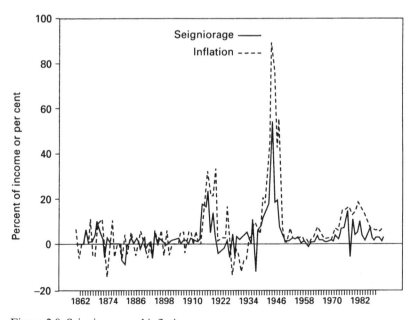

Figure 2.8 Seigniorage and inflation

actions. For example, on 1 May 1866 – six months after having signed the Latin Monetary Union agreement – Italy declared the inconvertibility of paper money into metal. The reason was a sharp deterioration in public finances. Budget deficits were also responsible for the monetary explosions of 1866–7 and 1870–2; the second inconvertibility in the middle of the 1880s, and the policy reversal of the *lira forte* (the strong lira) in the second half of the 1930s.[11] Fiscal discipline (i.e., low budget deficits), on the other hand, made possible the return to currency convertibilty of 1880, the steady and non-inflationary monetary policy from 1897 to 1913 and the 1950s, and the stabilisation policy of the 1920s and the *lira forte* of the 1930s.

Our position is that the relationship between the central bank and the Treasury involves a strategic conflict (Tabellini 1988). The central bank tends to interpret the public as wanting price stability or low inflation rates. The fiscal authorities, instead, interpret the public as wanting public expenditures. This difference in motives makes the Treasury seek as much seigniorage as possible from the monetary authorities. The greater the power of the fiscal authorities over the monetary authorities, that is the greater the degree of fiscal dominance, the lower the cost to the Treasury of financing a given budget deficit. According to this view, central bank independence and monetary accommodation are inversely related. Hence, central banks with a high degree of independence generate lower rates of inflation than dependent central banks (Alesina and Summers 1993; Fratianni and Huang 1995). Stated in a slightly different way, regimes of monetary dominance are associated with relatively low inflation, whereas regimes of fiscal dominance are associated with relatively high inflation.

Fiscal dominance has a long history in Italy. It can be traced to banks of issue such as the Banca Nazionale degli Stati Sardi (1850), the Banca Nazionale nel Regno d'Italia (1867) and the BI (1893). Each sought to become the only bank of issue. Good relations with the policy-maker were perceived to be an essential element of strategy. Politics was the relevant game and the Banca Nazionale first and later BI were the most adept at playing politics. The quest for the monopoly right of issue implied subservience to the political authority. Operational subservience meant the monopoly grantor would have ready and cheap access to credit, that is seigniorage.

In later chapters we provide detailed accounts of how banks of issue accepted fiscal dominance in exchange for market expansion. Here we offer a brief summary. The Banca Nazionale in the State of Piedmont successfully negotiated with the powerful Cavour the right to handle 'cash management' for the State and to make its notes legal tender. The same bank, after the political unification of Italy, never ceased to undermine the other banks so as to emerge as the issue monopolist. This goal was finally achieved in

1926 by BI, the successor of Banca Nazionale. However, BI continued to push for more power, in particular to have full control over the entire banking system. The political authority obliged with the Banking Law of 1936 and the creation of reserve requirements in 1947. The powers of BI continued to expand after the Second World War (De Cecco 1976). Yet, as these powers expanded so did BI's dependence on the Treasury. Dependence or fiscal dominance meant that interest rates had to be kept low so as to reduce the cost to the Treasury of financing budget deficits. Dependence also meant that interest rate targeting, rather than targeting monetary aggregates, was the preferred operating procedure.

The height of fiscal dominance was reached under the Governorship of Guido Carli (1960–75). In addition to monetising a large share of budget deficits, BI embraced the principle of administrative rules. Their aim was to redirect national saving away from the private sector and towards government, while keeping interest rates low relative to inflation rates. Banks were subject to ceilings on bank loans and minimum levels of purchases of government securities. An intricate web of regulations was enacted to prevent people from diversifying assets across currencies. Controls on exchange rates and capital movements were increasingly tightened to the point that the freedom to travel abroad was seriously compromised (chapter 8). Such actions were readily justified as the necessary price to keep interest rates below the level prevailing abroad and to allow the government to fund the excess of expenditures at 'reasonable' cost. Yet, the low cost of borrowing made it easy for the political authority to postpone needed adjustments. Hard decisions were not made and budget deficits rose. Fiscal dominance left a legacy of fiscal profligacy and the BI with low credibility. The entry of Italy to the EMS and the 'divorce' agreement of 1981 re-established some of the credibility the Bank had lost during the troubled 1970s. Under the push of the Economic and Monetary Union and the Maastricht Accord, the Italian central bank, with the permission of the political authority, has taken additional steps to enhance its independence from government. But these events are beyond the scope of our study.

Conclusions

The bulk of long-run money growth in Italy can be explained by the growth of the monetary base, which, in turn, can be explained by changes in its domestic source component. The actions of the monetary authorities during the fixed exchange-rate regimes were guided by the size of the government deficit and the desire to sterilise reserve flows.

Fiscal and monetary policies have often intertwined during the *History*. In the early days, the profit-seeking banks of issue were constrained by the convertibility clause and by a legal ceiling on their outstanding currency. Yet, these banks overissued from time to time. In our study of competitive central banking (Fratianni and Spinelli 1985, pp. 494–5) we concluded that:

The high probability, if not certainty, that government would legalise the excessive circulation, while maintaining the prices of bank notes unchanged, raised the expected profits of the overissuing bank. Had the latter faced a sharp drop in the price of her notes, its supply behaviour would have been different. The weak link in the system was government which maintained fixed relative prices among notes without actually controlling the aggregate amount of total currency in circulation. This weakness, in turn, had more of a political than an intellectual root: government borrowings were often the reason for breaking through the note ceiling.

Thus, larger budget deficits were the reason Italy got off the gold standard twice in the nineteenth century. The influence of public finances on monetary policy have become even stronger in modern times. Fiscal dominance, which is prevalent throughout the *History*, reached extreme forms in the 1970s. Budgetary improvements, on the other hand, set the grounds for lower money growth and the return to either the gold standard or stable exchange rates.

The stock of international reserves is the other key variable influencing the behaviour of the monetary authorities. This is true in the early as well as the later days of the *History*. In the early days the profit-seeking banks of issue had a bias for a low discount rate (i.e., high growth of the domestic source component), a policy that often ran into conflict with the maintenance of a stable ratio of specie to currency in circulation. The periodic balance-of-payments crises forced these banks to raise their effective discount rates, often to levels considerably higher than those prevailing in London or Paris. In modern times we have witnessed the massive deceleration of the monetary base from the end of 1963 to mid 1964 to stop the haemorrhaging of international reserves, and the web of exchange and credit controls woven around the Italian economy in the 1970s to prevent capital outflows.

The importance of the external constraint on monetary policy actions and outcomes emerge from two conflicting forces: the openness of the Italian economy and the desire of policymakers to achieve high growth rates of output and low unemployment rates. These conflicts have become more pronounced in modern times with the rise of Keynesian economics. Indeed, it is not surprising that the policy to decouple Italian financial markets from those abroad through a panoply of exchange controls and credit ceiling regulations coincides with the central bank adopting a wage-push view of inflation (chapter 8).

Changes in the money multiplier influence the growth of money more in the short than in the long run, a result that is in line with similar findings from other countries. Among the three ratios, the k ratio (public-held base money to deposits) has exerted by far the biggest impact on the money multiplier.

As to the interaction between the money multiplier and the monetary base, the latter was found to be Granger caused by the former. This finding is consistent with those policy regimes where interest rates and exchange rates, and not the monetary base, are the target variables.

Data Appendix *The monetary statistics of Italy, 1861–1991 (billion lire, year-end values)*

	BP	BR	BE	MBTR	MBOT	BF	D
1861	1.0566	0.00	0.00	0.040	0.8986	0.1180	0.1225
1862	1.1830	0.00	0.00	0.0370	1.0156	0.1304	0.1550
1863	1.1831	0.00	0.00	0.0420	0.9858	0.1553	0.1884
1864	1.1332	0.00	0.0074	0.0540	0.9420	0.1446	0.2000
1865	1.1619	0.00	0.0090	0.0620	0.9604	0.1485	0.2249
1866	1.6348	0.00	0.0095	0.6080	0.9147	0.1216	0.2247
1867	1.8033	0.00	0.0159	0.6700	1.0121	0.1371	0.2377
1868	1.8131	0.00	0.0113	0.7730	0.8229	0.2285	0.2766
1869	1.8344	0.00	0.0125	0.8250	0.7936	0.2283	0.2971
1870	1.9365	0.00	0.0312	1.2060	0.5133	0.2484	0.4961
1871	2.2059	0.00	0.0400	2.0870	−0.0650	0.2239	0.6379
1872	2.4208	0.00	0.0714	2.4600	−0.1749	0.2071	0.8905
1873	2.5154	0.00	0.0662	2.6680	−0.2982	0.2118	0.8197
1874	2.5365	0.00	0.0668	1.9730	0.4273	0.2030	0.8718
1875	2.5651	0.00	0.0586	2.2100	0.2693	0.1444	0.9685
1876	2.6073	0.00	0.0616	2.2404	0.2785	0.1500	1.0137
1877	2.6373	0.00	0.0621	2.2555	0.2936	0.1503	1.1405
1878	2.6481	0.00	0.0611	2.2634	0.2940	0.1518	1.2016
1879	2.6784	0.00	0.0745	2.2922	0.3120	0.1487	1.2747
1880	2.7250	0.00	0.0877	2.2903	0.3439	0.1785	1.3357
1881	2.6336	0.00	0.0865	1.5980	0.9838	0.1383	1.4155
1882	2.5141	0.00	0.0669	0.7800	1.6418	0.1592	1.4492
1883	2.4569	0.00	0.0781	0.7079	1.5043	0.3228	1.5969
1884	2.5502	0.00	0.0811	0.7438	1.5162	0.3713	1.7379
1885	2.6512	0.00	0.0918	1.0765	1.3277	0.3388	1.9041
1886	2.7505	0.00	0.0914	1.0531	1.4431	0.3457	2.1889
1887	2.7978	0.00	0.0954	1.3435	1.1704	0.3793	2.2734
1888	2.7888	0.00	0.1064	1.4085	1.0511	0.4356	2.3182
1889	2.9128	0.00	0.0835	1.2296	1.3278	0.4389	2.3133

Data Appendix (*cont.*)

	BP	BR	BE	MBTR	MBOT	BF	D
1890	2.9913	0.00	0.0782	1.5534	1.1063	0.4098	2.1869
1891	3.0163	0.00	0.0804	1.3299	1.3240	0.4428	2.0945
1892	3.0762	0.00	0.0710	1.3186	1.3813	0.4473	2.1995
1893	3.1292	0.00	0.0649	1.3810	1.3664	0.4467	2.1414
1894	3.1054	0.00	0.0679	0.7462	1.8904	0.5367	2.0806
1895	3.0678	0.00	0.0608	1.2428	1.3554	0.5304	2.2020
1896	3.0299	0.00	0.0650	1.1126	1.4233	0.5590	2.1433
1897	3.1588	0.00	0.0733	1.3306	1.3414	0.5601	2.1583
1898	3.2203	0.00	0.0745	1.4330	1.2947	0.5671	2.2579
1899	3.2893	0.00	0.0838	1.4562	1.3549	0.5620	2.5821
1900	3.3044	0.00	0.0780	1.4087	1.3941	0.5796	2.7050
1901	3.3478	0.00	0.0816	1.4214	1.4018	0.6062	2.9000
1902	3.4093	0.00	0.0876	1.5330	1.3205	0.6434	3.0219
1903	3.5582	0.00	0.0975	1.6703	1.1459	0.8395	3.2923
1904	3.7023	0.00	0.1056	1.8571	1.0879	0.8629	3.6227
1905	3.8360	0.00	0.1326	2.1199	0.7952	1.0535	4.1469
1906	4.1529	0.00	0.1348	2.0692	1.0202	1.1983	4.0269
1907	4.6147	0.00	0.1781	2.2527	1.1349	1.4052	4.3456
1908	4.6052	0.00	0.1894	2.4103	0.9280	1.4563	4.8231
1909	4.6915	0.00	0.1989	2.4113	1.0056	1.4735	5.2930
1910	4.9591	0.00	0.1989	2.8034	0.8664	1.4882	5.6054
1911	5.2532	0.00	0.2041	2.9494	0.9532	1.5547	5.9076
1912	5.2767	0.00	0.2319	3.0592	0.8593	1.5901	6.0531
1913	5.5049	0.00	0.2297	3.3743	0.7084	1.6519	6.3444
1914	6.4882	0.00	0.2761	4.5641	0.4687	1.7315	6.2106
1915	7.9192	0.00	0.3297	7.6266	−1.0666	1.6889	6.7164
1916	9.4563	0.00	0.4288	10.7910	−2.6323	1.7264	8.8759
1917	14.4586	0.00	0.4090	17.9178	−4.8337	1.7835	10.4735
1918	18.8585	0.00	0.5980	19.6112	−2.4853	2.3306	15.1427
1919	25.2392	0.00	1.0748	26.1171	−1.8480	2.0449	22.4748
1920	30.2692	0.00	1.4142	27.6348	1.9732	2.0754	27.8748
1921	30.3426	0.00	2.1901	24.7617	5.7724	1.9986	25.5397
1922	30.3321	0.00	1.1494	22.3396	7.1004	2.0415	27.2965
1923	29.2992	0.00	1.5397	20.1053	8.8862	1.8474	36.2903
1924	31.1745	0.00	1.7945	20.2077	10.9353	1.8260	42.7304
1925	31.9785	0.00	2.0139	22.0557	9.8959	2.0408	47.0603
1926	31.0754	0.00	2.6652	14.5060	16.7561	2.4785	55.89
1927	30.0675	0.00	2.8188	21.0030	−0.2226	12.1029	58.98
1928	29.9615	0.00	2.6702	14.4930	7.0679	11.0708	62.68
1929	30.7579	0.00	2.0103	18.3960	4.0310	10.3412	63.76
1930	30.8752	0.00	2.5548	21.1400	2.6657	9.6243	63.38

Data Appendix (*cont.*)

	BP	BR	BE	MBTR	MBOT	BF	D
1931	31.9927	0.00	1.6155	24.5230	1.2887	7.7965	61.32
1932	33.4282	0.00	1.9702	28.6690	−0.4146	7.1440	56.93
1933	34.6991	0.00	2.1243	33.4420	−4.0153	7.3967	58.11
1934	35.5857	0.00	1.8836	36.0370	−4.4509	5.8832	56.00
1935	39.4354	0.00	1.8002	36.1850	1.6559	3.3947	52.65
1936	43.6765	0.00	1.6915	47.9120	−6.5650	4.0210	57.41
1937	47.2456	0.00	1.5748	34.5970	10.1964	4.0270	54.17
1938	53.6937	0.00	1.2316	42.1500	8.9503	3.2460	60.97
1939	63.5887	0.00	1.4877	52.5340	9.2964	3.8250	55.53
1940	79.24	0.00	1.4697	70.39	7.9414	2.3770	72.46
1941	107.72	0.00	1.9418	94.32	12.9893	2.3470	93.63
1942	152.07	0.00	2.4287	129.96	21.8600	2.6720	117.95
1943	288.85	0.00	4.2975	216.56	64.8135	11.770	143.26
1944	426.29	0.00	4.7885	425.86	2.7820	2.4360	248.79
1945	549.31	0.00	9.4770	556.69	−0.3370	2.4360	406.59
1946	735.11	2.20	79.55	799.95	−8.8310	25.74	698.06
1947	1,066.13	73.30	204.67	1,027.29	231.29	85.51	1,013.89
1948	1,546.55	258.90	268.30	1,314.17	547.06	212.52	1,534.80
1949	1.933.47	349.90	311.70	1,512.32	673.39	409.36	1,972,40
1950	2,288.45	385.70	370.40	1,621.07	1,083.75	339.73	2,297.80
1951	2,443.65	457.30	466.40	1,753.92	1,247.17	366.26	2,726.60
1952	2,694.68	550.20	445.80	2,020.52	1,319.21	350.95	3,377.40
1953	2,926.12	658.00	453.00	2.262.59	1.340.15	434.39	3,946.70
1954	3,163.72	764.60	521.50	2,609.36	1,292.32	548.14	4,515.50
1955	3,399.32	885.60	563.10	2,845.22	1,263.89	738.90	5,218.60
1956	3,660.09	986.10	532.90	2,891.24	1,464.14	823.70	5,921.20
1957	3,826.44	1.094.40	611.70	3,070.22	1,397.62	1,064.70	6,590.70
1958	4,086.69	1,420.00	1,046.70	3,182.66	1,725.92	1,644.80	7,631.10
1959	4,453.22	1,692.00	1.302.40	3,082.97	2,089.95	2,274.70	8,930.80
1960	4,862.09	1,987.70	1,269.80	3.215.81	2.226.47	2,677.30	10,297.10
1961	5,500.83	2,282.80	751.20	3,399.64	2,508.99	2,626.20	12,057.40
1962	6,148.15	2,475.10	1,113.60	3,813.90	2,688.95	3,234.00	14,308.00
1963	6,935.32	2,782.70	783.00	4,627.40	3,357.62	2,516.00	16,174.40
1964	7,491.25	2,909.00	1.047.70	5,228.60	3,409.75	2,809.60	17,630.60
1965	8,266.53	3,390.30	1,118.00	5,833.10	3,505.13	3,436.60	20.728.00
1966	9,072.10	3,686.70	1,208.20	6,059.40	4,236.70	3,670.90	23,950.60
1967	10,030.00	3,873.80	1,154.60	6,367.00	4,777.60	3,913.80	27,407.30
1968	10,550.20	4,256.70	1,415.40	7,062.30	5,123.60	4,036.40	31,137.60
1969	11,629.50	4,754.70	1.090.00	7.704,60	6,383.00	3,386.60	34,670.00
1970	12,393.70	5,536.80	1,478.90	9,694.20	6,008.20	3,707.00	40,210.00
1971	14,216.70	6,698.70	1,845.00	11,117.50	7,579.80	4,063.10	47,372.00

Data Appendix (*cont.*)

	BP	BR	BE	MBTR	MBOT	BF	D
1972	17,075.90	7,936.00	1,849.40	13,523.90	9,690.30	3,647.10	56,203.00
1973	19,999.10	9,597.50	1,911.50	17,695.90	10,247.00	3,565.20	69,673.00
1974	22,042.60	11,091.70	2,481.20	22,757.00	12,440.80	417.70	81,381.00
1975	26,165.20	12,725.40	3,573.30	31,180.80	12,579.80	−1,296.70	101,558.00
1976	30,244.40	17,140.20	2,484.20	45,333.00	4,730.10	−194.30	124,059.00
1977	35,166.00	20,804.00	3,440.40	39,142.90	15,321.80	4,945.70	152,744.00
1978	43,146.20	25,880.30	5,312.70	55,086.50	8,395.90	10,856.80	187,934.00
1979	52,582.00	31,388.40	4,098.30	62,629.80	11,714.30	13,724.60	225,582.00
1980	58,216.50	34,434.80	4,677.70	73,745.80	9,152.70	14,430.50	255,314.00
1981	65,204.00	37,381.00	49,804.00	102,004.00	−8,872.00	14,357.00	276,434.00
1982	72,389.00	45,532.00	4,625.00	117,785.00	−3,946.00	8,707.00	332,079.00
1983	81,414.00	54,625.00	4,057.00	123,691.00	−1,142.00	17,547.00	376,613.00
1984	91,566.00	63,479.00	5,198.00	143,224.00	−5,669.00	22,688.00	421,529.00
1985	104,667.00	75,693.00	8,056.00	179,744.00	−338.00	9,010.00	466,104.00
1986	118,965.00	84,714.00	5,095.00	201,570.00	−5,350.00	12,554.00	506,036.00
1987	136,247.00	93,455.00	5,918.00	214,485.00	1,825.00	19,310.00	541,215.00
1988	151,674.00	102,898.00	4,982.00	235,016.00	−5,719.00	30,257.00	582,616.00
1989	177,468.00	112,645.00	5,413.00	257,255.00	−7,137.00	45,228.00	641,630.00
1990	191,946.00	125,490.00	4,284.00	270,231.00	−9,197.00	60,686.00	701,129.00
1991	210,679.00	128,915.00	5,107.00	301,234.00	−8,575.00	52,012.00	767,896.00

3 From political unification to 1913: creation of a new currency, multiplicity of banks of issue, banking legislations, monetary systems

Since its inception, (the Bank) has directed its activities to the well-being of the State.
Bank of Italy (1935)

Introduction

This chapter deals with the evolution of Italian monetary policy during the period from the political unification of the country to the eve of the First World War. Particular attention is given to the evolution of the legislation governing the activities of banks of issue, the monetary system, and the monetary relations with the rest of the world. As a result, the core of this chapter deals with the motivating factors and the practical repercussions of important new legislation passed in 1866, 1868, 1874, 1880, and 1893. We also emphasise the model of monetary policy adopted by the most important banks of issue in the country.

In view of the length of the period analysed, we shall deal separately with the two sub-periods 1861–96 and 1897–1913, in the hope that this demarcation will facilitate the reading of this chapter. Of course, we could have divided the period differently. Initially, in fact, we had considered 1893, the year when the Bank of Italy was formed, as the dividing line between the two sub-periods; but, as will be readily evident later, we have subsequently concluded that 1893 was not a significant year with respect to structural changes in monetary policy, nor did it bring specific new ideas with regard to real variables and the business cycle. For these reasons we decided to commence the second sub-period in 1897, a year that marked the beginning, in Italy and abroad, of a process of economic growth, which was one of the main features associated with the fifteen years preceding the First World War and an era usually known as the 'high tide' of the gold standard.

Banks of issue in the Italian states prior to political unification

Prior to political unification, Italy was divided into the several small states shown in figure 3.1. With some degree of approximation, the reader can

Figure 3.1 Italy at the time of unification
Source: Kindleberger.

visualise the process of unification as the result of the progressive expansion
of the Kingdom of Sardinia (or of Piedmont) which took place, for the most
part, in 1859–60. Our *History* begins in 1861, the birth date of the Kingdom
of Italy; but the process of unification continued in subsequent years. In
fact, in 1866 and 1870, through more wars, Venice and Rome, respectively,
were annexed; further annexations of territories in the north-east of the
country took place with the First World War.

In the following paragraphs we sketch the origins, evolution and main activities of the banks of issue in Italy's former states; this will provide us with some knowledge of the outstanding issues in pre-unified Italy, which will be developed in the following chapters, and the general circumstances which brought about the introduction of paper money in the period preceding 1861. These sections are structured to highlight the differences among the various banks of issue with respect to capital endowment, statutory and 'de facto' relations with government authorities, the degree of freedom in issuing paper money and their legal characteristics. The extent of information contained in each section is commensurate with the relative importance of each bank, both before and after unification.[1]

Banca Nazionale degli Stati Sardi (or Kingdom of Sardinia)

The first attempts to create a bank of issue in the Sardinian states date back to 1840. These attempts were not successful due to the opposition of political authorities. In 1844, however, the authorities approved the formation of a bank in Genoa, with capital of 4 million Italian lire entirely from private sources. Three years later, the establishment of a second bank, identical to the one in Genoa, was authorised with headquarters in Turin; it commenced its activities at the end of 1849.

The two banks, under the names Banca di Genova and Banca di Torino, respectively, were at the same time commercial banks and banks of issue. The main types of activities permitted by their statutes were discount operations, advances, deposit taking, the opening of non-interest-bearing current accounts and the issuance of bank notes. These notes were issued only in large denominations of 500 and 1,000 lire, in bearer form and convertible in bullion on demand. Their statutes proclaimed that the total amount in current accounts plus the notes in circulation, i.e., their demand liabilities, could not exceed three times the value of metal reserves held.

Even though they were formed to foster trade and stamp out usury, the two banks underwent a fundamental change of objectives in 1848, when the Treasury ran into financial difficulties due to the Kingdom of Sardinia's military confrontation with Austria. This was the beginning of an active and continuous process of reciprocal exchanges of favours and privileges, through which banks were gradually brought into the sphere of government interest.[2]

In the meantime, in 1849 the two banks merged into a new financial institution, under the name Banca Nazionale degli Stati Sardi, with capital of 8 million lire. The government strongly supported this merger as it recognised that it would benefit from a single, larger bank of issue.[3] Under normal circumstances, the notes of the new bank, which could now be issued in minimum denominations of 100 lire, had to be in bearer form and payable in metal on demand. The provisions of the old statutes, which limited total demand liabilities to a maximum of three times the metal reserves held, were maintained.

In a law passed in July 1850, the State formally introduced the system of a single bank of issue. Furthermore, the law imposed a new maximum limit of money in circulation, which was in addition to the existing statutory reserve ratio of one third. Finally, ties between the Treasury and the bank of issue were strengthened and the latter was authorised to carry out discount operations of Treasury bills, as well as advances against these instruments and a broader range of government securities coupons.

In July 1852 and April and October 1859 – on the occasion of new loans to the government – the bank obtained additional and significant concessions. In 1852 its capital was increased to 32 million lire, new types of activities were permitted and three new branches were opened. In April 1859 the inconvertibility of paper money was again proclaimed, but only until the end of the following October. In addition, a new principle was established whereby bank notes issued to meet the financial requirements of the government – also known as notes 'issued on behalf of the government' – were exempt from the regulations governing the quantity of money in circulation (both as maximum limits and in relation to metal reserves). This principle, which obviously also served the interest of the government, became a basic theme in the post-unitary history of controlling the outstanding stock of money. In October 1859, the bank was authorised to increase its capital to 40 million lire, as well as to expand its activities to Lombardy – in the event that this region would be annexed – and to issue notes also in smaller denominations of 50 and 20 lire. After the creation of the Kingdom of Italy, the relationship between the state and Banca Nazionale degli Stati Sardi was further strengthened.

The high initial growth of the bank is largely attributed to the initiative of Count Camillo Cavour, the prime minister of the Kingdom of Sardinia. Although an active advocate of free market forces, he believed that a strong pro-government central bank would bring about considerable benefits to the state (Corbino 1931, p. 281). Garelli (1879, p. 1148) wrote:

the Count of Cavour, being the practical statesman he is, considers that all governments have a powerful bank and resort as much as possible to its assistance in difficult times.

Since the majority of the Parliament of the Kingdom of Sardinia did not share Cavour's views, to attain his objectives the count sometimes resorted to his political influence, other times to diplomatic expedients and in other situations he simply postponed actions to a more opportune political period. For example, in 1851 – in connection with discussions about reinstating the convertibility of bank notes – he proposed to grant legal tender to notes issued by Banca Nazionale for a period of five years, as well as to authorise a capital increase from 8 to 16 million lire and to allow the bank to provide treasury services. Parliament did not approve these proposals as it considered them to be contrary to the principle of free enterprise.

During the years 1859–60, Cavour attempted, as much as possible, to extend the Banca Nazionale's presence in newly annexed territories. When circumstances were opportune, he exerted appropriate pressure on Parliament to pursue his strategy. In fact, as soon as the army of the Kingdom of Sardinia occupied Milan, a simple royal decree authorised the opening of a branch in that city. And even before the region of Emilia was annexed, the bank was already authorised to acquire the Banca degli Stati Parmensi and the Banca delle Quattro Legazioni, which operated in that region. On the occasion of the annexation of Italy's south, Cavour prevented the creation of a new bank of issue in the area, while making it possible for Banca Nazionale to pursue an aggressive expansion programme there.

And so, at the end of 1861, with eight full branches and 51 agencies, the bank had a presence throughout Italy, with the exception of Tuscany, where the opposition of local banks had been stiff. Even this resistance, however, would be overcome in 1865.

As Banca Nazionale became the 'de facto' pivotal force in a system of banks of issue in unified Italy, it is appropriate to elaborate further on the manner in which, until 1860, the bank pursued the objective of guaranteeing convertibility of its notes into metal, which also served the objective of protecting its own metal reserves. Until June 1857 in the Kingdom of Sardinia a usury law prevented banks from raising their discount rates above 6 per cent. Because of this law, it was difficult to assess how much Banca Nazionale was actually willing to change the interest rates to protect its reserves. We simply note that during the financial crisis of 1852–3, the discount rate was increased to the maximum of 6 per cent and, when necessary, the bank usually resorted to direct importation of metal from abroad. With the abrogation of the legislation on usury, which coincided with an intense financial crisis originating in the international market, the discount rate rose up to 10 per cent. It remained at that level for only one month and then quickly dropped to between 4.5 and 5 per cent. In the meantime, the metal inflow continued. Di Nardi (1953) rightly concluded, therefore, that the bank showed a clear and unjustified reluctance in fully relying on the interest rate mechanism.[4]

Banca Nazionale Toscana

The Banca di Sconto di Firenze was established in 1826 with capital of 1 million Tuscan lire.[5] In 1837 a similar bank was formed, the Banca di

Sconto di Livorno, with capital of 2 million. In 1857, the two banks merged and formed the essentially private Banca Nazionale Toscana, with capital of 3 million lire and branches in Florence and Leghorn. Between 1857 and 1860, the bank expanded its operations in Tuscany by acquiring four savings banks. Its capital was increased to 8 million lire.

The Banca Nazionale Toscana accepted deposits without interest but repayable on demand, or with interest but repayable with 30 days' notice. Its main source of income was the discount of bills of exchange. As a bank of issue, the institution, together with the Banca Nazionale degli Stati Sardi and the Banca dello Stato Pontificio, formed a group of banks authorised, in their respective states, to issue their own notes in bearer form and convertible into metal on demand. In the market place, bank notes circulated exclusively on a fiduciary basis. When presented to the Tuscan state, however, they became legal tender. By statute, total bank notes issued could not exceed three times the bank's paid-up capital, nor three times the value of metal reserves held.

Also by statute, the bank was not permitted to import metal from abroad. Consequently, to maintain the convertibility of its own notes – the only ones, in 1860, that had never been declared inconvertible – the bank could intervene only through the mechanism of interest rates. This crucial aspect of the notes represented a major difference between the Tuscan and Piedmontese banks. Another difference was the type of clientele: the former preferred to concentrate on its relationship with private clients, the latter dealt primarily with other financial institutions and with the government.

Banca Romana (or Banca dello Stato Pontificio)

The Banca Romana was established in 1833, with its head office in Rome. By statute, the bank was authorised to discount bills of exchange at a maximum rate of 5 per cent, extend advances, accept deposits in current accounts, and print various types of notes (payable to the bearer, or to order, on demand or maturing after a few days). The total value of notes in circulation could not exceed three times the value of metal held. At the beginning of 1848, due to the incompetence of its management, the bank was unable to guarantee the convertibility of its notes into metal. At this time, the Vatican government intervened and imposed a ceiling on the issuance of notes.[6]

In 1850, the Vatican government had to rebuild both the credibility and the net worth of the bank. Its capital was set at 1 million 'scudi'.[7] The bank's name was changed to Banca dello Stato Pontificio. The bank had the exclusive monopoly of issuing notes, accepting savings and providing credit facilities throughout the Vatican state. As in the case of the former Banca Romana, the stock of currency could not exceed three times the value of metal reserves.

The management of the new bank was not better than the previous one. In fact, between 1854 and 1856, the convertibility of notes into metal had to be limited to a daily fixed amount; this was equivalent to having part of the outstanding notes made inconvertible ('corso forzoso'). The same predicament reoccurred in 1866. In 1870, shortly after the Vatican government had increased the bank's capital to 10 million scudi, Rome was annexed to the Kingdom of Italy and the bank regained its former name of Banca Romana. The latter, against compensation, renounced its privilege of being the only bank empowered to carry out commercial banking activities and the issuance of notes in Rome.

The Banca Romana conducted its business in a shoddy and, often, illegal manner. In the 1850s and 1860s the bank did not appear to ever provide any significant financial assistance to the government.[8]

The bank had two branches, one in Ancona and the other in Bologna. In 1855 the Bologna branch was authorised to become private and to operate independently under the name of Banca delle Quattro Legazioni. By statute, this bank was empowered to issue fiduciary notes payable on demand to the bearer. Notes in circulation could not exceed three times the paid-up capital (200,000 scudi), nor the total value of bills of exchange outstanding in its portfolio.[9] As mentioned earlier, the bank was acquired by the Banca Nazionale degli Stati Sardi in 1861.

Banco di Napoli

In 1816 two banks were established under the same name of Banco delle Due Sicilie. One, known as 'dei privati' (for the people) took deposits from the public at large and from pawnbrokers; the other, known as 'di corte' (for the government) and falling directly under the management of the Minister of Finance, carried out treasury operations. The initial capital of the two banks was 7 million ducati.[10]

The government section of the bank was strengthened by a decree in 1818 which authorised discount operations at the bank 'di corte'. The new division, with capital of 1 million ducati provided by the Treasury, was empowered to discount bills of exchange to the public as well as to government bodies.

In 1862, the bank was named Banco di Napoli; its section 'di corte' was closed, while the bank continued to carry out its activities of a commercial bank. Its notes circulated virtually on a fiduciary basis and, for the most part, were even issued in the name of depositors.

Banco di Sicilia

The Banco di Sicilia was formed in 1850, owned by the government and under a different name, from the merger of various financial institutions established in 1843, which until this time had been part of the Banco delle Due Sicilie.

Until 1858, the bank operated only as a deposit-taking institution. Subsequently, it was authorised to discount bills of exchange and to issue notes in the name of clients (which were therefore transferable through endorsement) against deposits of metal. In 1860, the bank changed its name to Banco di Sicilia.

Stabilimento Mercantile di Venezia (or Veneto)

This bank was established in 1853 in Venice. The initial capital came exclusively from the private sector and amounted to approximately 3 million fiorini.[11] Between 1856 and 1863, the capital was first increased to 10 million and then reduced to 6 million fiorini.

The bank was the only exception in the Austrian–Hungarian empire, which included Lombardy and Veneto, where the role of bank of issue was performed exclusively by the Central Bank in Vienna. In fact, the Stabilimento Mercantile di Venezia was authorised to issue fiduciary notes in bearer form. The bank was acquired by the Banca Nazionale in 1866.

Banca degli Stati Parmensi

This bank was established in 1858 in Parma. Its authorised capital was 500,000 lire. The bank was empowered to issue notes in bearer form, payable on demand in metal money. The maximum value of notes issued was limited to three times the paid-up capital of the bank. In business circles, the notes could circulate only on a fiduciary (voluntary) basis. The bank was acquired by the Banca Nazionale in 1866.

Banca Toscana di Credito per le Industrie ed i Commerci d'Italia

Formed in Florence in 1860 by a provisional government, this bank began its activities only towards the end of 1863.[12] The bank's capital was 10 million lire, 3 million of which paid-up. It accepted interest and non-interest-bearing deposits and lent by way of discounting bills of exchange. It issued notes in bearer form and convertible on demand into metal. The fiduciary nature of the notes was emphasised in the bank's statute, which stated: 'Nobody is obliged to accept the Company's notes.' The statute also placed a ceiling, on total notes in circulation, of three times the bank's capital. On the other hand, no ratio was imposed on metal reserves in relation to the total value of notes in circulation.

Many or only one bank of issue in the new state?

Two important aspects are readily evident so far. The first is the wide diversity of banks of issue, stock of currencies and monetary policies in former states. Only some states had true banks of issue (i.e., banks that were authorised to issue notes in bearer form and with legal tender): the State of Sardinia, Tuscany and the Vatican State. The remaining states can be categorised into two sub-groups. In the first, banks were authorised to issue either registered notes, transferable through endorsement, or notes in bearer form, but circulating on a fiduciary basis (without legal tender). In the second sub-group, states had only metal monies. In these cases, the role of the bank was confined to a simple minting operation.

There were other important differences among the various banks of issue. Some were government owned, others privately owned, still others were of mixed ownership. Some had a large capital base, others did not. Their commercial activities and their relationships with public authorities were markedly different. But banks differed primarily on account of their interest rate policies, as well as in their objectives regarding the protection of metal reserves and convertibility of notes. As mentioned earlier, it was not by chance that notes issued by the Tuscan bank always maintained their convertibility into metal, while those issued by the Kingdom of Sardinia and Roman banks were proclaimed inconvertible on various occasions.

The second important aspect was that the process of political unification did not bring about a banking system whereby only one bank was authorised to issue notes. Of the banks of issue in former states, only the Stabilimento Mercantile di Venezia, the Banca degli Stati Parmensi and the Banca delle Quattro Legazioni – certainly three minor institutions – were liquidated. The remaining banks maintained their mandate to issue notes and a second Tuscan bank was added to this group. Through a persistent penetration into the regions gradually annexed to the Kingdom of Sardinia, the Banca Nazionale increased its size substantially and became much larger than the other banks of issue, but it did not become the only bank of issue in the kingdom of Italy. As shown in figure 3.2, the monopoly on issuing bank notes was reached only in 1926.

Why then, at the time of unification, was it not decided to establish only a single bank of issue? This is a critical question. In fact, as we shall see in the remaining part of this chapter, the option not to operate with one bank of issue often brought about strong negative repercussions on the quantity and

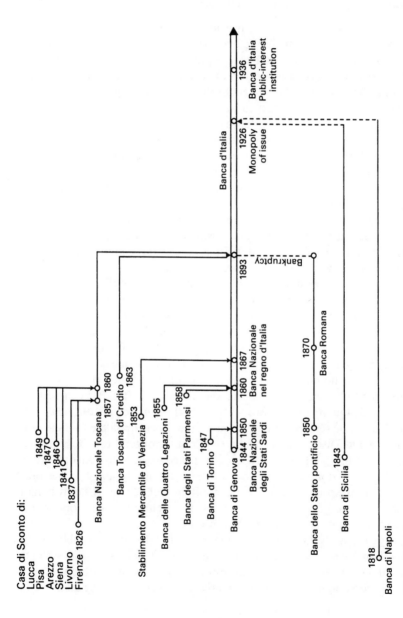

Figure 3.2 The origin of banks of issue and the evolution towards a single bank of issue
Source: De Mattia and Finocchiaro (1972, p. 339).

quality of currency stock, as well as on the stability of the country's whole banking system.

The answer to our question lies in the political circumstances and prevailing academic doctrines at the time. From the political standpoint, at the time of unification there were two opposing goals: the strengthening of the central regulatory authority over the whole new country and the respect for some important local aspirations, including those regarding the banks of issue. The creation of a single and strong bank of issue would certainly attain the first goal. With a statement that betrayed the Banca Nazionale degli Stati Sardi's dominating tendencies, but nevertheless emphasised the drive for a single bank of issue, the report to the annual meeting of shareholders in October 1863 indicated:

it is the strategy of this government that a single bank of issue should operate in Italy. While among various economic schools of thought it has not been resolved whether it is better for the nation to have one or more banks of issue, the government prefers the first alternative, but must concentrate its efforts on the political unity, which some internal factions, as well as external enemies, are opposing more than ever.

On the other hand – as recognised by Garelli (1879), Canovai (1912), and De Mattia (1959) – the strengthening of the country's political and economic unity could not totally disregard the opposing drive to respect local interests and jurisdictions.

A further obstacle to the notion of a single bank of issue stemmed from prevailing economic doctrines at the time. During these years, in fact, it was widely accepted that banks should be left free to issue their own notes. The most popular economist of this dominant liberal school was Francesco Ferrara, an expert in monetary matters, a member of Parliament and, in 1867, also Minister of Finance.[13]

The need to find a compromise between conflicting economic theories and practical requirements prompted political authorities to react with ambiguity and to change their position continuously with regard to either freedom for all banks or a monopoly for a single bank to issue notes. On the one hand, in the Kingdom of Sardinia and then in the Kingdom of Italy, the liberal doctrine generally prevailed to the point that: (a) the powerful Prime Minister Cavour himself had to repeatedly postpone his plan to strengthen the Banca Nazionale degli Stati Sardi; (b) a number of governments fell on account of proposed legislation interfering with the principle of plurality of banks of issue; and (c) in 1867 the Banca Nazionale degli Stati Sardi was not allowed to change its name to Banca Nazionale of the Kingdom of Italy, but was permitted to use the name Banca Nazionale in the Kingdom of Italy (Dell'Amore 1961, p. 476).

On the other hand, there were times when the faction supporting the notion of a single bank of issue prevailed. Let us review a few examples. In 1850, the Parliament of the Kingdom of Sardinia empowered only one bank, the Banca Nazionale, to issue notes. In 1863, thanks also to government mediation, the Banca Nazionale and the Banca Nazionale Toscana agreed to merge and form the Banca d'Italia. The agreement was approved by the Senate but was not ratified because of opposition in the House. In 1865, the same process took place. Parliament did not prevent Banca Nazionale degli Stati Sardi from expanding until it became by far the most important bank of issue in the country, and the only one with a presence all over the Italian kingdom.[14]

One bank of issue (BN) emerged as the dominant player. This outcome did not completely please either the competition supporters or the monopoly advocates. It was an outcome that reconciled the two schools of thought. Unfortunately, the country was too preoccupied to reach this compromise that did not pass the appropriate legislation to regulate banking and financial activities. This legislative inaction was the biggest flaw and induced more competition among banks of issue:

(i)   that were very different from each other in every respect;
(ii)   whose activities were regulated not by a central monetary authority but by common law and their own statutes (Di Nardi 1953, p. 119); and
(iii) that, being also commercial banks, they were in a position to shift the competition to the assets side of the balance sheet and, as a result, trigger some financial crises (Ripa di Meana and Sarcinelli 1990).

We shall return to this theme throughout the chapter.

The choice of a monetary system for the new state

The political unification of the country brought about the problem of creating a national monetary system. The solution to this problem entailed the choice of a 'base' for the monetary system and the elimination of existing regional differences with regard to currency stocks.

These initial differences, well analysed by De Mattia (1990), involved the circulation of both bank notes and metal currencies. As to bank notes, the fact of not having a single bank of issue and the lack of legislation to regulate money printing were clear indications that there was no willingness to have a single national currency. On the other hand, with regard to metal money, a decision was reached to unify the system. As this was, for the most part, only a mechanical process (i.e., withdrawing coins from former states and then smelting and minting them into a new metal currency), we do not consider it necessary to elaborate further on this matter.[15] Instead, it is appropriate to dwell on the problems connected with the choice of the base for the new monetary system. In fact, this choice had fundamental implications for the implementation of monetary policy. There were four possible solutions: inconvertible notes, notes convertible in silver, notes convertible in gold and notes convertible in gold and/or silver. For both practical and theoretical reasons, it became easy, almost automatic, to exclude the first solution.[16] The second, however, was feasible. In fact, a monometallism based on silver was clearly the most widely adopted system throughout the country. In the south, in particular, the only metal in circulation was silver. There were, therefore, basic good reasons for introducing a monetary system based on silver. However, there were strong opposing arguments coming from:

(i)   the authorities, who believed in the superiority of a gold-based system and, furthermore, were of the opinion that an imminent adoption of this system was inevitable at the European level;
(ii) the consideration that France, which had strong commercial, financial and political ties with Italy, had also always maintained convertibility in both gold and silver; and
(iii) the Banca Nazionale, in specific areas, was able to guarantee the convertibility of its notes only into gold.

In the end, the solution was again a compromise: convertibility into both gold and silver which, in practical terms, meant convertibility only into gold.

In the short run, it was not easy to extend the use of gold to the entire country. This was mostly due to the government's decision to impose a legal exchange ratio of gold–silver of 1–15.5. This ratio had been used in Europe since the beginning of the century and had been accepted almost as a natural law. Unfortunately, this ratio no longer reflected the relative market prices: silver was undervalued and, consequently, triggered the well-known mechanism of Gresham law.[17] A temporary and partial solution to the problem was found by reconciling a 'de facto' situation, where silver was the preferred metal, with a bimetallism that did not cause silver to disappear from circulation. In areas where gold was more widely accepted, the legal conversion rate of gold coins into silver was maintained, while in the rest of the country gold was allowed to be exchanged at a lower market value.[18]

The decision was reviewed a few months later. On 23 March 1862, the use of gold as a legal tender at its face value was extended to the whole country. On 24 August, to prevent the effects of Gresham law, the Parliament passed new legislation on the monetary system (De Cecco 1990, p. 76; Spinelli 1991). The legislation enforced the use of metal throughout the country, and, in so doing, introduced a gold-based monometallism in disguise. In theory, silver was given full legal tender at its face value; in practice, it assumed a very marginal role.

The kind of monetary system introduced resembled the French one, in terms of size and weight of metal coins, as well as the legal rate of exchange of gold–silver. In fact, however, the Italian system differed from the French in that it supported the role of gold without making it, as was done in France, the only metal in circulation.

The decision taken was the following: while Italian gold coins were the same (both in form and substance) as the French ones and had full legal tender, silver coins had limited legal tender and a nominal fineness of 900/1,000, but an effective content of silver of 835/1,000. As a result, the effective rate of exchange against gold increased from 1:15.5 to 1:14.38, in line with the market value of the two metals. Hence, silver was kept in the monetary system, but, in effect, gold became the only metal of exchange in international dealings.[19] In this respect, it is worth noting that the law also authorised the mint to issue a bigger silver coin with full legal tender and with an effective content of silver of 900/1,000, which could be used for international payments. However, the fact that this coin was heavy (Hawtrey 1927, p. 75) and, above all, could be minted only upon request, made it of limited practical use in the market place, considering the low price of silver.

The relationship with the Latin Monetary Union

In 1803 France introduced a new monetary system based on the principle of bimetallism, with an official gold–silver exchange rate of 1:15.5. From the very beginning, the government had great difficulties in maintaining this system in a world market where the price of precious metals was often subject to wide fluctuations.[20] Thanks to her political leadership, France was successful in convincing other European states to adopt a monetary system similar to her own. As a result, in the Kingdom of Sardinia, the Vatican State, Switzerland and Belgium coins were minted in such denominations, size and fineness that they were only slightly different from the French coins. By virtue of this basic uniformity of their monetary systems,[21] each of these states, including France, ended up also recognising as legal tender coins issued by other states. Consequently, coins could freely circulate from one state to another.

The new Kingdom of Italy was certainly in this position. In fact, it adopted a monetary system which had the two salient features of the French one: bimetallism and a gold–silver exchange rate of 1:15.5. Furthermore, the 1862 law, which defined and amalgamated the Italian metal monetary system, indicated:

by royal decree, the government has the power to give legal tender to foreign coins circulating in the state.

In December 1865, France, Italy, Switzerland and Belgium met in a monetary conference in Paris. The objectives, certainly ambitious, were to review the validity and the feasibility of bimetallism, to make their respective coins exactly the same, and to formalise their previous agreements on the international mobility of these coins, in order to arrive at an official monetary union. Italy and Belgium felt that the system should be changed to a gold-based monometallism. France, in spite of repeated past difficulties, insisted on bimetallism and, consequently, on the appropriateness of reviving the role of silver. The French position was predicated upon political and economic factors. On the political front, there was the underlying intention of creating a large monetary area to counteract Germany. On the economic side, the Bank of France maintained that it had more flexibility with bimetallism, while the two powerful private banks, Rothschild and Comptoir d'Escompte, preferred of course to continue benefiting from frequent arbitrage transactions which were made possible by a two-metal system.[22] France emphasised primarily the fact that, if bimetallism were adopted by several countries, it would become easier to control the precious metal market and therefore minimise the risk of triggering Gresham's law. On the basis of this argument, the French position prevailed.[23] As we have already seen, Italy's agreement with the French position, particularly with the idea of reviving the role of silver, was a mere formality.

With regard to the official gold–silver exchange rate, the fineness of the various coins and their legal tender, the monetary union decided to adopt the Italian system introduced in 1862. Finally, with regard to free currency movement from one state to the others, the four countries also undertook to extend it to silver and even copper coins. The only stipulation was that, within two years from an eventual termination of the agreement, each country commit to withdrawing its coins circulating in other states and converting them into gold or five franc silver coins or bills of exchange payable abroad.

At the 1865 Paris conference, the four countries signed an agreement called the Latin Monetary Union, which Greece joined three years later. Leaving aside the strategic and non-economic objectives pursued by France, the Union could bring significant benefits to each of the member states. The benefits were those usually associated with every monetary union, namely, the elimination of conversion costs in foreign exchange transactions and the reduction of international reserves. In the specific case of the Latin Monetary Union, these advantages did not materialise, as the modality and timing of this association soon made the agreement obsolete.

Ex-ante, member states erred by not coordinating their domestic economic policies.[24] The relationship between the Union and the rest of the world represented an additional problem. *Ex-post*, the French argument in favour of bimetallism proved to be completely misguided. After 1870, following the example of Germany, many countries chose monometallism based on gold. The price of silver dropped sharply and the Union ran the risk of becoming an area with a silver-based monometallism.[25] In view of these developments, member countries were forced to react and to make decisions, sometimes with others, sometimes on their own, that were always in contrast with the principle of bimetallism.[26]

The years 1861–1913: a quantitative overview

We shall now deal with a quantitative analysis of monetary and fiscal developments from political unification to the eve of the First World War.

The three fiscal ratios in the 1862–1913 period – government expenditures to national income, tax revenues to national income, and budget deficits to national income – were 13.5, 12.3 and 2.9 per cent, respectively. That is, government intervention was not only more contained in this subperiod than in the entire period, but also more conservative with regard to deficits (cf. table 1.4). This view is strengthened by the values of seigniorage and the inflation tax, 0.6 and –4.0 per cent of national income respectively, drastically lower than the corresponding 3.4 and 3.9 per cent of the longer period.

On the other hand, 82 per cent of the deficit was monetised, as opposed to 50 per cent for the longer period.

Out of 4.4 percentage points of the average money growth, approximately 3 percentage points were attributable to changes in the monetary base, of which the Treasury component was by far the most important force. The foreign component made a positive contribution, whereas the other elements of the domestic monetary base, mostly lending to banks, exerted a negative impact (cf. table 2.1). The money multiplier contributed on average 1.1 percentage points to money growth, a contribution which was entirely due to a secular decline of the k ratio. All in all, the main engines of money growth were the Treasury and the foreign components of the monetary base and the coefficient k.

From table 1.3 we see that money increased at an average which was about half the rate for the longer period. The velocity of money circulation, on the other hand, decreased at a rate that was almost twice that of the entire period. The average inflation was only 0.6 per cent against 6.9 per cent for the longer period (cf. table 1.3). As a whole, the period under consideration showed few monetary or real changes, a strong accumulation of money

(De Mattia 1991, p. 116) and exceptional price stability. The values of the standard deviations indicate that money supply, output and prices had a more stable growth than over the entire period.

Monetary base, money, output and prices from 1861 to 1896

We now analyse in more detail the years from 1861 to 1896. During this period, the monetary base grew at an average annual rate of 3.07 per cent and had a relatively high variability (the standard deviation was 6.73). In particular, the base grew quite sharply during the years 1866–7 and 1870–2, but dropped in absolute terms in 1864, 1881–3 and 1895–6.

The coefficient k showed a sharply decreasing trend (cf. figure 2.4). Between 1861 and 1872, it went from 8.53 to 2.5; in 1888, it recorded a minimum value of 0.95. This sudden drop was obviously indicative of an ongoing review of financial investment portfolios by the public. The negative trend in k came sometimes suddenly to a halt, the most significant example occurring between 1866 and 1867, when k rose sharply and remained at a relatively high level for the subsequent two years.

The coefficient re increased until 1872 and declined for the remainder of the sub-period (cf. figure 2.5). In the years 1864, 1873 and 1896, it was 3.7, 8.1 and 3.0, respectively. Thus, its variability was more contained than that of k. On the other hand, the movements of re were more unpredictable; the most significant deviations from its trend took place in 1867 and from 1879 to 1881.

The money multiplier increased rather regularly from an initial value of 1.12 to a maximum of 1.76 recorded in 1888; in 1896 it reached 1.67. Looking at the whole sub-period, the money multiplier had an average growth of 1.15 per cent and a standard deviation of 2.4. In sum, the ratio k, that is the public's behaviour, had a stronger influence than the ratio re, that is the banks' behaviour, on the growth of the multiplier.

As mentioned earlier, the behaviour of money reflected rather faithfully that of the monetary base, but was also amplified by the somewhat continuous growth of the multiplier. In 1861 and 1896, the stock of money was 1.18 and 5.17 billion lire, respectively. Its annual growth had a standard deviation of 6.4 per cent. As in the case of the monetary base, there was a rapid acceleration of the growth process in the years 1866–7 and 1870–2. In the years 1881–96 the trend of the multiplier, increasing at first and then decreasing, neutralised the effect of the sharp initial drop of the monetary base and its subsequent recovery on the quantity of money.

During the years 1861–96, there was a considerable decrease of the velocity of money, which went from a maximum value of 6.23 in 1861 to a minimum of 1.88 in 1889. All of this stemmed from the fact that in the first few decades following unification, money demand grew substantially, particularly the demand for bank deposits. In 1861, economic agents held a stock of money equivalent to 8.3 weeks of annual income; in 1889, it rose to 27.6 weeks' worth.

Between 1861 and 1896, real income, expressed in 1938 lire, grew from 49.0 to 60.1 billion. During the same period, the income deflator (1938 = 100) went from 15 to 17; therefore, we can safely say that, in the long run, prices were stationary. In the short period, however, there were wide and sudden movements in both directions; for instance, +11 per cent in 1872, –16 per cent in 1875 and +11 per cent in 1877. As was true for other countries during the years of the gold standard, price movements in Italy displayed jagged fluctuations (figure 1.2).

Exit from the gold standard

To understand the formulation and evolution of monetary policy during the initial years after unification, it is appropriate to focus both on the way banks of issue pursued their goal of defending the convertibility of their notes, and on the effects of fiscal policy. With Rome not yet part of the Italian state, there were only two real banks of issue: the Banca Nazionale Toscana and the Banca Nazionale degli Stati Sardi. Furthermore, considering that the latter had the bulk of financial resources, and the Tuscan bank increasingly tended to follow the directives coming from the former, we need concentrate only on the activities of the Banca Nazionale degli Stati Sardi.

The external constraint and interest rate policy

Due to the free flow of capital and gold between Italy and the rest of Europe, in principle the obligation of maintaining the convertibility of notes made it necessary for the Banca Nazionale (which we shall abbreviate BN) to monitor international money markets very closely. Consequently, also in principle, its discount rate policy had to follow the highs and lows of Paris, London and Berlin.

In practice, the importance of this external constraint already began to emerge between the end of 1860 and the first half of 1861 when, due to a surge in metal demand on the part of US grain exporters, all European banks considered it necessary to raise their discount rates (figure 3.3; Da Pozzo and Felloni 1964, p. 38). The importance of international relations was again evident on the occasion of the 1863–4 international monetary crisis.[27] Changes in the discount rate adopted by BN brought about fluctuations in the growth of the monetary base and the money stock. The 1864 decline, in absolute terms, of both variables therefore became understandable.

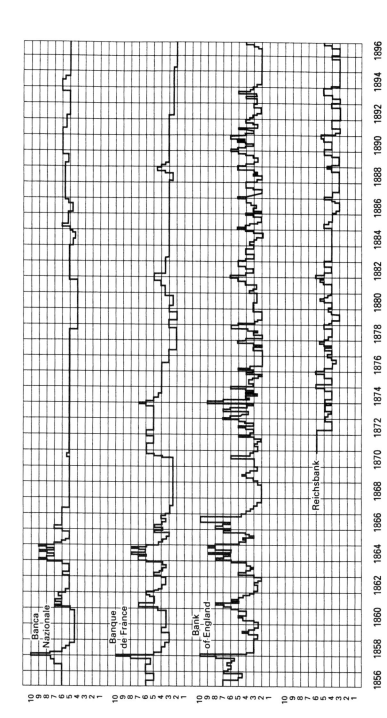

Figure 3.3 Monthly discount rate charged by European central banks, 1856–1896
Source: Da Pozzo and Felloni (1964).

Di Nardi (1953) analyses BN's behaviour during the 1863–4 crisis. It transpires that discount rates were raised late, when in fact it seemed more appropriate to restrain rather than prevent domestic repercussions arising from the international crisis. Furthermore, from figure 3.3 it is clear that, at the height of the crisis, the Italian discount rate was only equal to that prevailing in France and England and this was not sufficient to prevent the outflow of capital from Italy. In fact, as demonstrated by Lindert (1969), in those years the central banks of more financially developed countries were able to attract both foreign capital and reserves, even when discount rates in other countries were on the same level. Consequently, to stop the depletion of reserves, it was not sufficient to align the Italian discount rate with that of other European markets. This explains why BN's reserves dropped from 50 to 28 million lire. Overall, therefore, BN continued the lax monetary policy typical of the period preceding unification.

The short average holding period of bank notes was an indication of such a policy. In pre-unification states, the public showed a clear preference for coins (De Mattia 1991, p. 67). This propensity did not abate but rather increased after 1860; as a result, the average holding period of BN's notes was 121 days in 1860, 75 in 1862 and 65 in 1864. This is not the appropriate time to analyse the underlying reasons behind the initial, significant lack of success of bank notes.[28] However, we need to emphasise that it brought about a continuing depletion of metal reserves. For instance, with an average holding period of 75 days, each lira bank note was 'recycled' into metal (at the bank) almost five times a year. It should also be considered that, in similar circumstances, banks of issue should at least have tried to curb the creation of banknotes through the discount rate mechanism.

How could BN guarantee the convertibility of its own notes despite the increasing drain on metal reserves? In the absence of a discount rate policy, it resorted to direct importation of metal from abroad, just as it used to do during the pre-unification era. The bank imported metal for 49 million lire in 1860, 118 million in 1862 and 151 million in 1864. This meant that monetary policy did not follow the traditional rules of the game of the gold standard, and that the strategic objective of maintaining the convertibility of bank notes became increasingly vulnerable to the forces of international financial markets.

Fiscal policy and the premium for country risk

The pursuance of the convertibility objective should also be viewed in light of the government budget policy. During the early years of the new state, the government deficit was, on average, equal to 10.5 per cent of domestic income. This was not compatible with long-run price stability and a premium for Italian risk emerged. Consequently, it did not make sense for the country to remain in the gold standard.

Interest rates applied by BN were sometimes lower than yields on government securities and, between 1860 and 1865, its loans to the government increased from 16 to 28 per cent of the bank's total assets. Obviously, by taking advantage of the large government deficits, BN was determined to become the 'government's bank'. On the other hand, the differential between yields on Italian and foreign government securities remained positive. Between 1861 and 1865, the yield gap was such that it encouraged a total inflow of capital, and hence reserves, into Italy of approximately 600 million lire.

In their frequent placement of securities abroad, the Italian authorities relied primarily on the powerful French banking institution Rothschild. During 1865, Rothschild urged the Italian authorities to embark on a less expansive fiscal policy and, at the same time, it repeatedly declined new credit applications coming from the Minister of Finance and BN; see Gille (1968). These were signs forewarning a crisis that reached its peak between the end of 1865 and the following spring.

The crisis was triggered by the announcement of a large deficit for the fiscal year of 1866, coupled with a more widely spread perception of a new war with Austria and a general and sustained increase in interest rates on the international market. At first, it became impossible for BN and the Italian government to obtain foreign capital. Later, they could not stop a massive outflow of funds from the country. This change in capital movements was attributable to a new perception of the Italian country risk on international financial markets. Prices of Italian government securities dropped sharply on European stock exchanges, including the French stock exchange, which was of vital importance to Italy (Da Pozzo and Felloni 1964, pp. 81–2). The main bond traded abroad was the Rendita Italiana, and by far its largest volume of foreign trading took place in Paris. There, between 1860 and 1865, the price of this bond dropped from 80 to 65.4. At the end of April 1866, it plunged to 43.9. The negative differential between international and domestic prices of Italian government securities brought about easy opportunities for profit-taking and encouraged the outflow of metal. Italian speculators withdrew their bank savings and converted them into metal, which they used to buy securities abroad that were then sold in Italy (see Majorana 1893; Supino 1929; Cornaro 1931, p. 21). As a whole, as estimated by Corbino (1931, p. 168), a total of 400 million lire worth of Italian government securities found its way back into Italy during 1866.

Banks in difficulty and proclamation of inconvertibility

The process of converting savings into metal for further transferral abroad created great difficulties for the whole banking system. Ferrara (1868), Majorana (1893) and, before them, the House Committee inquiring into inconvertible paper money (which will be discussed later in this book) recognised that at least four banks showed signs of difficulties. Majorana mentioned that even BN was on shaky ground and Ferrara wrote that the solidity of 'the most creditworthy institutions' was in question. It was not clear whether he also referred to BN. It was true, however, that some of the troubled banks were controlled by BN, which had lost 30 million lire in metal reserves between October 1865 and April 1866.

The country resolved this crisis by abandoning the gold standard: a government decree of 1 May 1866 proclaimed banknotes no longer convertible into metal, effective the following day. This was a critical decision in Italian monetary history. Only in 1880 and 1927 were there resumptions of currency convertibility, and in both cases that ceased fairly quickly. Kindleberger (1984, p. 140) wrote that:

[The suspension of convertibility] represents a traumatic event for a country not so familiar with the use of paper money and afraid of its dangers transpiring from the French experience with John Law.

Economists, bankers and politicians were never unanimous in their views as to whether it would have been possible to avoid Italy's exit from the gold standard. On the premise that the conduct of fiscal and monetary policies remained unchanged, the country had no choice but to abandon the gold system. In fact, the fiscal authorities did not want or were unable to reduce the deficit to acceptable levels or to let yields on government securities rise to a level commensurate with country risk. On the monetary front, the banks of issue, primarily BN, were not prepared to bring discount rates to such levels so as to facilitate the protection of deposits and reserves (Corbino 1931, p. 272).

BN was not only 'reluctant' to increase rates to levels which would discourage discount transactions and advances; it did not even take any other action while the crisis unfolded. To protect its own reserves, the bank had increased the discount rate on bills of exchange to 10 per cent in 1857, 7 per cent in 1861 and 9 per cent in 1864. In January 1866, when the need for stronger measures started to become clear, the discount rate rose only from 6 to 7 per cent, then slid down again to 6 per cent in March. Rates applied on advances against securities (10 per cent in 1857, 7.5 per cent in 1861 and 9.5 per cent in 1864) increased only to 8 per cent at the beginning of 1866, and later dropped to 7 per cent. As these rates were not internationally competitive, it was obvious that 'arbitrage' transactions would quickly undermine the stability of the Italian monetary and financial system.

Overall, the departure from the gold standard was the logical and inevitable consequence of fiscal imbalances and the low interest rate policy. Again, the reader will remark that these two events are always concurrent in every monetary disorder in Italian history.[29]

Suspension of convertibility and BN

With regard to BN, *ex-ante*, the exit from the gold standard might have helped its plans for a dominant role in Italy by weakening the external constraint which invariably generated a depletion of its reserves. *Ex-post*, the bank enjoyed those advantages strictly connected with the decree suspending convertibility.

First of all, the decree specified (article 1) that BN should grant the government an extraordinary advance of 250 million lire in paper money (15 per cent of the total monetary base in 1865) at the annual interest rate of 1.50 per cent. The gold standard placed some restrictions on the ability to monetise government deficits. It did not come as a surprise, therefore, that the exit from the gold standard coincided with the decision to quickly accelerate the process of printing paper money.

The decree certainly strengthened the position of BN *vis-à-vis* other banks of issue. In fact, economic agents could refuse to accept the notes issued by other banks, but not those of BN. BN notes were used as reserves by other banks but these banks' notes were not accepted as reserves by BN on the principle of the 'riscontrata' (clearing). The result was that BN had a dominant position in the banking system.[30] It did not come as a surprise, therefore, that from 1 May the volume of other banks' notes in circulation could not keep up with BN's (Supino 1895). On the other hand, the decree had strong negative repercussions on BN's hegemonic plans, in that the number of banks of issue increased from two to five (Corbino 1931).

The ratio k

From December 1865 to December 1866, total monetary base increased by almost 40 per cent. This growth rate was by far the highest of the entire period from unification to the eve of the First World War.

There is evidence also that within the country people doubted the soundness of the Italian financial and banking system; the ratio k, which between 1861 and 1865 dropped from 8.53 to 4.99, rose to 6.86 in 1866. It increased further to 7.36 in 1867. The strong sensitivity of k to the country's financial instability is a recurrent theme of Italian monetary history. The money multiplier, which rose from 1.12 to 1.18 from 1861 to 1865, declined to 1.13 in 1866. In 1866, the quantity of money increased by approximately 29 per cent; similarly, this variable, too, recorded the fastest annual growth of the entire period 1861–1913.

Outflow of metal and illegal currency

Internal prices and, more suddenly, the lira exchange rate began to rise quickly. The monthly average rate with France (lire against 100 francs) was still equal to 99.85 in April; in May and June it rose to 103.88 and 112.75, respectively.[31] The average annual rate for 1866 was 108. The rapidity and intensity with which the lira exchange rate reacted to domestic monetary shocks represents yet another constant of Italian monetary history (Spinelli 1989).[32]

Metal outflow from the country continued. This was reflected in an exchange rate largely in excess of the gold export point.[33] Because of agreements under the Latin Monetary Union, the outflow of metal also involved coins of cheaper metal alloys. The economic doctrine at that time dealt extensively with the resulting difficulty of carrying out small commercial transactions and the fact that the market soon created surrogates of small denomination notes. (Ferrara 1868, p. 17; Ferraris 1879). De Mattia (1967) estimated that this type of currency, recorded as 'illegal' in official statistics, reached a volume of 18 million lire at the end of 1868. This was probably as much as the market required at that particular point in time.

We are not surprised with either the phenomenon of illegal surrogates, nor with their physical characteristics, nor with their total volume. It is worth noting that this phenomenon reoccurred first in the 1890s and again in the 1970s, that is when there was an excess demand of currency for small denominations. At this juncture, it is appropriate to dwell on a much more important aspect which almost invariably escapes the analysis of historians: the reason monies of small denominations disappear completely from the market place.

When a country goes from a gold standard to a system of inconvertible paper money, metal currency will not necessarily disappear. In general, a dual price system develops in the market: higher prices for payments effected with paper money and lower ones for those made with metal money. A clear example is given by the so-called greenback period in the Unites States which, incidentally, was almost contemporary with these Italian events. As noted by Friedman and Schwartz (1963), in such a situation metal money was not melted or transferred abroad, because the authorities did not impose a single level of prices which would have indirectly devalued the coins. In the case of Italy, however, article 3 of the decree passed on 1 May 1866 'provided' that one gold lira should have the same purchasing power as one paper lira. This legislation, therefore, forced the metal out of the market. The disappearance of large denomination coins may have been mitigated by the fact that, in private negotiations, a mutual trust between parties could overcome restrictions imposed by the law. Small denomination coins, however, were bound to disappear completely from the market place. This is attributable to the high component of fixed costs which made it uneconomical to convert money from legal to real value. Monies of small denominations were therefore either collected or smelted. Italy's membership in the Latin Monetary Union facilitated the disappearance of metal money as people who wanted to cash in the real market value did not even need to smelt coins or exchange them through foreign exchange transactions (Ferraris 1879b; Rolnick and Weber 1986).

The discount rate after the proclamation of inconvertibility

We close with an observation concerning the trend of the discount rate following Italy's exit from the gold standard. In light of what we have already mentioned about the underlying reasons for that event and the fact that the government had the final say on rates, it is not surprising that, as from May 1866, discount rate fluctuations became less frequent, remained decidedly within narrow margins and lost any relationship with international monetary events (see figure 3.3).

The 1868 law

In June 1867 the Minister of Finance, Ferrara, tabled a bill to end inconvertibility, although the necessary conditions for resuming convertibility did not exist. The bill, which also intended to put some order into public finances through the sale of assets obtained from religious bodies during unification, was not passed in parliament and Ferrara resigned. In March 1868, shortly after the proposal was resubmitted by Ferrara, a House Committee of Enquiry was appointed to review the matter (Spinelli 1989a). Within the first half of the month of April, the Committee was expected to issue a report on the money market and the internal situation of the banks of issue, as well as to formulate concrete proposals for a return to convertibility. The report, which was made public at the end of November, emphasised primarily the necessity of gradually reducing the amount of paper money outstanding in the country until the lira exchange rate was realigned to gold. Once the depreciation of the lira (relative to gold) was eliminated, it would be possible to resume convertibility 'at par'.

The suggestion to gradually reduce the money stock was accepted by Parliament on 3 September, that is before the Committee's report became publicly known. A new law was proclaimed to define an absolute maximum ceiling for the outstanding amount of BN's notes. This followed existing banks' statutory regulations and the provisions of a decree passed on 1 May 1866 regarding the ratio between reserves and currency stock. The new law was important because it marked the beginning of a process of direct control by Parliament on the quantity of paper currency outstanding in the market, a control that lasted almost until the Second World War. On the other hand, the law imposed partial control on the currency stock, as it regulated only notes issued by BN. In spite of this, the law produced positive results. For two consecutive years (1868 and 1869), the total monetary base did not increase and annual average growth remained around 2 per cent. During the same period, a reduction in internal prices and a significant improvement in the nominal exchange rate of the Italian lira also occurred. In April 1869, the Minister of Finance, Cambray-Digny, tabled another bill to end inconvertibility. However, the lira exchange rate indicated that such a move was indeed premature, and consequently the bill was not passed.

To justify the new law, it would have been sufficient to wait, as suggested by the Committee of Enquiry, until the rate of exchange dropped below the export gold point. Unfortunately, new circumstances dictated that it was no longer possible to continue with the ceiling set by the 1868 law. The determining factor which, at the beginning of the 1870s, fuelled a strong acceleration of the monetary base was the coming to maturity of government securities for approximately 500 million lire. This event and the intention of the new Minister of Finance, Sella, to drastically reduce yields on government securities explain why the monetary base suddenly exploded (the differential between domestic and external interest rates went almost to zero).

A law passed on 11 August 1870 authorised BN to lend 222 million lire to the government, partially in gold and partially in new notes, and brought the total limit of its paper currency from 750 to 800 million lire. On 28 August, an additional loan of 50 million lire by BN was authorised and its note ceiling was raised to 850 million lire. A law passed on 16 June 1871 approved a third loan of 150 million lire entirely in paper money; the ceiling of BN's outstanding notes was increased further to one billion lire. A law approved on 19 April 1872 authorised a fourth BN loan for 300 million lire in new notes and increased the BN's currency limit by the same amount. As a whole, during a period of only 20 months, BN was authorised to boost the total value of its notes from 750 to 1,300 million lire. It is also worth noting that BN was not obliged to keep metal reserves against new notes issued.[34]

During the three years 1870–2, the annual average growth rate of the monetary base remained in the 10 per cent range. The drastic reduction of the coefficient k contributed to increases in the money supply, for which the annual average rate was slightly less than 15 per cent (figure 1.1). Between 1871 and 1873, changes in domestic prices, both in absolute terms and relative to foreign prices, and lira depreciation reached values which are among the highest of the entire period 1861–1913. The combination of low nominal interest rates and high inflation generated seigniorage which was the highest for that period (figure 2.7). On the positive side, there was a substantial increase in the volume of stock exchange transactions as well as a sign of improvement in manufacturing activities which returned to previous values in 1873 (Da Pozzo and Felloni 1984, p. 124). These developments could be ascribed to the monetary surprise. In summary, the return to convertibility, which at the end of 1869 was within reach, became an impossible goal.

The 1874 law

Between the end of 1873 and the beginning of 1874, a number of aspects of Italian monetary policy proved to be highly problematic. Paper money was inconvertible and the exchange rate was above the export gold point. With regard to paper currency stock, there were inconvertible notes backed by metal reserves and notes with legal tender, supported partly by metal and partly by paper reserves. Furthermore, there were notes circulating all over the country and others confined to more limited areas. The value of notes issued by each bank had to adhere to limits imposed by its statute, obviously different from bank to bank, as well as to restrictions arising from the obligation, common to all banks, to respect a specific ratio in relation to reserves. For the stock of BN's notes, there was also a global limit imposed by parliament.

In addition, there were major deficiencies in supervisory and control functions over the activities of banks of issue. The Preface in De Mattia's volume (1967, pp. XIX–XX) recited:

For the banks of issue operating in pre-unification states, [government control] was generally carried out by an inspector who was appointed by the King and, paid by the banks, was based permanently at their executive offices. [Later on] the control function on the banks was retained by the Minister himself, who performed it through government inspectors, visits and controls of various kinds, assignments to local governors, peripheral offices and divisions of various ministries. In this way, the direct and ongoing control by a senior official invested with personal responsibility and acting on behalf of the Minister at each of the banks, was replaced by the faceless and undefined power of bureaucracy, with no delegation of authority.

An important indication of deficiencies in supervisory functions was given by the ministerial circular of June 1873, which reminded credit institutions of their obligation to contain the amount of paper money within the limits imposed by law and statutes. It was then clear that there was an 'illegal' currency stock created by the banks of issue, which existed in addition to the already mentioned illegal currency substitutes generated by ordinary banks, public institutions and private economic agents. The banks of issue's 'illegal' currency first declined to 9 million lire by the middle of 1870 and then increased to almost 47 million in June 1873. As a whole, ineffective government controls were responsible for an expansion in the stock of currency.

Many of the problems just outlined were interrelated. For example, it was not possible to guarantee that the notes of the various banks of issue had the same type of cover, the same legal characteristics, and the same ability to circulate over the entire country without first establishing a more equal balance of powers among the various banks. To do this, it was necessary that the government repay its debt to BN, which by now amounted to over one billion lire. Debt payment would also be an essential step to bring the total currency stock in the country, as well as domestic prices, in line with the gold parity of the lira, and then consider resuming convertibility. Another example, the elimination of illegal money substitutes made it necessary to determine how supervisory activities would be carried out and what freedom should be given to banks for issuing currency.

The legislator must have considered these problems in formulating the law of 30 April 1874, which authorised the establishment of a consortium of the six banks of issue for the purpose of issuing inconvertible notes for one billion lire.[35] These notes, which were basically 'government notes', as they were printed on behalf of the government, were given to BN in settlement of its credit position towards the government. BN undertook to withdraw from the market its notes originally issued to provide those credit facilities. Consequently, government notes replaced BN's paper currency in the market place. The law emphasised the fact that, with this change, BN 'was in the same general position as other institutions'. To further reduce BN's relative power, the law liberalised the process of territorial expansion for all banks and authorised the notes of each bank to circulate as legal tender in the areas where it had a presence. In this way, other banks were encouraged to open new branches.

To establish a level playing field for the various banks, the law imposed a maximum limit on the amount of notes issued by each bank. It stated that notes outstanding (plus any other demand liability) could not exceed three times the paid-up capital at the end of 1873, nor three times the value of metal reserves and consortium's notes held. A decree passed on 23 September 1874 checked into the capital base at that time and established the following limits: 450 million for BN, 63 for Banca Nazionale Toscana, 15 for Banca Toscana di Credito, 45 for Banca Romana, 146.5 for Banco di Napoli and 36 for Banco di Sicilia. Notes issued by the consortium on behalf of the government were exempt from any restriction regarding capital and reserves.

As the amount of capital eligible with regard to currency limits was not allowed to increase over time, the legislator was confronted with the problem of how to provide flexibility to the stock of currency. In this respect, the law indicated that, in exceptional circumstances, the government itself could authorise specific banks to exceed currency limits. New significant changes were also introduced with regard to the currency's legal characteristics. Inconvertibility was in fact reserved only for notes issued by the consortium. By contrast, notes issued by other banks were convertible: upon request, they had to be exchanged with 'notes of the consortium or metal money'. The problem of illegal currency substitutes was also tackled. The law provided that, for the whole duration of inconvertibility, no private or public entity, with the exception only of the six banks of issue, was allowed to issue bearer notes; for the first time, therefore, the function of issuing currency was restricted to a select number of banks. To fight illegal currency, the legislator specified a penalty equal to the value of such currency and attempted to strengthen supervision over the activities of the banks of issue. To this end, a regulation approved in January 1875 provided that supervision should be carried out through government inspectors who were based at the banks' head offices and who had extensive control powers but limited preventive authority.

Fiscal discipline and the return to convertibility in 1880–1883

While some aspects of the 1874 law were adequate to cope with the country's monetary problems, others were not. There was no doubt it was appropriate for the law to identify and restrict the number of banks authorised to issue paper money. However, as the new legislation related only to the period when the currency was inconvertible, it was not a crucial step against the existing principle of freedom in the issuance of currency. In other words, the government had not yet made a clear choice between monopoly and freedom for all banks to issue money. Second, the law placed too much reliance on the possibility that smaller banks would expand rapidly in other areas. Incentives offered by the law to these banks were fairly modest in relation to the difficulties of setting up and supporting the distribution of their own currencies on a national scale in competition with BN. The legislator did not have to wait long to realise that equality of power among the banks was not achievable at that time; for example, in September 1874 the government considered it appropriate to limit the 'riscontrata'. Third, not much progress was made under the new legislation, in terms of the variety of notes constituting the currency stock. In fact, the new government notes were different from those issued by banks, not only in their physical appearance, but also with regard to their legal characteristics and reserve requirements. Fourth, the conditions imposed by the law were too onerous for the banks to make the currency stock sufficiently flexible and remain at the same time within the boundaries of legality (Confalonieri 1974, p. 9). Fifth, the future of the monetary system remained unresolved. The law did indeed stated that 'within six months . . . the government . . . would have to submit a report on the matter of paper currency to the House, with recommendations aimed at ending inconvertibility'. But the law did not indicate how the new currency limits, which incidentally did not differ significantly from the status quo, would help attain that goal. Nor did it specify how to proceed with the replenishment of metal reserves necessary to the banks of issue for resuming convertibility.

In summary then, as also emphasised by De Rosa (1964b), we can say that the law dealt simply with regulating the currency stock during the inconvertibility period, but did not create the right environment for resuming convertibility.

In the long run, the negative aspects of the law prevailed over the positive ones. In fact, we shall see later how the financial crisis of the 1890s was mostly attributable to the former. By contrast, the positive aspects prevailed in the short term. This became evident in the foreign exchange market where, from March to June, the exchange rate with the French franc dropped from 115 to 110 lire. With regard to the medium term, it is not easy to express an opinion, as the law was introduced around the same time that the government balanced its budget for the first time since unification.

We already noted that Italian monetary policy was strongly influenced by budget trends and public-debt policy. In this respect, we reiterate the role that these two factors played in bringing about the monetary shocks of 1866 and 1870–2. The situation reversed as a balanced budget eliminated the pressure to raise the currency stock. Notes issued by the consortium on behalf of the government, which by law could only go up to one billion lire, were 880 million at the end of 1874 and remained in the range of 940 million from 1875 until the end of the decade and after. From December 1873 to December 1880, BN's notes increased by 111 million lire and slightly exceeded the legal limit on only one occasion. During the same period, the currency stock of other banks decreased (in total) by 26 million lire, but, with the exception of the Banca Romana's, remained regularly within the permitted maximum limits. During the years 1873–80, the average growth of the monetary base was 1.2 per cent and the average money growth was 2.8 per cent. As shown in figure 2.1, monetary growth was both restrained and stable. The wholesale price index fell from 21.7 in 1873 to 19.3 in 1880, while the income deflator dropped from 21 to 18.

The 1880 bill

On 15 November 1880 the Minister of Finance, Magliani, submitted a bill to resume convertibility, in the belief that the government budget and the monetary and financial situation could withstand the change (Rozenraad 1891). The bill contained three key points. First, it was necessary to replenish the country's metal reserves by launching a large issue on the international market. Second, the amount of outstanding paper currency had to be gradually but consistently reduced. Third, bank and government notes needed again to become convertible on demand.

The market reacted favourably to the bill, despite the fact that it was the last of a long series of such bills and did not indicate a resumption date. It was perceived that the bill would be approved by Parliament and it was noteworthy that the bill guaranteed the convertibility of paper money at its nominal value, despite the fact that at that time gold was worth approximately 10 per cent more than paper money. The rate of exchange reacted promptly and positively, reminding us of the English return to convertibility in 1819.[36] In fact, from a value of 109.57 lire in June 1880, the exchange rate with the French franc declined to 105.20 lire in the following November and 100.52 lire in June 1881. A number of authors focused on the rapid recovery of the Italian lira and indeed recognised the positive psychological implications of this bill (Canovai 1912, p. 62; Borgatta 1933, p. 157).

It was not only the exchange rate which reacted in anticipation of future developments. The monthly index of wholesale prices was 119.07 in June 1880, 108.92 in November and 105.93 in June 1881. Figure 2.7 shows that seigniorage dropped until it reached almost –9 per cent of national income.

A substantial and rapid increase in money demand transformed expectations into actual outcomes. Requests increased for the now rare coins primarily because of the necessity on the part of the Treasury and the banks to acquire as much metal reserves as possible in view of the return to convertibility. This was indeed the reason the government was authorised 'to acquire through treasury operations . . . the amount which was required for the conversion . . . of notes'. Furthermore, foreign borrowing was authorised as well. The banks had to move in two directions: to acquire as much metal money as possible and, if possible, to reduce the amount of their own notes in the market. It was not by chance, therefore, that the reserves to deposits ratio increased (figure 2.5).

International borrowing in 1881 and return to convertibility

As expected, the bill was approved by parliament and became law on 7 April 1881. While the consortium was being dissolved (it did in fact take place on

30 June), the solution to a bigger practical problem became more reachable: the placement abroad of part of government debt.

The transaction had been planned since the middle of the 1870s when, also upon the suggestion of major foreign financial advisors, the Italian authorities commenced redeeming government securities in order to stimulate an increase in their market prices. In fact, the price of Rendita Italiana 5 per cent, which was the type of security intended to be distributed abroad, increased from 79.15 in December 1875 to 83.71 in December 1878 and to 94.81 in October 1880. It was also in light of this performance that the authorities considered the circumstances to be most opportune for launching a large issue, and to rely yet again on the support of major foreign financial institutions.

The amount of this issue was certainly large: 644 million lire was slightly less than 7 per cent of the Italian domestic income in 1881. Contacts with international investors intensified during the formulation of the bill. As was well documented by Gille (1968), the authorities sought the opinion of the merchant bank Rothschild regarding the action plan contained in the bill. The French advisor took an ambiguous position which puzzled the Italian authorities. It is reasonable to assume that, initially, such a position was predicated upon the fact that Rothschild strongly favoured a return to a silver-based system, which was not contemplated in the Italian bill. In a subsequent phase, starting in February 1881 when France intervened in Tunis and political relations with Italy became strained, other factors obviously came into play. After some hesitation, the Italian authorities approached English and French banks less exposed to public opinion, and consequently in a position to overcome the possible vetoes of their respective governments (Gille 1968; Del Vecchio 1979). The transaction was concluded with three banking groups which undertook to deliver 444 million lire in gold and 200 million in silver (Corbino 1933, p. 395).

The agreement was signed in July 1881 and as of the following August the banks had commenced the delivery of metal to the Italian Treasury. Considering the magnitude of the amount involved, the incident with Rothschild which had been dealing with the Italian authorities for a very long time, and the development of unforeseen tensions in international financial markets, it is clear why all economic observers were unanimous in rating the placement of this issue as a technical and political success.[37]

In the authorities' plan, the imported metal served two important purposes: the withdrawal from circulation of about two thirds of the consortium's paper, and the subsequent injection into the monetary system of the metal necessary to maintain the convertibility of government and bank notes. The delivery of metal to the Treasury was completed, as agreed, in September 1882. In March 1883, the government responded with two decrees to the question of when convertibility would be resumed. The date was fixed for the following 12 April.

Despite this new legislation, business continued as usual. In particular, bank and Treasury offices were not crowded with customers. With the official return to convertibility, some important aspects of the monetary situation showed further signs of improvement. In April, the average monthly rate of exchange with France dropped to 99.85, below gold parity, and it is therefore correct to say that the paper lira was worth even more than the gold one. It was an event that had not happened since April 1866.

This new environment facilitated the re-establishment of business relations between domestic and international financial markets. In particular, foreign capital, attracted by higher interest rates in Italy and no longer restrained by volatility in the exchange rate, flowed into the country through new current accounts, forward contracts, rediscount of bills of exchange and investments in government securities. Supino (1895, p. 88) estimated that the inflow of funds was approximately 500 million lire, which was slightly less than the total amount of the foreign loan. In addition, if we consider that the public did not rush to convert large quantities of notes, it is not surprising that the banks' metal reserves increased substantially.

Again as noted by Supino (1929), for many observers these facts would prove the success of the foreign loan transaction.[38] However, this optimism is unjustified. In fact, it was clearly inappropriate to regard the monetary situation as normal. With the official end of inconvertible paper money, a number of large problems came to the surface, in addition to others inherited from the past.

Gresham's law, monetary disequilibrium and monetary control inconsistencies

The gold and silver content of the lira had not changed since 1862, and the same was true for the official exchange rate between the two metals. After 1880, however, the relative market price had dropped to 1:18.5. In 1886 it reached 1:21. Therefore, the official exchange price overvalued silver, and consequently the banks, free to choose the metal they could give in exchange for notes, did in fact prefer to utilise silver. This obviously discouraged the request of conversion by the public. Thus, the events of 1883 were not the return to normality, but another manifestation of Gresham's law. This is confirmed by the fact that, from 1883 to 1885, while the outflow of gold climbed from 8.2 to 101.3 million lire per annum, the inflow of silver increased from 50.7 to 103.7 million.

We have already noted that, at the time of the discussion in parliament of the 1880 bill, the metal was worth approximately 10 per cent more than the paper lira. We added that, with the return to convertibility, the value of paper money was aligned with that of metal through the decision to impose the conversion rate of notes at nominal value. Consequently, the return to convertibility produced the result of increasing the real value of the quantity of money outstanding. This increase also took place at a time of sluggish production and price declines. This aspect became even more evident and relevant after the enactment of the two decrees, one in August 1883 and the other in November 1884, which approved the banks' request to expand their paper currency stock. We have already mentioned that a large quantity of metal flowed into the banks, and the public refrained from converting notes on a large scale. As soon as they saw their metal reserves grow, banks began to exert pressure on the authorities to obtain an increase in the limit of their outstanding notes. As a result, the first of the two decrees authorised banks to issue additional notes up to 40 per cent of paid-up capital, with 100 per cent metal cover. The second decree removed all limits with respect to future issuance of notes.[39]

From 1879 to 1883 the monetary base declined. This can be attributed to the basic stability of currency stock (the amount of consortium's notes was constant and that of bank notes had already reached the maximum limits set by law) and to the flow of metal money into the Treasury. By contrast, from 1883 onward, both the monetary base and the quantity of money increased.

Why then, did the very sensitive barometer of the exchange rate fail to detect the beginning of turbulence in the internal monetary market? The expectation of a new monetary regime cannot explain the fact that the exchange rate remained within the gold points. The answer to this question must be that the loan, as well as the return to convertibility and the resulting initial inflow of foreign capital, had the same effect as a series of strong initiatives on the foreign exchange market in support of the Italian lira (Spinelli 1989). These were the initiatives that, for a few years, prevented the exchange rate from bringing to light the deterioration in the domestic money market.

As to the mechanisms of monetary control, it is useful to recall that in the gold standard the quantity of paper currency is an endogenous variable dependent upon both the metal reserves held by banks and the public's demand for paper money. Consequently, the stock of currency cannot and must not be set by law. On their part, the banks of issue must adjust metal reserves through the discount rate mechanism. The Italian experience after 1883 was anomalous in two ways. First, the paper currency limits introduced by the 1874 law were maintained, but banks were allowed to exceed these limits through issuance of notes fully covered by metal. Second, as shown in figure 3.3 and as we shall elaborate further in the next section, the banks of issue did not adjust interest rates in accordance with gold standard principles.

Banking crises

The decade lasting from the effective return to convertibility to the large banking crises and the establishment of the Bank of Italy has been analysed extensively in the economic literature.[40] Nevertheless, it seems there is still considerable confusion regarding some underlying aspects of the country's financial and monetary evolution during this crucial sub-period.

Underlying the banking crises, which also involved banks of issue, there were factors that could be categorised as external and internal. In turn, the latter could be of an economic, institutional, ethical and political nature. To begin with, the Italian banking system lacked a sufficient degree of specialisation. In particular, it did not have institutions in a position to meet the demands of medium- and long-term financing. In 1866 and 1869 there was an attempt to promote land and farm credit, but with little success. Even the demand for real estate financing, both residential and industrial, continued to be inadequately addressed by the banking system.

The fundamental institutional weakness of banks of issue acting as major credit institutions in the country was to shift competition and the collection of seigniorage to the asset side of the balance sheet (Ripa di Meana and Sarcinelli 1990). This phenomenon was enhanced by the existing deficiencies in supervision, as well as by some internal and external economic developments. Since the beginning of the decade, Italian agriculture had experienced difficulties due to high real lira appreciation and the price reductions of US agricultural products (Benini 1894). These difficulties increased in the subsequent few years because of the trade war with France.[41] The agricultural sector crisis had an impact on the banking system, which had allocated substantial resources to this sector.

In the 1880s, increasing demand for industrial and residential real estate financing gained momentum. The former stemmed from the country's industrial strategy (Di Nardi 1953, p. 321); the latter from strong urban expansion. Banks were confronted with soaring non-performing assets in meeting the medium- and long-term financing requirements of the manufacturing sector, and consequently suffered substantial losses in residential lending. In fact, a period of wild speculation in land development and construction, which relied for the most part on short-term bank credit, quickly generated an excess supply, with a subsequent drop in prices and an increase in failures of real estate companies and banks. The banks of issue, already burdened by their own losses and non-performing assets, were pressed by political authorities to come to the rescue of a number of commercial banks.

Starting in 1887, these rescue operations, which represented mere '*ad hoc*' interventions, produced the effect of placing further strain on the balance sheets of the banks of issue.[42] Ripa di Meana and Sarcinelli (1990) reckoned that, from 1884 to 1891, bad loans increased from 1 to 8 per cent for commercial banks and from 0.5 to 9 per cent for BN alone.

Among the reasons behind the crises, we must also mention those specifically attributable to the relationships with international financial markets. Let us reiterate that, thanks to foreign assistance, Italy was able to overcome difficult times such as those during the years 1860–5 and 1881 (placement of the issue). When this assistance was no longer available, such as in 1866, the inadequacies of domestic economic policy surfaced. The 1880s, therefore, started with ups and downs. Even though the placement of the international issue was completed, it became clear that financial assistance from Paris was less and less easy to obtain. The problem grew worse with the trade war between Italy and France, and with the strengthening of the political alliance between Italy and Germany. The latter did not bring about a full commitment on the part of the German financial market, in contrast with that previously provided by the French one (Gille 1968). In other words, as was later emphasised by De Johannis (1904, p. 300), while the international political centre for Italy became Berlin, her financial centre virtually disappeared.

In the meantime, there was also a return to government deficits. The highest value was reached in the fiscal year 1888–9, when the deficit was equal to 5 per cent of domestic income. The authorities were not willing to monetise their deficits. At the same time, in the hope of avoiding a worsening of the existing economic recession, they did not wish to consistently increase domestic interest rates. It followed that deficits had to be financed with foreign capital.

At first, Italy's loss of an international financial centre did not create a problem. In fact, after the country's return to the gold standard, the international financial community continued to support Italy. However, problems were encountered as soon as foreign financial markets entered a period of instability characterised by frequent and stringent credit restrictions or even by the cancellation of existing loans. The opening of this new phase, already evident in 1885, can be attributed to both external and internal events. Among the former, it is worth noting the financial and stock exchange crises in various countries. Among the latter, we find, as indicated earlier, both the attempt on the part of some Italian banks to shift abroad the financing of Italian real estate speculations and the large placement of Italian government securities in foreign countries.

The gradual lack of availability of international financing and the depreciation of the lira over the export gold point took place concurrently and, as a result, influenced each other. This meant that, against a stronger incentive to transfer gold abroad, there was a weaker incentive in foreign markets to send metal to Italy. Furthermore, as had happened previously, the cancellation of international credit was accompanied by new large differentials between the internal and external price of Rendita Italiana. In turn, these differentials encouraged arbitrage operations which necessitated the re-exportation of capital. Total metal reserves held by the Treasury and the banks dwindled rapidly from 913.7 million lire on 1 April 1883 to 596 million in December 1887. From the end of 1883 to the end of 1887, the percentage ratio between reserves and total amount of bank and government notes dropped from 52.7 to 40.5.

More on the inadequacy of interest rate policy

We have already observed that, from the end of 1880 to the end of 1881, BN, under market pressures, chose to exceed the limits set by the 1874 law instead of substantially increasing interest rates. The inadequacy of the interest rate policy became even more obvious with the effective return to convertibility. At first, when banks held large reserves, the problem was simply ignored. Later, when the lira depreciated again and reserves dropped, the banks of issue, which still had to guarantee convertibility and maintain a specified ratio between reserves and currency stock, were again obliged, by law in June 1885, not to change discount rates without the government's prior approval. This decision left no doubt that the way authorities viewed the protection of reserves, and hence convertibility, was wrong. We must emphasise that all of this took place despite the fact that the authorities recognised the traditional cause–effect relationship linking interest to exchange rate and consequently to metal reserves.[43]

In the spring of 1885, when the lira was weak, BN proposed to raise the discount rate, which in fact went from 5 to 6 per cent. However, the trend reversed itself one month later. In 1886, the discount rate was lowered to 4.5 per cent. Subsequent developments were summarised by Di Nardi (1953, p. 353) as follows:

From December 1886 to February 1889, for 27 consecutive months, the discount rate did not show any change, stabilising at 5.50% while the exchange rate remained constantly above the gold export point for the whole period. . . . From February to July 1889, the exchange rate returned to within the gold points and banks hastened to lower the discount rate to 5%. They raised it again in November, with three months delay from the time it exceeded the upper gold point. The exchange rate remained at that level for the entire 1890 period and until August 1891, during which time it was always above the gold point, but with a clear tendency to deteriorate. The discount rate was then lowered in September 1891, while the exchange rate had not shown any sign of improvement.

In any event, the fact remains that, as shown in figure 3.3, the year 1883 did not bring either a meaningful improvement in the flexibility of the Italian discount rate, nor a better correlation with foreign rates.

In the past, the banks of issue endeavoured to compensate for deficiencies in the discount rate policy with the direct importation of metal. With a change in circumstances, this alternative was no longer feasible. In the 1930s (see chapter 5), banks succeeded in maintaining a given ratio between reserves and the amount of currency outstanding, and counteracted a fall in reserves through a progressive reduction in the currency stock. But now, in view of the current economic recession, this alternative was not feasible. The only way out for the banks, then, was simply to refuse to convert notes into metal money. This was obviously an illegal solution to the problem of a continuous and growing depletion of reserves. Nevertheless, this was the systematic response from the middle of the decade onward. According to Benini's estimates (1894), the total amount of conversions for the six banks of issue went from 153 million lire for the period June 1884–June 1885 to 100 million in 1888–9, then dropped again to 51 million during the years 1891–2.

Ethical–political crisis and Banca Romana's failure

In addition to convertibility obstacles, an exchange rate above the gold export point, and the failure of some banks and the rescue of others, there were other crisis indicators such as the return of illegal currency. Owing to the depletion of their reserves and the increase in non-performing loans – partly attributable to a total lack of regulations – banks of issue had an incentive to print paper money in excess of legal limits (Di Nardi 1953, p. 332). Each of these currency excesses or violations was tacitly approved, *ex-ante* or *ex-post*, by the authorities. The most remarkable example was given by the June and July 1891 decisions to increase the currency limit from three to four times the size of paid-up capital. For the six banks, this meant that the new stock of currency was 1,064 million lire, or 309 million lire in excess of the limit permitted by the 1874 law.

The weakness shown by the authorities in coping with the crisis also emerged from their measures regarding the 'riscontrata'. Since 1887, Banca Romana exerted pressures on the authorities to induce them to limit the clearing process. The government intervened and persuaded BN not to demand conversion of Banca Romana's notes against its own, first for 4, then for 6 and later for 15 million lire. In August 1891, this process was extended to all other banks and taken to the extreme with the decision to completely void the 'riscontrata' of any effect. This decision was even more serious as it was made after the 'riscontrata' had been ascertained at least to have helped constrain the currency stock of smaller banks, and after the

Banca Romana was found to have been continuously involved in serious irregularities.

The connection between the ethical and financial aspects of the crisis was strengthened by the fact that the results of the 1889 government inspection on the banks of issue were taken lightly. It was soon clear that this official examination, which formed part of the periodic controls carried out on banks of issue to comply with the law, was different from a routine inspection. In fact, inspectors brought to light irregularities, illegal transactions and a seriously deteriorated financial situation (Vitale 1972). Nevertheless, the only practical consequences of that inspection took place in February 1890, when the two southern banks were liquidated. Prime Minister Giolitti, in open contrast with the opposition in Parliament (which heard about the inspection report and demanded drastic and immediate action), decided not to make these findings public, nor to undertake any legislative reform regarding the banks of issue.

The ethical–political crisis reached its final stage when, towards the end of 1892, Giolitti sponsored the governor of the Banca Romana for a senatorial appointment. Maffeo Pantaleoni, an influential economist, then considered it appropriate to pass a copy of the 1899 inspection report to some right- and left-wing opposition members in the House. From this point on, events unfolded rapidly. On 20 December 1892, the opposition attacked the government, accused it of connivance with Banca Romana, and demanded that a parliamentary enquiry be authorised to fully investigate the affairs of the banks of issue and the intermingling of political and financial interests. The opposition also proposed a new law to regulate the banks of issue. The government was prepared to pass a new law, but had no intention of proceeding with the parliamentary enquiry. On 30 December, the government ordered a routine administrative enquiry, which was just enough to trigger a series of unexpected reactions.

In fact, during the early days of the enquiry, inspectors uncovered such irregularities in the affairs of the Banca Romana that the immediate involvement of the law courts was warranted. On 19 January 1893, the bank's governor (who was also a senator of the Kingdom) and the chief cashier were arrested. In the following days, a legal investigation quickly extended to various levels and bodies of the government's political and administrative structure. On 20 March 1893, Giolitti presented the results of the administrative enquiry to Parliament. A sealed envelope contained documents relating to connections between politicians and Banca Romana. Another envelope, open and directed to members of Parliament, included information on the financial condition and currency stock of the various banks of issue.

With regard to assets, the position revealed a total of approximately 200 million lire in non-performing loans and 60 million in losses. In addition, Banca Romana had issued duplicate notes for 41 million, and created an excess of more than 100 million lire in relation to the maximum amount of currency.

Irregularities at Banca Romana also included, for example, a cash shortage; discount transactions extended at reduced rates to politicians, bank managers and their relatives; collateral valued at higher than market prices; renewal of discounted transactions relating to unpaid bills of exchange; and farm loans disguised as discount operations.

The 1893 law, establishment of the Bank of Italy and the new exit from the gold standard[44]

On 21 March 1893 a House Committee was appointed to enquire into political and moral responsibilities arising from the crisis of the banks of issue. The Committee report of 23 November 1893 gave credence to the suspicion that Giolitti himself abused his position to obtain personal gains. With the resignation of Giolitti and his government on 24 November, the moral and political crisis of the country reached its climax.

Before we analyse the repercussions of these developments on the trend of the lira exchange rates, it is appropriate to step back and outline the provisions of the new law, enacted on 10 August 1893, which governed the banks of issue. The salient points of the law were the following:

(i)   BN and the two banks in Tuscany merged to form a single bank by the name of Banca d'Italia, while Banca Romana ceased to exist. The banks of issue were consequently reduced from six to three;

(ii)   The illegal currency of the former Banca Romana was made legal by raising the issue limits for Banca d'Italia, Banco di Napoli and Banco di Sicilia; the new ceilings were now set at 800, 242 and 55 million lire, respectively;

(iii) These limits remained valid for four years, after which time they were automatically reduced every second year so that, within 14 years, they reached a level three times the amount of the three banks' paid-up capital;

(iv)   The currency tax was 1 per cent, while a penalty on currency 'excesses' was set at twice the official discount rate;

(v)   To avoid duplication of notes and eventually stop any increase over the limits in the stock of currency, the State assumed the right to issue banknotes. To avoid any possible conflict of interest, members of Parliament were not allowed to accept appointments, remunerated or not, in banks of issue;

(vi)   Upon the public's demand, the banks of issue were obliged to convert notes into metal, under conditions to be specified in subsequent regulations;

(vii) The banks of issue had to keep reserves for a value that, within one year, were to reach 40 per cent of the total of currency outstanding plus other demand liabilities. To enable part of the reserves to earn interest and to encourage the accumulation of stock in foreign currencies, the law provided that 7 per cent of reserves could be denominated in foreign currencies.[45] The remaining 33 per cent had to be in metal (three quarters of this percentage in gold);

(viii) The official discount rate was required to be the same for the three banks of issue and was always under government control. The preferential discount rate, on the other hand, was left to the banks' discretion. The government also reserved the right to appoint the manager of Banca d'Italia;

(ix)   Transactions carried out by the banks of issue were clearly defined. Discount operations could not exceed the term of four months, advances six months, foreign exchange trading three months and the purchase of government securities was limited to a maximum of one third of the paid-up capital. The banks were allowed to accept deposits in interest-bearing current accounts. If the total amount of these deposits exceeded the limits set by law, the currency stock had to be reduced by three quarters of the excess.[46]

To avoid any misunderstanding, the law reiterated that the banks could not engage in financing farm land. The banks were given up to ten years to place their books in order. The penalty for carrying out an illegal transaction was three times the official discount rate multiplied by the value of the transaction.

Deficiencies in the law and market reaction

Contrary to what happened in 1874 and again in 1881, the impact of the new law was extremely negative in the short run. The criticism directed at the legislator was substantive and covered different aspects of the law. First, there was still ambiguity between monopoly and competition in issuing notes. In this respect, the legislator would have had an easy task, perhaps, in resolving a controversy which had been going on for over 30 years. In fact, the difficulties encountered in controlling a few banks of issue simultaneously had been of such a magnitude as to convince even economist Francesco Ferrara to support the idea of a single issuer.

Second, the law did not eliminate the deficiencies in regulations. Pressures from the political arena and from an economic system in a state of recession played an important role in bringing about the deterioration of the financial affairs of the banks. This and events at Banca Romana should have dictated new stringent regulatory rules.

Third, excess currency was once again officially ratified *ex-post* and the reduction of stock to levels below the limits considered appropriate in the circumstances was postponed to a later date.

Fourth, the law was rather cryptic about the convertibility of both bank and government notes, as indicated in the Committee report:

in present circumstances, if the obligation of conversion would be fully effective, metal reserves could run the risk of disappearing. Conversely, by not imposing such an obligation, it could be interpreted as a tacit acceptance of inconvertibility.

The dilemma was not resolved and, as a result, the law obliged banks to convert notes, at the same time indicating that the regulations dealing with the conversion rate would be issued only on a later date.

Fifth, the law did not formulate a strategic plan to facilitate the recovery of the banking industry (Confalonieri 1975, p. 83).

In sum, the new law raised uncertainties in financial markets, at least in the beginning, about the stability of the system and the ability of the authorities to deal with the situation.[47] Since the enactment of the law coincided with the ethical–political crisis, it is hard to isolate the specific consequences of the legislation on the behaviour of the exchange rate. The Italian lira/French franc rate, after increasing progressively to 104 from the summer of 1891 to the spring of 1892, experienced a high depreciation beginning in July 1893, in conjunction with the approval of the bill by the House Committee and the commencement of Parliament proceedings (figure 3.4). At the end of August, the rate had already reached 110; in the third week of November, which marked the apex of the ethical–political crisis, the rate was more than 115 lire.

Figure 3.4 illustrates another phenomenon, concurrent with the depreciation of the lira: the appearance of a significant differential between domestic and international prices of Rendita Italiana. In particular, during the first six months of 1893, the average price of the Rendita at the Paris stock exchange was equal to 92.23; in the second half of the year, it dropped to 83.59, with a minimum of 78.70. In comparing the two lines of the figure, we note that, commencing from the month of July, the ratio between domestic and international quotations remained above the exchange rate. This means there was an incentive to engage in arbitrage activities.

The reason for the higher fall in foreign prices is obvious: international financial markets were in the process of reviewing the Italian country risk.[48] The consequences of the ensuing arbitrage operations are also obvious.

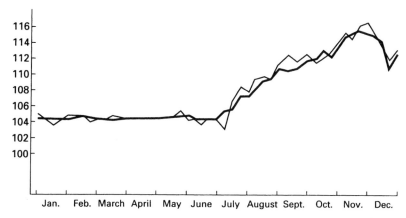

Figure 3.4 Weekly exchange rate between the lira and the French franc (–) and the ratio between domestic and foreign prices of the Rendita Italiana 5 per cent (–)
Source: Pantaleoni (1895, allegato E).

First of all, the country lost capital and therefore metal, including silver. Da Pozzo and Felloni (1964) estimated that during those months, Rendita for 2.4 billion lire found its way back into Italy. Secondly, commercial and other banks had to cope with a massive withdrawal of deposits. Caught between the cancellation of foreign lines of credit and a run on domestic deposits, some of the banks had no other choice but to wind up their operations. Among the most noteworthy failures were Credito Mobiliare, the second largest bank in the country, on 29 November 1893, and Banca Generale on the following 18 January.

The government proceeded to take '*ad hoc*' measures as it was incapable of formulating a viable strategy to rescue the banks, and the currency stock was already at the maximum legal limits. On 23 January, a first decree authorised Banca d'Italia, Banco di Napoli and Banco di Sicilia to exceed their currency limits. To further enhance the ability of the banks of issue to intervene in favour of ailing banks, the decree repealed the section of the 1893 law which imposed a reduction of the currency stock in the event that interest-bearing current accounts exceeded a specified amount.

On 21 February, a second decree containing two important innovations was enacted. First, the legislator dispelled doubts about the real nature of the monetary system, and dictated that the banks of issue were indeed obliged to convert their notes into government notes or into metal, but at market prices. This was, in fact, a return to inconvertibility. Second, the Treasury was authorised to increase the amount of government notes from 340 million lire, as set by the 1881 law, to 600 million. The confusion increased shortly thereafter when the legislator first mitigated the effects of some of these decisions, then introduced a withholding tax on interest accrued on public debt.

More on the nature of the crisis: money in the decade 1884–1894

Let us now look at the evolution of monetary aggregates during the period 1884–94, i.e., from the return to convertibility to the time of the bank failures. This period included a complete growth cycle of the monetary base (figure 2.6). In fact, the base declined in absolute terms from 1880 to the end of 1883 when it recorded a value of 2,535 million lire. Then, it began growing and reached a local maximum of 3,194 million in 1893. In 1894, the monetary base was declining and ended up at 3,173 million. Between the minimum and maximum points, there was an annual average growth of 2.3 per cent. To put this growth in perspective, recall that the monetary base increased at an annual average rate of 9.73 per cent during the whole 1862–1991 period, 3.25 per cent during the 1862–1913 period, and 3.07 per cent during the 1862–96 period. From this broad comparison, it is evident that the crisis was not reflected in the trend of the monetary base.

During 1884–94, the ratio re continued to fall, and the ratio k reached a minimum value of 0.95 in 1888 and then increased to end at a local peak of 1.12 in 1894 (figures 2.4 and 2.5). The reversal in the trend of the k ratio coincided with the country's financial crisis, particularly with the bank failures.

The money multiplier peaked in 1888 and then reached a trough in 1894. The quantity of money outstanding grew until 1889 and then remained quite stable: 4,053.8 million in 1883, 5,270.6 million in 1893 and 5,186 million in 1894. Between the minimum and maximum points, the annual average growth was 2.6 per cent. By contrast, money grew on average at 10.5 per cent from 1862 to 1991, 4.4 per cent from 1862 to 1913 and 4.22 per cent from 1862 to 1896 (table 2.1). These data strengthen our judgement that the crisis did not quite result in a loss of monetary control.

Further evidence on this point comes from an analysis of price trends. The income deflator remained stable from 1878 to 1892 and reached a low in 1894, when the financial and political crisis was at its highest point. Wholesale prices declined until 1887, rose in the subsequent three years and then again started to decrease until, in 1894, they reached the absolute minimum of the entire period 1861–1913. According to the monthly index of wholesale prices computed by Cianci (1933), there was only one significant increase from June to July 1889 when the index went from 103 to 110. Later, prices fell almost continuously.

Let us now go back to the government inspection of the banks of issue submitted to the House on 20 March 1893. There were no doubts about the seriousness, depth, and widespread nature of the financial crisis. The situation for the stock of currency, by contrast, did not appear to be out of control, nor seriously jeopardised. In fact, as already mentioned, the outstanding currency of the two banks in Tuscany and BN was maintained within legal limits. The volume of currency issued by Banco di Sicilia showed an excess of 2 million lire and that of Banco di Napoli an excess of 15 million. In relative terms, these were fairly negligible amounts. Only in the case of Banca Romana was the excess significant, where unauthorised currency reached 100 million lire. However, this value had to be placed in relation to a total bank and government paper currency stock of approximately 1,500 million lire, and to a total monetary base of more than 3,000 million. For the six banks together, the currency fully backed by metal was slightly more than 40 million lire. Finally, currency issued on behalf of the Treasury, which by law could go up to 130 million lire, was below 100 million. The banks' metal reserves, even though had fallen continuously since 1883, seemed to be adequate enough to guarantee the convertibility of paper money under normal circumstances. At the end of 1889, the percentage ratio between the banks' metal reserves and the total value of their currencies was 39.41. In 1893 it was equal to 36.88. Similarly, the ratio of the combined reserves of the banks and Treasury to total bank and government notes was 41.00 in 1889 and 37.3 in 1893.

This elucidates two underlying problems. The first relates to the inability of the political leadership to isolate the money market as much as possible from the financial crisis. It may be helpful to reiterate that such a crisis was also the result of a monetary control system which encouraged the various banks to compete with one another on the assets side of the balance sheet. The second observation, closely related, is the scant attention given by the profession to the need to distinguish the monetary from the non-monetary aspects of the crisis. With better vision and determination, the political leadership could have avoided some consequences of the financial crisis on the money market. The disorderly succession of decisions, which often served to disguise the true nature of the crisis, might have deceived some historians. To our knowledge, Confalonieri (1974) and Ripa di Meana and Sarcinelli (1990) alone separated the financial and political elements from the monetary aspects of the crisis. In general, other historians tended to make no distinction and did not even catch the significant diverging trends between the exchange rate and the general level of prices.

Monetary base, money, production and prices from 1897 to 1913

The growth of the monetary base recorded three brief pauses in 1900, 1908 and 1912, and displayed a decidedly more sustained trend from 1903 onward. In absolute terms, the monetary base increased from 3,094.9

million lire at the end of 1896 to 5,734.6 million at the end of 1913, a higher growth rate than the one relating to the sub-period 1862–96.

The ratio k started again to decline after the temporary upswing between the end of the 1880s and the beginning of the 1890s. The decline in k stopped in 1906–7 when the value reached 0.48 (figure 2.4). In the new environment, investment portfolios displayed a clear preference for bank deposits over cash. The ratio refell until 1901, then rose until 1907, and started to decline again in the final part of the sub-period. In 1897 and 1913, the ratio was 0.034 and 0.036, respectively. Finally, the monetary multiplier increased from 1.65 in 1897 to 2.07 in 1913. In the mid-period, its performance continued to be dominated by the trend of the ratio k. As for the short period, the multiplier recorded a significant drop in 1906–7, concurrent with an increase in k and re.

The quantity of money rose in a very regular fashion, with only two pauses in 1906 and 1912. The first is attributable to a multiplier decline, the second to the temporary set-back in the growth of the monetary base. From the end of 1896 to the end of 1913, the quantity of money jumped from 5,173.2 million to 11,849.3 million lire, a rate higher than in the 1862–96 sub-period.

The velocity of circulation continued its long-term decline from 1.90 in 1897 to 1.67 in 1913. With regard to real income, the sub-period was characterised by more sustained growth. After increasing from 48.9 billion to 60.9 billion (in 1938 lire) during the years 1861–96, real income reached 94.4 billion in only 17 years. Finally, both the income deflator and wholesale prices remained stable until 1904 and grew during the last part of the period.[49]

We have already mentioned that the literature considers the period between 1897 and the First World War as the best era of the gold standard. In particular, it is normally emphasised that those years were characterised by high growth rates in industrial output and remarkable monetary and financial stability. All of this was true for Italy. In fact, the annual average growth of real production increased from 0.62 per cent during the years 1861–96 to 2.58 per cent for the 1897–1913 period. The country succeeded in recovering from a clearly difficult financial situation.

Genesis of a monetary policy model

We analyse monetary and financial factors by relying on the Banca d'Italia's Annual Reports. For brevity we identify Banca d'Italia with the initials BI, and the Annual Reports with the initials R.A., followed by the year which is the subject of the report, rather than the year of publication.

It is appropriate to remind the reader that BI was created as a joint stock company and, as such, had a profit objective. This was clearly highlighted in the bank's first R.A. and was confirmed by its behaviour during the early years of operation.[50] In subsequent years, the bank focused its attention on a plan to improve its overall financial position and raise its reserves. Furthermore, shareholders became less influential in the decision-making process (Bonelli 1991, p. 42). With the appearance on the scene of Stringher, appointed BI's director in 1900, the original profit goal lost a great deal of impetus (Confalonieri 1975). As a result, as time progressed, the Bank's activities were more directed towards the control of the domestic money market.

In reviewing the bank's annual reports, the following monetary policy 'model' emerged. BI sustained domestic output by adjusting the stock of outstanding currency both to the legal ceilings and to the stock of international reserves. This strategy was consistent with profit maximisation, and was effective until such time as the Bank ran into problems with respect to its metal reserves, the country's balance of payments, and the exchange rate. It was only then that monetary policy would become restrictive. In chapter 8, we remark on a strong similarity between the monetary policies of these years and those of the 1970s.

The question of direct interest involves the way BI's monetary policy reacted to domestic and international macroeconomic variables. The Bank was quick in realising the importance of the external constraint on policy:

In the past year, we have seen how much attention our institution must devote to political and economic events in other countries. In fact, it has been ascertained, without any doubt, that these events affect our country, directly or indirectly, primarily on account of the large quantity of Italian securities traded abroad. (BI R.A. 1899, p. 20)

It is also significant that, at the beginning of this century, BI started a tradition of including in its annual reports an analysis of international political and economic developments. Clearly, the Bank was sensitive to the performance of exchange rates. *Ceteris paribus*, it was willing to reduce the discount rate if prices of Italian bonds traded abroad had improved and the lira had appreciated in foreign exchange markets (BI R.A. 1894, pp. 24–5). In particular, the Bank was very reluctant to reduce the discount rate when it approached the upper gold point (BI R.A. 1908, p. 25).

When the recovery of domestic economic activity was in conflict with keeping reserves from flowing out of the country, BI did not hesitate to favour the latter objective (BI R.A. 1896, p. 24; 1898, p. 6; 1900, p. 19; 1904, p. 26; 1907, p. 26; 1908, p. 17; 1909, p. 8; 1910, p. 5; 1910, p. 33; 1911, p. 9; 1912, p. 11; 1913, p. 7). When such a conflict did not exist, the Bank viewed its role as moderating the domestic monetary market in a counter-cyclical fashion (BI R.A. 1899, pp. 23–5; R.A. 1906, p. 14). It therefore protected its stock of metal reserves by raising the discount rate when domestic credit demand was strong (BI R.A. 1902, p. 15).

A careful reading of the annual reports also reveals how international monetary policy was transmitted to the domestic market. On the one side, there was the traditional mechanism, starting with changes in foreign interest rates which triggered movements of capital and the lira in the exchange market, which in turn prompted BI to react. On the other side, there was a mechanism more specific to Italy; that is, sharp fluctuations in the price of Italian securities traded abroad brought about by international financial turbulence. As a consequence, these price fluctuations led to instability in the Italian capital flows and in the lira exchange rate.

The authorities tried to lower their dependence on foreign financial markets by reducing the stock of Italian securities held by non-residents. This strategy was also reflected in the prudent fiscal policy pursued from 1896 onward. The positive effects of this approach were highlighted at the beginning of the twentieth century (BI R.A. 1902, p. 7; Spinelli 1989).

A second event which contributed to making the country less vulnerable to international monetary disorders was the large increase in metal and foreign currency reserves at the banks of issue. From 1899 to 1908, the ratio of metal and foreign currency reserves to BI's paper in circulation increased from approximately 43 to 78 per cent. The accumulation of reserves stemmed from exogenous events and monetary policy choices. The former included a massive increase in world gold production, of which all central banks took advantage (BI R.A. 1909, p. 6). The latter included the Italian authorities' decision to increase metal and foreign currency reserves for the purpose of eventually intervening in the foreign exchange market.

The appropriateness of these initiatives was mentioned in BI R.A. (1898, p. 9), in which the Bank complained that wide and frequent fluctuations in the lira exchange rate were attributable to external factors and then added:

We believe . . . that the public authorities should consider whether it would be appropriate to confer powers to the Bank, so that it could intervene, more promptly and effectively, to mitigate the frequent, damaging fluctuations in premiums.

BI's statutory requirements to intervene in the foreign exchange market were in fact formalised in 1903. In 1907, these were extended to cover the forward market. Furthermore, incentives were introduced for banks of issue to accumulate reserves to operate effectively in the foreign exchange market (De Cecco 1990; Bonelli 1991). Banks of issue already had the right to convert metal reserve surpluses into notes fully backed by metal. They were also allowed to hold part of their legal reserves in foreign currencies. Additional incentives were introduced by laws passed in August 1895 and January 1897. The first law authorised the inclusion of foreign lines of credit

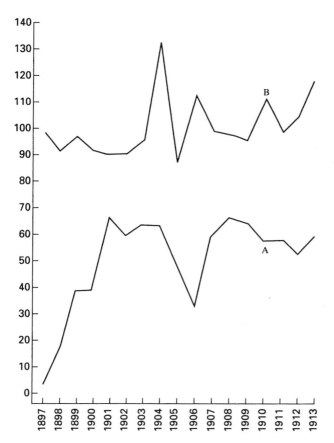

Figure 3.5 Treasury bills issued by foreign governments in the portfolio of Bank of Italy (A) and the total foreign credit of the Bank of Italy (B)
Source: Banca d'Italia R.A. (1913).

in legal reserves. The second increased the limit of reserves to be made up of bills of exchange payable abroad and foreign loans from 7 to 15 per cent. It also provided that collections on bad loans could be, for the most part, invested in foreign treasury bills, bills of exchange or foreign current accounts. The effects of the two laws are clearly illustrated in figure 3.5.

Finally, a number of factors had an extremely positive effect on the lira exchange rate: strong economic growth, prudent fiscal policy which at times resulted in budget surpluses, reduction of foreign debt and the ensuing appreciation of Italian securities on international stock exchanges, and the large accumulation of metal and foreign currency reserves. The increase in reserves and the appreciation of the lira strengthened each other.

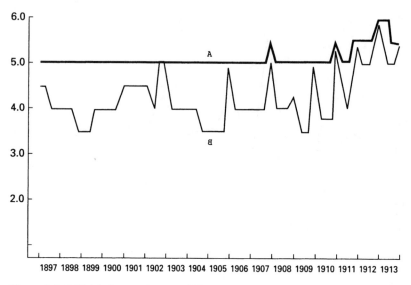

Figure 3.6 Official discount rate on bills (A) and most favoured discount rate
charged by Bank of Italy (B) (end of quarter date)
Source: De Mattia (1967, Tavola 20).

A 'partial' revision of interest and discount rate policy

So far, interest rate policy has been identified with the official discount rate.
However, this was not the only rate in the market as banks of issue were
increasingly allowed the discretion of applying 'special' and 'reduced' discount rates (BI R.A. 1905, p. 27; Einaudi 1960b, p. 148; Bonelli 1991, p. 532).

Figure 3.6 illustrates the trend of both the official and 'special' discount
rates applied by BI. The first continued to be inelastic, the second appeared to
be decidedly more flexible. By contrast, figure 3.7 shows the value of discount
transactions at official and 'special' rates. In the main, the practice of applying
interest rates seemed to follow the following path. First of all, the number of
transactions eligible for preferential discount rates would be curtailed at the
approach of a credit squeeze. If the quantity reduction was not enough, preferential rates would be raised to the official discount rate level. If that turned out
to be inadequate as well the official discount rate would be increased.

The R.A. for 1907 confirmed that past practices had by now changed:
that was a year characterised by a strong financial crisis, both in Italy and
abroad. The report included a reference to Walter Bagehot, an eminent
theorist of the principle that, should a liquidity crisis develop, the central
bank should not restrict credit, but should rather extend it at progressively
higher interest rates. In the R.A. for 1910, BI indicated that circumstances

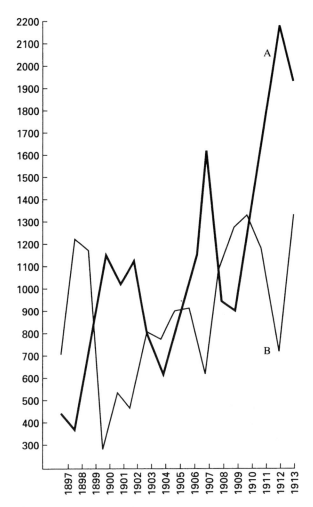

Figure 3.7 Amount of discounts by the Bank of Italy at the official discount rate
(A) and the most favoured rate (B), 1897–1913
Source: Banca d'Italia R.A. (1913).

had dictated an increase in both preferential and official discount rates. On
page 9 the Bank stated:

At that particular time, what was important to the Italian business community was
not so much to obtain funds at reasonable conditions, but to know that credit was
still available for good risk transactions. And the [Banca d'Italia] did not fail to
provide this type of credit.

This was Walter Bagehot's (1873, p. 51) theory in action.

Conclusions

The evolution of the banks of issue, and hence the behaviour of the money supply, was not stimulated and guided by specific and consistent government actions. Instead, the money-issuing system evolved in a laborious manner. The process was heavily influenced by the goals pursued by various institutions, as well as by the interaction among the banks and between banks and the political system. In light of this, it becomes clear why problems relating to monetary control dragged on. For instance, no decision was reached as to whether to continue with a competitive system of money issuing or to grant the monopoly to one of the banks. Furthermore, banks of issue were also operating as commercial banks. On the other hand, the major bank of issue, BN (which later became BI), was a joint stock company and, consequently, had a profit motive.

There was also no clear demarcation between the short and long-term supply of credit. Rather, the supply of both types of credit was inadequate. The 1907 crisis illustrated precisely that the problem was not even resolved with the establishment of the large, merchant banks, such as Banca Commerciale Italiana and Credito Italiano (Castronuovo 1975; Confalonieri 1982b).

The state of public finances, the state of international financial markets and the flows of metal reserves were the key factors underlying money growth. In particular circumstances, the extent to which banks abided by the rules governing the ceilings of paper circulation was also important. Yet, the behaviour of public finances was a dominant force behind money creation, not only in purely quantitative terms, but also in determining the nature of the monetary regime. In fact, public deficits were directly or indirectly responsible for the country's exit from the gold standard in 1866, and for the monetary shocks of 1866–7 and 1870–2. They were also responsible for the *de facto* suspension of convertibility from the mid-1880s onward, for the deterioration of the monetary situation at the beginning of the subsequent decade, as well as for the improvement in monetary policy in 1910–12. Similarly, the improvement in public finances coincided with a period of relative monetary stability following the enactment of the 1874 law, and with the 'good era' after the establishment of BI.

The systematic role played by the international financial markets and the availability of metal reserves cannot be ignored. That is, things did not change much when Italy left the gold standard. This is for two reasons. First, the quantity of currency outstanding was to a large extent endogenous and demand-driven because the banks of issue and in particular BI had a lira exchange-rate target. Second, gold remained very important despite the fact that Italy did not have a real gold standard, except for short periods of time. The importance of gold was connected with the fact that, although currency creation was constrained by legal ceilings, these ceilings could be ignored if banks had the appropriate backing of metal reserve.

Finally, as noted by Supino (1895, p. VII):

In Italy money evolved by way of a continuous series of efforts on the part of the banks of issue to create as much paper money as possible, regardless of business requirements in the market place. Each violation was legalised by subsequent legislation, and this placed banks outside of the common law.

However, there was a shift over time towards more discipline in the issuance of paper money. Some constraints on currency creation were introduced in 1866. In 1868, BN's currency creation was restricted. In 1874, the law for the first time fixed the number of banks of issue, regulating at the same time the volume of their outstanding currencies. In 1893, the government established that an official representative must be present when a bank of issue creates new currency. Statutory requirements and legal restrictions did not guarantee a stringent control on monetary aggregates.

We also emphasise the persistent willingness of the banks of issue and political authorities to restrain interest rate movements. More than once the legislator defined precise ceilings on paper currency growth, freezing at the same time the levels of interest rates. In general, it is fair to say that monetary policy aimed at controlling both the quantity of money and the levels of interest rates. Often, the interest rate target was more important than the money target (Di Nardi 1953; Confalonieri 1974, 1975, 1982a, 1982b).

How did the notion of money evolve over time? Even at the very beginning, when metal money was considered to be the only 'true' currency, the government quickly realised it was also appropriate to control the quantity of paper money. By contrast, there was some delay, as in other countries, in recognising the nature and role of the so-called bank money, i.e., bank deposits. In 1893, limits to the growth of bank deposits were introduced, but only with respect to deposits held at banks of issue. Furthermore, the main purpose of the new law was to prevent the stock of paper currency from reaching the legal limit. Constraints on deposit growth were less effective. After the 1907 crisis, BI proposed to somewhat restrain the deposit growth of commercial banks. However, this was construed as a ploy by BI to protect its own market share, and consequently, its request was dropped.

The economic system underwent an intense process of money creation. Money demand grew systematically in excess of nominal income (Muscatelli and Spinelli 1993). At the same time, the demand shifted clearly towards bank deposits. The velocity of circulation moved along its trend with little variation around it. In particular, lacking a real specialisation in the credit supply and with interest rate cycles being neither long nor significant, velocity did not exhibit a cyclical behaviour.

In contrast, the ratio between the publicly held monetary base and bank deposits was much more volatile than velocity. Deviations of k from trend were undoubtedly related to the country's financial stability. The stability of velocity and the volatility of k implied that the private sector was more concerned with financial than monetary stability.

Turning to the effects of monetary policy, at first glance it did not seem to influence real income, which instead responded to real factors or world developments. By contrast, although generally tied to the international cycle, prices were visibly influenced by domestic monetary policy. In the short run, however, the variable which was most affected by actual or expected monetary impulses was the lira exchange rate. The years from 1861 to 1913 were undoubtedly characterised by wide fluctuations in the real lira exchange rate, owing to similarly wide variations in the nominal rate, which were in turn related to major legislation or innovations or monetary policy shocks.

Finally, we add one general remark on the gold standard. On at least three occasions – 1866, 1881 and 1894 – it was critical for the market to know whether convertibility did in fact exist, *de-jure* or *de-facto*. At the same time, however, the experience after 1893 showed that monetary stability could be achieved even without officially being on the gold standard.[51]

4 The First World War: inflation and stabilisation

The Management has been able to carry out a number of expansions and changes in printing facilities, overcoming quite a few obstacles in fitting premises, acquiring new machinery, obtaining supplies and training personnel. As a result, against an output of five million notes, recorded in 1913, eighteen million were issued this past year. The Management is satisfied with the outcome of its endeavours. (Banca d'Italia R.A. 1917, p. 48).

Introduction

The world war shattered the domestic and international mechanisms which for two decades gave Italy monetary stability, both in absolute terms and in relation to the rest of the world. Between 1914 and 1920, the inflation rate, measured in terms of the national income price deflator, rose progressively from zero per cent in 1914 to 34.7 per cent in 1920 (figure 1.2). Over the same period, the lira price of the pound climbed from 25.3 to 77.5.

This chapter deals with the evolution and consequences of macro-economic policy during the war. With regard to the first aspect, we shall emphasise fiscal policy as this appeared to be the dominant and destabilising impulse. We shall then examine monetary policy by illustrating the limits of funding the massive increase in government spending through additional taxes or the placement of public debt. With respect to the second aspect, we shall focus on the process of internal and external depreciation of the lira.

As usually happens when the economy is in a state of emergency, during the period Italy resorted to policies of direct control of domestic prices and exchange rates. Consequently, we shall attempt to assess both the effectiveness of such policies (during and immediately after the war) and their possible side effects. Furthermore, we shall explain the unusual occurrence of the temporary but very rapid drop in inflation which took place between the end of 1918 and the spring of 1919, concurrently with a clear deterioration of the lira exchange rate and a persistent disarray in fiscal and monetary matters. Finally, we shall identify the reasons which in 1920–1 caused the inflation rate to rapidly fall to zero, as well as the eventual costs associated with the deflation process.

In contemporary historiography, the strong social tensions of the immediate post-war period which brought about the advent of fascism are usually ascribed to political factors. In contrast, in reiterating a theory proposed by the economic literature of the 1920s and 1930s (Supino 1920; Amantia 1933), we will focus on the role of the largely unexpected inflation during the war. Naturally, unexpected inflation and political turmoil interact.

The First World War in a long-run perspective

Figure 4.1 illustrates the trend of industrial output in the period under consideration. The rapid economic growth, which characterised the beginning of the century, came to a sudden halt in 1909. The country was still going through a recession when war broke out. This triggered a strong increase in production which stopped in 1916. In the subsequent five years, industrial output contracted; its index dropped from 71 to 54. In 1922, the growth process resumed with a trend line which was basically parallel to that recorded in the first decade of the century. On average, during the years 1914–20, real income had zero growth (table 1.3)

The state of public finances began to deteriorate visibly in 1914. The largest imbalance was recorded between 1917 and 1918, when the deficit climbed to more than 60 per cent of domestic income. Then the fiscal imbalance improved slowly but consistently, until it showed a small surplus by 1924. On the basis of the stylised facts of chapter 2, the sub-period 1914–20 was characterised by:

(i)   an average ratio of government revenues to national income that was moderately lower than that of the entire 1861–1991 period, and a ratio of government expenditures to income which was approximately double (table 1.4);

(ii) an average deficit to income ratio of 29.3, approximately four times the entire period value; and

(iii) budget deficits monetised on average at 38.2 per cent, a percentage decidedly lower than that relating to the entire period.

Figure 4.2 illustrates the behaviour of the two components of the total stock of currency (that is, government and bank notes) held by the public. We utilised quarterly data to more precisely identify the dates of the most significant turning points in the variables. Until the summer of 1914, the stock of currency showed an obvious but very slight tendency to increase. Later, when war broke out (but prior to Italy's involvement), total currency

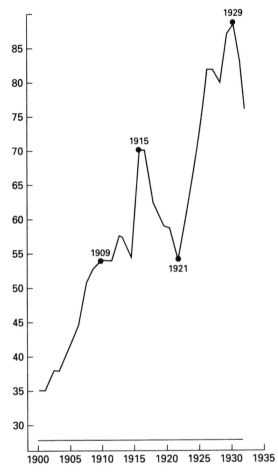

Figure 4.1 Index of industrial production, 1900–1931 (1938=100)
Source: ISTAT (1957).

began to grow very rapidly. After Italy's massive defeat at Caporetto at the
end of 1917, there was further acceleration. The process of currency growth
did not show any significant and lasting respite, even at the end of the war.
In fact, while the total amount of government notes soon stabilised, the
stock of bank notes continued to grow until the final quarter of 1920.

The stock of government notes increased from slightly less than 500
million lire in May 1914 to about 1,300 million in December 1916 and
approximately 2,200 million at the end of 1918. The total amount of paper
currency outstanding also doubled in only two years, from 2,539 million lire
in May 1914 to 4,984 million in May 1916. In August 1917 it was 7,470

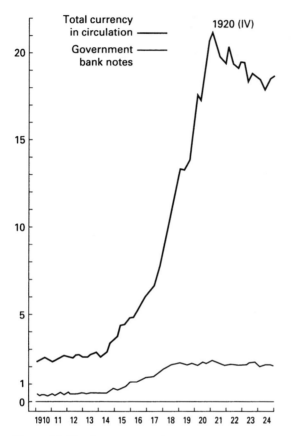

Figure 4.2 Total currency in circulation and government bank notes net of
holding of banks of issue, 1910–1926
Source: De Mattia (1967).

million and four months later it exceeded 10,000 million. In December 1920
it reached the maximum value of 21,753 million. Consequently, in only six
years and seven months, the currency stock increased by 860 per cent.
Within the same period, the ratio between reserves at the banks of issue and
total currency outstanding dropped from approximately 70 to 10 per cent.

From 1914 to 1920 the annual average growth of the monetary base was
24.4 per cent, which was almost three times the average for the entire period
(table 2.1). The Treasury component contributed more than 100 per cent to
this growth. Thus, not only was there vast monetary disorder, but also clear
dominance of fiscal impulses.

The end of hostilities brought only a slow-down in the acceleration of
outstanding currency; a reduction in growth rates took place only in 1920,

well after the war. In 1921, the quantity of money decreased in absolute terms. Until 1920, the behaviour of the money stock reflected more the dynamics of the monetary base than those of the multiplier. This was particularly evident if one considers the crucial year of 1917. Besides, money grew on average by 22.7 per cent, that is slightly less than the monetary base. The money multiplier contracted, on average, by 1.7 per cent.

The effects of the war on the trend of the domestic and international purchasing power of the lira were bound to be dramatic, considering the sharp increase in the monetary aggregates and the slump in real output. Our measure of the inflation rate fluctuated around the zero mark until 1914, then rose suddenly, with a peak occurring in 1917. With the end of the war, inflation at first fell by ten percentage points, then rose again until it reached almost 35 per cent in 1920. In the following year, inflation dropped very rapidly to zero. On average, the annual inflation rate in the sub-period was 21.1 per cent, more than three times that of the entire period (table 1.3).

Italian inflation systematically exceeded our measure of foreign inflation with an average differential of 7 percentage points (table 1.2). This differential rose to almost 20 per cent in 1922. Therefore, it is not surprising that at the outbreak of hostilities the Italian lira began to depreciate on the foreign exchange market. On average, lira depreciation with respect to the British pound was in the order of 15.8 per cent per annum (table 1.2).

Viewed relative to the entire period 1861–1991, the war years produced:

(i)   a lower average real growth (0.0 per cent versus 2.2 per cent for the entire period);
(ii) twice as high monetary growth (22.7 per cent versus 10.5 per cent); and
(iii) the same average trend in money circulation velocity;
(iv) three times as high an inflation rate (21.1 vs. 6.6);
(v)   contained variability in the growth rates of the four variables of the exchange equation (table 1.3).

In sum, the war period showed strong dynamics in monetary variables, a slump in production and limited variability in these variables.

The fiscal shock and problems in financing government deficits

Let us now investigate the fundamental topic of fiscal shock. Table 4.1 shows government budget data on a cash basis and on an accrual basis, as well as deferrals from 1910 to 1930. The budget was balanced up to the fiscal year 1914–15; afterwards it deteriorated. The largest deficit took place in 1918–19, with a ratio between revenues and expenditures of one to seven. The end of hostilities brought about a significant, albeit temporary,

Table 4.1 Central government budget, 1910–1930 (million lire)

Fiscal year	Accrual			Residuals			Cash		
	Receipts	Expenditures	Balance	Receipts	Expenditures	Balance	Receipts	Expenditures	Balance
1910–11	2,499	2,717	−218	334	872	−538	2,636	2,698	−62
1911–12	2,614	2,936	−322	279	887	−608	2,770	2,906	−136
1912–13	2,607	3,233	−626	267	962	−695	2,719	3,138	−419
1913–14	2,789	3,063	−274	259	953	−694	2,879	3,080	−201
1914–15	2,776	5,937	−3,161	347	1,280	−933	2,667	5,586	−2,919
1915–16	2,978	11,067	−8,089	885	1,406	−521	3,401	10,867	−7,466
1916–17	3,193	18,085	−14,892	1,592	2,976	−1,384	4,848	16,441	−11,593
1917–18	4,148	25,735	−21,587	1,979	5,733	−3,754	7,379	22,848	−15,469
1918–19	4,701	33,410	−28,709	1,465	11,487	−10,022	10,423	27,428	−17,005
1919–20	6,174	24,892	−18,718	5,488	15,267	−9,779	11,654	20,905	9,251
1920–21	15,087	38,942	−23,855	10,395	31,593	−21,198	14,226	20,716	−6,490
1921–22	16,206	36,702	−20,496	14,136	42,861	−28,725	16,366	25,398	−9,032
1922–23	16,605	24,219	−7,614	5,361	24,421	−19,060	27,545	41,272	−13,727
1923–24	17,453	23,334	−5,881	3,568	15,532	−11,964	26,294	30,571	4,277
1924–25	17,141	21,268	−4,123	3,714	16,046	−12,332	22,296	20,638	1,658
1925–26	16,846	22,404	−5,558	3,785	18,021	−14,236	22,803	19,861	2,942
1926–27	18,823	23,403	−4,580	3,851	18,240	−14,389	21,650	21,823	−173
1927–28	20,785	21,952	−1,167	4,553	15,903	−11,350	20,575	23,378	−2,803
1928–29	18,924	21,452	−2,528	3,753	10,374	−6,621	21,331	24,752	−3,421
1929–30	19,154	20,971	−1,817	3,779	9,604	−5,825	20,197	21,176	−979

Source: Ministero del Tesoro (1969, Tables 3, 5 and 6).

improvement of the situation. Only with fiscal year 1923–4 did the cash budget return to a durable balance.

Deferrals grew until 1921–2, when they even exceeded the accrual budget values of 'expenses' and 'balance'. This illustrates that, as the war progressed, budgeted expense items were progressively postponed. The success of such a policy explained the different, at times even opposite, trends of cash disbursements and budget figures. In any event, whether we consider cash or accrual disbursements, there is no doubt that the war created formidable financing problems.

When dealing with a large fiscal shock, the obvious question is whether it would have been possible to finance the war without resorting to the inflation tax. Einaudi (1933) was among the few economists to have answered the question affirmatively. He relied heavily on two facts: (i) in the years 1914–24 the average ratio of total expenditures to national income was approximately 36 per cent; (ii) in the years 1928–30 the government was able to finance expenditures of more than 27 per cent of national income, without creating inflation. From that Einaudi drew the conclusion that, to cope with war expenditures, it would have been sufficient to increase the average tax burden to 36 per cent of national income, a level that would have been tolerated by the country. Consequently, inflation was not inevitable.

This may be true, but only in the narrow technical sense that, more than being generated by external events, inflation was invariably the result of economic policy decisions. Furthermore, these decisions were clearly predicated upon the actual and perceived permanence of the fiscal shock, that is the length of the war. From this viewpoint, it is difficult to argue that *ex-ante*, the war was expected to last for some time. In fact, as we shall recall shortly, the perception was that it would not continue for long. Apart from the fact that from 1915 to 1919, the average ratio between expenditures and national income was 42 per cent, and not 36 per cent, Einaudi (1933, p. 27), contradicting his own argument, wrote:

> If everyone were convinced that the war would be long and costly, and that because of it taxes should be drastically increased . . . the country would be able to cope with . . . the harsh sacrifices imposed by the situation.

To underline the importance of public perceptions to economic policy decisions, it suffices to mention that in the summer of 1915 there was widespread and strong belief in Italy that the war would not last more than four months and would not cost more than four million lire (the 26 June, *Economist*). Given these expectations, it would be difficult to believe that the population would have put up with a substantial increase in the tax burden (Heilperin 1968, p. 98).

There were also institutional problems, such as the absence of an income tax system which, by contrast, existed in the United Kingdom and the United States.[1] Strong political constraints on government initiatives were in place as well. Particularly at the beginning of the war, there was a widespread perception that an increase in tax rates would be extremely unpopular.[2] This is important because it may lead us to believe that miscalculations in forecasting the duration (and hence the cost) of the war could perhaps have been intentional, at least in part.[3]

In addition to public opposition to a tax increase for political reasons, one must not forget the economic crisis which preceded the First World War (Parlato 1982, p. 314). As shown in figure 4.1, after rising by more than ten points from 1905 to 1908, industrial production remained stable for the subsequent five years. The index of real wages went from 2.8 in 1905 to 3.5 in 1909, then fell for a few years and returned to 3.5 in 1914. In the first half of 1914, the awareness of a precarious economic situation spread and stirred up popular discontent (*Economist* of 14 March).

Employment declined at the outbreak of war. Emigration of eligible conscripts was halted by government, and a great number of emigrants were forced to return home, primarily from Germany and Austria–Hungary, but also from Switzerland and France. It was estimated that, from August to the first half of September 1914, slightly less than half a million workers returned to Italy and that 60 per cent of them ended up on the unemployment list (Parlato 1982, p. 319).

In conclusion, considering all the problems at odds with the feasibility of quickly and substantially raising tax revenues, we agree with Bruins (1920, p. 5) and Cassel (1922, p. 9) on the difficulty of financing war expenditures through new taxes, and concur with De Angelis (1982a, p. 229) that criticism levelled at the then ruling class was largely unwarranted.

The placement of public debt in the domestic market and abroad

Let us consider the public debt policy pursued by the Italian government during the war. Government foreign debt, converted into Italian lire at the then current exchange rate, climbed from 7.4 billion in 1917 to 66 billion in 1918, and then to 101 billion in 1924. The medium- and long-term portion of the domestic debt increased from 14.8 billion lire in 1914 to 34.4 in 1919, and to 60 billion lire in 1924. Treasury bills jumped from 380 million lire in 1914 to 15 billion in 1919, and to 22 billion in 1924 (table 4.2).

Foreign debt increased up to 1924. Medium- and long-term domestic debt also rose until 1923; short-term debt climbed until 1922, and notes issued by the government or by banks on its behalf increased until 1920. Nevertheless, the ratio of foreign to domestic debt remained equal to one from 1919 to 1924.

Table 4.2 *Central government debt on 30 June (million lire)*

	1914	1915	1916	1917	1918	1919	1920	1921	1922	1923	1924
External[a]	–	–	–	7,382	19,868	29,520	66,148	80,783	84,061	93,651	101,222
Domestic											
Longer term											
Irredeemable	9,922	9,992	9,992	17,064	23,752	23,514	43,275	44,382	44,448	44,445	44,465
Redeemable	4,918	6,005	9,869	5,171	5,113	5,067	5,020	4,971	4,920	4,867	4,064
Others[b]	–	–	–	2,422	3,078	5,835	4,013	5,619	7,232	10,718	11,977
Total	14,840	15,997	19,861	24,657	31,943	34,416	52,308	54,972	56,600	60,030	60,506
Short term											
Treas. bills[c]	380	401	785	4,291	7,812	15,054	9,079	19,777	25,312	24,713	22,226
Currency issued on behalf of state	–	1,613	2,157	3,295	6,481	8,026	10,333	8,722	8,049	7,764	7,447
State currency	486	754	1,124	1,451	1,966	2,267	2,267	2,267	2,267	2,428	2,428
Others	60	–	–	–	200	450	509	622	425	351	555
Total	926	2,768	4,066	9,037	16,459	25,797	22,188	31,388	36,043	35,256	32,656
Total domestic debt	15,766	18,765	23,927	33,694	48,402	60,213	74,496	86,360	92,643	95,286	93,162
Total debt	15,766	18,765	23,927	41,076	68,270	89,733	140,644	167,143	176,704	188,937	194,384

Notes:

[a] Converted in lire at the exchange rate prevailing on 30 June.

[b] 3-, 5-, 7- and 9-year Treasury bonds.

[c] 3- to 12-month maturity.

Source: US Congress (1925, vol. I, pp. 381–2)

Foreign debt consisted mainly of loans granted by England and the United States to the Italian ally. Funds were obtained through issues of so-called Buoni Speciali del Tesoro (BST) or special Treasury bills. At the beginning, these bills had a three or 12-month maturity, and were issued at discount.[4] Later, they were also issued with a maturity beyond 12 months, in which case the interest was paid by way of coupons through the Treasury's foreign correspondents. BSTs could be in bearer or registered form as well as in foreign currencies. The large growth of foreign debt from the end of the war onward was accompanied by a considerable depreciation of the Italian lira in the exchange market.

At home, six long-term issues were launched: the first in 1914 for 1 billion lire, the second in June 1915 for 1.1 billion, the third in December 1915 for 2.1 billion, the fourth in January 1917 for 2.5 billion, the fifth in 1917 for 3.6 billion, and the sixth in 1919 for 8.7 billion. Furthermore, there were placements of short- and medium–long-term Treasury bills, the latter with a maturity of three to five years at first, then seven, and later nine years. Table 4.2 shows that, from 1915 to 1918, medium- and long-term securities for approximately 17,000 million and short-term Treasury bills for about 7,500 million were issued.

The effective yield at the time of issue on the first five domestic securities was between 4.6 and 5.8 per cent. On short-term securities, such as the 10 to 12 month Treasury bills, the yield fluctuated between 3.5 and 5 per cent, from 1915 to 1918. The spread between long- and short-term securities was very small and inadequate in compensating the investor for the lower liquidity and higher risk associated with the long securities. The question raised, is why did investors continue to prefer long bonds?

One possible answer is that investors held the view, throughout the war, that prices would return to their pre-war 'natural' levels once hostilities had stopped. Consequently, yields on long securities were 'expected' to rise above the value indicated above. From this viewpoint, it made good sense that, once (by 1919) deflationary expectations proved to be unrealistic, investors' preferences would shift massively towards short-term securities.

In view of the difficulties of quantifying medium-run deflationary expectations, we focus on short-term debt yields, so that we can evaluate how the authorities pursued the objective of war financing through public debt placements. From 1915 to 1918, the average inflation rate was approximately 23 per cent, whereas nominal short-term yields ranged from 3.5 to 5 per cent. With the exception of 1916, the differential between domestic and international rates remained positive and, on average, was equal to about 0.5 per cent. An altogether different picture emerges when one considers the more important differential between real interest rates. Starting from 1916, the latter was consistently negative and, on average, was equal to approximately –6 per cent (table 1.2). These differentials were indicative of a monetary policy which had abandoned the objective of defending international reserves and supporting the lira exchange rate (BI R.A. 1915, p. 53). They were also indicative of stringent restrictions on capital movements that permitted the existence of highly segmented financial markets in Italy and abroad.

In sum, the government's decision to issue new public debt to reduce the inflationary consequences of the war was only partially successful. In fact, during the war, inflation was, on average, 26 per cent of domestic national income computed at constant prices, while seigniorage grew rapidly until it reached 25 per cent of national income in 1917 (figure 2.7). Subsequently, seigniorage declined, but remained around an average value of 7–8 per cent.[5]

The monetary shock: legislation and quantitative and qualitative issues

During the war, the government passed additional legislation to allow the stock of notes issued 'on behalf of trade' to grow over the limits set by existing regulations. Particulars of the new legislation are given in Spinelli and Fratianni (1991, pp. 281–4). The maximum limit, which stood at approximately 900 million lire for almost three years, was doubled in only three months. The tax on notes creation was 1 per cent on the first two increases and 2 per cent on the third. The last of the decrees passed by the government also repealed the important part of the legislation which set a ratio between current account deposits and maximum currency limits allowed.

Legislation relating to notes issued 'on behalf of government' was also thoroughly revised within a few months' period. First, the maximum amount of statutory advances to the government (also called 'ordinary' advances) was raised from 155 to 485 million lire. Second, only one month after Italy entered the war, the so-called 'extraordinary' advances were introduced, on which neither reserve requirements nor a tax applied. In three years, their ceiling reached almost 5 billion lire. Following the Italian defeat at Caporetto in November 1917, new advances for 1.5 billion were authorised within a few hours.

Despite the fact that the last official decision with regard to extraordinary advances was taken in June 1918, two additional large advances were approved after the war.[6] The first, for one billion lire, had the purpose of redeeming a similar amount of Treasury bills purchased previously by the banks of issue. The second, for 800 million, had the objective of withdrawing from the market paper currency issued by Austria–Hungary and circulating in annexed territories.

Furthermore, the government launched 'extraordinary for special needs' advances, which was another way of saying twice 'extraordinary'. In August 1914, the Treasury was authorised to ask the three banks of issue to supply notes for 300 million lire, for extraordinary and special reasons. With this amount, the government intended to establish a multi-purpose fund to assist savings banks and pawn banks in dealing with the deposit withdrawal during the first days of the war, to purchase foodstuff by public bodies to control prices, and to provide incentives for the production of grains and replenishment of live stocks in areas invaded by the enemy. The limit for extraordinary advances for special reasons was revised upward several times until it reached 1,850 million lire in November 1919. Notes issued against these advances were exempt from currency tax and reserve requirements. Finally, during the war, there was a frantic succession of new laws regarding the issuance of government notes. After a period of stability around the 500 million lire mark, the note ceiling grew fivefold.

As a result of this legislation, the outstanding amount of government notes (including bank notes issued on behalf of government) and bank notes issued on behalf of trade increased dramatically, even before Italy entered the war.

The authorities could have tried to restrain the monetary shock by at least curbing the volume of trade notes through the discount rate mechanism. In fact, as noted in the 1915 BI's Annual Report, during and after the war this mechanism was never given serious consideration. On the contrary, the ordinary discount rate applied by BI became less flexible starting in 1915 and, from 1916 to 1921, it tended to be even lower than the one offered by the Bank of England. This latter bank, of course, not only operated in a stronger and more reliable financial environment,[7] but also had to cope with an inflation much lower than the Italian one. From 1915 to 1917 discount transactions at preferential rates rose from 31 to 46 per cent of the total, while the interest charged on them declined from 5.35 to 4.86 per cent.

As a whole, events seemed to evolve as follows. On the one hand, the government purposely kept public debt yields low so that, to meet its financial needs, it had to issue new paper currency, either directly or through bank notes printed on its behalf. On the other hand, by also maintaining a low discount rate, the authorities encouraged the demand for public debt which the public acquired through bank loans. From an accounting point of view, this process amounted to disguising under 'Trade Notes' a portion of the currency which would have otherwise appeared under 'Government Notes'.[8] The League of Nations (1922), US Congress (1925), Alberti (1931), Bresciani Turroni (1931), Del Vecchio (1932) and Einaudi (1933) underlined this aspect and basically agreed, albeit with differences in emphasis, with Riccardo Bachi (US Congress 1925, p. 165) who wrote that:

a portion, at times not negligible, of notes issued by banks apparently for business reasons turned out to be in fact issued to meet government requirements.[9]

This was confirmed by BI itself (R.A. 1919, p. 90). Consequently, the war blurred the distinction between new notes issued for business or government purposes. Up to then, this distinction was considered important (and rightly so) in matters of monetary control (Del Vecchio 1932, p. 157; Einaudi 1933). In addition, the war had very strong repercussions on the quantity of money outstanding.

An analysis of banking operations also revealed a deterioration in the credit quality. Some large commercial banks went beyond their statutory objectives and invested heavily in equities. The results of these transactions became dramatically evident at the end of the war, when some industrial groups had to restructure. Loans became doubtful and some banks failed. The biggest failure was that of the Banca Italiana di Sconto in 1921, which resulted in the creation of 1.7 billion lire of monetary base by BI.[10]

In summary, the war period produced a very serious deterioration of the monetary situation, both in qualitative and quantitative terms. The period saw a succession of new laws aimed at broadening the already existing channels for currency creation or at introducing new ones. All of this took place in a confused and disorderly manner. The war, therefore, marked a very sharp change with respect to the 1861–1914 period, when the authorities endeavoured to clearly define powers and responsibilities to make the decision process transparent and the money market stable.

The ratio k and the accumulation of inflationary potential

For the first time since 1866, there was a strong shift of the public's preference from bank deposits to notes: between 1914 and 1917, the ratio k increased by about 50 per cent. The propensity of Italians to hoard notes did not escape the attention of contemporary economic observers (*Economist*, 22 April 1916), who suggested two possible explanations. The first emphasised the systematic decline, from the beginning of the war onward, of the volume of private dealings relative to those within the public administration or involving it. As the public administration was inclined to pay in cash rather than by bank cheques (unlike the private sector), the relative contraction of the private sector shifted the money demand toward notes. This was not a convincing explanation because (a) k increased from the very early days of the war, when the government purchasing apparatus had not yet been put in motion; (b) the ratio fell at a similarly rapid pace before the end of the war, when such apparatus was dismantled; and (c) the public accumulated a substantial amount of notes.

A more plausible explanation – suggested by Alberti (1931), Del Vecchio

(1932), Amantia (1933) and Einaudi (1933) – emphasised instead the erosion of public confidence in the ability of the banking system to survive the shock. This lack of confidence, which was eventually made concrete by bank failures such as Banca Italiana di Sconto in 1921, triggered a run on deposits at the beginning of the war, and after Italy's defeat at Caporetto. In the course of time, therefore, public confidence was reflected in the behaviour of the ratio k.

Warnings of a confidence crisis came as early as August 1914, when the BI's manager sent the following letter to its branches (Toniolo 1989, p. 125):

[The withdrawal of large quantities of notes from the banks] has taken place not because larger liquid resources are required to satisfy the increased needs of industrial and commercial enterprises, but rather because the great majority of people, in emergency situations, withdraw funds previously deposited with various financial institutions and keep them in cash.

It should be mentioned, however, that sharp increases in the ratio k occurred during wars even in economic systems where the government was not greatly involved in commercial transactions.[11]

There are other aspects of the behaviour of k worth emphasising. To begin with, even within the shorter period of 1914–18 (when there was a strong increase in the ratio and a consequent reduction in the monetary multiplier), the massive growth of the monetary base was such as to give a strong push to the total money stock. Consequently, the hoarding of paper currency by the public did indeed have a mitigating effect on the money creation process, albeit slightly. Second, between 1915 and 1916 there was also an increase in money velocity, implying a decline in the overall demand for notes and deposits. Third, given the inflationary expectations that a war generates, it was reasonable to expect that the propensity to spend out of money hoarding was bound to rise. But the inflationary consequences of money dishoarding, in particular of a rapid decline in k, did not materialise. As mentioned earlier, economic agents remained convinced that, at the end of hostilities, not only would monetary stability be restored, but that prices would return to pre-war levels. Thus, deflationary expectations acted as a stabiliser during the war, curbing the effects of the monetary expansion, albeit only in part. However, when at the end of the war it became evident that these expectations were not grounded in reality, the demand for money was sharply reduced; as a mirror image of this, the velocity of circulation rose from 1.3 to 1.75 between 1919 and 1922.[12]

Price and exchange-rate controls

With the start of the war, a more sustained demand for goods and a riskier environment brought about an increase in international prices of raw materials, finished products and freights. In Italy, the first significant rise in wholesale prices was already recorded in August 1914. As months went by, a domestic inflationary impulse, much more pronounced, followed the international one. On the foreign exchange market, the depreciation of the Italian lira gained momentum.

In part, authorities reacted in a traditional manner, in the sense that they did not remove the primary causes of the problem. Rather, they reacted to the symptoms by rationing goods and imposing controls on prices and exchange rates. The intensity of the controls reached a level never seen before and clearly in violation of the long-held principle of government non-interference in economic matters (Corbino 1938). On the other hand, what happened in Italy was basically in line with events elsewhere (Cassel 1922, p. 22; Robbins 1935; Rasi 1982a). In Italy, the policy of goods rationing and price controls found its natural complement (and its claimed justification) in an active promotional campaign against an alleged monopolistic determination of prices, commercial speculation and merchandise hoarding.

Despite the full determination of the authorities in implementing the price control policy on a broad range of goods and despite a favourable public opinion towards such policy, the general price trend was unaffected. Spinelli and Fratianni (1991, figure 6.1) explain this in terms of the difficulty of implementing price controls in an agricultural country with a highly decentralised system of production and consumption. Einaudi (1933, p. 192) arrived at the same conclusion.[13]

On the other hand, price controls did change the relative price structure. In fact, while the price index for industrial raw materials increased from 121 to 1,465, for goods-in-process it grew from 119 to 861 and for finished products from 100 to 395. Furthermore, prices of raw materials for food processing grew less than those for industrial usage, while the prices of finished food products increased even less (Cianci 1933; Spinelli and Fratianni 1991, table 6.9). In conclusion, this is yet another of the innumerable episodes in history during which price controls fail to restrain inflation, but instead alter the structure of relative prices in an arbitrary way, with negative repercussions on the real economy.

The lira exchange rate was also subject to strong and increasing interference by the authorities. There were exchange restrictions, and government intervention on exchange rates through the utilisation of either its own resources or new borrowings.

Table 1.2 has already shown the large average depreciation of the Italian lira relative to the pound sterling. To pursue our analysis further, we have prepared table 4.3, which shows data on the nominal and real exchange rate of the lira *vis-à-vis* the British pound (semi-annual from 1914 to 1918 and

Table 4.3 *Nominal and real exchange rate of the lira price of pound sterling, 1914–1923 (average monthly values)*

Year and month[a]	Exchange rate			Year and month[a]	Exchange rate	
	Nominal	Real[b]			Nominal	Real[b]
1914 M	–	–		1919 M	30.86	77.6
J	25.26	99.2		J	37.33	92.3
S	–	–		S	40.94	103.8
D	25.86	109.0		D	50.08	115.3
1915 M	–	–		1920 M	70.55	140.0
J	28.53	103.6		J	67.14	119.4
S	–	–		S	80.86	134.9
D	31.00	94.5		D	99.96	129.3
1916 M	–	–		1921 M	102.51	123.8
J	30.41	95.1		J	75.77	102.4
S	–	–		S	87.82	106.6
D	32.62	97.9		.D	93.95	98.5
1917 M	–	–		1922 M	86.07	99.1
J	33.98	95.3		J	89.48	104.5
S	–	–		S	106.36	106.8
D	39.67	90.1		D	91.56	96.2
1918 M	–	–		1923 M	97.01	104.2
J	43.68	91.8		J	101.00	114.3
S	–	–		S	102.94	122.5
D	30.25	70.8		D	100.48	116.3

Notes:
[a] M, J, S, D denote March, June, September and December.
[b] Ratio of UK wholesale prices, expressed in Italian lira, and Italian wholesale prices (1901–5=100). A higher ratio denotes a real depreciation of the lira.
Source: US Congress (1925).

quarterly from 1919 to 1923). In nominal terms, the lira depreciated since the beginning of the war. The devaluation process continued in 1915 and stopped in the the first half of 1916, when a loan from the British government brought valuable foreign currency to the Italian Treasury (Toniolo 1989). However, the devaluation process resumed and went through a second, momentary pause at the time when the United States joined the war. It then accelerated sharply soon after the Italian defeat at Caporetto. As a whole, between June 1914 and June 1918, the nominal exchange-rate lira lost more than 40 per cent of its value.

At the beginning of the war, the authorities confiscated all foreign currency denominated securities held by Italian residents. In August 1917, banks were obliged to officially record all foreign exchange transactions. At the end of the same year, as the devaluation process accelerated, the Treasury was empowered to purchase foreign exchange proceeds arising from exports. Furthermore, an import list was drawn up, indicating goods for which foreign currencies would be made available for payments to foreign exporters. The 'Istituto Nazionale per i Cambi con l'Estero' (National Institute for Foreign Exchange) was then established and empowered with the monopoly of all foreign exchange transactions. This entity operated until six months after the end of the war.[14] The potential effectiveness of this Institute's activities was considerable. In fact, in addition to a large control network, it could rely on favourable public opinion which saw in speculation the main cause of the lira problems. Furthermore, the Institute could capitalise on the fact that the government was directly involved in a great deal of international trade transactions and could count on the cooperation of similar official bodies established in other countries. Yet, as soon as the Institute commenced its operations in March of 1918, it became clear that it was not in a position to curb lira depreciation. Consequently, in the following June, the authorities went back to negotiate new financial agreements with the Allies. The obvious purpose was to obtain the necessary resources to carry out massive interventions in the foreign exchange market. This explains the substantial appreciation of the lira rate during the second half of 1918 (table 4.3).

The real and nominal exchange rates appreciated as the lira price of the British pound rose. There were two spikes, one in the second half of 1915 and the other, even more pronounced, in the second half of 1918 when the real exchange rate dropped from 91.8 to 70.8. The second spike coincided with the massive official interventions in the exchange market mentioned above. This sharp real appreciation of the lira brought about an equivalent loss of competitiveness of Italian exports.[15]

In conclusion, the price and exchange control policy left the country, by the end of 1918, with an artificial structure of relative prices and an artificially high real value of the lira.

The end of the war: unexpected inflation and social conflict

At the end of the war, there was a resurgence of the nominal depreciation of the lira exchange rate; the real exchange rate this time moved in sympathy with the nominal rate. The authorities' response was to apply even stricter controls. Five decrees were passed between 13 May 1919 and 24 April 1920. These abolished the monopoly of foreign exchange trading, but transferred this function to a selected group of banks under the supervision of the

National Institute for Foreign Exchange; prohibited the transfer of lire abroad; restricted the availability of foreign currencies to those who could provide justification; and introduced the requirement of the currency of denomination for export invoices (essentially the lira could be chosen as an alternative to foreign currencies). The tighter controls notwithstanding, in 1919 the lira price of the pound rose from 30 to about 50, while the real rate jumped by 45 points.

The end of the war brought a smaller improvement in public finances than had been anticipated. In fact, while military expenditures remained high, large amounts of funds were also required to reactivate annexed territories devastated by the war. Furthermore, with the large lira depreciation, the price controls policy generated increasing operating losses, because of the authorities' decision not to adjust domestic prices of select imported goods to reflect their higher cost in lire. In fiscal years 1918–19 and 1919–20, the government's current account still showed a large imbalance. Money growth reached its peak in 1919.

Under these circumstances, one would have expected a further increase in the inflation rate. That did not happen: between 1917 and 1918, the annual inflation rate actually dropped by more than 10 percentage points. The monthly wholesale prices reported in Cianci (1933; Spinelli and Fratianni 1991, table 6.11) records a maximum value in November 1918, then a decline until the following March and subsequently a resumption of an upward trend. In October 1919, the price level was the same as in November 1918. These facts came as a surprise, in light of the trend of the lira exchange rate and of the fiscal and monetary policy at the time.

The explanation lies with the deflationary expectations we have repeatedly alluded to and which characterised the behaviour of Italian economic agents during the war. As Cassel (1922, p. 45) and Einzig (1935, p. 98) also emphasised, for the whole period people remained firmly and generally convinced that at the end of hostilities prices would return rapidly to their prewar level. That level was perceived to be 'natural' and was therefore expected to resume as soon as the exceptional circumstances of the war faded away.

The empirical justification of regressive price expectations goes back to the experience of the gold standard, when the price level was stationary. The authorities not only refrained from changing these expectations but tried to strengthen them (Cassel 1920, p. 27). The Italian government, sometimes through sheer misinformation, reinforced in the public's mind the notion of a 'normal' price level. Furthermore, there was also the peculiar belief in the population that Germany was storing away large quantities of goods for the purpose of flooding the Italian market and causing prices to plunge at the end of the war. In an attempt to show the irrationality of this belief and to

minimise its potential negative consequences, Einaudi put forth the following question in the *Corriere della Sera* of 1–2 May 1915:

There are many people in allied countries who fear a colossal sale of merchandise,
which Germany is allegedly manufacturing and storing for flooding foreign markets
at very low prices. This danger is nine tenths the product of unsound imagination.
How can Germany, with a very reduced workforce and dreadful military and agricultural needs, afford to manufacture goods with raw materials which she does not
have for the sole purpose of building up a large inventory?

When the war ended almost unexpectedly, there was a surge in the supply
of goods accompanied by cautious consumers who were expecting that
prices would fall imminently and substantially (Bachi 1926, p. 166). In such
conditions, the general level of prices stopped growing at first and then
began falling in absolute values.[16]

What happened when crude economic reality prevailed and prices
resumed their upward trend and, as a result, economic agents had to
thoroughly revise expectations that they had had for many years? We have
already mentioned that the price control policy implementation was accompanied by a promotional campaign. This campaign had the purpose of
instilling the notion of 'fair' prices in the business community, but also
made people very suspicious towards the commercial sector. Thus, it did
not come entirely as a surprise that people blamed the commercial sector for
the return of inflation. Bachi (1926, pp. 168–9) described these developments very well:

In the face of an inevitable increase in prices, people rediscovered their old faith in
price controls. The sense of violence, so widespread during the war and in subsequent social and political disorders, inspired a new faith in a 'direct action' also in
commercial matters....

Hence, we had the widespread popular riots which wildly exploded during the
early days of July 1919 to protest price increases. Social confusion developed and
spread throughout Italy in a few days. It also reached peripheral areas and even
small mountain villages, but culminated primarily in large cities, some of which were
plundered for many days. . . . In many places, labour associations systematically
directed the operations, and often disguised them as quasi-legal activities. They
ordered the requisition of consumer goods from shops, stored them in their own
premises and sold them to association members at very low prices. In the second
phase of this movement, the turmoil prompted the intervention of municipal
authorities. This was a new artifice to legalise this absurd movement, in which the
authorities imposed a strong reduction in prices in order to please the masses and
pacify the population at large. It was perhaps in Bologna that municipal authorities
introduced the awkward practice of reducing existing prices by 50 per cent across the
board. This practice spread rapidly throughout the country, so that in myriads of
small villages, towns and large cities, municipal bulletins were posted in the streets
saying that prices . . . had been magically reduced by half.

Cianci's (1933) wholesale price data lead us to conclude that the practical consequences of these events on price trends were less significant than those that transpired from Bachi's remarks. In fact, the various price indexes declined in absolute terms, or slowed down only slightly and for a short period. Prices of raw foodstuff were stable in the second half of the year, while those of finished food products did not appear to be affected by controls.

The problem of bread price and the end of the crisis

There was a strong tendency to ascribe the resumption of inflationary processes to the relaxation of the rationing policy and a partial return to market-economy principles, two events which took place at the end of the war. As indicated by Bachi (1926, p. 175), in June 1919, the executive council of the Italian municipalities' association reached the conclusion that if the authorities' action in providing supplies: 'was disorganised and inadequate during the war, it was even more so after the armistice, when it was necessary to quickly introduce fundamental measures aimed at preventing price increases for almost all consumer goods'.

On this occasion, demand from the public strengthened government policy of selling consumer goods below cost. Thus, on 15 August 1919, the authorities decided to broaden the basket of goods subject to price controls and on 5 April 1920 rationing resumed. Against these measures, on 23 November 1919 in the daily *Corriere della Sera* Einaudi wrote the following famous statement: 'the remedy, unum et necessarium, is to put the printing press [of the notes] out of order'.

In theory, the only way out was to reinstate tight control over monetary policy. In practice, however, this process was made particularly difficult by the very same large costs brought about by the price control policy. As mentioned previously, with the end of the war and the resulting strong nominal and real depreciation of the Italian lira, government had accumulated massive losses stemming from the domestic sale of imported goods at controlled prices. Thus, the problem of the bread price became extremely relevant.

The authorities had controlled this price for a number of years by purchasing wheat mostly abroad at market prices, then selling it domestically to bakeries below cost. At the end of the war, the cost of this intervention increased from 1.9 billion lire in fiscal year 1918–19 to 2.7 in the following fiscal year. In the spring of 1920, the projected loss for 1920–1 reached 4.5 billion. To appreciate the meaning of such figures it suffices to recall that, at the end of March 1920, the total amount of publicly held paper currency was 17.7 billion lire. It was not a surprise, therefore, that a perception began to develop that the bread price problem could lead to hyperinflation.

The first bill aimed at reducing government losses on bread was tabled for discussion in parliament in June 1920, but this simply sparked a government crisis. However, a second attempt at the end of the year was successful because it proposed a gradual solution, while benefiting from the relatively (to anticipations) poor showing of the left parties in the elections. Consequently, the retail price of bread was raised to fully cover the purchasing cost of domestic wheat. For imported wheat, break-even was reached through sharp increases in taxes.

The reaction from financial markets was positive: the lira price of the British pound dropped from the average value of 102.51 in January 1921 to 75.77 in the following June, which was sufficient in itself to eliminate government losses on imported wheat. Secondly, thanks to an abundant world crop and a worsening of the international recession, the foreign currency price of wheat dropped substantially in 1921. In fact, a recession started in Britain in the second quarter of 1920, in Germany in 1919, in Sweden around the middle of 1920 and in the Lower Countries in the autumn of 1920. In many countries prices declined even in absolute terms (Einzig 1935, p. 223). In the United States, for instance, wholesale prices in June 1921 were 56 per cent of their May 1920 level. Finally, there was an exceptionally large domestic crop (5,200 million kilos against 3,850 of the previous year), which consequently reduced the country's dependence on imported wheat. The concurrence of these factors determined a turning point in the fiscal situation: the government even started to show a budget surplus. The end of the crisis should therefore be interpreted as a combination of economic policy decisions and a favourable economic cycle (Bachi in League of Nations 1922, p. 23). In this connection, it is significant that, while the general price index began to decline in November 1920, the stock of currency started to drop only in January 1921.

The Banca d'Italia's Annual Reports

The Annual Reports of the Banca d'Italia reveal an inability to analyse both the economic developments and the policy options open to the monetary and fiscal authorities. As also transpires from two recent retrospective assessments undertaken by the BI itself (Toniolo 1989; De Mattia 1991), BI appears resigned to the minor role of only printing notes. For example, on page 48 of the 1917 Report, we read:

The Management has been able to carry out a number of expansions and changes in printing facilities, overcoming quite a few obstacles in fitting premises, acquiring new machinery, obtaining supplies and training personnel. As a result, against an output of five million notes (recorded in 1913), eighteen million have been issued this past year. The Management is satisfied with the outcome of its endeavours.

While BI emphasised these types of activity, it purposely avoided tackling the problem of war financing, to the point of failing to report even a single price graph (De Mattia 1991, p. 561). BI did not deal with the inflation issue from the autumn of 1918 to the summer of 1919, nor did it explain why the process came to an end. When the Bank eventually brought up the subject of prices, it usually referred to international prices (the Sauerbeck index). Typical of the poor quality of BI's economic analysis is the following sentence (BI R.A. 1919, p. 7): 'The amount of public debt has increased substantially, the stock of paper currency has grown, foreign exchange rates have generally deteriorated, and the prices of goods have gone up everywhere.'

A decade of nominal and real exchange rates and the Phillips curve

In this last section, we deal with the relationship between the trends of nominal and real lira exchange rates, as well as the relationship between production and price level changes.

We have already studied the negative correlation between the nominal and real exchange rates of the lira from the outbreak of hostilities to the summer of 1918. In turn, the stickiness of the nominal rate and, hence, the appreciation of the real rate were attributable to massive systematic government interventions. From the summer of 1918 to March 1920, the correlation between nominal and real exchange rates became positive: the nominal rate rose more than the difference between Italian and UK inflation rates. The underlying reasons were the end of government interventions and the pressure of the nominal exchange rate to rise to a higher equilibrium level.

But if we expand our field of observation to the whole 1914–24 period, we come to see a first sub-period from 1914 to 1920, when the lira depreciated in nominal terms at an annual rate of 15.8 per cent and in real terms by approximately one half of that. Subsequently, the correlation between nominal and real exchange rates switched from positive to negative. In fact, the lira continued to depreciate in nominal terms, but appreciate in real terms.

The switch in the sign of the correlation was due not so much to a different intervention policy, but to a shift in monetary policy that took place between the end of 1920 and the beginning of 1921.

In figure 4.3 we display the annual growth rate of the price deflator and real income from 1913 to 1923, a period which encompassed a complete cycle, at least with respect to these two variables.[17] Different types of short-term behaviour emerge. Overall, movements between the south-west and the north-east regions appear to dominate. Hence, a Phillips curve relationship is evident. On the other hand, there are also movements in the

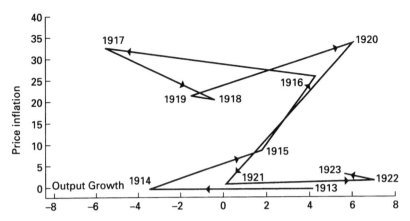

Figure 4.3 Inflation and output growth (annual growth rates)
Source: Chapter 1.

opposite direction. In particular, the years 1916–18 and 1920–3 reveal a 'perverse' negative correlation between production and inflation.

The 1920–3 period is undoubtedly more interesting: it was a time of peace and is illustrative of the behaviour of the Italian economy during the post-war stabilisation process. Here we note both a decline in the inflation rate by approximately 35 percentage points and a basic stability in output growth.

Therefore, the evidence does not lead to a rejection of the hypothesis of a drastic change in the macroeconomic environment, either real or perceived by economic agents. Such a change reduced considerably the stabilisation costs. Furthermore, the new environment could be associated with the solution of the bread-price problem at the end of 1920 and the benefits derived from the implementation of domestic fiscal and monetary policies.[18]

Conclusions

The fiscal impulses were a predominant factor in Italian monetary history during and immediately after the war. In the face of substantial expenditures, which the government was unable or unwilling to finance either through new public debt issues or by increasing the tax burden, the monetary authorities chose an accommodating policy. Hence, there was a sharp increase in money growth. The concomitant reversal in the trend of the k ratio generated a considerable monetary shock, whose inflationary impact was amplified by an output slowdown.

The authorities reacted by imposing direct controls on prices and foreign exchange rates. Three important remarks should be made in this respect. First, this policy was ineffective in curbing prices, even when people resorted to violence. Second, at the end of the war the price control policy itself came close to bringing about hyperinflation. Third, government interventions and exchange controls led first to a cumulative real appreciation of the lira, and subsequently made the process of monetary stabilisation more difficult.

In any event, economic agents remained strongly convinced that, at the end of hostilities, prices would return to their pre-war levels. To quash this belief, it was necessary to go through the inflation behaviour of the years 1919–20, both in Italy and abroad, and the subsequent failures of many governments, before prices and exchange rates could be restored to pre-war levels.

The Italian experience of 1919–20 represents a classic and very important case of a causality running from unexpected inflation to social conflict, and not vice versa. It also supports what Amantia (1933, pp. 29–30) had to say about the effects of inflation:

entrepreneurs and businessmen get rich; savers suffer substantial losses; old pensioners and all fixed income earners get poorer and poorer, while additional paper currency is issued; the middle class . . . faces lower standards of living; the working class, if there is a solid unionised structure in the country, succeeds in obtaining nominal wage increases to realign earnings to their existing real purchasing power, and sometimes even to higher levels than necessary. . . . Inflation disturbs . . . the social balance among the various classes.[19]

Finally, the return to fiscal and monetary stability was in part attributable to the initiatives of those responsible for economic policy and in part to mere exogenous factors. The cost of deflation appeared to be modest, thanks to the quickness in the revisions of inflation expectations.

5   The 1920s and 1930s: foreign exchange policy and industrial and financial restructuring

Mr. Mussolini threatened to take the lira back to its former value. Fortunately, . . . the lira does not pay attention even to a dictator and one cannot treat the currency with castor oil. (Keynes 1923)

the time came for Mussolini to regain control of the lira. In a speech delivered in Pesaro in August 1926, he stated his intention to defend the lira at all costs. Soon after, the currency showed a strong improvement. (Einzig 1935)

Introduction

There are many salient characteristics of the Italian monetary history of the 1920s and 1930s. First of all, the purchasing power of the Italian lira was lower at home than on the international markets. This problem emerged slowly between 1922 and 1924, then exploded in the subsequent two years. For the most part, this situation was inherited from the war as it stemmed from the process of normalising both domestic and international monetary relations. The authorities also faced difficulties in dealing with an obsolete industrial and financial structure existing at the end of the war. Second, the authorities initially reacted to the lira collapse by launching a monetary stabilisation program, but then went much further and aimed at a fundamental restructuring of the industrial system. Thus, from 1926 to 1936, the authorities tried to harmonise monetary policy, industrial restructuring and the resumption of the process of capital accumulation.

This chapter consists of five major parts. We begin with a comparison of the Italian economy and the economies of the United Kingdom and the United States. Then, we analyse the causes of domestic inflation and lira depreciation from 1922 to 1926. The third section lists the important decisions made by the authorities from 1925 onward to first stop and then reverse the depreciation of the lira. A cost–benefit analysis of the strong lira policy follows. Finally, we outline the new financial innovations which culminated with the 1936 Bank Legislation still in existence in the early 1990s.

The three stages of the Italian economy and a comparison with the USA and UK

Table 1.3 shows that, for the sub-period 1921–37, monetary growth was at its lowest during the 131 years covered in the *History*. The average inflation rate was equal to zero, and the growth of real income did not differ from its long-run average. Furthermore, we know from table 1.2 that during the same period, Italian economic growth was, on average, in line with the British one, while Italian inflation exceeded that of Britain by approximately three percentage points. As the lira depreciated in foreign exchange markets by an annual 1 per cent, on average, it gained approximately 2 per cent per annum in real terms.

However, average values for the period do not reveal the ups and downs of the Italian economy. From a statistical viewpoint, many of the variables appeared to go through three distinct stages defined by the sub-periods 1921–6, 1927–33 and 1934–7. In short, the first stage coincided with the lira's domestic and international depreciation. The second was associated with the stabilisation programme and a strong lira policy on the domestic front, and with the worldwide great depression. The third stage corresponded to the disintegration of the domestic monetary control mechanism and the resumption of inflation.

In Italy, the growth of the money stock was high in the first, low in the second and again high in the third stage (table 5.1). Velocity growth showed a positive correlation with money growth, exacerbating the swings in the rates of price change: +5.2 per cent in the first sub-period, −7.4 per cent in the second, and then back again to +5.4 per cent in the third. In addition to such a wide fluctuation band, there is no precedent in our *History* for the price level dropping so sharply and so continuously for seven consecutive years as it did from 1927 to 1933. The dynamics of real income did not differ qualitatively from those of the money stock, but the correlation between money and prices was much stronger than that between money and output.

To better grasp the meaning of the evolution of the variables of the exchange equation, it is also useful to consider what happened abroad. The work of Friedman and Schwartz (1982) enables us to analyse the United States and the United Kingdom (table 5.1). With regard to money, velocity and prices, there was more similarity between Italy and the United States than between Italy and the United Kingdom. Italian inflation, however, lagged behind that of the other two countries. In fact, while in Italy on average the price level grew at 5 per cent in the first sub-period, in the United States (and more so in the United Kingdom) it declined in absolute terms. In the third sub-period, inflation resumed everywhere, but more vigorously in Italy. With regard to industrial output, in the United States the depression

Table 5.1 *The exchange equation for Italy, US and UK, 1921–1937 (annual percentage changes)*

	Money	Velocity	Price level	Output
Italy				
avg. 1921–6	6.7	1.9	5.2	3.4
std. dev.	(2.6)	(3.7)	(2.4)	(1.3)
avg. 1927–33	0.9	−7.9	−7.4	0.4
	(0.9)	(2.2)	(1.4)	(1.7)
avg. 1934–7	2.2	6.8	5.4	3.6
	(2.4)	(4.6)	(2.1)	(2.7)
US				
avg. 1921–6	3.8	−1.9	−2.9	4.8
	(2.1)	(3.2)	(2.8)	(6.1)
avg. 1927–33	−4.3	−5.4	−4.7	−5.0
	(2.9)	(3.6)	(2.1)	(3.4)
avg. 1934–7	8.7	5.4	2.5	11.6
	(1.8)	(1.8)	(1.7)	(1.5)
UK				
avg. 1921–6	−2.0	−3.1	−6.6	1.5
	(0.7)	(3.7)	(2.9)	(2.1)
avg. 1927–33	1.6	−2.0	−1.9	1.5
	(0.7)	(1.8)	(0.5)	(1.9)
avg. 1934–7	3.6	1.9	1.1	4.4
	(1.3)	(1.6)	(1.0)	(1.3)

Sources: Table 1.3 for Italy and Friedman and Schwartz (1982, tables 4.8 and 4.9) for the US and the UK.

had a magnitude and duration decidedly more pronounced than in Italy. British depression turned out to be the least severe.[1]

Government deficits between the two wars were also the most contained of the 131-year history. Yet again, in our three sub-periods there was a marked difference with regard to both endogenous and policy variables. For each of the sub-periods, table 5.2 gives the annual averages of the ratio of budget deficit to national income, the monetisation ratio and the contributions of the determinants of money growth.

The government's budget was balanced in the first stage, but showed an increasing deficit in the second and third stages. The extent to which the deficit was monetised, i.e., the evolution of MBTR, was not always the main factor underlying the growth of the total monetary base. In particular, during the sub-period 1927–33, MBTR indeed grew at an average annual rate of 10.3 per cent, but such growth was more than offset by the sizable

Table 5.2 *Budget deficits, money and its contributions, 1921–1937*

Variable	1921–6	1927–33	1934–7
DEF/Y	0.0	3.5	5.4
(dMBTR/DEF)×100	–61.8	84.1	–235.5
Money	6.7	0.9	2.2
Monetary base	1.0	1.2	7.0
Multiplier	5.7	–0.3	–4.8
Contributions to money growth			
MBTR	–6.2	10.3	3.4
MBOT	7.1	–12.0	5.8
MBF	0.2	2.9	–2.1
k	5.7	–0.6	–5.1
re	–0.1	0.3	0.2

Notes:
Except for the first two lines, all others refer to period averages of annual
percentage changes. Contributions to money growth were computed by setting to
zero the interaction terms.

reduction in the 'Others' component. As we shall see later, this means that
the monetary authorities were in a position to unload on the banking
system the increased indebtedness of the Treasury *vis-à-vis* the Bank of
Italy. The multiplier's average rate of change moved in the opposite direction of the monetary base's. This mainly reflected the considerable reduction of the ratio k in the first stage and its very strong growth in the third.[2]

Prices and the exchange rate from 1922 to 1928

Figure 5.1 compares the monthly average lira/dollar rate with the level of
Italian wholesale prices from January 1922 to December 1928.[3] From the
spring of 1922 there was strong deterioration of domestic prices and the
exchange rate. Between May and November, the price index increased from
630 to 715; it then dropped back to its February 1921 and March–April
1920 values. Between May and October, the dollar price increased from
approximately 18.5 to 24 lire. The price of the pound sterling reached a
minimum value of 81 lire during the third week of April, and a maximum of
112 lire in the first week of November 1922 (figure 5.2). That the lira was
under pressure was therefore obvious; previously, the market had never
recorded rates of 24 lire against the dollar or 112 against the pound.

The Mussolini government came to power on 31 October 1922. This date
marked not only the end of an era of political and social instability, but also

Figure 5.1 Index of wholesale prices and dollar exchange rate, 1922–1928 (monthly data)
Source: Cianci (1933) and Borgatta (1933).

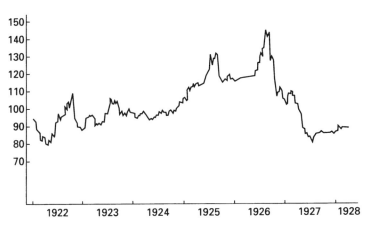

Figure 5.2 Average weekly sterling exchange rate from 1922 to the first week of March 1928
Source: Spinelli and Toso (1990).

the beginning of a new political regime. According to Alberti (1931), the event had a positive effect on market expectations. In the previous two months of the year, the dollar rate had dropped to 20 lire; it then remained stable until the summer of 1923, when it again started to increase. Between August 1923 and August 1924, the dollar rate stabilised around 23 lire. The rate against the pound improved until the penultimate week of 1922; it increased until the second week of July 1923, then fluctuated (around the 100 lira mark) until the end of August 1924. The beneficial impact of expectations showed up also on prices which continued to decrease until June 1924.

Then, in autumn 1924 the situation degenerated so rapidly that, by 1925, prices and exchange rates had returned to pre-fascist levels. At the end of 1924, the annual inflation rate was already above 7 per cent; in the third quarter of 1925, it reached 15 per cent. In June and July 1925, the rate against the dollar climbed from 24.5 to 27.5 lire. In the last week of June, the rate against the pound sterling reached 136. At this point, a series of massive interventions by the authorities in the foreign exchange markets at first reduced then stabilised the dollar and pound rates at 25 and 120 lire, respectively. On 13 May 1926, confronted with an untenable situation, the authorities were forced to suspend their official interventions. The repercussions of this decision on the lira rate were traumatic. On 28 July, the dollar and pound rates climbed to 31.6 and 153.7 lire.

On 18 August, Mussolini delivered a widely publicised speech in Pesaro, through which the government officially declared its commitment to 'fight' in defence of the lira. As illustrated by figure 5.1, the results were spectacular. The lira appreciated during the days immediately following the speech. By the end of the year, the pound had already dropped to 107 lire; at the beginning of May 1927, it was around 90 lire; in June, the authorities had to intervene to prevent a further currency *appreciation*. Between August and December 1926, the dollar rate fell to 22.5; in the following June, it recorded a value of 18.

In the second half of 1927, exchange rates remained stable. At the end of the same year, the authorities fixed the new gold parity of the lira and sanctioned the end of flexible rates which had prevailed officially since 1894 and *de facto* since 1866. The commitment was to stabilise the dollar rate at 19 and the pound rate at the 90 lire mark (the so-called 'quota 90').

Domestic prices fell quickly and sharply. In less than a year the wholesale price index dropped from 831 to 615 (figure 5.1). The annual inflation rate, computed on the basis of the same index, had already turned out to be negative by the end of 1926 and equal to −28 per cent in the third quarter of 1927. Consequently, in a period of only 15 months, it dropped by 34 percentage points. Between 1926 and 1927 the income deflator also displayed a wide and sudden directional change in behaviour: annual percentage change dropped from +17 to −13.

The behaviour of prices and exchange rates from 1922 to 1927–8 raises some interesting questions. What were the underlying reasons for the initial decline of the domestic and international purchasing power of the lira? What was the influence of Mussolini's Pesaro speech on prices and exchange rates? What actions did the government take? Did the targeted rates of 19 lire per US dollar and 90 lire per UK pound represent equilibrium levels? We shall deal with such questions in the rest of this chapter.

The resumption of inflation and of exchange-rate depreciation

The resumption of inflation after its drop in 1921 (figure 5.1) was the result of international and domestic inflationary impulses. The world disinflationary process came to an end in 1922. This process characterised the immediate post-war period and, as an example, resulted in a drop of almost 50 per cent in the Sauerbeck price index.[4] In an industrial economy such as that of Italy, the end of declining world prices, concurrent with the start of a depreciating lira exchange rate, could result only in increased production costs and lower stability in domestic prices.

Domestically, the behaviour of the monetary base suggests that monetary policy was restrictive, at least until the beginning of 1924. In fact, the annual percentage change of this aggregate was 2.6 in 1921, –3.3 in 1922, and –2.1 in 1923. A more in-depth analysis, however, reveals that policy was not so restrictive. In chapter 4, we noticed that between 1914 and 1917 the ratio k increased so significantly that, from 1918 to 1920 inclusive, the public reduced its own currency holdings in relation to deposits. This process resumed in 1922 and continued in a sustained fashion until 1928. Over these years, k decreased by almost two thirds.

In the meantime, the ratio re also dropped by approximately 50 per cent. Consequently, the money multiplier grew rapidly. In the early years of the inter-war period, the multiplier's strong growth not only counteracted the reduction in the monetary base, but also succeeded in fuelling the money stock's strong upward trend. This trend, as we have already noted, placed Italy in an anomalous situation in international markets. In 1923, annual money growth reached almost 13 per cent against a real income growth of only 5.6 per cent. Thus, it appears that the authorities could not, or did not want to, offset the expansionary impulses stemming from the conversion of the monetary base into bank deposits. Thus, we can say that, contrary to what the trend of the monetary base would lead us to believe, monetary policy was expansionary from 1921 to 1924. Both Del Vecchio (1932, pp. 337–8) and Alberti (1931, pp. 146–7) expressed views similar to ours and drew attention also to the low interest rate policy and the tendency for velocity to rise. In fact, domestic real interest rates declined until 1925, when they stabilised at –11 per cent, whereas velocity rose significantly from 1924 to 1925, when it recorded the maximum value of the inter-war period.

In part, the fact that the monetary base did not contract to the point of offsetting the expansionary effects of the reduction of k and re can be related to the activities of the 'Sezione Autonoma del Consorzio per sovvenzioni su valori industriali' (a Division of the Consortium for Financing Industrial Enterprises). The 'Sezione', established in March 1922, was a financial entity which funded itself directly through the banks of issue in order to grant loans to (or to liquidate) companies and banks in precarious positions, such as Ansaldo, Banca Italiana di Sconto, Ilva, and Banco di Roma. The maximum amount that banks of issue could provide to the 'Sezione' was at first fixed at 1 billion lire, and then raised several times (De Angelis 1982b). As a result, the Sezione's notes grew from 898 million lire at the end of 1922 to 3,306 million at the end of 1923, and reached a maximum of 4,081 million at the end of 1924. At that point in time, the value of the Sezione's notes, which were not guaranteed by collateral and were not subject to reserve requirements, represented more than 20 per cent of total currency outstanding.

In principle, there should not necessarily have been a close relationship between the Sezione's notes and the overall stock of paper money. In fact, the authorities could have reacted to the creation of new notes by the Sezione by eliminating some other component of the monetary base. In practice, however, in view of the nature and urgency of the Sezione's activities, such a close relationship could not but exist. This was also later admitted by BI's Governor, Menichella (1956). Supino (1929, p. 240) speaks of a 'deterioration of currency quality' and Alberti (1931, p. 188) of 'currency dilution'.

Whereas monetary policy was expansionary during the early years, fiscal policy moved in the opposite direction. Our measure of the government budget deficit dropped from approximately 15 per cent of national income in 1921 to 0.6 per cent in 1923; two years later, there was a substantial surplus. Table 4.1 indicates that the fiscal impulse was in a contractive phase. Finally, a strong recovery in world demand provided strong external expansionary impulses to the Italian economy.

The two impulses, i.e., monetary and external, turned out to be predominant. As a result, domestic production started to grow at a rate never experienced before: the industrial output index was 53 in 1921, 61 in 1922, 73 in 1924, and 83 in 1925. Furthermore, between the end of 1922 and the end of 1925, unemployment dropped from 540 to 122 thousand units.

Conditions were therefore favourable for the resumption of the domestic inflationary process. Menichella (1956) explicitly mentioned that a situation developed in which 'the available physical resources were no longer sufficient to cope with the demand, so that prices started to grow rapidly'.

Filosa, Rey and Sitzia (1976) were also of the view that excess demand was the main reason behind the resumption of the inflationary process. By contrast, Rey (1978, p. 284) wrote that, starting in 1922:

The excess demand triggered an inflation rate of 7.4 per cent per annum in consumer prices, and such excess was particularly evident in capital goods, where the pressure on prices was very sustained in 1925 (+19%) and continued further in 1926.

Given the usual close relationship between import demand and domestic output, the strong recovery also generated strains in the balance of payments (Filosa, Rey and Sitzia 1976, p. 56; Rey 1978, p. 284). These problems were made worse by the growing disparity between Italy's free trade policy and the increasing protectionist approach of other countries; a decline in revenues from tourism and, more importantly, from emigrants' remittances; and the frequent placement of foreign loans in Italy. The latter phenomenon was clearly justified by the differential between domestic and international real interest rates.

The twin problems of domestic inflation and external imbalance brought about an increasing depreciation of the Italian lira exchange rate. In August 1925, in the face of a sharp increase in the exchange rate (which was also related to social disorders in Britain), the Treasury began to intervene on the exchange market and purchased abroad all available Italian lire through forward exchange contracts. This was made possible by a credit facility at Morgan Bank. The interventions reached exceptionally high figures, estimated to vary between 2.5 and 3.5 billion lire. BI's 1925 R.A. also confirmed that interventions were 'of an unusual magnitude and frequency' (Volpi 1928, p. 257; De Maria 1928). Furthermore, there was a shift of international speculative pressures towards the Italian lira (after the crash of French and Belgian francs), and a deterioration of the Italian foreign trade imbalance. Mussolini stated that lira depreciation was not mainly attributable to political reasons and stated: 'It appears, instead, that the bug eroding the lira's defence mechanism must be found in the increased disequilibrium of our trade balance' (De Felice 1968, p. 231). On 13 May 1926 the authorities suspended their interventions which were hardly proving effective. In his memoirs, the Governor of the Bank of France, Moreau (1986, p. 157) wrote that:

Chalendar has been able to obtain the graph of foreign exchange transactions carried out by the Italian Treasury during the years 1925 and 1926. This graph reveals the inefficacy of those interventions on the market.

Soon after, the final crash of the lira occurred and, in August, the Pesaro speech followed.

The stabilisation programme: expectations and actions

Let us now consider two questions: How was the trend of domestic prices and foreign exchange rates reversed; and: What was the connection between the Pesaro speech and the grand reversal? The depreciation of a currency depends, among other factors, upon expectations. If the authorities have any credibility, they are in a position to significantly influence the evolution of the exchange rate through manipulation of expectations. On the other hand, because expectations are ultimately endogenous, these government signals will have no effect unless they are accompanied, and preferably preceded, by concrete measures which tackle the ultimate causes of the depreciation process. Thus, the best results may be achieved by first taking concrete policy actions and subsequently, when these actions begin to affect market behaviour, by further altering expectations through appropriate public announcements.

An approach of this type was adopted between the spring and summer of 1925, when the authorities took concrete measures, and, in August 1926, when they made a formal commitment with regard to monetary stabilisation. If we lose sight of this aspect, we are bound to either underestimate the authorities' knowledge of the economic system, or to attribute the lira recovery only to Mussolini's persuasiveness. In this respect, see Keynes' and Einzig's citations at the beginning of the chapter, as well as the positive assessment expressed by De Mattia (1991, p. 572).

The details of the stabilisation programme can be summarised as follows. First, between 7 March and 17 June 1925, the official discount rate applied by BI was raised from 5.5 to 7 per cent, a level never recorded since 1866. Second, the budget surpluses of fiscal years 1924 and 1925 made it possible not only to put the brakes on the reaction of the government's monetary base, but also to reduce the stock of public debt (from 94 billion lire in June 1925 to 84 billion at the end of 1926). Third, both the banks' and government's paper currency stocks began declining after October 1925. The same applied to 'Sezione Autonoma del Consorzio' notes which peaked at the end of 1924. The total monetary base, after peaking at the end of 1925, declined from a value of approximately 34 billion lire to 32.6 billion in the next three years. Fourth, on 9 July 1925 Mussolini accepted a proposal from the Association of Italian Industries to place Volpi in charge of both the Ministry of Finance and the Treasury. Volpi was a man of great technical ability and well connected in international financial circles. Fifth, in November 1925 and January 1926, agreements were officially concluded with the United States and Britain to settle Italy's war debts. These agreements were important for a number of reasons. They dissipated some of the uncertainty surrounding the solution of the difficult problem of war debts (BI R.A. 1924, p. 10). Also Italian companies and municipalities resumed their dealings with US financial markets after the US Congress had closed them in 1922 because of outstanding war debts vis-à-vis the US. The reopening of US financial markets and the resulting inflow of foreign reserves strengthened the lira in both the short and long run. In the long run it allowed Italian companies to radically restructure the manufacturing sector, which, in turn, had a favourable impact on the balance of payments through higher economic growth (Tasca 1927). Sixth, with the Decree Law of 6 May 1926, which came into effect the following 1 July, BI became the only issue bank (Supino 1929, p. 254). With that decision the era of multiple banks of issue in Italy came to an end. A number of factors came into play and brought about that key innovation. There was widespread perception that the economy needed a broad stabilisation plan that was best suited to a single bank of issue. Additionally, the basic philosophy of the Fascist regime was very favourable to a centralisation of power; the absence of regional political opposition facilitated its implementation (Stringher 1926; Minister De Stefani's correspondence with Mussolini reported by Marcoaldi 1986). Even the US financial community looked favourably upon the notion of centralising issuing facilities in a single bank (Migone 1971, pp. 49–50 and 64). Finally, new and significant developments occurred in the Treasury bills market. In December 1925, the total value of these securities reached 17.3 billion lire, an amount slightly less than the total stock of paper currency outstanding. As the stabilisation programme got underway, it became increasingly evident that the massive quantity of Treasury bills caused monetary policy to be less effective. In fact, when these securities were held by the banks, they were utilised as reserves and consequently reduced the financial institutions' reliance on the central bank. When held by the public, Treasury bills could, of course, be converted into paper currency at regular and very short intervals. In other words, Treasury bills revealed their true nature as being financial assets that could be exchanged for monetary base at low cost (Spinelli 1989; BI R.A. 1926, pp. 66–7). The authorities reacted decisively and effectively to the situation, first by gradually reducing the stock of Treasury bills outstanding, and then, through legislation passed in November 1926, by consolidating all short- and a good portion of the medium-term debt.

The strong lira policy and industrial restructuring

Far from being an isolated and new event, the Pesaro speech was part of a broader and structural economic policy design. This policy went beyond the objectives of mere monetary stabilisation. To grasp this second and important aspect, it is useful to recall some of the underlying reasons behind the industrial crisis of the early 1920s to understand the link between the above design and the need to restructure the country's industrial system.

The underlying reasons behind the industrial crisis of the 1920s have been analysed by Filosa, Rey and Sitzia (1976), Ciocca (1976), Rey (1978), and above all Gualerni (1976, 1982). It is worth starting with a citation from Gualerni (1976, pp. 39–44):

the President of the [Association of Italian Industries], Olivetti, stated the situation in these terms: 'The years from 1923 to 1925 may be defined as the era of productiveness. This is an awkward word to indicate the tendency to maximise the country's productive capacity. This is the period when the government aimed at removing the obstacles and harnesses created by the war, and restored the possibility for individuals to strive for the very best and to achieve maximum performance.

. . . But in the process, traditional industries received preferential treatment, with the result that steel and heavy machinery manufacturers were continuously rescued and the textile industry created a productive capacity which remained mostly unutilised. In practice, the application of the most advanced techniques, the renovation and expansion of manufacturing facilities took place primarily in those sectors which had become obsolete in terms of potential growth and economic leadership. . . . At first, the results seemed to confirm the success of the policy adopted by the government. The expansion in industrial production experienced between 1922 and 1925 was among the largest recorded in the history of Italian industry.

But, as already noted, the problems of domestic inflation, balance-of-payments crisis and lira depreciation appeared at the same time as the production expansion took place. In part, the balance of payments' perennial problem stemmed from the already noted high elasticity of import demand with respect to domestic output. There was something new, however, due to latent protectionism and sudden changes in comparative advantages, which reduced the number of potential markets for traditional Italian exports (Paradisi 1976, pp. 274–5; Tattara and Toniolo 1976, p. 115; Gualerni 1982, p. 28).

In the intermingling of monetary and structural problems, it became increasingly evident that there was a need for deflation, for a review of the role given by economic policy of the early 1920s to the foreign component of aggregate demand, and for fundamental industrial restructuring. An economic programme was then implemented, which was articulated to meet the requirements of a new growth model. The following were the essential components of this programme. First, there was monetary deflation. With this, the government attempted not only to achieve stability of domestic prices, but also to attract foreign capital to a stable and possibly strengthening currency (Migone 1971, p. 46; Ciocca 1976, p. 33; Rey 1978, p. 286). Wage control and social harmony, which the fascist regime had no difficulty in guaranteeing, also served the dual purpose of stopping currency depreciation and attracting foreign capital. In addition, the strong lira policy had the objective of containing the lira costs of imports of the raw materials and machinery necessary to carry out the industrial restructuring programme. According to Grifone (1971), the whole scheme was a reflection of the increased influence of those industrial sectors which were to benefit from low importation costs. The Treasury Minister, Volpi (1928, p. 259), stated:

'there is no doubt that for Italy, largely a nation importing raw materials absolutely necessary for its very existence and work force, it is beneficial that its currency has a higher purchasing power abroad'. But the strong lira policy also had obvious costs: it penalised the exporting sectors while encouraging demand for imports. The first problem was resolved (partially) through dumping and a tax'. (Filosa, Rey and Sitzia 1976, p. 62; Rey 1978, p. 291).

Having said that, we must quickly add that it would be wrong to ascribe the strong lira policy exclusively to domestic factors. Gualerni (1976, p. 48) wrote: 'the real reasons behind the drive for a strong currency were structural and of an international nature'. Ciocca and Toniolo (1976, p. 17) confirmed that: 'The turning point stemmed from the inability of the industrial system to adapt to the new structure of world demand, as well as from the determination of the international financial community to pursue the normalisation process of financial markets commenced around 1924.' In essence, the 'quota 90' programme also turned out to be a prerequisite in attracting foreign capital. We have repeatedly emphasised the need for Italy to receive massive capital inflows to finance the restructuring of its manufacturing sector: clearly the demand was there. The works of Meyer (1970), Migone (1971) and, indirectly, Moreau (1986) point out that the external supply of funds was able to satisfy the domestic demand and, thus, dispel the myth that the drive for a stronger lira was purely a national matter. Furthermore, they prove the key role played by the international financial community, particularly the US, in stimulating and supporting the new Italian economic policy.

At the end of the war and for the first time in its history, the United States found itself not only at the centre of the international financial system, but also in a position to export capital. Consequently, it resolved to maintain monetary and social stability in Europe in order to invest its excess financial resources there (Migone 1971, pp. 43–4). It is not surprising, therefore, that the US financial community monitored the evolution of the Italian crisis with interest, and encouraged Italian authorities to proceed with the stabilisation programme. The governor of the New York Federal Reserve Bank went as far as to suggest to the Italian authorities that they should discuss the programme and reach an agreement with the French and Belgian governments in order to minimise both the amount of foreign currencies required and the chances that the programme might fail (Meyer 1970, pp. 45–6). The governor's suggestions, which included the important proposal of conferring only to BI the power of issuing paper currency, were quickly followed by financial assistance extended to Italy during the implementation of its stabilisation plan.

Decisions taken after the Pesaro speech

The Pesaro speech, delivered on 18 August 1926, represented the most critical, theatrical and explicit part of the process aimed at restoring the authorities' credibility about their commitment to maintain monetary stability. The ultimate goal of this process was to reverse expectations of a lira depreciation and, hence, to facilitate the success of the stabilisation programme.

The authorities had a number of factors on their side. There was no political opposition nor freedom of the press to counteract the effects of government propaganda. Furthermore, the speech was preceded by a number of important decisions which were also meant to carry a strong psychological message. It suffices to recall the balancing of the budget, the settlement of war debts, the concentration of money creation privileges at Banca d'Italia and the appointment of Volpi as Finance and Treasury Minister. Finally, the publicity and emphasis given to the speech were of the type employed on great occasions, as is evident from its well-known central core:

I want to tell you that we are fully determined to carry out our economic fight in defence of the lira, and from this square I confirm to the whole civilised world that I shall defend the lira to the end. I shall never inflict the moral shame and the economic disaster of a currency failure to the wonderful people of Italy, who for four years have been working as heroes and suffering as saints. The fascist regime will oppose with all its strength attempts made by hostile financial circles, and is determined to eliminate opposing forces whenever they are identified in our midst. The fascist regime is willing, from top to bottom, to endure all necessary sacrifices, and our lira, which represents the symbol of our nation, our wealth, our work, our efforts, our sacrifices, our tears and our blood, must and will be defended.

A decree law passed on 7 September 1926 strengthened the psychological effects of the speech and broadened the scope of the stabilisation programme already underway. In fact, the legislation provided for the complete withdrawal of government notes or bank notes issued on its behalf. Therefore, the law created the premise that, in future, all paper currency would be issued only by BI and exclusively for commercial purposes. There was an obligation on the part of BI to abide, starting on 15 September, with a limit of 7 billion lire with respect to the stock of paper currency. The eventual excess over that limit, not fully backed by metal reserves, was subject to an extraordinary levy equal to the discount rate increased by one third.

With a second decree law passed on 7 September, followed by another on 6 November, the authorities started a massive reorganisation process of the country's financial structure and a review of the regulators' control functions, which would result in the 1936 reform of the banking system. We shall deal with the reform later in this chapter. It suffices to mention here that regulatory control would apply to the establishment of new banks as well as to the entire spectrum of activities of all financial institutions. In particular, the banks were subject to new restrictions with regard to bank deposits. These could not be more than 20 times the banks' equity value; any excess had to be invested in government securities.

In November, the authorities made the historic decision of consolidating a good portion of the public debt. We have already underscored the fact that a considerable amount of Treasury bills held by banks and the public at large hindered the implementation of the monetary stabilisation programme. Between the spring and August of 1926, following a reduction in the stock of paper currency and more frequent lira depreciations on the foreign exchange markets (which precluded a possible debt consolidation), holders of Treasury bills became more and more inclined to cash them at maturity.[5] A decree passed on 6 November, which had the expressive title of 'Authorisation to Issue a New National Bond in Defence of the Currency', provided for the mandatory conversion into perpetual debentures not only of short-term Treasury bills, but also of securities with five and seven years' maturity, for a total value of 20.5 billion lire.[6] Later, Del Vecchio (1928, p. 285) would write: 'the consolidation was meant to be the most significant deflationary measure under the circumstances. Treasury bills had so far constituted the largest drain in the dam of monetary control, but now suddenly they became the most formidable and unsurmountable barrier.'[7] Thanks to the consolidation, the public debt structure improved significantly between June 1926 and June 1927. In fact, while at the beginning of this period the floating debt was 27.9 billion lire against a total domestic debt of 91.3 billion, at the end the floating debt had dropped to 6.2 billion against a total of 90.8 billion (Spinelli 1989).

On 6 November, the government passed another decree to wind up the 'Sezione Autonoma del Consorzio' and established the 'Istituto di Liquidazione' (Liquidation Institute). As stated in the decree, the government wanted to pursue 'the opportunity of restoring the health of the currency' by accelerating the liquidation of the former 'Sezione Autonoma's' assets, and the withdrawal of its notes from circulation.

A continuous revaluation of the lira?

At the Pesaro speech and during the following weeks when the lira gained value rapidly both domestically and internationally, the authorities were quite secretive about their intentions regarding the target level of the lira exchange rate. The *Economist* of 2 October asked the question: 'Will the government continue to pursue a deflationary policy until the lira regains the old parity, or will it stop before then?'

As the lira strengthened, supporters of the stabilisation programme became less cohesive. Some of them, obviously led by exporters, wished to avoid a situation in which the programme would continue indefinitely to pursue a policy of currency revaluation and, worse still, real currency appreciation. Consequently, they pressed the authorities to announce their ultimate target with respect to exchange-rate levels. In February 1927, there was a rumour that the goal was 125.66 lire for 1 pound sterling. An official press release dismissed this rumour as 'stupid', but did not indicate an alternative figure to be used as a general reference point for the market. The following 26 May, after a further lira appreciation (figure 5.2), Mussolini only mentioned, during a long-expected and important speech in Parliament, that: 'We shall remain at the level of 90 *vis-à-vis* the pound for the time necessary for all economic variables to adjust to this level.' It was only in August, after many weeks of interventions to stabilise the rate at 90 lire to the pound, often against the lira, that the government announced its intention not to proceed further with the revaluation process. However, these interventions remained sustained until November, when the rate rose above 90 lire. For the rest of the year, authorities became convinced that the rate at 90 lire was defensible and it was time to turn to other aspects of the programme.

With a decree law passed on 21 December 1927, the authorities specified the new gold content of the Italian lira and, hence, the new exchange rate with other convertible foreign currencies. In addition, the decree reinstated the principle of free convertibility of the paper lira into coins and gold. The gold content of 100 lire was reduced to 7.919 grams from the previous 29.03. Consequently, the lira lost 73 per cent of its value with respect to gold. The new metal parity implied a lira–pound rate of 92.46, a lira–dollar rate of 19 and a lira–French franc rate of 3.66.

The decree also included provisions relating to the composition and limits of BI's reserves. Against its demand liabilities, BI was required to keep reserves exclusively in gold and convertible currencies, but no longer in government securities. Reserves were not allowed to drop below 40 per cent of the total notes outstanding or below demand liabilities. The decree gave BI adequate time to arrange new lines of credit for a total of 125 million dollars with foreign commercial and central banks. Thanks to these transactions and the revaluation of existing metal reserves, BI brought its reserves almost to the level of outstanding notes by the end of December.

The decree passed on 21 December was entitled 'End of Inconvertibility . . .' and recited: 'Given the urgent necessity to resolve the Italian currency situation and to make the lira convertible into gold or equivalent currencies', a preamble that revealed the authorities' intention to reinstate the full gold convertibility of the lira. The decrees passed on 26 February 1928, which specified actual convertibility procedures, highlighted the formal differences between the traditional and the new gold standards, respectively:

> The Banca d'Italia must ensure, through gold trading or interventions in the foreign exchange market, that rate fluctuations of the Italian lira with respect to foreign currencies . . . remain within set limits.
> The upper and lower gold points, in relation to gold parity, are set as follows: 19.10 lire for exports and 18.90 lire for imports against the dollar.

The authorities were therefore obliged to guarantee, at a fixed price, the convertibility of the lira into other currencies, but not into gold, as was in fact required in a true gold standard. But the difference was purely formal. In substance, there was no significant difference in the long run between the traditional gold standard and the newly adopted Italian system (De Maria 1928, p. 176; Del Vecchio 1932, p. 451). In the very short run, by contrast, the legislation seemed to satisfy a dual need: minimising the cost of keeping adequate reserves, while at the same time attempting to prevent further upward pressure on the lira. In turn, because of the large real interest rate differential in favour of Italy, this was intended to restrain foreign capital inflow.

Domestic prices and the cost of stabilisation

A substantial appreciation of the lira implied a reduction in domestic-currency inflation, which in fact brought about a higher purchasing power of the currency in the foreign exchange market. To encourage lower domestic prices, the authorities adopted a number of measures. In assessing the overall situation, the *Economist* of 11 June 1927 reported:

> A very interesting feature of the current price adjustment process in Italy is the massive involvement of the government, other public bodies, unions and the press. Sometimes, the Americans undertake large promotional campaigns aimed at pursuing specific economic or political objectives. However, what is going on in Italy to lower both prices and costs is something really unique.

The data analysis, as well as the economic literature at that time, agreed on the magnitude and speed by which salaries and prices were adjusting. The particular nature of the political system and centralised negotiations made it easier for the authorities to influence the process of salary adjustments. According to Zamagni (1976, pp. 337–8):

> the first adjustment took place 'spontaneously' when fascist associations 'accepted' (but in effect proposed) a salary reduction of approximately 10 per cent in May, 1927. As this was not adequate, in October 1927 the fascist party caucus imposed a salary cut (including the previous one) of 20 per cent. . . . It is worth noting that this second adjustment was a 'preventive' measure which proved to be off-target . . . and

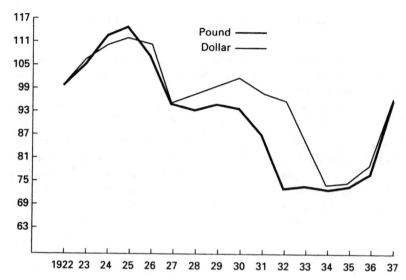

Figure 5.3 Real exchange rate *vis-à-vis* the dollar and the pound calculated with wholesale prices, 1922–1937
Source: Mitchell (1962); Commission on the Role of Gold in the Domestic and International Monetary System (1982); and Banca d'Italia R.A. (various years).

produced a reduction in real salaries. By contrast, a further decrease in November (of about 8 per cent) was almost technically perfect and maintained real salaries virtually unchanged.

Figure 5.3 illustrates the behaviour of the dollar and pound real exchange rates, calculated on the basis of domestic and international wholesale prices. The value of 100 for 1922 can be interpreted as an approximate equilibrium value of the lira exchange rate in the strict meaning of purchasing power parity.[8] Let us now examine the subsequent behaviour of the lira exchange rate. Between 1922 and 1925, the nominal depreciation of the lira appeared excessive relative to the inflation differential; hence a real depreciation of the lira. Then, from 1925 to 1927 the lira appreciated by 18 per cent relative to the pound, despite the fact that Italian wholesale prices dropped by a larger amount (14 per cent) than British wholesale prices (11 per cent). The critical factor underlying the real appreciation was a nominal appreciation of the lira of 21 per cent. In sum, there was general deflation in Italy and abroad and a very large appreciation of the lira in the exchange markets.

By 1927 the real exchange rates had come full circle, that is, they had returned to approximately the 1922 value (figure 5.3). This fact did not escape the attention of a number of economists of the time who underscored the purchasing power parity of the exchange rate. According to Del Vecchio

(1928, p. 286), domestic prices dropped quickly to the level corresponding 'to the increased international value of the lira'.[9] Tagliacarne (1928) stated that the lira ceased to be undervalued between 1926 and 1927. Alberti (1931, p. 277) considered that the domestic price adjustment was already adequate in December 1927. Finally, Baffi (1965, p. 175) summarises the various viewpoints: 'economists refer to 1928 or 1929 as the year during which exchange rates closely reflected price comparisons between different countries, and money stocks were also adequate to specific countries' requirements'.

The consequences of the real appreciation of the lira on output and employment were unfavourable. The industrial production index climbed by 29 points between 1921 and 1925, remained stable in 1926 and declined by four points in 1927. The number of unemployed was 122,000 at the end of 1925, rose to 181,000 by the end of 1926, and to 439,000 at the beginning of 1928. The monthly average number of corporate bankruptcies went from 602 in 1925 to 1,040 at the beginning of 1928.

It is difficult to make a comprehensive cost–benefit analysis of the stabilisation programme and, hence, to arrive at a precise conclusion. The unresolved issues are the costs associated with not changing course, the magnitude of the monetary adjustment, as well as developments in the great international economic depression that would follow. With regard to the domestic situation, two facts lead us to believe that, even in the absence of a monetary adjustment, the Italian economy would have soon entered a period of industrial stagnation.[10] In the middle of the 1920s the structure of the Italian economy was dated and could not deliver the historical growth rate; an adjustment had to be made sooner or later. The 1925–6 recession made it impossible to defer action in cooling off the economy. As to the size of the adjustment, one might recall that a similar but more contained measure (almost concurrent with the Italian one) put one million people out of work in Britain.

Notwithstanding the above remarks, the total cost of the stabilisation programme was substantial and was magnified by the real lira appreciation. The interesting question is: Why did the authorities insist on the '90' level with respect to the pound and why did they want to get there so rapidly? To answer satisfactorily, it behooves us to recall the prevailing doctrine, so brilliantly outlined by Cassel (1928). This excluded the possibility that any currency might experience a slow revaluation, because sooner or later speculators would succeed in anticipating the exchange-rate target and would force the market to trade at that price (Nurkse 1944, p. 32). The authorities would then feel obliged to accelerate the deflationary process in order to maintain domestic prices in line with the exchange rate. The degree of acceptance of this theory was reinforced by the failure of the slow revaluation plans carried out in Denmark and Norway during that period. Furthermore, the international policy climate was strongly in favour of revaluing currencies up to the pre-war rate levels, despite opposing views expressed at the 1922 Genoa International Conference and open criticism voiced by economists such as Cassel and Keynes.

The deterioration of the 1930s

Between 1927 and 1930, the lira's real exchange rates remained relatively stable and close to the 1922 values. By 1930, the lira was slightly undervalued against the dollar, but overvalued by about seven percentage points against the pound. Later, the situation drastically changed, and the strong lira policy became less and less sustainable and increasingly controversial.

The first serious problems emerged with respect to the British pound. On 21 September 1931, the pound abandoned the gold standard and the Italian lira began to revalue both in nominal and real terms. Between 1930 and 1932, the annual average lira–pound rate dropped from 90.83 to 68.48. During the same period, the real rate declined from 93.56 to 72.09. The US dollar depreciated against gold on 19 April 1933. From 1933 to 1934, the annual average lira–dollar rate fell first to 15.59 and then to 11.69 lire; the real rate decreased from 85.1 to 73.7. Overall, the lira appreciated against the dollar and the pound by about 25–30 percentage points in 1934. There is only one other precedent in the *History* set by the real exchange rate recording such a wide variation with respect to its purchasing power value, and this was in 1920.

In the 1930s, a number of important developments would provide the Italian authorities with valid reasons for relaxing the strong lira policy. First, with the Great Depression came a sudden collapse in world trade, which amplified the inherent difficulties of that policy. Second, the international movement of capital (including that flowing from the US to Europe, which was the most important from the Italian viewpoint) petered out. Under these circumstances, it became more difficult to pursue a strong lira policy and, in any event, it was clear that such policy could not attract the foreign capital required. Third, not only did the two key currencies of the international financial system depreciate (and a number of other currencies with them) but they also triggered off a chain of competitive devaluations. Fourth, protectionism became widespread; this, coupled with devaluations, penalised mainly countries such as Italy, whose exports were relatively elastic with respect to prices.[11]

In sum, the fundamentals were inconsistent with a strong real lira. In the short run, the strong lira could be defended only through a continuous haemorhage of international reserves. The measures adopted by the authorities and by business, aimed at mitigating the negative effects of the exchange policy, proved to be inadequate in relation to the gravity of the situation and, often, were even in conflict with each other. The action most widely utilised by business was dumping.[12] While Italy's terms of trade – the ratio of export to import prices – were stable in 1931 and 1932, they subsequently rose as the lira appreciated in real terms. At least until 1936, the increase was negligible relative to the lira appreciation.

The authorities revised their trading policy, but not adequately with regard to the extent of the lira appreciation and the on-going trade war (Mochi 1982, p. 131; Gualerni 1976, 1982; Guarnieri 1953, p. 256). Instead, they aimed at containing production costs by favouring a strategy of industrial and financial concentration.[13] Despite these measures, Italian exports became less competitive; their international market share dropped from 2.8 to 2.3 per cent between 1931 and 1934.

International reserves

Metal and foreign currency reserves of BI rose dramatically in 1926–7, thanks to international borrowings, the transfer of some reserves from the Treasury and the revaluation of the overall stock. Altogether, incremental reserves totalled about 10 billion lire in 1927. Subsequently and until 1933, gold reserves grew slowly, but foreign currencies dropped substantially. The reduction of total reserves accelerated from 1933 onward; by 1936, the total stock was 2.8 billion lire, that is, 22 per cent of the reserves existing in 1927.

The trends of the trade and the current account balances help us to identify the reasons behind the depletion of reserves. Between 1928 and 1930, both accounts improved rapidly and significantly, but still showed large deficits. A further improvement of the current account took place in 1931. Subsequently, the trend was reversed. These observations and those relative to the 1930–1 relaxation of foreign exchange regulations lead us to believe that the continuous drain of reserves from 1928 onward could be primarily attributed to the current account until 1930, to capital outflows in 1930–1 and to a combination of current-account deficits and capital outflows from 1931 onward (BI R.A. 1934, pp. 13–14).

Legislation on reserve requirements would have been sufficient in itself to ensure a certain degree of tightness in the money market. That would have made the multiplier of currency with respect to reserves equal to 2.5. On the other hand, the initial situation in 1928 was such that the ratio between reserves and bank demand liabilities was well over the 0.4 set by law. Because of this, the authorities believed they could afford to reduce the currency stock by an amount less than reserves for a number of years. In fact, between 1929 and 1934, reserves fell from 10.3 to 4.9 billion lire, while the amount of currency outstanding declined from 16.9 to 13.1 billion. In 1934, once the legal reserve ratio fell to 0.4, the strategy of overstabilising currency was no longer feasible.

Collapse of monetary control

New international reserve restrictions were concomitant with a clear deterioration in the overall macroeconomic situation. This deterioration was triggered, yet again, by fiscal policy. The year 1927 saw a return to budget deficits. From 1929, the deficit–income ratio took an upward trend; in 1935–6, concurrent with the colonial war in Ethiopia, the ratio reached 12 per cent.

It is interesting, at this point, to revisit table 5.2 and observe the quantitative relationship between fiscal policy and money growth. We have already dealt with the general progression of budget deficits during the 1930s. By focusing on the three sub-periods indicated in the table, we note the change from a budget which was balanced, on average, during the years 1921–6 to those showing increasing deficits in subsequent years. But we also note that the significant difference was more in the behaviour of the monetary base's Treasury component than in the size of the deficits. The authorities restrained this component in the first and third sub-periods, but relaxed their control in the second. Consequently, from 1927 to 1933, 84 per cent of budget deficits were monetised. However, in spite of this and the large foreign component of the monetary base, the money stock showed a very modest change in comparison with the next sub-period. The key variable was the remaining part of the domestic component of the monetary base, MBOT, which the authorities used as a buffer. In fact, MBOT virtually offset the combined growth of MBTR and BF.

The relationship among the three monetary base components changed drastically in the 1934–7 period. As already noted, the foreign component contributed negatively to the growth of the monetary base, while the Treasury component neutralised this effect. The contribution of MBOT was largely positive and of such a magnitude as to increase the total monetary base at an annual average rate of 7 per cent. As a result, despite a lower multiplier caused by an increase in k (which characterised a deterioration of the domestic macroeconomic situation), the monetary base stabilised at average values 2.5 times larger than those recorded in the previous sub-period. All of this took place while the velocity of money again began to rise rapidly. The income deflator change was –12.0 per cent in 1931, –6.5 per cent in 1933, but +10.2 per cent in 1937.

The behaviour of MBOT was obviously tied to the official discount rate policy. Between the spring of 1932 and the autumn of 1934, the rate was lowered from 7 to 3 per cent to facilitate also the conversion of the 'consolidated debt 5 per cent' into redeemable securities at 3.5 per cent. Subsequently, the rate was raised, but never above 5 per cent. From 1932 onward, the domestic real interest rate declined on a continuous basis, and so did its differential relative to the foreign rate, which became zero by 1934.

The authorities reacted in two different ways to the depletion of foreign reserves. First, between May 1934 and December 1935, they restricted commercial and financial dealings with the rest of the world (Abrate 1978, pp. 40–1; BI R.A. 1934, pp. 34–5 and 1935, pp. 37–9). For the first time, therefore, the government introduced a protectionist policy in international trade and foreign exchange activities.[14] The second reaction was to remove the 40 per cent reserve requirement against paper currency. This historic decision was embodied in a decree passed on 21 July 1935, and enabled the authorities to monetise a larger portion of the 1935 and 1936 budget deficits.

As a result, monetary policy became fully dependent on purely domestic political considerations. BI (R.A. 1935, p. 63) openly adapted itself to the political reality, as transpires from the following excerpt:

Credit and monetary policies are no longer governed by a numerical ratio related to the value of metal reserves held, a ratio that often imposes hardship on the country's economy. In a fascist political regime, credit is more closely tied to the nation's resources and economic needs, while the currency's purchasing power is also protected by an adequate control over price levels.

Devaluation

Beginning in 1934, the probability of a lira devaluation rose. To be sure, the authorities were strongly opposed to this solution, even at the cost of introducing protectionist measures. But the Ethiopian war placed the government in a difficult situation. On the one hand, the increase in monetary base and domestic prices strengthened the possibility of a massive lira devaluation. On the other, the need to purchase large quantities of military equipment abroad and the existing international sanctions were good arguments for keeping the exchange-rate parity. In the short run, the latter considerations led the authorities to postpone the devaluation.

This took place in October 1936, after raw materials had been replenished. Various countries, such as Belgium, France, Switzerland and Holland had devalued their currencies with respect to gold from 10 to 40 per cent. The sanctions had been removed and international trade again started to grow.

The decree passed on 5 October 1936 reduced the metal content of 100

Italian lire from 7.919 to 4.677 grams of fine gold. This implied a devaluation of 40.9 per cent, which was exactly the same as the 1934 dollar depreciation, thus restoring the gold parity of lira–dollar to 19 lire and setting the lira–pound parity at 93 lire. Following the devaluation, the real value of the lira *vis-à-vis* both the dollar and the pound quickly returned to the 1922 value. Thus, the strong lira policy came to an end.

Unlike what happened in 1927, the decision to devalue the lira was not taken as an integral part of a monetary stabilisation programme. For example, there was no significant improvement in fiscal policy. Furthermore, contrary to the provisions of the previous devaluation decree, the legislation passed in October 1936 did not impose either a reserve ratio or a maximum limit on notes creation by BI.

Less stringent monetary control became even more evident in a decision taken on 31 December 1936 aimed at amending provisions regarding BI's advances to the Treasury. A previous decree passed in June 1928 set the maximum limit for ordinary advances at 450 million lire and prohibited so-called extraordinary advances. The new decree brought the limit of ordinary advances from 450 million to 1 billion lire and provided that Treasury could obtain further funds against collateral of an equivalent amount of Treasury bills. Yet again, we see monetary policy being subjected to political considerations (and consequently to fiscal policy). In summary, contrary to what happened in 1914, the country approached the Second World War with a shattered system of monetary control.

The 1936 banking legislation

Between 1926 and 1936, the country's financial structure was drastically changed. The changes primarily involved two closely related areas. Longer-term industrial financing was separated from traditional banking activities; that is to say, merchant banking as such came to an end. Furthermore, the role of the central bank was strengthened within the overall financial system, with banking activities being more thoroughly regulated. For our purposes, the second institutional changes are more relevant than the first and thus we will emphasise them in the following discussion.

Historic legacy has a great deal to do with the decision to separate medium- and long- from short-term financing. We have seen repeatedly that the effects of sectoral crises, particularly in industry, tend to spill over on to the country's financial system. The underlying reason for this transmission process lies in the disproportionate share of loans allocated to these sectors by the country's large banking institutions. In all such cases, even when the financial system succeeded in correcting the shock and retaining stability, there was always a persistent deterioration of paper currency in circulation, in both quantitative and qualitative terms. At the root of the problem was not only an inadequate legislation, but an undeveloped capital market that propelled Italian banks to the fore stage of long-term financing. At the end of the 1920s and at the beginning of the 1930s, the authorities intervened on three occasions to rescue industrial enterprises as well as their respective bankers. The first of these rescue interventions took place when, in the early 1920s, the Italian manufacturing sector had to grapple with a transition to a 'peace' economy and with structural changes to international trade. The second intervention was connected with the implementation of deflationary measures to reach 'quota 90'. These measures caused a collapse in capital goods prices as well as publicly quoted shares and, consequently, the failure of a large number of companies. The final rescue operation was concurrent with the Great Depression of the early 1930s.

We have already dealt with the 'Sezione Autonoma del Consorzio' and its large exposure to BI at the beginning of the 1920s. Ten years later, the 'Istituto di Liquidazione' (a liquidation entity which replaced the 'Sezione') was created to prevent rescue operations. In fact, these activities expanded considerably. At the beginning of 1933, the total value of BI's rescue interventions to ailing companies and banks was around 7.5 billion lire, almost 50 per cent of outstanding notes. With the establishment of Istituto Mobiliare Italiano (IMI) and Istituto Ricostruzione Industriale (IRI) industrial-sector financing was separated from commercial banking activities. This marks the end of universal banking in Italy (until the EC Second Banking Directive of 1989 and the Italian Reforms of the 1990s which are beyond the scope of the *History*). Consequently, central banking restricted its area of operations to commercial banking and monetary policy became potentially more effective.

We recall that the monetary stabilisation programme of the mid 1920s focused on two aspects: protection of bank depositors[15] and a stricter (and politicised) control over the central bank and the banks. The 1936 Banking Law (decrees n. 375 of 12 March 1936 and n. 1400 of 17 July 1937) brought about an even more structural reform of the whole banking system, including BI.

The main features of the legislation were as follows. First, deposit-taking and credit activities were officially recognised as public services, even though they were provided by the private sector. Second, longer-term financing was sharply separated from short-term financing. The Italian banking system was divided between institutions that were lending for eighteen months and longer ('credito mobiliare') and commercial banks that were limited to lending for eighteen months and shorter ('credito ordinario'). Third, the supervisory role over banking activities was delegated to the 'Ispettorato per la Difesa del Risparmio e per l'Esercizio del Credito'

(Office of the Inspector for the Protection of Savings and the Business of Banking) which had the critical task of ensuring that the banking system would fulfill the economic objectives set by political authorities. Finally, BI was transformed into a public interest institution, functioning as the bank of banks.

The purpose of the new legislation was twofold. It showed, as a matter of principle, the authorities' commitment to protect small depositors and to regulate banking activities. But it also brought all financial institutions, regardless of their legal status, under the supervision of one single entity, the 'Ispettorato'. The separation of industrial banking and commercial banking was made to formalise the functions of IMI and IRI. The role of 'Ispettorato' was to ensure consistency and discipline in the activities of financial institutions across the system, as well as to enable political authorities to exercise more direct and effective control over credit strategies. The supervisory functions, which in the past were performed by a number of ministries and BI, were consolidated within the newly formed 'Ispettorato', headed by the Governor of BI.

The type of banking restrictions envisaged by the 1936 Banking Law became evident when the Ministerial Committee, through the 'Ispettorato', was empowered to intervene on a number of issues, such as interest rates applied by banks, charges relating to various banking services, the allocation of credit facilities to different sectors of the economy, the geographical distribution of banking services, the collection of bad debts, and so on. The intent of the law, therefore, was not only to safeguard the stability of the banking system, but also to subjugate it to political will, with its attendant and arbitrary influence on prices and quantities of banking services. It makes sense in interpreting the new legislation as a sort of nationalisation of the banking industry.

Finally, the 1936 law strengthened the role of BI, now a public-interest institution, at the top of the financial system. While the relationship of BI *vis-à-vis* the Treasury was rather open ended, the legislation restricted BI's activities with the public and the banks. To the former BI could only make advances against the collateral of securities; to the latter credit was limited to rediscount facilities. In essence, the label of public-interest institution meant that government had privileged access to BI's credit. The dependence of BI on government had its legislative roots in the 1936 law.

Conclusions

In the first sections of this chapter we identified the reasons behind the reoccurrence of a strong lira depreciation process, both domestically and internationally, which characterised the early 1920s. We then analysed the various aspects of the stabilisation programme launched in the spring of 1925, but officially announced by Mussolini in his Pesaro speech in August 1926. We noted that, through this programme in general and the strong lira policy in particular, the authorities pursued objectives which extended beyond the stabilisation and included a massive restructuring of the country's industrial system.

The strong lira policy, known also as 'quota 90', was undoubtedly supported by the international economic doctrine of the time, which favoured revaluations of currencies to their pre-war levels. In the long run, however, it became difficult to sustain such a policy. Consequently, in the 1930s, the Italian authorities found it necessary to implement an income policy, introduce new tariffs, and progressively embark on the road of trade and financial protectionism. The final and decisive blow came from a new and traumatic fiscal shock. In 1934 the government abandoned monetary control, which in fact was the main tool that sustained the strong lira policy; the lira devalued in 1936.

A second theme of the chapter was an overview of the major structural changes relating to the financial sector, and the relationship between the banks and BI, as well as between the latter and the country's political system. We have emphasised the important legislation of 1926 and, even more, that of 1936 which fundamentally changed banking and central banking up to the present time. Among other things, the new law formalised the ultimate power of government over banking matters. The central bank and commercial banks assumed the status of public institutions, and bank officials received the status of public servants. The 1936 Banking Law legitimised the supremacy of politics over banking. Perhaps, it is not surprising that the fascist regime would pass such a legislation. What is surprising is that such a law lasted through almost 50 years of republican life.

6   The Second World War and the 1947 stabilisation

During the past few months and days, the recurrent question has been . . . what does the BI's governor do, when he repeats the old 1920 cry 'let us break the printing press' and then continues to sign notes endlessly . . .? (BI R.A. 1946, p. 254).

Introduction

This chapter deals with the 1938–49 years, a period full of extremely important events. On the political–military front, there was the outbreak of the Second World War, the shifting of military operations from the African colonies to domestic soil, the fall of the Mussolini government and the resumption of conflict on the side of western powers. Then there was the German occupation, the rebirth of the Fascist regime in the north, the end of the war and the advent of the Republic. On the economic front, mostly as a result of political events, we register first a collapse in industrial output and then a surge in the velocity of money. These two occurrences caused the gap between aggregate demand and aggregate supply to grow wider, in turn generating an inflationary process, which turned out to be the most intense of the entire *History*. The country suddenly returned to price stability in the last quarter of 1947, concurrent with the implementation of a stabilisation programme that has been closely associated with Einaudi and Menichella. This programme has been the subject of controversy in terms of the underlying objectives, impact on monetary and credit aggregates and net benefits for the country.

This chapter begins with an overview of the war period. It then deals with the aggregate supply of goods and services. It continues with an analysis of fiscal policy and its impact on monetary policy. After describing the relationship between aggregate supply and aggregate demand, we analyse the various episodes of the lira depreciation process, both domestically and internationally. This analysis will also bring to light the autonomous and critical role of a very pronounced deviation from trend of money velocity in the depreciation process.

The concluding and more problematic part of the chapter deals with the 1947 stabilisation; in particular, we discuss its timing, its impact on money and credit aggregates, the role played by expectations, and its cost in terms of foregone output.

The Second World War from a longer-term perspective

There is no doubt about the great peculiarity of the war period with regard to the behaviour of aggregate supply. In fact, the industrial production index fell from 110 to 29 between 1940 and 1945 (ISTAT 1957, table 16). It was only in the early 1950s that output returned to levels which would have been reasonable to expect by extrapolating the 1930s data. In contrast with the first conflict, the Second World War did not begin when the economy was stagnating. Partly as a consequence of the higher initial level of output, the subsequent drop was more pronounced in the Second than in the First World War.

Another peculiarity of this period was the government budget, whose deficit began to deteriorate considerably before the outbreak of hostilities. This, naturally, contributed to making the situation even worse; the deficit climbed rapidly to over 34 per cent of national income. Similarly to what happened in 1918–19, the end of the war did not facilitate a return to full control of government finances; one would have to wait until 1950–1 for that to happen.

Price inflation rose in 1940, recorded a maximum value of 90 per cent in 1944, then fell to 39 per cent in 1946 to rebound to 60 per cent in 1947. In the two subsequent years, inflation sharply declined by about 50 percentage points; this time the decline was permanent in the sense that it lasted through the fifties and the sixties (figure 1.2).

The Italian inflation differential remained systematically positive; it grew from 1939 until it reached 80 percentage points in 1944 and then petered out by 1948–9. The nominal lira exchange rate remained stable until 1943, thanks to a stringent exchange-market control policy. In subsequent years, the lira depreciated, on average, more than the inflation differential. The rate finally stabilised in 1949.

It is useful to compare the inflation performances in the world wars. To begin with, the Second World War started with a high level of inflation relative to the First World War. Inflation was much more contained during the First World War (35 per cent being the top rate) than during the Second World War. In both cases, there was a significant rebound of the inflationary process after the end of hostilities; the Second World War rebound lasted longer than the First World War rebound. The lira depreciated more, on average, during the Second World War than the First World War; in both instances, the depreciation accelerated toward the end of the hostilities. Finally, the Second World War was followed by a period of great exchange-rate stability in the 1950s and most of the 1960s, whereas great exchange-rate instability followed the First World War.

The monetary base grew by about 500 per cent between the end of the 1930s and the end of the 1940s; by contrast, it had grown by about 300 per cent between 1914 and 1920. Money growth, which in 1937 was less than 0.3 per cent, reached almost 50 per cent in 1943. It fell to 24 per cent in 1949, after fluctuating regularly around 40 per cent for five years. As we shall see in chapter 7, monetary expansion settled at around 10 per cent within a few years. As a comparison, the highest money growth during the First World War was about 35 per cent, and that took place after the conclusion of military operations.

Money velocity declined until 1943. Then, it increased suddenly and sharply until 1947 when it returned to the 1875 value, and fell again in 1948–9. The size and speed of the velocity was a most unusual occurrence in the *History* (table 1.3).

So far, from the perspective of the 131-year history, the Second World War shows a faster growth of nominal variables, a lower growth of output, a four-year reversal in the secular downward trend of money velocity, and an altogether more uncertain economic environment (cf. standard deviations of table 1.3).

Both government expenditures and the budget deficit, as a proportion of national income, are more contained, on average, during the Second World War than the First World War (table 1.4). The average monetisation ratio of 57 per cent is in line with the historical average, but is higher than the First World War monetisation ratio. The monetary base grew at an average annual rate of 33 per cent, that is, 3.5 times faster than in the whole period (figure 2.2). In contrast, the multiplier declined by an average annual rate of 2.6 per cent (figure 2.1). It is obvious, then, that the monetary base was the dominant force underlying the average annual money growth of 30.4 per cent. The domestic monetary base contributed 32 of the 30 percentage points of money growth, 27 of which related to the monetary base created by the Treasury (table 2.1). Finally, with regard to the multiplier, the contracting effects came from all of the three ratios – k, rr and re. The reserve requirement coefficient, which came into play only toward the end of the sub-period, had the largest impact on the multiplier.

Recovery, or return to normalcy, began between 1946 and 1947 with regard to output, between 1946 and 1948 for prices, in 1948 for money velocity and in 1949 for money. As was true for the First World War, output adjustment appears to have led monetary policy adjustment. More on this later.

Table 6.1 *The Barberi indices of agricultural and industrial output (1938=100)*

Year	Agriculture	Industry	Average
1939	103	107	105
1940	97	109	103
1941	95	96	95
1942	86	75	81
1943	77	65	71
1944	78	36	57
1945	58	23	40
1946	77	38	58

Source: Bank for International Settlements (1947, p. 12).

The collapse of industrial output

Industrial output fell so drastically during the conflict as to qualify as a very large supply shock (Southard 1946; Foa 1949; V. Lutz 1950; Baffi 1950). Given the centrality of this shock, this chapter will reverse the usual order with which aggregate demand and aggregate supply factors are analysed.

We begin with an estimate of the size of the output collapse.[1] We searched for studies that utilise alternative data sets from ours. One such study is Barberi, then general manager of the National Institute of Statistics, who provided the estimates shown in table 6.1 with regard to agricultural and industrial output from 1939 to 1946. Between 1940 and 1945, the two indexes fell from 97 to 58 and from 109 to 23, respectively. Their simple average, which is relevant because the weights of the two sectors are quite similar, dropped from 103 to 40. A second study is Coppola d'Anna (1946a) who gave an estimate of the ratio between real net national product in 1945 and 1938. According to his calculations, shown in table 6.2, that ratio was around 50 per cent. In fact, we believe the ratio should be less than one half if one considers that the expansion phase of the business cycle preceding the war lasted until the end of 1940. Both of these sources concur with our view that the war brought about a precipitous drop in industrial output. In the Marshallian graphical representation of aggregate demand and aggregate supply, we can portray the war as a massive shift of the aggregate supply curve in the north-westerly direction.

Table 6.2 *Coppola d'Anna estimates of net national product (billions of 1938 lire)*

Sector	1938	1945	(1945/1938)×100
Agriculture	43,1	25,7	59,6
Industry	40,0	10,0	25,0
Commerce	10,4	4,5	43,3
Housing	6,7	5,7	85,0
Professionals	18,2	13,5	25,4
Total	118,4	59,4	50,7
Adjustments	−1,8	−0,8	−
Net total	116,6	58,6	50,3

Source: Coppola d'Anna (1946a, pp. 4–8).

Fiscal shock and government deficit financing

Turning to an analysis of aggregate demand, we consider the role of fiscal policy. Government expenditures increased from 29 per cent of national income in 1938 to over 50 per cent in 1941–2; they subsequently fell and settled around 20–1 per cent of income between 1946 and 1949. Therefore, while expenditures climbed steeply during the war, revenues could not keep up with prices. In fact, revenue as a proportion of national income dropped from 20.5 in 1939 to 8.0 in 1944, generating a substantial budget deficit.

The slow growth of tax revenues was due to a number of factors. Some of them were technical in nature and analogous to those already seen in chapter 4; others were not. On this point the Bank for International Settlements (1947, pp. 38 ff.) wrote:

Indirect taxation in Italy has always been more important than the direct one, as in other countries with low living standards. . . . In 1938–9 trade taxes, custom duties and income derived from the tobacco monopoly made up 60.7 per cent of total revenue. . . . Furthermore, inflation and rent control shifted income from capital to labour, and this reduced the benefit of progressive taxation. For these reasons, it even became difficult to keep revenue in line with the nominal growth of domestic income.

In fact, the proportion of direct to total tax revenues fell from 22.7 to 14 per cent between 1938–9 and 1945–6. More importantly, Italy had to cope with the administrative disruption following the collapse of the Fascist regime in 1943 (Foa 1949, p. 75).

The direct capital circuit

Let us examine the alternative measures taken by the government once it realised that it was impossible to fully finance the war through taxation. The government could no longer resort to foreign assistance, which by contrast financed a good portion of the First World War expenses (Thaon di Revel 1942, p. 215). At least initially it also opposed the idea of financing the war through inflation. Instead,the authorities endeavoured primarily to stimulate domestic savings and to channel them to the Treasury through the so-called capital circuit. The Minister of Finance, Paolo Thaon di Revel (1942, pp. 226–7) explained the concept of capital circuit as follows:

in wartime, expenditures are usually in excess of what can be collected through taxes, and it is therefore necessary to resort to borrowing. But financial requirements are also more than the normal saving capacity. As a result, there is a need to liquidate assets or print new currency to provide the initial stimulus to the capital circuit process in order to finance the war. It will then be necessary, by way of taxes or new borrowings, to recover the whole amount spent in excess of the normal budget revenue. To retrieve notes previously issued and to meet new expenses, the government must prevent any type of investments other than those in government securities and savings accounts that finance the state.

It is therefore necessary to . . . (a) restrict the construction of industrial plants to those sectors related to the war and ban real estate investments; (b) discourage speculative purchases/sales of land and buildings; (c) contain prices, salaries, service costs, rents . . . (d) reduce civilian consumption by the amount additionally required for military use. If all these restrictions would be fully implemented, the capital circuit should work perfectly, and the Treasury would regain . . . not only the excess of expenditures over budget revenues, but also the amount of savings corresponding to the proceeds from the liquidation of some government assets.

The placement of government securities became an essential financial tool. It was sustained until the end of 1942 (BI R.A. 1945, pp. 105–7) in spite of large negative real yields. The initial effectiveness of the capital circuit policy was also illustrated by the fact that, while government deficits increased from 11 to 34 per cent of income between 1939 and 1942, the portion covered through the new monetary base fell from 55 to 34 per cent.

By the end of 1942 the capital circuit no longer provided the government with an adequate flow of savings. In its 1942 Annual Report (pp. 125–6), BI remarked that 'widespread rumours . . . of extraordinary taxation . . . have encouraged . . . accumulation of currency'. A substantial increase in the supply of new currency was already in evidence during the last two months of the same year. Through these developments, BI realised that a clear shift was taking place in the war financing policy: in the 1942 Annual Report the

Bank acknowledged the 'hard reality' of having to continuously raise the stock of currency.

In 1943, there was further strong evidence that the capital circuit was not working. With military defeat becoming increasingly clear, the collapse of the Fascist regime created a psychological and administrative vacuum, thus reviving the fires of the inflationary process. These events constituted a strong obstacle in collecting taxes and in placing government securities. As a result, the monetisation ratio jumped to 90 per cent (it would reach 107 per cent in 1944). Seigniorage exploded: in only two years it rose by more than 40 percentage points of national income (figure 2.7). The monetary regime had definitely changed.

The indirect capital circuit

The change in monetary regime was officially christened as the 'indirect capital circuit', that is a circuit in which banks and the central bank would play a critical role (Mancini 1947; De Vita 1949). In practice, the government raised interest rates on deposits at BI, created new forms of required bank deposits with BI, and prohibited inter-bank accounts. Furthermore, it exerted pressure on banks to invest customer deposits exceeding 20 times their net worth in government securities or in deposits with BI. In January 1943, the authorities introduced the requirement that banks holding customer deposits over 100 million lire should transfer, every month, 75 per cent of additional funds collected in the previous month to BI. In other words, the indirect circuit policy acted primarily as a form of mandatory, but transitional, reserve, the purpose of which was in fact to temporarily reduce the money multiplier.

The authorities increased even further rates on deposits with BI branches in the spring of 1944, as it became particularly difficult to collect taxes and to place government securities and post office certificates in the south. Furthermore, the Treasury decided to absorb interest costs paid by BI on required deposits held by banks. As a result of these decisions, bank deposits with BI grew from 4.6 billion in December 1942 to 131.8 billion in December 1945 (BI R.A. 1943; Mancini 1947).

There is no doubt that the indirect circuit policy was successful in stemming the monetary avalanche which engulfed the country from 1943 onward. At the same time, however, this policy also created the preconditions for a subsequent monetary-base explosion, which would ignite when the required bank deposits with BI were eventually transformed into liquid reserves at the central bank.

The k ratio and the inflationary potential

Let us now analyse the relationship between the growth of the monetary base and that of money stock. The ratio k, which shows a sharply declining historical trend, was rising at the outbreak of the war (figure 2.4). In 1943, the most unsettling and traumatic year of the war, the coefficient had a sharp upturn, then quickly fell.

Temporary (albeit vigorous) and permanent factors influenced the behaviour of k. Among the former, we record the high degree of uncertainty regarding the political and military outcome. In fact, monthly data show that the coefficient rose sharply in September 1938, just before the Munich agreement; in August and September 1939, concurrent with the outbreak of hostilities; in June 1940, when Italy joined the conflict; in September 1942, when the Allies began bombing Italian cities; in July 1943, when Allies invaded Sicily and the Mussolini government fell; and, finally, in September–October 1943, when the country was basically divided into two regions. On the latter occasion, for the first time, it was necessary to impose a moratorium on bank deposits in the north.

One of the more lasting phenomena affecting k involved the substitution of currency for cheques 'for payments relating to clandestine transactions of raw material, finished products and foodstuff' (Azzolini 1943, p. 59). This was the result of the stringent price control policy and consumer goods rationing. Furthermore, the war brought about massive population movements, which necessitated the use of cash more than of bank deposits. In general, the countryside clearly became more important for trade and the distribution of wealth in general. People there had always displayed a higher propensity to hoard cash.[2] A final fact that was responsible for the increase in k was the fall in the real yield on bank deposits.[3]

The money multiplier declined continuously and consistently up to and including 1943; that is, as long as the ratio k was rising. But the multiplier reduction did not counteract the expansive effects of an everincreasing monetary-base creation on the stock of money. As a result, money accelerated until 1943. In the subsequent three years, the monetary base slowed down while the multiplier rose quite significantly, owing to a downward adjustment of k. In the end, there was only a slight deceleration of the money stock.[4] The situation reversed itself in 1947–8, when monetary-base creation began again to accelerate and the multiplier resumed a downward trend due to the introduction of reserve requirements. Money growth did not differ from that of the previous two years. As already noted, the real turning point in money growth took place only in 1949, when a slight upturn of the multiplier occurred concurrently with a sharp slowdown of the monetary base.

Inflation and the lira exchange rate in 1943

It does not come as a surprise that the lira underwent a very strong domestic and international depreciation process in these years, following a series of very intense shocks which affected both aggregate supply and aggregate demand. As to domestic prices, we have already commented on the trend of the price deflator. Wholesale prices showed even wider fluctuations, with a maximum growth of 130 per cent in 1944 (De Mattia 1977, table 7). The inflation explosion of 1943 constituted a clear turning point. But 1943 also marked a change for the lira exchange rate. In fact, the official exchange rate with the dollar, which remained stable at 19 lire until 1940 and was not even quoted up to 1943, was fixed at 100 in the summer of the latter year (Spinelli and Fratianni 1991, table 8.5).

Why the changes in 1943? At the outbreak of the war, the authorities imposed price and wage freezes. These proved to be quite effective in curbing inflation, as long as the government administrative structure was working. Coppola d'Anna (1946b, p. 25) wrote:

Wholesale prices and the cost of living showed fairly modest . . . increases until the end of 1942 and part of 1943. This growth was . . . much lower than that shown by the money stock during the same time. In fact, at the end of 1942, the legal currency stock increased by more than three and a half times and bank deposits by almost twice, while wholesale prices rose by 50.5 per cent with respect to 1938, and the cost of living by 63.7 per cent. The situation began to be critical during the second semester of 1943.

In those months, Italy gradually fell under the US administration, which removed controls and permitted prices to reach their market levels. But the Germans and the Italian Social Republic continued to curb prices in the areas they controlled. The Italian economic system quickly became characterised by two price levels: higher to the south and lower to the north of the frontline, which obviously made any arbitrage transactions much more costly (Baffi 1965, pp. 240–1; Bank for International Settlements 1947, p. 30). Figure 6.1 illustrates the price differential between north-of-the-frontline Milan and south-of-the-frontline Rome that lasted until the summer of 1945, thus corroborating the view that the gradual removal of controls made explicit an inflation that had been repressed earlier.

As for the lira's international purchasing power, Italy joined the war with an official parity of 19 lire against the dollar and a market price of 19.8. At that time, the lira was already overvalued by about 30 percentage points, according to Barberi's (1947) calculations. Subsequently, the government discontinued quoting the lira against all currencies, with the exception of the Deutsche Mark. Barberi indicated that, when the Allies landed in Sicily,

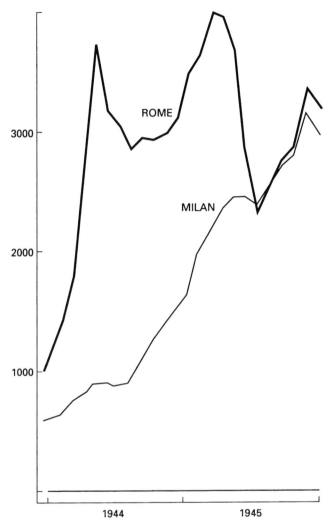

Figure 6.1 Index of cost of living, 1944–1945
Source: Banca d'Italia R.A. (1945, p. 123).

the market price of the dollar was around 45–50 lire. The Allies imposed a rate of 100 lire; this decision was later viewed harshly by some commentators.[5] Due to the high inflation differential against Italy, the lira undervaluation dwindled and disappeared altogether within a short period of time. In fact, the currency returned to being overvalued when the Allies entered Rome.

In summary, the turning point in the domestic and international depreciation of the lira was linked to the political and military events of the summer
of 1943.

1944 and the end of the war: the stabilisation debate

The stabilisation debate developed during the last phase of the war and
touched upon several of the country's economic problems: public finances,
the inflationary process, wide fluctuations in the velocity of money and
purely technical problems concerning note issuance. Furthermore, there
was concern that BI was unable to guarantee the required flow of new
notes, whereas the German military authorities could issue Italian lire
and flood the country with paper money, if the conflict continued even
after the complete withdrawal by Germany from Italy (BI R.A. 1945,
pp. 77–8).

A variety of proposals circulated to stabilise the economy. The ones that
attracted most attention were: (i) make an inventory of all outstanding
notes and stamp them; (ii) substitute new notes for old notes; (iii) temporarily freeze all bank deposits; (iv) impose a wealth tax, including cash holdings; and (v) impose a tax on cash holdings, to be collected when old notes
would be replaced with new notes. These proposals and their underlying
analyses were often manipulated for political purposes. Treasury, whose
Ministers were generally conservative, strongly opposed them, but other
Ministers, particularly from the left, enthusiastically supported them. The
few serious and technical discussions revolved around the potential effect
which the implementation of some of the proposals would have on money
velocity. From this viewpoint, Treasury Ministers often seemed obsessed by
the fear that the public might refuse to use cash.

It was not until the spring of 1947 that an extraordinary tax was introduced. The tax consisted of a flat 4 per cent rate, plus a surtax varying from
6 to 41 per cent applied to one's taxable income. Money holdings were taxed
only indirectly, that is, by adding a fixed 12 per cent to non-liquid wealth
(Foa 1949, p. 98; Baffi 1965, p. 183). This measure was totally inadequate in
terms of bringing the budget under control and in abating inflation. The
tax, however, succeeded in insulating the money market from the shock of a
freeze and/or note replacement. The market's fear that the more radical proposals, examined above, would come to light petered out.

Inflation slowdown and resurgence – fiscal and monetary policies

In 1944 money growth remained more or less at the 1943 level; there was a
slowdown in the monetary-base growth, but the multiplier accelerated.

Industrial output continued to decline, and the inflation rate reached maximum values for the period under consideration. In 1945 the monetary situation improved, thanks to the placement of the so-called five year 'liberation' loan. In fact, the monetisation ratio contracted by 60 percentage points, with predictable consequences for the creation of the total monetary base. Industrial output declined further. The inflation rate dropped abruptly, perhaps more than what would have been reasonable to expect, considering the evolution of both output and economic policy.

What were the reasons underlying this decline in inflation? According to Foa (1949, p. 67), the inflation slowdown had to do with the recovery of the aggregate supply (which, in turn, was reacting to a partial improvement in trade volume, the UNRRA's assistance programme and a reduction in the stock of speculative merchandise) as well as with a decline in inflation expectations. Baffi (1965, p. 247) believed expectations were the dominant factor.

Then, inflation rebounded between the spring of 1946 and the spring of 1947. This rebound is reminiscent of a similar phenomenon, analysed in chapter 4, that took place between the end of 1918 and the beginning of 1919. A number of factors were responsible for the 1946–7 inflationary resurgence. First of all, the monetary base grew by 58 per cent in 1946, against 26 per cent in 1945, propelled by a 73 per cent monetisation ratio. The growth in the base, in turn, was fully reflected in higher money growth, given the approximate stability of the money multiplier. Beyond money, the government issued a 30-year 'reconstruction' bond, yielding at first 3.5 per cent and later 5 per cent, with interest exempted from future extraordinary taxation.[6] The issue brought 112 billion lire to the Treasury, approximately one fifth of the 1946–7 fiscal year budget deficit. The poor performance of the underwriting reflected, as well as strengthened, a pessimistic outlook about market conditions (Foa 1949, p. 97). Market participants, furthermore, could not shake the fear of a future extraordinary tax rate and/or a currency replacement (De Vita 1949, p. 40; Gangemi 1961, p. 409; Castronuovo 1975, p. 378). Finally, several sectors of the economy were experiencing shortages and delays, with inevitable repercussions on prices. In the 1949 Annual Report, Governor Menichella summarised the inflationary environment of 1946–7 as follows:

credit expansion and persisting budget deficits had their impact on prices, even though the economy started from a very low level of industrial resources, and some of the most important shortages, such as coal, steel and foodstuff were gradually met with American assistance. The country was almost overrun by an inflationary process, to the surprise of those who contended that the increase in money demand should not push prices upward in an environment where industrial resources remained unutilised. (pp. 230–1)

Partial liberalisations and the two-tier foreign exchange market

In the short run, the government's micro-structural interventions in the economy impacted negatively on the country's overall monetary stability. These interventions focused primarily on exchange rates, administered prices, and the financial market.

The liberalisation process for the foreign exchange market began in January 1946, when the dollar rate was raised from 100 to 225 lire for exporters. At the end of March, exporters were allowed to retain at least 50 per cent of export proceeds in foreign currency and to convert them at market rates, which began to be quoted from May. Thereby, a two-tier foreign exchange market came into existence: one freely quoted (so-called 'quota libera'), and one official.[7] The average of these two rates climbed to 386 lire per US dollar in 1946; just as in the June–September period the lira of the 'quota libera' depreciated by 54 per cent.

Agricultural prices received by farmers tripled in May, but prices paid by consumers were left unchanged (BI R.A. 1946, pp. 108–9). Since lenders to government agricultural pools were able to automatically rediscount their receivables at BI, the resulting loss was financed by the Treasury through creation of monetary base, thus contributing to the inflationary process.

Finally, government introduced a number of measures, such as the elimination of taxation on income from bearer securities and stocks and the repeal of the extraordinary tax on war gains and the surtax on securities trading. Furthermore, the government removed restrictions on the distribution of profits and the 50 per cent tax reduction on equity transactions. These measures briskly raised the demand for equities, the value of which more than doubled between April and the end of August 1946 (Baffi 1965, p. 254). Share prices recorded a further 50 per cent increase during the last two months of the year. Volume trading peaked in December, despite the concurrent launch of the reconstruction loan. The price hike continued during the first months of 1947 (BI R.A. 1946, pp. 180–2). Thus, goods–price inflation went hand in hand with asset–price inflation. Money velocity surged between 1946 and 1947 (figure 1.1).

The high degree of liquidity of the money market is reported by Baffi (1965). The public had large holdings of cash and bank deposits, as well as deposits of banks with BI. Due to the strong credit demand generated by speculative activity in securities trading and the industrial recovery, banks found it to their advantage to withdraw deposits from BI. These funds were held at BI not to comply with the 1926 law (which was ineffective by this time), but as a result of industrial stagnation and the indirect capital circuit policy. The loan–deposits ratio rose from 42 to 75 per cent between the summers of 1943 and 1947. This growth is even more significant considering that, in the meantime, the k ratio had declined. There is no doubt, therefore, that the role of the banking system was to finance purely speculative transactions on merchandise and securities, in addition to the industrial recovery (V. Lutz 1950, p. 313).

There is no evidence that the authorities tried to stop speculative activities. De Cecco (1968, p. 129) hypothesises that the authorities' laissez-faire policy stemmed from their theoretical attachment to the monetary rather than the banking school. Consequently, they were inclined to ignore the movements in the credit multiplier. But there is no indication that the monetary authorities, particularly Einaudi (1947), were unaware of the role of the credit multiplier or that they were ideologically committed to the monetary school. Hence, we believe that the reason for their laissez-faire policy lies elsewhere.

The 1947 stabilisation

We will now devote some space to the 1947 stabilisation, which has attracted considerable attention in the literature; see, for example, F. and V. Lutz (1950), Bank for International Settlements (1947), Hirshman (1948), Simpson (1949–50), V. Lutz (1950) and Baffi (1965). We follow F. and V. Lutz (1950) in dividing the period which is associated with the stabilisation into four separate phases:

1 June 1946–September 1947, when inflation was rising;
2 October 1947–December 1947, when the new rules on reserve requirements came into effect;
3 January–December 1948, when prices were stable;
4 January–August 1949, when prices declined in absolute terms.

Tables 6.3 and 6.4 facilitate the description of the programme and its effect on different economic variables. For each of the four sub-periods, table 6.3 gives average growth rates of the monetary base, money multiplier, money, bank credit, and credit multiplier. The second table shows monthly variations of wholesale prices and nominal and real lira exchange rates, as well as monthly indexes of share prices and industrial production from June 1946 to August 1949. Neither the Lutzes nor the other historians mentioned above fully utilised monthly data.[8]

During the first sub-period, money grew at an annual rate of over 40 per cent. The growth was attributable to the monetary base increase for about three quarters and to the multiplier for the remaining one quarter. Bank credit grew by almost 62 per cent, much more than money growth. The credit multiplier rose three times as much as the money multiplier. Wholesale prices went up at an average monthly rate of slightly less than 6

Table 6.3 *Money and bank credit: June 1946 to August 1949 (period averages; annual percentages changes)*

	June 1946 Sept. 1947	Oct. 1947 Dec. 1947	Jan. 1948 Dec. 1948	Jan. 1949 Aug. 1949
Monetary base	29.2	73.0	35.7	26.6
Money multiplier	11.3	–31.6	–2.1	–0.3
Money	40.5	41.4	39.9	26.2
Credit multiplier	32.6	–85.5	–6.4	–1.0
Bank credits	61.8	–12.6	35.7	25.8

Source: BI, *Bollettino Statistico*, various issues.

Table 6.4 *Prices, exchange rates, equities and industrial production from June 1946 to August 1949*

Year and month	Monthly percentage changes			(1938=100)	
	Wholesale prices	Nominal exch. rate	Real exch. rate	Stock market	Indust. Product.
1946					
June	0.4	3.6	4.9	557	
July	3.2	26.8	34.1	726	
August	4.3	5.6	4.8	994	
September	7.9	18.0	14.0	885	
October	5.5	0.7	3.3	860	
November	6.3	–5.3	–7.5	1032	
December	8.9	0.0	–8.0	1373	
1947					
January	2.1	–7.0	–8.7	1443	71
February	3.6	0.8	–0.7	1523	67
March	6.4	13.7	10.8	1890	83
April	9.5	15.2	4.5	2835	93
May	14.8	30.0	14.8	3145	104
June	2.4	–7.2	–9.3	2744	103
July	8.4	–7.8	–14.2	2370	110
August	1.9	–7.0	–6.9	2370	93
September	5.3	–7.5	–10.3	2285	100
avg. 6/46–9/47	5.7	4.5	1.6		
October	–3.1	–7.3	–3.5	1680	105
November	–6.0	–2.4	4.3	1434	94

Table 6.4 (*cont.*)

Year and month	Monthly percentage changes			(1938 = 100)	
	Wholesale prices	Nominal exch. rate	Real exch. rate	Stock market	Indust. Product.
December	−2.1	−4.6	−0.3	1325	91
avg. 10/47–12/47	−3.7	−4.8	0.2		
1948					
January	−2.8	−0.3	4.0	1216	89
February	−0.3	0.0	−2.6	1206	90
March	−0.6	0.2	−1.1	1097	96
April	−1.5	0.0	2.4	1743	97
May	−1.1	0.2	2.0	1736	97
June	−0.8	0.0	2.2	1437	99
July	0.0	0.0	1.5	1436	101
August	−1.0	0.0	−10.5	1586	91
September	11.1	0.0	−1.6	1613	110
October	−0.8	0.0	−1.3	1609	109
November	−1.0	0.0	0.3	1609	106
December	0.5	0.0	−1.6	1629	105
avg. 1/48–12/48	0.3	0.0	−0.3		
1949					
January	0.0	0.0	−1.1	1031	100
February	−0.7	0.0	−0.9	2049	96
March	−1.8	0.0	2.0	2004	103
April	−3.0	0.0	2.1	1944	98
May	−2.1	0.0	1.3	1754	112
June	−1.2	0.0	0.5	1608	111
July	−3.5	0.0	2.8	1676	110
August	−2.9	0.0	2.5	1745	90
avg. 1/49–9/49	−1.9	0.0	1.1		

Notes and sources:
Wholesale prices: BI (R.A. 1947, p. 264; R.A. 1948, p. 304; R.A. 1949, p. 349).
Nominal exchange rate: export exchange rate from F.A. and V. Lutz (1950, table XI) up to August 1949 and from BI (R.A. 1949, p. 352) for the remainder.
Change in the real exchange rate is equal to the change in the nominal exchange rate plus the change in US wholesale prices minus the change in Italian prices.
Stock market: index of the Milan Stock Exchange from Smid (1948, p. 13) and BI (R.A. 1949).
Industrial production: general index from Rasi (1982d, pp. 220–2).

per cent, and the lira depreciated by a monthly average of 4.5 and 1.6 per cent (in nominal and real terms), respectively. The share price index rose by about 560 to almost 2,300. In the first nine months of 1947 alone, the general industrial production index climbed from 71 to 100.

In May 1947, in the midst of the inflationary and speculative frenzy, the fourth De Gasperi government was formed, with Einaudi and Del Vecchio heading the Budget and Treasury ministries, respectively. Menichella replaced Einaudi as Governor of BI. The three together formed an illustrious troika in charge of economic policy.

On 4 August, the Interministerial Committee for Credit and Savings met for the first time, under Einaudi's chairmanship. This Committee was approved on 2 August, and replaced the old Ministerial Committee established under the 1936 Banking Legislation. In subsequent days, the Interministerial Committee aimed at implementing a credit squeeze, with new rules which came into effect at the end of September: credit institutions had to deposit with BI or purchase government securities for an amount equal to 20 per cent of the difference between their deposit base and ten times their net worth, and 40 per cent of any subsequent increase in deposits. Amounts deposited with BI yielded the interest applied on short-term Treasury bills less 25 basis points. With these decisions, BI became a true central bank, in the sense that it also assumed the role of custodian for the reserves of the banking system.

In addition to decisions regarding bank deposits and credit, the official discount rate was raised from 4 to 5.5 per cent, effective 6 September; rates applied by banks increased to levels higher than those experienced during the war; the official dollar rate was raised from 225 to 350 in August, when the US currency was exchanged at over 700 lire in the free market. From November onward, the two rates were combined and fixed at the free market of average price for the previous month.[9]

The second column of table 6.3 illustrates the effect of the stabilisation measure on money and bank credit. The significant fall of the money multiplier, caused by the increase in reserve requirements, did not completely offset the effects of the very large rise in the monetary base. As a result, money supply accelerated its upward trend. The bank credit multiplier, more sensitive than the money multiplier to the increase in reserve requirements, fell by 86 per cent and caused a drop in credit in absolute terms.[10]

From table 6.4, we note that price changes were –3.7 per cent in the second sub-period, the lira appreciated in nominal terms, but remained the same in real value. The share price index was 2.285 in August, and dropped to 1.325 in December. The industrial production index fell from 105 to 91 between September and December. As a whole, therefore, the stabilisation measure had an immediate and very strong effect on the business cycle.

In 1948, a significant slowdown of the monetary base was coupled with substantial stability of the money multiplier. Money growth was not very different from the previous two sub-periods. The credit multiplier was rather stable and credit growth was recorded at about 36 per cent, a figure not dissimilar from that for monetary growth. Price levels and the lira exchange rate remained stable (table 6.4). Share trading climbed by about 30 per cent and, in September, industrial output returned to the maximum value recorded in July of the previous year.

In the last sub-period – from January to August 1949 – monetary-base growth settled at around 27 per cent; money and bank credit increased more or less by the same percentage, thanks to the high stability of the respective multipliers. Domestic prices declined at an average monthly rate of 1.3 per cent. The lira nominal rate remained constant and, consequently, the fall in domestic prices brought about a real depreciation of the lira. In August, share trading was even higher than in the previous December. As to industrial output, the values remained rather stable, except for the seasonal contraction in August.

The issues

Our data raise a number of questions which the literature has either avoided or only partially answered. To begin with, would it have been possible to carry out the stabilisation programme prior to 1947? To be more precise, was it feasible to prevent the great 1943–5 inflation by adopting a price control policy or a monetary squeeze? Second, was the 1946–7 inflation accidental or 'intentional'? And how accurate are historiography and contemporary critics in regarding Einaudi, then BI Governor, as a vigorous proponent of price stability? Third, is it true that the 1947 summer measures were introduced expeditiously and were, therefore, almost unexpected? Why were the measures passed at that particular point in time? What was the role played by international events? Fourth, did the measures bring about a permanent monetary squeeze? Why did they turn out to be so powerful as to subdue inflation? What was the connection between the high unemployment rate at the end of the 1940s and the 1947 measures? Finally, why did prices remain stable from 1948 onward, despite the sustained growth of money and bank credit relative to output?

We deal with the first set of questions in this paragraph and tackle the others subsequently. In theory, there were two ways to prevent a resurgence of inflation: enacting price controls or squeezing quickly and decisively the excess liquidity out of the system. The first alternative was not feasible because, as De Cecco (1968, p. 110) notes:

The price control mechanism . . . disintegrated completely due to administrative inefficiency, concrete difficulties, as well as ideological resistance to controls and to the Allies' presence (several hundred thousand soldiers with a purchasing power a hundred times higher than the local population's . . .).

Other authors like Foa (1949) and Rasi (1982c) emphasised the psychological aspects of the situation and suggested that, with the collapse of the regime, inevitably economic agents and public authorities instinctively moved away from the constraints and political interference which had characterised the Fascist regime. It was not by chance, therefore, that liberal economists re-emerged in the political arena, quite apart from their past opposition to Fascism.

There are two further considerations against price controls. The first is that between 1943 and 1944 the resurgence of inflation would have occurred, and would have broken through price controls, regardless of political change. This is confirmed by the fact that in the north, where government bureaucracy was still effective and price control policy continued, prices were allowed to increase in 1944 to levels well above those prevailing in the free market in the rest of the country (figure 6.1; Catalano 1975, pp. 128–33). The second consideration is that, even if controls would have continued to be effective, they would have only delayed the quest for a permanent solution to the inflation problem.

In considering the monetary squeeze alternative, it is useful to distinguish the situation spanning 1943 and part of 1944 from that of the subsequent two years. Money grew in real terms until 1943–4. It would have been ideal, therefore, to drastically reduce liquidity before it had an impact on prices; but that was not possible for two reasons. First of all, the liquidity squeeze would have affected only part of the country; second, the authorities would have had difficulties in tightening money and simultaneously financing the deficits and the continuing war.

Surge in velocity and authorities' responsibilities

The situation changed radically at the beginning of 1944. The inflationary process was not only gaining momentum, but soon reached such a magnitude as to represent a massive reduction in real money balances. During 1944–5 velocity increased by about 42 percentage points, compared with a 170 percentage point increase for the price level (figures 1.1 and 1.3). In the subsequent two years, the connection between velocity and the price level became even tighter, the two rising, respectively, 75 and 95 percentage points.

These facts suggest that part of the inflation process was not the direct result of the authorities' actions, at least for the period up to the end of 1945.

It is true that, at times, the authorities gave the impression of supporting an increase in velocity, as in the case of their proposals regarding the extraordinary tax and the change of money. But it is equally true that the surge in velocity had a lot to do with the war, the collapse of the Fascist regime, administrative disorders, and frequent proposals to adopt the principles of a planned economy (Rossi 1954, p. 648).

As we progress into 1946 the argument that the inflationary process was beyond the authorities' control becomes less and less credible. In fact, the question that immediately arises is how could a monetary inflation persist and deteriorate under the leadership of Luigi Einaudi who was BI Governor from January 1945 to May 1947? The economist-publicist *par excellence*, Einaudi had been an unbending proponent of price stability since the beginning of the century and, above all, during and immediately after the First World War. Historiography, both written and oral, depicts Einaudi as the unconditional inflation fighter of the 1947 stabilisation programme that he personally engineered and implemented. But was Einaudi indeed an inflation fighter at all costs?

Einaudi and inflation

Our view on Einaudi as an inflation fighter differs from much of the literature. Hence, we go to some length to corroborate our thesis that the monetary authorities were more than willing to let inflation go, to extract actual and perceived benefits. Our most convincing evidence comes from Einaudi himself as the author of the Final Remarks of the 1946 Annual Report.[11] This document is a masterpiece of diplomacy and not easy to grasp. It has two parts, one where Einaudi defends himself and the other where he attacks his critics as well as the government. It begins with Einaudi's question:

How is it possible that the governor . . . could witness a rise in currency stock of 103,813 million lire between the end of May 1946 and 20 January 1947, without intervening . . .?   (p. 222)

A third of this increase was attributable to the rediscounting of agricultural bills from government pools, another third to purchases of foreign currency and the remaining third to banks' withdrawals of their deposits from BI. On the basis of this, Einaudi begins his defence by asking:

could the Bank refuse to rediscount receivables from government pools?   (p. 224)

Of course, the answer was that it could not, as it was obliged to rediscount such receivables by law (p. 224); and Einaudi goes on:

Could the Bank refuse to provide the Italian Exchange Office with the funds necessary to purchase foreign currencies . . . from exporters . . .?   (p. 224)

Again, the answer is negative. Then, Einaudi asks the crucial question:

could the Bank refuse to reimburse large deposits held by credit institutions . . .?
                                                                                   (p. 225)

   In this case, the reply should have been unequivocally positive. In fact, it
was Einaudi himself who sent a letter to the major banks in January 1947 –
that is, two months before the Final Remarks – reminding them that existing legislation provided for such refusal (BI R.A. 1946, pp. 169–70). In an
attempt to extricate himself from an indefensible position, Einaudi adds:

If [the central bank] would not have reimbursed the deposits, it would have acted
against the law and in such a harmful manner as to trigger a credit crisis, with very
serious consequences for the country.   (p. 225)

We had no other choice; we could either increase the currency stock or unleash economic chaos. Both were evils, to be sure, but the latter would have been far worse.
                                                                                   (p. 231).[12]

These statements were particularly striking as they were not substantiated
by analytical and empirical evidence, and contrasted clearly with Einaudi's
prior positions.
   At the end of his self-defence, Einaudi attacked the policy of government
pools, as well as bread price controls. His criticism evolved into an open
exhortation to the government to reduce operating losses arising from this
policy. At this point his speech turned to inflation. Einaudi emphasised its
negative repercussions and repeatedly asked that inflation be eradicated.
This could easily be interpreted as additional evidence that the BI's governor was passionately opposed to any form of price increases. Such an interpretation, however, would distort the message delivered by Einaudi. What
he really meant was that inflation brings about substantial benefits which
dissipate when inflation reaches a certain limit. When this threshold is
reached, inflation must be stopped.
   It is not difficult to understand why the anti-inflationist Einaudi was keen
to mainly emphasise inflation benefits. To start with, he was not acting in his
former capacity as a freethinker, academician and journalist, but as the
central bank governor who also posed as a politician. Inflation provided an
output stimulus that might have saved Italy from a violent Communist take-
over (Carli 1993, p. 15). Inflation, furthermore, was eroding rapidly the real
value of public debt: domestically held public debt as a percentage of
national income declined from 122 to 25 between 1942 and 1947, thanks
primarily to high inflation (Spinelli and Vismara 1990). Finally, and this
was also clear from his Final Remarks, Einaudi reached the conclusion that

inflation could stimulate savings and consequently could enhance private demand for government securities.

Einaudi proposed controlling only future inflation, because he believed that Italy had reached 'the critical inflation point when its effects become negative even for government' (p. 249). Additional evidence of the governor's acquiescence to, if not complicity with, the inflationary process comes from the resignation of the Treasury Minister, Epicarmo Corbino, in September 1946. Corbino quit, not only because he did not get along with Finance Minister Scoccimarro and the Left, but also because he had a different view of inflation. Corbino would comment later on his resignation (1962, p. 331) as follows:

I was convinced that inflation was not . . . necessary . . . . But I was aware that the other members of the government and almost all parties supporting it were not of the same opinion.

While this statement might appear at first to be self-serving, it is hard to dismiss it, especially when an authoritative and independent observer such as the Bank for International Settlements (1947, p. 32) reported that, in the summer of 1946, there were mounting political attacks on Corbino, 'whose policy was to policy was to oppose inflation'.

Was the stabilisation really unexpected?

It would be wrong to conclude that the August 1947 measures were introduced suddenly and, consequently, forced the economic system to adjust quickly with resulting high costs. The economic community in general, and banks in particular, had received several warnings that the stabilisation was in the offing and that reserve requirements would play a pivotal role. It suffices to say that representatives from the major credit institutions had been invited several times by the government, between February and August 1947, to participate in discussions regarding the regulations it was about to introduce.

The programme was launched in August 1947 because international reserves had petered out between the spring and summer of that year (Baffi 1965, p. 266). The shortage of reserves was jeopardising not only economic recovery, but also the high export potential of the Italian manufacturing industry. The shortage also explained the way the measures were articulated, through a combination of credit squeeze, lira devaluation, and amnesty for foreign-exchange crimes aimed at encouraging repatriation of foreign-currency assets.

The data on the Italian balance of payments, emphasised by V. Lutz (1950), concur with the thesis that the timing of the measures was primarily attributable to international factors. Lutz dwelled mainly on the behaviour of the current account, which was divided into an ordinary and an extra-ordinary part. The latter, which included the important items of foreign assistance (including the Allied Military Relief Programme, European Recovery Programme, and UNRRA), switched from a positive balance of about 250 million dollars to a negative one of approximately 400 million between 1946 and 1947. If we also consider capital movements, there was an overall loss of reserves of about 65 million dollars in 1947.

More evidence on the role of external factors in instigating the stabilis-ation programme comes from a report of the Bank for International Settlements (1947) which forecasts a deficit of about 300 million dollars in 1947, excluding the inflow of foreign assistance and loans. After pointing out that actual Italian reserves totalled only about 200 million dollars, the report continued:

Approximately 100 million [of those reserves], equivalent to 34 weeks of imports, represents the bare minimum which is always prudent to have available. . . . An addi-tional 100 million was spent in the early months of 1947. Consequently, the residual negative balance for the second part of the year, which can be met only through foreign assistance, amounts to about 200 million dollars.   (p. 60)

The already difficult situation deteriorated further during the days im-mediately after the preparation of the report when the British government proclaimed the inconvertibility of the pound. Consequently, a substantial part of the already limited Italian reserves could no longer be utilised. Furthermore, all this took place against a widespread perception that the Marshall Plan, announced in June 1947, would take longer to implement than initially anticipated.

As with 'Quota 90', the stabilisation programme, and its timing, were influenced by the international search for monetary stability, pushed pri-marily by the International Monetary Fund (IMF), which Italy had recently joined.[13] The IMF membership imposed new obligations on Italy. There were short-term commitments, such as the deposit of reserves, the rapid abolition of the two-tier foreign exchange system and the adoption of fixed rates.[14] There was also the strategic commitment of pursuing monetary stability.

Also, the United States pressed for monetary stability in Italy (Castronuovo 1975, p. 358). At the beginning of 1947, De Gasperi and Menichella went on an official visit to the United States. There, the repre-sentatives of the Italian government received offers of cooperation aimed at easing Italy's burden in the implementation of an eventual stabilisation pro-gramme. The offers resulted in the abolition of existing sanctions against Italian exports to the United States, in the reimbursement of 50 million dollars for expenses borne by Italy during the allied military occupation, and in a 100 million dollar loan (the exact amount mentioned in the preliminary negotiations leading to 'Quota 90').[15]

Was it really a strong credit squeeze?

The 1947 measures were considered by part of the literature, and perhaps more so in oral tradition, to be a strong credit squeeze. But were they really so? The data of table 6.3 suggest otherwise. Nonetheless, given the importance of this aspect, we examine the issue in some detail.

Bank credit stopped growing in the last quarter of 1947, but rose again at the rate of 36 per cent in 1948, and at the rate of almost 26 per cent during the first eight months of 1949.[16] The monetary base grew by 73 per cent between October and December 1947, by 36 per cent in the subsequent year and by 27 per cent during the first eight months of 1949. With regard to the money stock, the corresponding percentages were 41, 40 and 26. Certainly, these figures do not indicate a strong credit squeeze.

A time series analysis, based on monthly observations, of the monetary base, money and bank credit reveals no information concerning the beginning of the credit squeeze (Spinelli and Fratianni 1991, figures 8.14–8.16). In fact, one is hard pressed to determine whether the credit squeeze actually occurred, a point emphasised by Foa (1949, p. 65), BI (R.A. 1949, pp. 231–2), F. and V. Lutz (1950, p. 12), Hildebrand (1965, p. 33) and Baffi (1965, p. 275). But if that is the case, how can we explain that government decisions produced such powerful results?

As the literature recognises, the answer lies in the reversal of inflation expectations.[17] The announcement of government actions had a larger influence on the market than their implementation. As a result, economic agents readjusted their portfolios by shifting from real to financial assets. The credibility of government was sufficient to cause a slowdown in the velocity of money and, consequently, to stop the inflationary process.

There is, however, a risk of exaggerating the effect of the government's programme on expectations. In this regard two considerations must be made. The first is that it is not possible for expectations alone to bring about a rapid and lasting abatement of high inflation unless the latter is not primarily due to an unusually high level of velocity (that is, if inflation is 'excessive' with respect to the trend of real and monetary variables). We know this condition was met when the measures were announced. Moreover, at that time the duration and magnitude of velocity deviation from its trend had already generated a substantial decline in the real quantity of money. On this point BI (R.A. 1948, p. 103) commented:

in the third quarter of 1947, prices reached a level that could not be sustained by the market purchasing capacity without further expansion of existing mediums of payment.

This meant that the situation in the market place was such that velocity could decrease significantly and permanently so as to trigger an increase in the stock of real money balances.

This leads us to the second consideration. Government decisions were made when the inflationary process was already 'self-destructive'. In principle, such a process could have developed into hyperinflation, or might have continued until money lost virtually all its value. In practice, however, neither outcome was realistic. According to data reported in table 6.4, the economy had already reached a turning point in May–June, that is, before the decisions were made. In fact, in June the inflationary process was at a standstill, the lira exchange rate began to appreciate in both nominal and real terms, and industrial output was slowing down. BI (R.A. 1947), Hirschman (1948), V. Lutz (1950) and F.A. and V. Lutz (1950) attributed these phenomena to an initial improvement in expectations, triggered by the economic plan of the fourth De Gasperi government and the formation of the Menichella–Einaudi–Del Vecchio team. But liquidity had been tightened as well.

The fact that there was not a strong credit squeeze, and that the August 1947 measures acted mostly on expectations in a climate of economic recession suggest that government was not motivated primarily by domestic political considerations.[18] There is no doubt that significant pressures were building to form a social consensus before the 1948 general elections. It is also true that centre parties, which constituted the political majority in the summer of 1947, believed they could benefit from a newly found price stability. Yet, we have demonstrated that a cyclical turning point of the economy had occurred before the measures were passed; that the timing of the programme had been dictated mostly by international constraints, as well as by the May 1947 government crisis, and not by the elections of the subsequent spring; and that the measures were calibrated so as not to spark a severe recession.

The following paragraph will deal with the stabilisation costs.

Stabilisation costs

The most controversial of the many questions surrounding the 1947 programme is that regarding its impact on the country's output. The debate was lively both in Italy and abroad and addressed short- and longer-term consequences of the stabilisation. De Cecco (1968, pp. 133–4) made a negative assessment of the program, at least for the short term:

In the winter of 1947–8, prices . . . fell . . . and unemployment increased daily. The 18 April 1948 elections resulted in a clear victory for the centre parties coalition. But in the subsequent three years, all economic indicators revealed the price that the Italian economy had to pay for such a victory.

On the other hand, Hirschman (1948), Simpson (1949–50), Hildebrand (1965) and Baffi (1965) expressed very different views. Hirschman recognised the significant fall in production and warned that

it is almost impossible to stop a dramatic inflationary process without triggering a recession.   (p. 605)

Simpson went even further by illustrating that if seasonal factors were considered neither industrial output nor unemployment demonstrated a trend such as to validate the hypothesis that the programme had entailed a sustained cost. Hildebrand (p. 5) shared Simpson's conclusion:

the measure did not generate a substantial fall in production. The industrial output dropped by 11 per cent during the two quarters following the announcement, but this was partly attributable to seasonal factors. At the end of 1947, the output already exceeded its 1947 peak by almost 6 per cent.

And so did Baffi:

The industrial production index, net of seasonal adjustments, declined by some points in the last quarter of 1947 and remained at that level for the following winter months. After a temporary upturn, the index reflected a shortage in hydroelectric power and the effects of international recession around the end of the year. The expansion resumed more steadily in the spring of 1949.   (p. 276)

In view of the above considerations and the fact that a firmly established inflation of more than 60 per cent was reduced to zero in the span of three months, the balance of the arguments is to judge the measures, on the whole, to have been very successful. This is well illustrated by the relationship between growth of real income and inflation during 1938–49 (see figure 4.3). At first, real growth dropped from about 4 to –30 per cent, while inflation climbed from 5 to 90 per cent. In 1946 and 1947, real growth turned positive as inflation decreased by 20–30 percentage points. In 1948–9, price growth was zero, while real growth remained around 7.5 per cent. As already indicated in chapter 1, the joint movement of the two variables along the south-east/north-west line may be interpreted as the result of a significant shift of the aggregate supply curve in the north-westerly direction. In 1946–7, the supply curve showed a second, equally strong shift, but of opposite sign. This reflected changes introduced by the new measures, which made it possible to subdue a 60 per cent inflation in a short period of time without a significant loss in production.

Turning to the longer-run consequences, the 1947 decisions gave the country a stable macroeconomic environment which facilitated the subsequent stage of sustained economic growth uninterrupted by tight monetary situations arising from periodic balance-of-payments crises. The 1926 stabilisation provides an illuminating comparison in this regard. The cost–benefit analysis of the 1926 programme would have been partial and myopic without taking into consideration the economic situation that would otherwise have existed in the 1930s. Similarly, an assessment of the cost of the 1947 measures cannot disregard what the 1950s would have been in the absence of the 1947 stabilisation (Gualerni 1980, p. 69; BI R.A. 1951, p. 71).

Finally, the Italian industrial sector was positioned favourably with respect to foreign competition, owing to extensive restructuring in the 1920s and 1930s and the fact that the sector came out of the war basically undamaged. Hence, it was not reasonable to expect a large drop in aggregate demand.[19]

Foreign criticism

By 1949, the debate on Italian economic policy had shifted to the unemployment problem. This was sparked primarily by the publication of the 1948 Hoffman Report, submitted to the US Congress in February 1949, as well as by a paper on the state of the European economy, which was prepared by the United Nations Economic Commission (1950). Both documents criticised Italian policymakers for their insistent 'fear' of a resurgence of inflation and the depletion of international reserves. These reports deemed such fears justifiable in 1947, but not in 1948; consequently, economic policy in general, and monetary policy in particular, should have been more 'aggressive' in facilitating the return of the unemployed to work.

International criticism prompted a number of authoritative responses in defence of the government's 'fears' and prudence. Bresciani Turroni (1950) reiterated the non-deflationist nature of the 1947 measures and ridiculed the analysis of the United Nations Commission:

Italian unemployment is not attributable to the economic cycle, but to a permanent, chronic disparity between the labour force and market demand. Appropriate measures can reduce this imbalance, but not eliminate it altogether.   (p. 282)

Simpson (1949–50, p. 219) and the Bank for International Settlements (1950, p. 76) agreed that unemployment in Italy was not of a Keynesian nature.

F.A. and V. Lutz (1950) focused on the strategic importance of the capital accumulation process as an alternative to the stimulation of domestic demand to obtain a permanent solution to unemployment. V. Lutz (1950, p. 360) and Baffi (1965, p. 277) stressed that the continual Italian government's concern regarding the level of reserves should not be considered excessive. Hildebrand (1965, p. 43) expressed the view that the long period of non-inflationary economic development enjoyed by Italy in the 1950s proved that the government's initiatives were correct with regard to 'both the diagnosis and the cure'.

We reported the main lines of the debate less to voice, yet again, an overall favourable opinion on the 1947 stabilisation programme, than to underscore the difference in the intellectual debate of the time. Keynesian doctrine and advice appears to have been more prevalent in the United States than in Italy. Italian policymakers, far from blindly fearing inflation, were formulating and applying general principles of optimal monetary policy. As an illustration, the Governor in his Final Remarks for 1948 raised the important question of the role of monetary policy:

> we cannot expect that monetary policy resolve all those fundamental problems connected with high economic growth. These are primarily the responsibility of others to tackle . . . and resolve these problems with the awareness that, in future, no difficulty can be overcome or even mitigated through inflationary practices.
>
> (BI R.A. 1948, p. 207)

Simply put, monetary policy should not be directed at overcoming supply bottlenecks and structural problems that affect the country's economic growth. If it did, not only would policy fail, but it would exacerbate inflation. To underline the maturity and modernity of such a concept, it suffices to recall that other central banks would come to this conclusion thirty years later, that is, only after the so-called monetary revolution.

The reconstitution of real money balances

Why did inflation not resume in 1948 and 1949, when growth rates of monetary aggregates were high relative to output growth? The answer lies in the mere necessity for economic agents to reconstitute real money balances, greatly curtailed by the high inflation during the 1943–7 period. In other words, after 1947, the monetary aggregates could afford to grow at relatively sustained rates in the face of an excess money demand. Velocity in 1948 and 1949 was still high relative to the pre-war period; and many years would elapse before velocity would return to its historical trend path.[20]

Compare, again, the 1926 with the 1947 stabilisation. In 1925–6, the lira depreciated in real terms and the policy objective was to stop devaluation expectations. In 1946–7, the general price level increased more rapidly than money and the challenge was to break inflation expectations. Hence the similarities between the Pesaro speech and the decisions made in the summer of 1947.

However, there is also a substantial difference between the two measures. Not content with having stopped the nominal devaluation of the lira, 'Quota 90' started a policy of continuous revaluations. As a result, the stock of money outstanding not only failed to grow, but actually declined. In 1947, policy virtually froze the level of prices. Consequently, the need to replenish real money balances necessitated additional growth in the nominal money stock.

The lira from 1947 to 1949

In April 1947, Italy and the UK signed an agreement whereby Italy accepted the convertibility of the pound sterling and the need to maintain a cross-currency parity of 4.03 between the US dollar and the pound (F.A. and V. Lutz 1950). The agreement fell through the following August, when the British currency was again proclaimed inconvertible. The lira then began to appreciate against the pound, whose value dropped to a minimum of about 1,700 lire in January 1948. As the lira exchange rate with the dollar was fixed at 575 as of December 1947, the dollar–pound parity declined to about 3.0. In November 1948, Italy and the UK reinstated their former agreement and, as a result, the pound recovered lost ground with respect to the lira.

Around the middle of 1949, the lira was in a state of approximate equilibrium with the dollar (steady at 575), but was undervalued against other European currencies (BI R.A. 1948, p. 67). On 18 September 1949, the pound was strongly devalued to 2.80 against the dollar, triggering a chain of devaluations. The Italian government allowed the dollar exchange rate to slide upward to prevent a real appreciation of the lira and a consequent loss of international competitiveness for Italian exports (BI R.A. 1949, p. 137). The lira–dollar rate was fixed at 625 in October, and remained at that level for over twenty years.

Bank of Italy, banks and politics

We conclude with some remarks on the relationship between BI and the political system, as well as between BI and the banking industry. These relationships evolved on account of new legislation and changes in the economic environment.

Decree No. 1 of 1945 – passed on 4 January - stated that 'the Bank of Italy's governor, general manager and deputy general manager . . . would be appointed or removed . . . upon the recommendation of the Prime Minister, in consultation with the Treasury Minister and with the concurrence of the Cabinet'. This indicated more political intrusion in the internal affairs of the central bank and, consequently, less independence and power on the part of the latter. However, there were also other developments on the positive side, certainly more substantive. First of all, we have to remember that, at the end of the war, BI absorbed the Consortium for Financing Industrial Enterprises and took over many of the functions previously performed by the dissolved Ministry of Trade and the Foreign Exchange, as well as the Office of the Inspector of Savings and Credit. The Consortium had been in operation since 1936 as a division of IMI (Istituto Mobiliare Italiano), but was brought into BI's jurisdiction by way of a decree passed in 1945. The governor of the central bank also became the president of the Consortium (BI R.A. 1945, pp. 44–5). As the latter could previously carry out rediscount operations with BI, the new structure enabled the Bank to better control its monetary base. By contrast, the Ministry of Trade and Foreign Exchange was dissolved and part of its foreign exchange powers transferred to BI. The importance of this institutional change soon became clear, as BI could now directly influence the allocation of scarce foreign currency reserves.

BI also benefited from amendments affecting the 1936 Banking Law. We recall that this legislation sanctioned the power of the political system over monetary policy and the central bank. This power was exercised through the Ministerial Committee and the Office of the Inspector of Savings and Credit, which provided, in fact, the link between politics and monetary policy. These two bodies were significantly affected by two decrees. One, passed on 14 September 1944, dissolved the Office of the Inspector and transferred its functions to the Treasury, with the exception of the supervisory role over credit institutions, which was delegated to BI. De facto, the Ministerial Committee lost its powers, as it could operate only through the Office of the Inspector. A second decree, passed on 17 July 1947, created the Interministerial Committee for Credit and Savings, which assumed responsibility for the country's monetary and foreign exchange policies.

All the above changes gave BI broader powers and responsibilities (Marconi 1979; Minervini 1987). De Cecco (1968, pp. 44–5) summarised the new environment as follows:

The 1936 Banking Law had the primary function of subjecting the banking system to government strategic planning. Banks regained autonomy when the decision-making government bodies were dissolved. It is true that the central bank remained under government control, as monetary policy was still the responsibility of the Ministerial Committee. However, this committee no longer had an operational arm, and the recording of monetary policy decisions was, in fact, delegated to the central bank. Various ministers could make use of their own research departments, but these had not yet been formed. . . . Consequently, the central bank governor found himself in a privileged position. He could rely on a well-organised economic research department and, additionally, had first-hand knowledge of all information regarding credit, currency and foreign exchange.

Furthermore, a law passed in March 1947 had formally sanctioned Italy's participation in the Bretton Woods Agreement and indicated the ministries responsible for liaising with the International Monetary Fund and the World Bank. The same law empowered the ministries to delegate part of their functions to BI, enabling BI to represent Italy in international conferences and to directly access privileged and valuable information.

We recall that the institution of required reserves consolidated BI's position enormously. Even before 1947, the Bank had begun to strengthen its role in the banking system by enhancing the development of local banks and, consequently, reversing the trend of bank concentrations.

With regard to the relationship between BI and Treasury, extraordinary advances had formerly been permitted only in emergency situations and under specific legislative authority, while ordinary advances had to be maintained within the limits set by law. The ministerial decree, dated 31 December 1936 (cf. chapter 5), had amended the legislation by indicating that:

When government requirements of an extraordinary and exceptional nature would dictate providing the Treasury with additional funds (in excess of the maximum limit set for ordinary advances), these would be made available against the collateral of Treasury bills, as agreed between the Finance Minister and the Governor of Bank of Italy.

In other words, the decree had eliminated any maximum limit for extraordinary advances and replaced the specific legislative authority with a mere 'agreement' between the Finance Minister and the Governor. As a result, the Treasury had formally deprived the central bank of any control over the process of monetary-base creation. In 1947, all of this was in contrast with the policy of monetary stability and the introduction of reserve requirements. This contradiction was partially resolved by way of two decrees passed in December 1947 and May 1948. In particular, the second decree indicated that the Treasury could request advances from the central bank for a maximum of 15 per cent of approved budget expenditures; eventual excesses over this limit had to be covered within 20 days and, if this did not occur, the Bank could refuse any new drawings: 'no new extraordinary advance could be extended by the Bank of Italy to the Treasury without a specific legislative approval that would also set the amount'. In essence, 'the authority and, consequently, the ultimate responsibility [in granting extraordinary advances to the Treasury] were transferred to Parliament' (Ciampi 1983, p. 91).

The new legislation only partially enabled BI to recover its former autonomy and hence regain control over the process of monetary-base creation. To defend the Bank's independence, art. 81 of the new Republican

Constitution mandated that any expenditure decision had to indicate, concurrently, the corresponding source of funds.[21]

BI took advantage of the fact that industrial reconversion had already taken place. Monetary policy assumed the important and legitimate role of ensuring that price and foreign exchange instabilities would not interfere with domestic economic growth and expansion of Italian exports in foreign markets. From this viewpoint, the 1947 measures proved very valuable in revealing the power of monetary policy and its capacity to maintain stability.

Finally, BI, besides using 'fear' for inflation as a political leverage, was bestowed with competent senior management. In the inter-war period, the Bank had submissive executives who yielded to pressures exerted by economic ministers such as De Stefani, Volpi di Misurata, Jung and Thaon di Revel. These ministers had strong personalities, technical abilities and close relations with the domestic and international financial world. After the Second World War the situation was reversed: it was governors Einaudi and Menichella who possessed remarkable personalities, technical abilities and strong ties with the domestic and international financial communities; and the economic ministers who were technically weak and uncertain even about their own political mandate.

Conclusions

This chapter revolved around two major issues. The first was the impact on the economic system of the real, fiscal and monetary shocks connected with the Second World War. As to the quantitative repercussions of these shocks on the domestic and international depreciation process of the lira, the period stands out as a unique event in the entire *History*. This was attributable to a strong upward shift of the aggregate supply curve, the political-administrative-military collapse of the Fascist regime, and to an upsurge in the velocity of money.

As a whole, these events brought about growth rates in money and prices that were three and five times, respectively, higher than the 131-year historical averages; an average output growth which was one-fourth of the historical average; a markedly higher instability in the growth process of key macroeconomic variables.

The second topic involved the stabilisation programme of 1947, which rapidly put an end to a situation which had the potential to degenerate into hyperinflation. In particular, we underlined that the decisions government took in the summer of 1947 could have been taken earlier. We elaborated on the government's possible complicity with the inflationary process, and expressed our disagreement with most of the literature on the subject. We explained that the 1947 stabilisation did not come as a total surprise, nor did it result in a wild credit and monetary squeeze; but rather was characterised by a favourable cost–benefit relationship for the economy, since it acted primarily on inflation expectations.

The final part of the chapter focused on three important post-war issues: the need for the market to reconstitute its real money balances, which had been drastically depleted by the great inflation; a central bank managed by people of great prestige and having increased influence on bankers and the politicians; and a general desire for monetary stability. With this background, it will be easier to understand the monetary developments of the 1950s, which will be discussed in the next chapter.

7   The fifties and sixties

Introduction

Two important events give a distinctive character to the last 40 years of the *History*. First, between the sixties and seventies and, again, between the seventies and eighties, the monetary regime went through two drastic changes, which involved the formulation of the intermediate and final objectives of monetary policy. Second, during the eighties, BI was no longer submissive to the political system. Consequently, for the first time and for a long period afterwards, monetary policy was in conflict with fiscal policy.

In this chapter, we deal with the years 1950 to 1969, during which monetary policy was tailored to a longer-term strategy, at least in the first decade; was able to guarantee an almost absolute price stability; and contributed to regular and sustained economic development. Chapter 8 will examine the seventies during which monetary policy privileged the short over the long horizon; was not only incapable of counteracting domestic and international shocks, but was in itself a cause of instability; and contributed to an inflationary process that had no precedents in peacetime. The monetary authorities did not pursue price stability; instead they favoured employment as its primary target. Furthermore, they acquiesced to a regime of fiscal dominance by developing a new intermediate objective that gave virtually absolute priority to government lending.[1] Chapter 9 deals with the eighties and will give insight into the nature of the second drastic change, a counterrevolution which produced a number of innovations in the conflict of monetary policy, but most significantly gave the monetary authorities independence from the fiscal authorities.[2]

We begin with an analysis of the evolution of some key variables to underscore the structural break at the end of the sixties. We then focus on the period 1950–69, with a quantitative analysis of the behaviour of those variables as they relate to the equation of exchange and the process of money creation. The 1950–69 years coincide roughly with the Bretton Woods era. There are two distinct phases in this era, one of currency inconvertibility

(1950–7) and the other of full currency convertibility. We adhere to this classification in the chapter so as to separate those policies aimed at bringing
about free trade and the external convertibility of the lira from the ordinary
practice of running a fixed exchange-rate regime. After analysing the
process of money creation under fixed exchange rates, we end the chapter
with an account of the interaction between the business cycle, external constraints and monetary policy in the convertibility period of 1958–69.

The 1950s–1960s versus the 1970s

The break at the end of the sixties can be easily ascertained by looking at
fiscal and monetary variables. On the fiscal side, between 1950 and 1969 the
budget deficit remained low and stable at about 2.8 per cent of national
income. By contrast, in subsequent years, it increased rapidly and reached
values in excess of 22 per cent of national income towards the end of the
1970s (table 1.4 and figure 1.4).

On the monetary side, the growth of the monetary base tended to decline
until 1969 (figure 2.2). The trend was reversed in 1970; between this year and
1978, the base growth went from 8 to about 22 per cent. There is a positive
correlation between the size of the budget deficit and monetary-base
growth. Similar observations hold for money growth. In particular, 1969
represented the end of a historical phase characterised by growth rates
increasingly tending downward. Starting with 1970, money growth
increased sharply and, within a few years, reached a rate of 11 to about 21
per cent;[3] the annual growth began to contract in 1979.

Output growth does not reveal a specific turning point, although it is
evident that owing to the first oil shock and the 1975 recession the seventies
had, on average, lower economic growth than in the rest of the period (figure
1.3). Thus, there is an increasingly diverging trend between monetary aggregates and real output as we move from the fifties and sixties to the seventies.
It is not surprising, therefore, that inflation started to rise just towards the
end of the sixties, and reached almost 20 per cent in 1980, after fluctuating
for twenty years around an average value of 4–5 per cent (figure 1.2).

We recall from chapter 1 that the Italian inflation of the seventies could
not be primarily attributed to international factors. To be sure, core inflation rate in the industrialised world rose, but the Italian inflation rate was
strongly and positively correlated to its differential with respect to the
United States (table 1.2). Besides being more inflation-prone on average, the
Italian economy was decidedly more unstable than that of the United
States, which, in turn, was not the most stable among the industrialised
countries during the seventies.

The statistical break-point of the exchange rate coincided with the end of the Bretton Woods system and took place later than the break-point of the inflation differential. In fact, the lira price of the dollar remained stable at the 600–25 mark until President Nixon made the decision in August 1971 to end the gold convertibility of the dollar. After that, the exchange rate first declined slightly and then began to increase at an annual rate that in 1976 reached almost 25 per cent; its level peaked at 882 lire in the following year. Altogether, the change in the exchange rate followed the inflation differential in the long run. Over shorter periods of time, however, there were wide and sustained deviations between the two variables; in particular, between 1976 and 1980, the real value of the lira first sharply depreciated and then appreciated.

Real interest rates, and their differential *vis-à-vis* US real rates, were only sporadically negative in the fifties and sixties; in the seventies the opposite is true. This phenomenon reflects the financial segmentation of the country and points to controls on capital movements and on the exchange market as the means through which this isolation was achieved. Financial segmentation, in turn, made it easier for the authorities to extract a high level of seigniorage. The latter climbed to 6 per cent of national income in the seventies and touched 15 per cent in 1976 (figure 2.7).

We end our brief data excursion by pointing out that the progressive deterioration of both the inflationary process and its trade-off with the unemployment rate is vividly illustrated by the shape of the Phillips curve, shown in figure 7.1. The observations regarding the seventies lie to the north-east of all other observations, reinforcing the peculiarity of this decade.

The sub-period 1950–1969: a quantitative overview

Let us now place the years from 1950 to 1969 within a long-term perspective.[4] On average, money and income grew by 18 and 160 per cent, respectively, more than during the entire period of the *History*; prices, however, rose by only half as much. Money velocity declined at almost double this rate: –3.2 versus 1.7 per cent of the entire period. Thus, the fifties and sixties had strong economic growth with low inflation.

The high-growth years were also accompanied by a less volatile economic environment. Obviously, this does not mean that business cycles were made obsolete. For instance, money growth was equal to 16 per cent in 1950, 8 per cent in 1957, 15 per cent in 1962 and again 8 per cent in 1964. Prices displayed more or less the same pattern. According to official statistics, output contracted significantly between October 1963 and January 1965. Finally, velocity of money declined relative to trend in 1952, from 1959 to 1961, and again from 1965 to 1968.

Government expenditures increased from 22 per cent of national income in 1950 to 27 per cent in 1968. Tax revenues also grew in a fairly regular

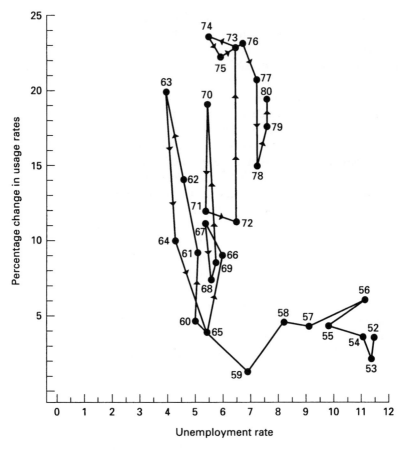

Figure 7.1 The Phillips curve, 1952–1980
Source: ISCO for unemployment rate and ISTAT for wages.

fashion. Budget deficits, as a percentage of income, were higher at the beginning than at the end of the sub-period (figure 1.4). Deficit monetisation
declined progressively until 1959 and then rose, leaving the period average
no different from the long historical average.

  Money grew at an average annual rate of 12.4 per cent, fuelled by a strong
expansion of the monetary base (9.6 per cent). The growth of the multiplier,
while small relative to that of the monetary base, was unusually high in relation to the long historical experience and contributed to an annual 2 percentage faster growth of money. The steep and concomitant decline of k, rr
and re made this possible (table 2.1). This, in turn, reflected the fact that
Italy was developing into a more mature financial economy.

The fifties: trade normalisation and monetary stability

In our review of the fifties, we shall focus on three aspects: the move to free trade, the conduct of monetary policy, and the return to the external convertibility of the lira.

Progress towards freer trade

In 1950, Italy took a decisive step towards liberalising trade. On 15 July, 39 per cent of imported finished products were allowed freely into the country. This followed the previous 1949 liberalisation, which involved 11 per cent of finished products, 77 per cent of raw materials and 52 per cent of agricultural foodstuff. The same day, new *ad valorem* custom duties replaced existing quotas. On 20 September, the percentage of unrestricted importation was raised to 66 per cent for finished products, 82 per cent for raw materials and 73 per cent for agricultural foodstuff. Italy then became the leader, within the OECD, in the liberalisation of trade. This leadership was strengthened further in subsequent years: by 1953, 99.7 per cent of Italy's imports were unrestricted, against 92 per cent for Germany, 75.3 per cent for Britain and 52 per cent for France.

That trade liberalisation was a deliberate government policy aimed at energising Italian industry is clear from the following statement by Governor Menichella (BI R.A. 1953, pp. 402–3):

It is also necessary to be vigilant against easy and recurring illusions that the equilibrium of our balance of payments may be restored through export subsidies . . . or the granting of large long-term credit facilities to exporters, or the practice of restricting imports through higher custom duties or even quotas. Such measures, prompted by a purely simplistic notion of the balance of payments . . . are not appropriate to solve our fundamental problems. Our problems require . . . that our productive sectors (manufacturing as well as agriculture) develop and become stronger only through a real, and not artificial, ability to compete internationally. To this end, these sectors should be even more willing to welcome, not to oppose, outside competition.

Besides exerting pressures on the industrial sector to meet higher levels of international competitiveness, liberalisation was grounded on the opportunistic view that Italian manufacturing – which was efficient and almost undamaged by the war – would take advantage of great opportunities on international markets. In some quarters, there was fear that freer trade would expose the country to the influence of international cycles. But a stable currency and a considerable stock of foreign reserves seemed to provide an adequate insurance against those risks.

It should not be overlooked that Italy was an enthusiastic signatory of the European Payments Union in 1950 and that an Italian, Guido Carli, was appointed to preside over the board of that institution. The European Payments Union was very successful, not only in multilaterilising the system of credits and debits that European countries had carried out on a bilateral basis up to that time, but also in creating a much more open trade environment. Much of the credit goes to the US government which, using the carrot of the Marshall Plan, was the catalyst in the trade liberalisation process (Carli 1993, pp. 95–101).

Monetary stability

The importance of a stable currency and abundant foreign reserves became evident in connection with the Korean cycle of the early fifties (Baffi 1965). Italy continued her steady monetary policy, in contrast to most other countries which instead had to tighten up. A similar situation occurred in 1955–7, when a deep international recession, worsened by the Suez political crisis, caused inflationary tensions and external imbalances. In this instance as well, monetary conditions in Italy remained basically the same, while other countries had to adopt restrictive monetary measures. Finally, in 1958 monetary policy abroad became very expansive in reaction to a contraction in industrial output; yet, Italy managed to make a small downward adjustment of only 50 basis points in its discount rate.

Monetary policy of the fifties did not show the drastic changes that characterised the following two decades. A number of authors, particularly Baffi (1965, 1973) and Ackley (1972) dwelled on this aspect. The latter expressed his surprise that during an entire decade the Bank of Italy was never compelled to intervene with open market operations, and only once changed the official discount rate and reserve requirement ratios.

The regularity of Italian monetary policy was partly attributable to the way in which it was applied, and partly to favourable economic conditions that facilitated the task of the authorities. Overall, monetary policy set long-term objectives, namely to maintain price stability subject to the balance-of-payments constraint. We recall that under a fixed exchange-rate regime there is a negative correlation between the foreign and domestic components of the monetary base. This correlation comes about when an excess of domestic money spills over into other countries' money markets through a deficit in the current account and/or a net outflow of capital, that is, through a loss of foreign reserves (for a review of these issues, see Fratianni and Spinelli 1984). However, monetary policy did try to mitigate the repercussions of the flow of reserves on monetary aggregates. But there is a second reason the foreign and domestic components of the monetary base are inversely correlated: the desire of the monetary authorities to delay or avoid the transmission of monetary impulses from one country to another. Both effects were present in the fifties. As noted by Baffi (1965, pp. 35–53), the sterilisation activity of BI was asymmetric, and thus only partial, in the sense that it expanded money and credit when foreign reserves increased, but did not contract money and credit when reserves declined.

The legacy of past monetary policy actions, the strong hold of BI on the banking industry, and the newly found independence of the central bank from the fiscal authorities were the favourable circumstances that made it easier for monetary policy to be stable. The positive impact of the 1945–7 great inflation and the subsequent stabilisation occurred in a variety of ways. We have already mentioned the flexibility in actions the authorities gained from having at their disposal a large stock of foreign reserves. In addition, at the beginning of the fifties, market participants were reconstituting their real money balances; the demand for financial assets with respect to income was rising rapidly; a prudent fiscal policy was curbing the supply of government securities; and finally market expectations leaned towards price stability. In these circumstances, monetary authorities used their credibility to keep the fiscal authorities on a prudent path.

The relationship between the central bank and credit institutions was addressed by Governor Menichella (1956) himself. Menichella outlined the policy instruments available to BI: that is, the power to grant discount and advance facilities to credit institutions; the discretion of making foreign currency loans to credit institutions through the Ufficio Italiano Cambi (Italian Foreign Exchange Office), of which the BI governor was the *ex-officio* head; the ability to issue directives with regard to the banks' foreign indebtedness; the authority to relax capital–loan ratios for the banks; and the power to influence the amount of deposits banks kept with the central bank.

The panoply of monetary instruments was so ample as to make it unnecessary to resort to changes in reserve requirement ratios. As Menichella indicates in the following quotation, BI seemed to prefer moral suasion, grounded in its great prestige and institutional authority over the credit system, and to call upon reserve requirement ratios when alternatives failed:

the central bank would not hesitate to intervene by raising the amount of required reserves, if it would become clear that commercial banks did not follow its suggestions.

The road to convertibility

Currency convertibility emerged as an important issue at the beginning of the fifties because it was seen as the natural complement, at times even as a precondition, of the process of trade liberalisation in general, and of economic integration between the sterling pound and dollar areas in particular

(De Angelis 1982c, pp. 230 ff.). We have already mentioned the important role played by the European Payments Union and the US government in the process of trade and currency liberalisation. The first concrete steps towards currency convertibility were taken between 1953 and 1954. At that time, Italy still had a system of multiple exchange rates tailored to support her international trade. The authorities applied different rates, according to import or export trade, countries of origin or destination and type of goods (Holbrick 1959).

A number of significant innovations were introduced in January 1955, signalling the government's intention to move the lira towards convertibility. The tax on foreign exchange transactions was reduced, and exporters were allowed to utilise 50 per cent of their proceeds in Swiss francs as they wished. In February 1956, non-residents with investments in Italy were permitted to repatriate the initial capital and accrued profits at the official exchange rate. In June, a free market of foreign banknotes was established. In March, the authorities set a fixed exchange rate between the lira and the currencies of the European Payments Union. In July, banks were authorised to carry out foreign exchange transactions. Carli (1993, pp. 120–3) considers this decision as nothing short of the creation of a true foreign exchange market, even though tightly regulated by the Italian Exchange Office (UIC). The law made transparent the rule that what was not explicitly permitted had to be considered prohibited, a rule that remained in force until the end of the 1980s when exchange markets were liberalised. A month later exporters were given the choice to sell their entire foreign currency proceeds on the free market.

In February 1957, the bilateral payments system came to an end and multilateral lira foreign accounts were permitted. The actual convertibility of the lira and other European currencies was sanctioned in December 1958, when the European Monetary Agreement prescribed that member governments had to convert national currencies held by non-residents. At that time the lira–dollar rate was pegged at 625, with intervention limits of plus or minus 0.72 per cent (620.5 for purchases and 629.5 for sales). The intervention limits for other currencies were derived implicitly through triangular arbitrage. On 28 January 1960, BI was authorised to value its gold reserves at the price of 703.297 lire per gram, which was equivalent to a parity of 625 lire per dollar.[5] The appreciation in value of gold reserves was credited to the Treasury.

Two decisions taken in 1959 further liberalised foreign exchange transactions; with the first, resident companies were authorised to purchase shares of companies incorporated abroad with the same business objectives; with the other, Italian banks were permitted to hold monetary balances in foreign currencies.

The attitudes of the monetary authorities towards lira convertibility reflect the prevailing mistrust for fully unrestrained freedom of capital movement (BI, Final Remarks 1959). Governor Menichella excluded the possibility of exploiting the convertibility of the lira to raise the foreign share of Italian government securities. The governor was mindful of the constraint on monetary policy resulting from having a large portion of the country's national debt in foreign hands; unrestrained capital mobility can quickly affect the share of foreign ownership, as often occurred in the nineteenth century (cf. chapter 3).[6] The governor's reservations about free capital movements, especially those of a short-run nature, are clearly captured by the following quotation from page 339 of the aforementioned Final Remarks:

we cannot allow unlimited freedom for Italian investments abroad, although it is logical that existing restrictions be gradually and adequately reduced, in view of improvements in foreign currency reserves. . . . In fact, these reserves constitute the base for new investments which we consider possible to undertake in the near future, in order to turn around the present, still uncertain recession.

Two closely related issues gained importance with the external convertibility of the lira. The first pertained to the determination of the money supply in an open economy; the second related to the way the country's international openness constrained monetary policy. We turn our attention to these issues in the next sections.

The money supply process in an open economy

The process of money supply creation involves the joint interaction of the monetary authorities, the banking system, and the public. The authorities are constrained by the size of the fiscal budget and balance-of-payments imbalances. While it is true that the authorities can exert some influence on the long-run outcome of budget imbalances and the choice of an exchange-rate regime, these must be considered as constraints on day-to-day monetary policy actions. The authorities, in turn, generate regulations that act as constraints on the behaviour of the banking system and the public, e.g., the legislation on reserve requirements of 1947. Finally, the banking industry may collectively decide to set limits to competition, as in the case of interbank agreements to fix interest rates, both on the deposit and lending sides.[7]

The analytical structure adopted so far for the process that determines money supply is relatively simple. As this was thoroughly discussed in chapter 2, we shall reiterate here only its salient points. The quantity of money is defined as the product of the monetary base and the multiplier. The multiplier is equal to $[(1+k)/(k+rr+re)]$ and the monetary base is the sum of a domestic and a foreign component.

At this juncture, we need to go beyond the basic analytical structure adopted so far and elaborate further on the process of money creation in an open economy. We begin by introducing the concept of adjusted monetary base, BMA, that is the monetary base net of the banks' borrowings from BI and net borrowings from the rest of the world. The motivation underlying this choice is that BI has no direct control over banks' domestic borrowings, although it can influence them through its cost and availability. In an open economy net foreign borrowings are substitutable for domestic borrowings; hence, net foreign borrowings escape also the authorities' direct control.

In sum, BI can control BMA but not the total monetary base. For a given value of the foreign component of the monetary base (BF), the authorities can generate the desired level of BMA by adjusting the level of the Treasury component, MBTR. The constraint of a fixed exchange rate, however, makes it impossible for the monetary authorities to control the sum of MBTR and BF in the long term. The authorities can act independently on MBTR but must bear the consequences of changes in BF. The decision to expand MBTR is constrained by the fact that the maximum sustainable losses in international reserves are limited by BF.[8] Between the short and long run, the authorities may strive for a desired level of international reserves. In this case MBTR becomes the strategic variable the authorities must control, while BF reflects developments in the balance of payments, as well as of the authorities' decisions to sterilise flows of international reserves. In contrast to what happens in the long run, the constraint on monetary policy imposed by fixed exchange rates depends on the degree of substitutability between domestic and foreign financial assets. The fundamental implication of the monetary theory of the balance of payments, that it is impossible to control the total monetary base in a regime of fixed exchange rates, depends on the perfect nature of this substitutability. If it is less than perfect, however, the authorities can achieve a desired value of BMA in the medium run (Fratianni 1976).

To elaborate on these points, suppose a lira increase in MBTR affects prices, income, and interest rates in such a manner that, given the responsiveness of the various accounts of the balance of payments to these variables, BF declines by 1 lira. Under these circumstances, and barring any changes in the money multiplier, monetary policy is totally ineffective. These are the well-known implications of the monetary theory of the balance of payments: monetary policy is at the complete mercy of the rules governing the regime of fixed exchange rates. This is also the long-run implication of a model in which domestic and foreign assets are less than perfectly substitutable in the short run.

Monetary policy is instead effective whenever the offset coefficient between changes in MBTR and changes in BF is different from –1. If it were between –1 and 0, policy would work in the 'normal' direction with the usual application of brakes and gas pedals. Relatively low values of the interest elasticity of the capital account and/or low values of the price and income elasticity of the current account assure that 'normal' conditions hold. It is also possible that the offset coefficient be algebraically smaller than –1. Such a result could be generated by a hypersensitive response of BF to changes in prices, income and interest rates. Monetary policy would still be effective, but in a perverse manner: the working of the brakes and gas pedals would be reversed with respect to the 'normal' case.

With these considerations, we can write the alternative formulation of the money supply equation as

$$M=ma\,(MBA) \tag{7.1}$$

$$ma=(1+k)/(k+rr+re\,-\,bh\,-\,bf) \tag{7.2}$$

$$MBA=BD\,-\,ABI\,-\,ARW+BF=MBTR+MBF \tag{7.3}$$

where the new symbols have the following meaning: MBA=the adjusted monetary base, ABI=banks' borrowings from BI, ARW=banks' net foreign borrowings, MBF=adjusted foreign component of the monetary base, bh=ratio of ABI to deposits, and bf=ratio of ARW to deposits.

The public and the banks compete with each other for a share of the available supply of monetary base. Reserve requirements impose a minimum on the demand for monetary base by the banks. Banks can add to their reserves by borrowing from either the central bank (ABI) or from the rest of the world (ARW). For the banks these two components are interchangeable, to a degree depending on domestic and foreign interest rates as well as on the cost of borrowing from BI. In Italy, the published discount rate is only part of the total cost of borrowing from the central bank. BI over the years has considered banks' borrowing more a privilege than an unconditional right; as a result, BI has preferred to control the expansion of ABI through quantitative ceilings instead of raising the official discount rate. For a period of twelve years ending in August 1969, the official discount rate remained unchanged at 3.50 per cent.[9]

BI introduced non-price constraints also on ARW. Often banks were told to 'zero' their net foreign position. At other times, when they were net importers of funds, banks were prohibited from converting foreign reserves into domestic reserves. In other words, the central bank sterilised bank-held foreign reserves. Finally, when they were net exporters of funds, banks were allowed to convert foreign reserves into domestic reserves, but only for an amount not exceeding their net foreign balance.

To better understand the consequences of sterilising bank-held foreign reserves, let us define the balance-of-payments surplus as

$$BOPS = T + K$$
$$= d[FRCB + sFRB] + d[(1-s)FRB + FAB - FLB] \qquad (7.4)$$

where $BOPS$=balance-of-payments surplus, T=current-account balance, K=capital-account balance, s=proportion of bank-held foreign reserves eligible for lira conversion, $FRCB$=foreign reserves held by the monetary authorities, FRB=foreign reserves held by banks, FAB=foreign assets held by banks, FLA=foreign liabilities held by banks, and d=first-difference operator.

The expression $[FLB - FAB - (1 - s) \times FRB]$ is equal to ARW. The country's volume of international reserves is given by the sum of $FRCB$ and FRB; the foreign component of the monetary base, BF, is the sum of $FRCB$ and $sFRB$; the difference between international reserves and BF, $(1 - s)FRB$, represents what the authorities sterilise. If the authorities do not sterilise, $s = 1$ and the balance-of-payments surplus $BOPS$ translates entirely into a monetary-base increase. If the authorities sterilise, then $s < 1$ and $BOPS$ does not fully translate into an increase in monetary base. Consequently, the rule imposed on credit institutions to balance their net foreign holdings may be redefined in terms of sterilisation policy. When a bank is a net importer of funds, that is, when FLB exceeds the total of FAB and FRB, foreign currency holdings cannot be converted into lire and s is therefore equal to zero. If, on the other hand, banks are net exporter of funds (FLB is less than the sum of FAB and FRB), foreign reserves can be converted into domestic currency only up to the amount of the banks' net asset position. In sum, the authorities can influence the extent to which external monetary imbalances affect BF and hence the monetary base.[10]

Typically, BI tended to react to balance-of-payments surpluses by sterilising their reserve inflows – that is, $s < 1$ – and by inducing banks to be a net exporter of funds. By contrast, during periods of balance-of-payments deficits, BI tended to raise s and, concurrently, to remove restrictions on banks to repatriate funds from abroad.

To verify how the open-economy formulation of the money supply differs from that of a closed economy we employ quarterly data over the post-convertibility period, that is, 1958 to 1969. Quarterly data have a potential advantage over annual data in identifying the degree to which banks substitute domestic for foreign assets. The algorithm is similar to that employed in chapter 2. Here are the sample averages of the contributions of the determinants of money growth under the alternative formulations shown in table 7.1.

These are the salient results. First, the multiplier has a larger influence on money growth in a fixed exchange-rate open economy than in a closed economy; the opposite holds for the monetary base. Second, in an open economy the banking system can borrow either from the central bank or

Table 7.1 *Annual growth rates, 1958:2–1969:4*

Closed-economy model	Open-economy model
Money=12.9	Money=12.9
k=1.51	k=1.84
rr=0.42	rr=0.48
re=1.26	re=1.37
interaction=0.04	bh=0.84
MB=9.74	bf=–0.68
	interaction=–0.09
	BD=8.01
	ABI=–1.97
	BF=2.72
	ARW=0.15
	interaction=0.21

from the rest of the world. The above decomposition indicates that domestic and foreign borrowings are substitutes. Third, in a closed economy or in an open economy with flexible exchange rates the monetary authorities have direct control over MB and rr; these two variables account for 79 per cent of the average money growth from 1958 to 1969. But in an open economy the authorities can only control $MBTR$ – that is, the domestic component of the base net of banks' domestic borrowings – and rr; these two variables account for 50 per cent of the average money growth. The inference is that monetary control is more difficult in a fixed exchange-rate open economy than in a closed economy or in an open economy operating under flexible exchange rates. To achieve a given target value of money under fixed exchange rates the authorities have to offset changes in MBF (the algebraic sum of BF and ARW), k, re, bh and bf with appropriate movements in $MBTR$. Finally, $MBTR$ and MBF move in opposite directions in 21 out of 47 quarters, especially in 1963 and 1969 when Italy suffered large balance-of-payments deficits. Yet, the average contribution of $MBTR$ and MBF, across the 12-year period, is positive. In sum, the open economy formulation of the money supply process underscores the wider range of borrowing opportunities available to banks and the increased difficulty of the monetary authorities to control the money stock.

In what follows we give specific examples of how the Italian central bank tried to delay or avoid the automatic money supply adjustments implied by a fixed exchange-rate arrangement. In particular, we emphasise the motivation and technique of the monetary authorities in sterilising the effects of foreign reserve flows on money.

Monetary policy and the balance-of-payments constraint

In the fifties, the monetary authorities' prudence and their pursuit of long-run objectives, in conjunction with favourable economic conditions, made the foreign constraint irrelevant in the conduct of monetary policy. BI never had to resort to restrictive actions to curb domestic demand. Monetary policy stability was the ultimate outcome.

In the sixties, and more so in the seventies, monetary policy became less prudent, aimed at a multitude of overly ambitious objectives, and focused on a short-term horizon. An activist monetary policy led to balance-of-payments crises which were met by policy reversals.

The validity of our thesis that monetary policy was a determining factor in accelerating foreign exchange crises will emerge from our discussion of specific episodes. Additional evidence comes from the literature on the central bank's reaction function. Despite differences in approaches, time periods, data and evaluation methods, this literature concludes that BI was primarily concerned with and reacted to deviations of international reserves from their desired level.[11] Furthermore, this literature indicates that BI violated the 'rules of the game' of the fixed exchange-rate regime by imposing balance-sheet constraints on the banking system, in essence by altering the value of the sterilisation parameter s (table 7.2).

The monetary authorities also engaged in foreign currency-lira swap operations with the banks to modify the composition of the banks' balance sheets. On several occasions, UIC supplied foreign exchange to banks at subsidised terms. A sale of foreign exchange against lire by the authorities to banks, with an opposite transaction in the future at agreed-upon prices, lowered MBTR while leaving BF unchanged. The forward transaction produced opposite results: an increase in MBTR and no change in BF. While the monetary base did not change, the swap operation could have had a lasting effect. For instance, if banks had used foreign currencies to reduce their indebtedness to foreign creditors, there would have been a permanent reduction in the monetary base held by banks. On the other hand, if the currencies were deposited with foreign banks (with a consequent reduction of the banks' net foreign debt position), there would have been no change in monetary base held by domestic banks; but the composition of the monetary base would have shifted in favour of the foreign component.

We illustrate these aspects of Italian monetary policy with an analysis of specific episodes. To facilitate the interpretation of events, we refer to figure 7.2 and table 7.3. Figure 7.2 shows the movement of the inflation rate against a measure of utilised productive capacity in the industrial sector, which is our proxy of business cycle conditions. The sub-period under consideration began with an expansion that lasted until autumn of 1963 and

Table 7.2 *Two indicators of sterilisation activity,*
1958–1969 (billion lire)

Year/quarter coefficient s	Sterilisation	Sterilised reserves
1958 1	1.00	0.0
2	1.00	0.0
3	1.00	0.0
4	1.00	0.0
1959 1	1.00	0.0
2	1.00	0.0
3	1.00	0.0
4	1.00	0.0
1960 1	1.00	0.0
2	1.00	0.0
3	0.93	149.7
4	0.93	163.1
1961 1	0.92	185.4
2	0.92	195.9
3	0.92	198.0
4	0.92	205.8
1962 1	0.92	216.7
2	0.92	217.2
3	0.93	199.0
4	0.99	0.4
1963 1	1.00	0.0
2	0.99	0.4
3	1.00	0.0
4	0.86	392.5
1964 1	0.90	238.8
2	0.93	177.0
3	0.89	297.0
4	0.90	283.3
1965 1	0.92	219.3
2	0.95	131.8
3	0.98	41.5
4	0.94	208.9
1966 1	0.93	241.0
2	0.92	283.4
3	0.93	263.0
4	0.92	294.1
1967 1	0.92	285.2
2	0.89	425.4
3	0.91	367.4

Table 7.2 (*cont.*)

Year/quarter coefficient s	Sterilisation	Sterilised reserves
4	0.90	421.7
1968 1	0.90	415.2
2	0.91	387.7
3	0.94	228.0
4	0.93	264.4
1969 1	0.95	190.7
2	0.90	402.9
3	0.88	425.5
4	0.87	497.6

Table 7.3 *Balance of payments, 1958–1969 (million dollars)*

Year	Current account balance	Capital movements balance	'Official' settlements surplus	Changes in foreign reserves	Changes in banks' net foreign position
1958	564.2	270.4	895.4	865.4	30.0
1959	755.0	231.6	850.3	897.3	−47.3
1960	317.3	166.5	442.5	174.4	268.1
1961	508.5	202.4	577.4	617.1	−39.7
1962	276.4	−308.7	50.4	480.7	−430.3
1963	−791.0	−485.4	−1,251.8	−602.0	−649.8
1964	619.6	110.3	773.9	442.3	331.6
1965	2,209.1	−454.8	1,594.2	959.7	634.5
1966	2,117.2	−1,276.5	695.6	287.8	407.8
1967	1,599.1	1,023.4	323.6	519.1	−195.5
1968	2,626.9	−1,690.7	627.3	−60.8	688.1
1969	2,368,5	−3,432.8	−1,391.2	−704.6	−686.6

was followed by a recession which proceeded until the early part of 1966, then by a second expansion phase, which came to an end in autumn 1969. Table 7.3 provides data pertaining to the balance of payments as well as to changes in international reserves and the banks' net positions abroad (in the sense that these variables are defined in equation (7.4)). The fourth column is of particular interest as it illustrates the two foreign exchange crises, which we shall discuss shortly.

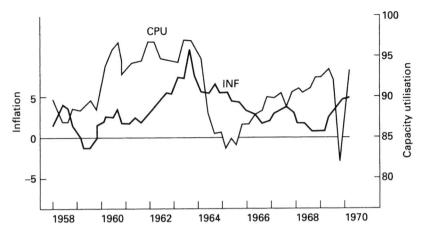

Figure 7.2 Capacity utilisation (CPU) and CPI inflation rate (INF), 1958–1969
Source: Brunner *et al.* (1973).

1958–September 1963

From 1958 to 1961 the balance of payments showed large surpluses (table 7.3, fourth column). Domestic output grew rapidly and our index of utilised productive capacity remained above 95 per cent from 1960 onward. The banking system was left completely free to deal with the rest of the world until August 1960. Subsequently, in view of the large external surpluses, the monetary authorities asked the banks to bring their net foreign debt position down to zero by the end of the year. To assist in this process, UIC sold foreign-currency assets to banks at particularly favourable terms, producing a decline in the domestic component of the monetary base. Approximately 8 per cent of foreign reserves were sterilised (table 7.2).

UIC changed its policy in the spring of 1961 when it began to stimulate the process of monetary base creation by depositing with the banks' large foreign-currency deposits. Furthermore, 200 billion lire of monetary base were 'freed' as BI reduced the reserve requirement ratio from 25 to 22.5 per cent in January 1962. In October 1962, banks were again authorised to take net debt positions *vis-à-vis* the rest of the world. Banks reacted expeditiously: their aggregate net position changed from 55 million at the end of 1961 to –357 at the end of 1962 and to about –1,200 million dollars in August 1963.

The sharp increase in banks' net foreign indebtedness financed in excess of 50 per cent of the very large balance-of-payments deficit of 1963 (table 7.3). But the banks' increased indebtedness generated additional liquidity at home that the authorities did not sterilise (table 7.2 indicates that, between 1962 and 1963, the parameter s rose towards unity). BF did not show any significant change from the fourth quarter of 1962 to the third quarter of 1963. These facts are consistent with the view that the monetary authorities wanted to avoid balance-of-payments deficits spilling over into a domestic monetary contraction.

The current account was primarily responsible for the balance-of-payments reversal between 1962 and 1963. In addition, there were negative developments in the capital account. A 1962 regulation, aimed at stimulating non-residents' demand for Italian securities and thus capital inflow, produced perverse results. The regulation offered opportunities for tax-induced arbitrage; Italian residents found it advantageous to sell securities at home and repurchase them through foreign intermediaries, primarily Swiss ones.[12] To avoid detection, capital moved out of Italy in the form of hard-to-trace banknotes, sometimes carried in suitcases across the Swiss border: 1.58 billion dollars were exported in this fashion from the first quarter of 1963 to the first quarter of 1964.

Were the monetary authorities disregarding the external constraint? Governor Carli made no mention of the deteriorating balance of payments in his Final Remarks delivered in May 1962. A year later, at the peak of the balance-of-payments crisis, Carli sounded a tepid warning during his delivery of the Final Remarks (BI R.A. 1962, p. 512):

> the bank of issue would fail to perform its duty, if it would not point out that public and private sectors' requests for capital are uncoordinated and in excess of available savings. In the current balance-of-payments situation, the Bank could not satisfy such requests through injections of liquidity, as this would in turn generate a more acute imbalance of demand over supply. . . . Such an action could lead to a situation that, although presently under control (and controllable despite some difficulties), might cease to be so.

It is hard to understand how the situation was 'under control' or 'controllable' when bank loans were growing at an annual rate of 25 per cent and imports in excess of 30 per cent. The monetary authorities were either ignoring the problem or hoping for a miracle.

October 1963–end of 1965

Between summer and autumn of 1963 it became obvious that the policy of defending reserves by exclusively relying on banks to attract funds from abroad was no longer sustainable. The authorities seemed reluctant to undertake any classical action, such as raising the official discount rate, or devaluing the lira, or altering reserve requirements, or imposing constraints on capital outflows. Their preferred action was to invite banks – and this occurred at the end of September – to gradually reduce their net credit position *vis-à-vis* the rest of the world. In the following December and June, additional regulations were put in place to freeze that exposure at lower levels. As none of the banks had a net credit exposure, the regulation had an effect of sterilising 392 billion lire of monetary base, equal to approximately 14 per cent of the country's stock of international reserves (table 7.2).

The banking system was very quick in responding to the authorities' directives, because of the higher level of interest rates abroad and an increasing premium to cover foreign exchange risk. Net foreign indebtedness declined from 1,200 million dollars in August 1963 to 634 million at the end of 1964. The combination of this net outflow of bank capital and the drain of official reserves produced a sharp decline in the foreign component of the monetary base. From the last quarter of 1962 to the first quarter of 1964 MBF exerted consistent negative pressure on money growth.

The monetary contraction came late, but was very intense. The total monetary base decelerated by a ratio of five to one before and after September 1963. Interest rates rose sharply, both in nominal and real terms. Industrial output had four consecutive quarters of negative growth; utilisation rates in manufacturing dropped to 85 per cent. Inflation slowed from 7.8 per cent in the third quarter of 1963 to 5.8 in the last quarter of 1964. Finally, and perhaps most significantly, the external imbalance switched from a deficit of $1.25 billion in 1963 to a surplus of $0.77 billion in 1964 (table 7.3).

The quick turnaround in the balance of payments led the authorities, in the summer of 1964, to bring pressure on banks to become net creditors on the Eurodollar market. Monetary policy became expansive again between October 1964 and the end of 1965. As a senior BI official, later to become a governor, put it:

The improved foreign exchange situation and the abated inflationary process, together with a rise in unemployment and a reduction in investments, created a climate where public opinion became favourable to an expansionary policy through higher government deficit.   (Fazio 1970, p. 277).

Our last episode involves the monetary cycle that started in 1966 and was carried out through a complete interest rate pegging policy.

1966–1969

During these years there were consistent balance-of-payments surpluses. The substantial accumulation of international reserves was accompanied by a lower than average growth of domestic base, the net result being a smooth growth of the total base. A sterilisation policy was pursued by subjecting banks to zero their net foreign position. The rule, in turn, implied that bank-held foreign reserves could be converted into domestic monetary base to the extent that banks had an excess of foreign assets over liabilities. UIC established maximum limits for its foreign exchange transactions with banks, and provided advantageous (i.e., at subsidised terms) foreign exchange–lira swaps only to those financial institutions willing to reduce their net foreign exposure.

Interest rate pegging was the most visible aspect of monetary policy in those years, and had numerous practical implications. In the intent of the authorities, pegging would have to aim at long-term interest rates to encourage a larger flow of investments. The rationale was based on the trade-off between average and variability of returns; namely, holders of financial assets were willing to accept lower average yields if these yields were to be more stable. Consequently, interest rate stabilisation would have enabled business and government to issue debt at a lower real cost, in turn spurring investment. On this point, it behoves us to quote Fazio (1979, p. 280), an advocate of this policy:

In addition to an increased stability in yields and aggregates, the advantage of an [interest rate] stabilisation policy, compared to a purely quantitative policy, is that it can reduce the level of liquidity in the economy at any time by suspending interventions. . . . By contrast, the policy has the drawback of not adjusting the size of the monetary base to business cycle considerations. Furthermore, once the interest rate level has been set, it becomes difficult to change it without altering markets' expectations.

In the initial phase of the stabilisation policy, the authorities did not run the risk of losing control over the monetary base creation process; this was so because the targeted long-term interest rate (about 6.5 per cent) was widely recognised as being close to market equilibrium. In fact, the central bank was often a net seller of securities. But a number of problems emerged in 1967 when an increase in foreign interest rates influenced an outflow of capital. The fact that Italian banks were by now active players in the Eurodollar market heightened the impact of rate differentials on reserves flows. Table 7.3 illustrates that the net outflow of capital was substantial between 1967 and 1969, so much so that the external imbalance changed from $324 to –$1,391 million, despite a positive current-account balance. The decision of the authorities was motivated by reducing the expected drain on official foreign reserves. Again, it is worth mentioning how the 'rules of the game' of the fixed exchange rates were violated for the benefit of domestic objectives.

In the first quarter of 1969, the authorities requested that the banks first reduce their net foreign credit position and then bring it down to zero by the end of June. UIC first raised the premium on its swap transactions and later flatly refused to sell foreign currencies to banks which were net exporters of funds.

Once more, the policy turn around was fast and clear. And the reason for monetary tightening is the 'classical' one of preventing a depletion of foreign reserves; the adoption of administrative rules served to postpone the full consequences of the automatic adjustment mechanism inherent in a fixed rate system.

Interest rate pegging ended in May 1969, after a three–year experiment. As a result, BI started again to purchase and sell short-term Treasury bills (BOTs) at rates which were consistent with a given target of the monetary base.[13] Short-term interest rates began to rise. Two months later, long-term rates were also allowed to move freely.[14] In the summer of 1970, there was a tax hike.

The monetary squeeze was again very effective in reversing foreign exchange flows. In fact, the external imbalance recovered from –$1,391 million to $356 million in the span of twelve months.

Conclusions

Italian monetary policy started to change at the end of the fifties, when it became more aggressive. Price stability was considered to be among the objectives pursued by the authorities, but not necessarily the most important one. Furthermore, the policy was formulated with a short-run horizon. The end result was a series of 'stops-and-gos' for both money and economic activity.

This chapter has underscored how monetary policy contributed to periodic foreign exchange crises. The fact that these crises caught the authorities by surprise shows the authorities' unwillingness or inability to implement a monetary strategy compatible with the external constraint. When the crises exploded, they were handled not with traditional methods, but with administrative rules that usually forced domestic banks to change their net foreign exposure. Once the drain on foreign reserves came to an end, monetary policy was immediately redirected to pursue 'real' objectives, such as investment and employment. This, in turn, paved the way for a new crisis.

The next chapter deals with the deepening of these policy shortcomings in the seventies.

8 The seventies

We have asked ourselves whether the Bank of Italy would have been able or could have refused to finance public deficits. . . . Such an action would place the government in the impossibility of paying salaries to public servants . . . and pensions to people. While this action would have the [technical] appearance of a monetary policy initiative, in practice it could be construed as an act of subversion, for it would bring about a paralysis in the institutions.   (BI R.A. 1973, p. 418)

Introduction

In this chapter we investigate the seventies. The distinctiveness of this decade is not the output slowdown, but the high inflation rate, relative to both Italy's recent past and the experience of other industrialised countries. The key factor underlying the high inflation turns out to be, once again, a profligate fiscal policy and a central bank subservient to the financing needs of the fiscal authorities. The monetary authorities adopted a new intermediate target, total domestic credit, which sanctioned the supremacy of fiscal policy over monetary policy.

A high seigniorage is the natural corollary of fiscal disorder and a compliant monetary policy. This was indeed true for the seventies; to collect such a seigniorage the country was financially isolated from the rest of the world through a pervasive and complex web of capital and exchange-rate controls.

The seventies versus the fifties and the sixties

The obvious point of departure for our comparison of the fifties–sixties and the seventies is government finance, which is the largest shock for the economy. Government expenditures were 28 per cent of national income in 1970; by 1978 they had almost doubled. Tax revenues grew as well, but at a much lower rate than expenditures. In fact, the former went from a low of 21 per cent of national income in 1973 to a high of 34 per cent in 1980. From the long perspective of our *History*, the behaviour of government expenditures

Table 8.1 *Annual growth rates, 1970:1–1980:4*

Money	=	17.4		
k	=	1.77	MBTR	= 15.9
rr	=	0.14	MBF	= −1.28
re	=	0.31	interaction =	0.33
bh	=	−1.66		
bf	=	1.47		
interaction =	−0.11			

and revenues appears decidedly anomalous, with obvious repercussions on the size of budget deficits. These rose from 3.9 per cent of national income in 1970 to 22 per cent in 1978. Large budget deficits, as we will see in the next chapter, will persist through the eighties.

Monetisation was close to the long historical average of 50 per cent. There were, however, two distinct periods: the first, from 1970 to 1976, when the monetisation ratio was 74 per cent, and the second, from 1977 to 1980, when the monetary authorities began to free themselves from the influence of fiscal policy. In this second period monetisation was low relative to the historical average. Thus, during the first part of the seventies the large size of the government budget reinforced the high monetisation ratio in establishing an accommodating monetary policy. After 1976, the low monetisation ratio reduced the influence of fiscal policy on monetary policy.

The multiplier and the monetary base grew at an annual average rate of 1.8 and 15.6 per cent, respectively. Again, the monetary base had a dominant influence on money growth, despite the fact that the multiplier's average growth was twice as large as that of the long period.

We can also examine money growth in terms of the open-economy model developed in chapter 7. These summary statistics are shown in table 8.1.

The Treasury, MBTR, and the net foreign component of the monetary base, MBF, tended to move in opposite directions, more so in the seventies than in the 1958–69 period analysed in chapter 7. In fact, there were 27 quarterly occurrences in the seventies when the influence of MBTR and MBF on money growth had opposite signs. On average MBTR contributed 15.9 percentage points to money growth, while MBF contributed −1.28 percentage points. A declining *k* and *re* were responsible for the above average growth of the money multiplier. Reserve requirement ratios were stable and made a marginal contribution to the growth of the multiplier. The domestic and net foreign borrowing ratios almost offset each other, again confirming that the Italian banking system used them as substitutes. The difference is that in the seventies the contribution of *bh* and *bf* to money growth had opposite signs with respect to their counterparts in the period 1958–69. In sum, the Treasury component of the monetary base accounted for almost the totality of the 17 per cent average annual growth rate of money; this is evidence of the dominance of fiscal impulses.

Moving to the other three variables of the equation of exchange, velocity continued its long-run decline, although at a lower pace. Real income grew at an annual average of 3.2 per cent. In the seventies economic performance, measured by the growth of real income, fell short of the performance in the fifties and sixties by 2.4 percentage points per annum; yet, the 3.2 annual average is 50 per cent higher than the long-run average. The average annual inflation of 13 per cent was the highest recorded during peacetime and exceeded the long-run average by 6 percentage points.

The seventies were years of stagflation compared with the previous two decades. This was true for Italy and basically for all other industrialised countries. However, while the slowdown in Italian economic growth was in line with what was happening in other industrialised countries, inflation was distinctively higher. In chapter 1 we saw, in fact, that the economic growth differential between Italy and the United States remained positive during the seventies and dropped by only 0.7 percentage points, while the inflation differential jumped from 1.1 to 6.2 percentage points (table 1.2).

In sum, relative to the fifties and the sixties the seventies witnessed an explosion of expenditures and budget deficits. Fiscal dominance led to a high growth of the Treasury monetary base, which accounted for almost all of the high money growth. The continued decline in velocity meant that prices accelerated more than monetary aggregates. Economic growth declined but remained well above the historical average. Variability increased across the board.

High inflation as the true Italian peculiarity

A flexible exchange-rate system enables a country to adopt its own inflation rate. In the approximately flexible exchange-rate regime of the seventies the Italian inflation differential with respect to the rest of the world reached its highest point of the *History* during peacetime.[1] The true peculiarity of Italy in the seventies is her high inflation rate and not the decline in economic growth.[2] This peculiarity has domestic roots, in particular the explosion of government deficits which are unmatched in other industrialised countries.

Inflation is a public-choice response to bulging budget deficits, and the *History* has offered several examples of such a response. However, the pursuit of inflation was never as resolute in peacetime as it was in the seventies. Inflation was the natural consequence of an emasculated monetary policy which was at the mercy of fiscal requirements. We can epitomise the

Table 8.2 *Budget deficits in Italy and other EC countries, 1971–1980*

Country	Deficit/ Income	Cycle- adjusted	Cycle and inflation adjusted
Italy	–8.3	–8.3	–6.3
Belgium	–5.0	–5.5	–3.6
Denmark	0.9	1.2	1.3
Germany	–2.1	–2.3	–1.6
France	–0.3	–0.7	–0.4
Netherlands	–1.5	–2.0	–2.3
UK	–3.1	–3.2	–2.3
EC average	–3.1	–3.3	–2.4

Source: European Economy, November 1984, p. 125.

economic policy of this decade with two complementary labels: fiscal dominance and budget deficit monetisation. The formulation and use of total domestic credit, TDC, as an intermediate target of monetary policy, made it much easier for government to obtain credit from the central bank. Monetary policy went further by relying on administrative rules and foreign exchange restrictions that insulated the Italian financial and money markets from those abroad. Financial segmentation, in turn, prevented domestic investors from substituting foreign assets for domestic assets; monetary segmentation impeded domestic money holders from switching into more stable monies. In this manner, government could maximise seigniorage.

In the following section we shall dwell on the four topics just mentioned: the explosion of government deficits, TDC, seigniorage and the country's monetary and financial isolation from the rest of the world.

Government deficits, their financing and total domestic credit

The deterioration of public finances in the seventies is not a phenomenon unique to Italy; the intensity is. For this reason we have prepared table 8.2 which illustrates three different types of budget deficit measures for EC countries.[3] In the first column we see that Italy's deficit was by far higher than that of all other countries. The second column shows that the deficit was not the result of a particularly unfavourable business cycle. The third column indicates that Italy continued to represent the most anomalous case even when deficits were adjusted for inflation.

There were three fundamental factors behind the sharp increase in Italian public deficits. First of all, a new layer of local governments, the Regions, was created in April of 1972. Regional diversity and autonomy has always been an integral part of Italian history; hence the desire to give autonomous decision-making powers to regions was widely shared across the political spectrum. As Putnam (1993, p. 20) puts it:

Populists claimed that regional government would raise the levels of *democracy*. . . . Moderates argued that decentralisation would increase *administrative efficiency*. Southerners believed that regional government could speed *social and economic development*. . . . *Regional autonomy* appealed to whichever group happened to be 'outs' in national politics.

In a span of a few years the central government shifted to the Regions authority in areas such as health, housing, urban planning, agriculture, public works and education (Putnam 1993, p. 24). The territorial redistribution of functions was accompanied by a massive transfer from the centre to the periphery. While the intent of the regional law aimed at expenditures being made by the Regions to replace, for the most part, central government expenditures, in practice the two levels of expenditures became to a significant extent complementary.

The second factor underlying the rise in government expenditures had to do with the diminished incentives in controlling the growth of expenditures. The power to impose taxes was retained by the central government, yet a sizable and rising proportion of expenditures was decided at the regional level which did not bear the burden of raising taxes for the creation of new programmes or the expansion of old ones. An example will illustrate the importance of decoupling expenditures from revenues. Health expenditures as a fraction of net national income doubled from 1960 to 1977. Part of the increase, to be sure, can be explained by an enlarged coverage of benefits and an improvement in the quality of services. Objective indicators such as infant and pregnancy mortality rates indicate, however, that quality improvements were modest (Cotula *et al.* 1979). The critical intervening variable was the Hospital Reform Act of 1968 which freed health-care units from quantitative budget limits. Hospitals charged the central government on the basis of actual costs without any incentive to control such costs. Theory could have predicted that hospitals would become revenue maximisers and expand budgets, as indeed they did (Fratianni and Spinelli 1982).

The third and most important reason government expenditure rose is that the political system became decidedly more active in redistributing income and wealth. The range of transfer payments to individuals and firms was enlarged, while their average size was made more generous. Politicians literally bought votes by subsidising inefficient firms, pumping resources into the south, expanding the safety net and public-sector employment, liberalising the social security system and granting indiscriminately disability pensions. For example, there were 28 pension recipients for every 100 people in 1977, approximately twice as many as in 1960. Among those, 5.3 million were classified as disabled; in 1960 the number of disability pensions was less than one-quarter of the 1977 figure. No data confirm that the risk from injury had quadrupled over a 17-year period. Disability pensions simply became a 'covert' way to redistribute income or the price for a vote in an election.[4]

As already mentioned, there was a strong acceleration of monetary aggregates and budget deficits in the first six years of the seventies relative to the previous period. The year 1976 is the beginning of a monetarist 'counter-revolution', which coincides with the creation of a secondary market for public debt. This innovation enabled BI to sell government bonds on the open market, thus offsetting, in part, the monetary base which the Bank was forced to create by either absorbing the unsold portion of government debt at public auctions or lending directly to the Treasury through the Treasury account ('conto corrente di Tesoreria'). After 1976 the strength of monetary and fiscal impulses began to decline.

The TDC model

Let us elaborate on the significance of TDC as an intermediate target so that we can fully grasp its role in linking budget deficits to money creation. TDC became an official intermediate target when the Italian authorities negotiated a loan from the International Monetary Fund in 1974. The memorandum of understanding underlying the loan makes explicit reference to the fact that Italy must maintain TDC below a prescribed ceiling. In what follows we present a simple model, based on Penati and Tullio (1983), of how the monetary authorities viewed TDC and its role.

We begin by rewriting the basic national income identity as

$$S-I=DEF+X-IM=d(AF)-d(PFI+PFE) \tag{8.1}$$

where S indicates private sector's savings, I investments, DEF public-sector deficit, X exports of goods and services, IM imports, AF private-sector lira and foreign-currency financial assets, PFI and PFE financial liabilities denominated in Italian lire and foreign currencies, respectively, and d the first-difference operator. PFI is traditionally defined as the sum of loans made by Italian commercial banks and Special Credit Institutions. The total demand of financial assets is

$$AF=f(Y, RE)+AF_{t-1}, \tag{8.2}$$

where Y is nominal national income and RE the foreign interest rate. The economy is open and the exchange rate is controlled by the authorities. Controls in the exchange market see to it that the domestic interest rate falls short of RE, implying that the domestic interest rate adjusts to the foreign interest rate. Being beyond the authorities' control, BE can be dropped without fundamentally altering the structure of the model.

The supply of financial assets is obtained by rearranging equation (8.1)

$$AF = DEF + X - IM + d(PFI + PFE) + AF_{t-1}. \tag{8.3}$$

Finally, the import function has the simplest Keynesian formulation

$$IM = IM(Y). \tag{8.4}$$

We also recall that

$$DEF = d(MBTR) + d(S), \tag{8.5}$$

where $MBTR$ is the Treasury component of the monetary base and S is the stock of government securities held by the public and the banks.[5] The model is closed by equating the demand for and supply of financial assets and then solving for dY

$$dY = [1/(f_Y + IM_Y)]d(TDC + TFC), \tag{8.6}$$

where TDC = total domestic credit = $d(MBTR) + d(S) + d(PFI)$, TFC = total foreign credit = $X + d(PFE)$, f_Y = marginal propensity to hold financial assets with respect to income, and IM_Y = marginal propensity to import with respect to income.

Equation (8.6) has a strong similarity to the Keynesian IS model. In contrast with the Keynesian model, however, (8.6) emphasises credit flows to the economy and not expenditure flows. In principle, these credit flows ought to be autonomous or controlled by the monetary authorities, to the same extent that government spending in the Keynesian IS model was controlled by the fiscal authorities. In practice, the definition of TDC included funds that firms could obtain either by issuing equity or by borrowing abroad and, thus, left open two avenues for weakening monetary control by BI.[6] But the more fundamental weakness is that TDC made monetary policy subordinate to fiscal policy.

TDC's endogeneity and BI's subservience to fiscal authorities

It is clear from the model presented above that government budget deficits were taken by the monetary authorities as exogenous. The critical issue then is how the monetary authorities reacted to changes in budget deficits. Theoretically, the monetary authorities could have maintained a given target of TDC by reducing the flow of credit to the private sector every time the budget deficit exceeded its target. In practice, however, such

Table 8.3 *TDC and public-sector requirement targets versus realisations, 1974–1980*

| | TDC | | | | Public-sector requirements | |
| | Targets | | Realisations | | | |
Year	Flows (billions)	Percentage changes	Flows (billions)	Percentage changes	Targets (billions)	Realisation (billions)
1974	22,400	18.6	20,015	16.6	9,200	8,796
1975	24,700	17.6	35,633	25.4	8,000	14,237
1976	29,500	17.5	34,048	20.2	13,800	24,200
1977	30,600	15.1	35,703	17.6	13,100	17,923
1978	38,000	12.9	49,240	20.6	–	31,707
1979	53,000	18.4	53,252	18.5	31,000	28,503
1980	59,300	17.4	63,150	18.5	37,900	34,008

Source: Caranza and Fazio (1984).

compensatory movements were deemed unfeasible, because they would have quickly deprived the private sector of any credit, considering the rapid increase of government deficits in the 1970s. The final effect was that TDC accommodated fiscal policy almost in full.

Table 8.3 illustrates this observation. The first columns compare targets with realised values of TDC. For three of the years under consideration, the difference between realisations and targets was contained within two percentage points; for the remaining years, the differential was wider. In 1975 and 1978, the discrepancy reached about 50 per cent of the initial budget. The second part of table 8.3 provides information about the public-sector requirement which in 1974 fell short of target; a similar pattern holds for TDC. In the subsequent three years, public-sector requirements exceeded target values; again, a similar pattern holds for TDC. In 1979–80, public-sector requirements fell short of projected values, and TDC expanded in line with the monetary authorities' objectives.

Consider now the reasons for the discrepancy between realisations and target values of TDC. Targets for the public-sector requirements were not set in 1978, but we may consider 1975, when the discrepancy between realised and target values of TDC was very large. The monetary authorities had no difficulty admitting that the TDC's dependence upon government deficits, and the consequent loss of control over credit flows, were the result of a strategy aimed at containing the political costs of budget deficits. In a retrospective article Fazio (1984, pp. 707–8) wrote:

one thing is the analytical validity of a target, another how this is implemented. In our specific case, the deviation [of TDC from its target] is dependent upon economic policy choices and not on technical difficulties. The fact that Treasury has been allowed to finance its deficits during the past few years, regularly in excess of budgeted and reported levels and with no serious repercussions on the economy, has been criticised by some observers. . . . If Parliament sets specific budget deficit targets, even in contrast with the executive's announcements, it is not possible for public officials, albeit with large decision powers, to disregard such a target or to operate inconsistently relative to these norms.

BI's 1973 Annual Report contained the passage we have cited at the beginning of this chapter. We have given sufficient prominence to these citations because they are highly representative of the prevailing attitude in BI, that is, one of monetary policy subservience (or endogeneity) to fiscal authorities. Our *History* shows that monetary accommodation has been the most recurrent principle of Italian monetary policy.

Interest rates and monetary aggregates

The policy of monetary accommodation has always required the pegging of interest rates. This is the reason the TDC model attributed a secondary or insignificant role to interest rates. Credit had to be rationed through an administrative measure called 'massimale' (ceiling). The logic of the model proceeds as follows. Given public deficits, a contraction of TDC implies a reduction of private-sector credit and, hence, a lower investment flow. Income declines and so does the demand for financial assets; lower income, on the other hand, raises the current-account balance and the supply of financial assets. In this manner equilibrium is re-established (Cotula and Micossi 1977; Penati and Tullio 1983).

The TDC model was predicated on the premise that the link between money and nominal income was loose and variable and that there would be no point in controlling monetary aggregates. Fazio (1969, p. 105) attributed the poor quality of the transmission mechanism from monetary base to income to the inelastic demand for credit:

credit supply is more sensitive than demand to interest rate levels. This produces the effect that monetary base variations, if not accompanied by changes in credit demand, have a limited impact on the actual credit amount.

Governor Carli, in a speech delivered in Brescia in 1973 (Mengarelli 1976, p. 258), brings into question the very stability of the demand for money:

The monetary aggregate . . . consists at present of different assets with regard to their use and type of investors. For some of them, such as legal currency, the role as a medium of payment is dominant and its relationship to income is extremely stable.

Other assets, such as interest-bearing deposits, are for the most part forms of investment more or less stable. Their relation to income is less stable. There are no simple rules, therefore, which link the volume of payment media to monetary income value. Attempts by monetary authorities to accelerate or slowdown the money growth rate invariably produce inverse movements in interest rate levels and the flow of funds through non-banking institutions. This means that, within limits which vary according to countries and circumstances, changes in volume of payment media bring about opposite variations in velocity of circulation. As a result, the impact of money stock movements on volume of transactions is in part mitigated.

It is worth noting that the TDC model ignores the integration, partial or complete, of the financial markets in the world. The assumption of financial segmentation makes it easy for the model to ignore the role of interest rates and to disavow the use of monetary aggregates; at the same time, financial segmentation accentuates the authorities' propensity to depreciate the lira to correct external imbalances. The latter are identified by current-account deficits (Azzolini and Marani 1982). Had financial integration been explicitly recognised, the model would have had to concentrate on the overall balance of payments, rather than on the current account. The introduction of capital movements in the analysis would have made it impossible to ignore the role of interest rates. Above all, it would have been necessary to recognise the relationship between the money and the overall external imbalance.

The 'massimale' and portfolio constraints

We have seen that the quantitative loan ceiling or 'massimale' was justified by the ultimate and declared purpose of monetary policy to keep interest rates low. Since this objective became elusive under the pressure of rising budget deficits and debt-to-income ratios, the authorities found it necessary to further constrain banks on the asset side of the balance sheet. The basic problem was the need to create a large demand for government securities at low interest rates. A captive market could be easily created by obliging the Italian banking system to invest a fixed amount of its earning assets in government securities. The *vincolo di portafoglio* or 'portfolio constraint' was intended to achieve exactly that. It turned out to be a bureaucratic mess, involving a Soviet-style succession of increasingly complex regulations.

The initial portfolio constraint came to life in June of 1973 when banks were forced to purchase long-dated securities for an amount equal to 6 per cent of bank deposits as of 31 December 1972. Simultaneously, BI issued regulations that determined the maximum growth of aggregate loans. As the constraints were affecting various sectors of the economy differently, the pressure mounted to make the regulations more sector or firm specific.

Soon the monetary authorities fell into the business of micro managing credit allocations; the criteria for the allocations ranged from whether the firm was private or public to firm size. The resulting web of micro credit allocations was arbitrary and reflected the bargaining power of the various groups more than their respective value added in the economy. In 1980 banks that violated rules on credit allocations were subject to placing a non-interest-bearing deposit with BI for an amount equal to the loan in excess of the ceiling. Also in 1980 the portfolio constraint was extended to include debt issued by (mostly) government-owned mortgage and agricultural credit institutions.[7]

The long-run result of this process of 'banking by regulations' was to destroy bankers' human capital, undermine loan origination and loan monitoring activities, and reduce the efficiency of financial markets. The rules of the game were penalising risk taking and rewarding bureaucratic behaviour aimed at interpreting and satisfying regulations on credit ceilings and portfolio constraints. The TDC model continued for some time to guide monetary authorities, despite the fact that its flaws had been fully and explicitly recognised by the new Governor Paolo Baffi.

Italy's monetary and financial isolation

We saw how the predominance of fiscal impulses manifested itself through a high level of deficit monetisation and domestic savings channelled to the public sector to keep interest rates low relative to the inflation rate. Two factors would have automatically emerged in an open economy – where complete freedom of movement of goods, services and capital existed – to make the consequences of fiscal dominance more conspicuous and unsustainable: the depreciation of the lira in the foreign exchange markets, and the alignment of domestic real interest rates to the level prevailing abroad. In the absence of this alignment, domestic savings would have been diverted to foreign investments, with a resulting loss in foreign reserves or upward pressure on domestic real interest rates. Inevitably, the open economy would expose the contradiction between a spendthrift fiscal policy and the monetary policy response to mitigate its effects on credit and financial markets.

One way out of the impasse is to put a wedge between domestic and foreign financial markets. The Italian authorities did just that during the seventies. Old restrictions on foreign exchange and capital flows were tightened and new ones were added to insulate Italian monetary and financial markets from international ones. These limitations must be viewed simply as the natural complement of the *massimali* and the portfolio constraints discussed above, that is, as administrative measures aimed at containing the

Table 8.4 *Balance of payments, 1970–1980 (billion lire)*

Year	Current account	Capital movements	Balance
1970	476	−148	222
1971	981	−374	491
1972	1,169	−1,571	−748
1973	−1,473	1,737	−206
1974	−5,212	1,559	−3,715
1975	−377	−527	−1,439
1976	−2,343	1,484	−1,531
1977	2,175	−54	1,730
1978	5,261	1,319	6,996
1979	4,553	−2,404	1,824
1980	−8,291	2,749	−6,258

Source: BI R.A. various years.

upward pressure on domestic interest rates. In fact, domestic real rates were negative for extended periods of time and lower than those abroad.[8]

We recall that Italian monetary authorities had retained vast discretionary power over foreign exchange transactions. Italian foreign exchange law had been inspired by two principles. The first was that the Italian Exchange Office, but essentially BI, was entrusted with the monopoly of all foreign exchange transactions. Individuals, firms and banks did not have the unconditional right to hold foreign currencies, foreign-currency denominated assets, or to be indebted abroad. Exceptions required explicit approval by the monetary authorities. The second principle was that what was not explicitly permitted was considered forbidden.

To have a better appreciation of the administrative measures introduced by the authorities, it is best to keep in mind the balance-of-payments data for the period under examination (table 8.4). The first balance-of-payments crisis began in 1972, before the upsurge in oil prices, and continued until the end of 1976. The second crisis exploded in 1980 and lasted until 1982, with the overall imbalance swinging from a surplus of 7,000 to a deficit of 6,300 billion lire between 1978 and 1980. As we shall see in the following section, these sharp balance-of-payments reversals reflected the combination of internal and international developments.

As far back as March 1969, Italian credit institutions were already forbidden to participate in foreign securities placements. The monetary authorities had permitted foreign mutual funds to operate in Italy, but on the condition that at least half of their portfolios be invested in Italian securities. In February 1970, payment terms relating to imports and exports were shortened; credit for repatriated banknotes could be obtained only at BI's Head Office (with the obvious intent of raising the cost of capital outflows).

At the end of 1971, investors were impeded from purchasing unlisted foreign securities. Ceilings were set on loans to and by non-residents. Banks were compelled to balance foreign assets and foreign liabilities on a daily basis; and their forward transactions were subject to ceilings. To other entities forward transactions were limited to 'visible' trade. Even tourists were not spared: their travel allowance could not exceed 1 million lire during a given year.

As had happened in the sixties, monetary authorities resorted to moral suasion to encourage government agencies and banks to either raise funds abroad (1970) or repay indebtedness (1971). The purpose of these 'exhortations' was to offset the behaviour of current-account items.

The exchange restrictions led inevitably to an illegal outflow of capital. This took place primarily by the overinvoicing of imports, the underinvoicing of exports, or the outright physical transfer of banknotes abroad. In June 1972 the authorities proclaimed the inconvertibility of repatriated Italian lire.

A two-tier foreign exchange market was created in January 1973. The authorities continued to intervene in the exchange market to stabilise the commercial exchange rate, leaving the financial rate to fluctuate freely. At the same time, payment terms for exports and imports were tightened once more. In February, as the dollar began to depreciate against other currencies, the commercial rate was also allowed to fluctuate; however, it traded below the financial rate for the duration of the two-tier market, that is, until almost the end of March.

Arbitrage activities involving different currencies became more prevalent. In July 1973 the authorities tried to put a stop to these activities by compelling banks to hedge separately their dollar positions and positions denominated in European currencies. Investors in foreign financial assets were obliged to keep a non-interest-bearing deposit for 50 per cent of the investment value. Italian banknotes were quoted abroad at a discount of 7 to 11 per cent in relation to the official rate. Tourism became a convenient way to export capital abroad after the June 1972 decision. With a view to stop this trade of Italian banknotes abroad, the authorities introduced a ceiling of 20,000 lire for cash carried by repatriating residents and non-residents leaving Italy (March 1974). This amount was raised to 35,000 in May 1974. Only bureaucrats of planned economies could conceive a micro-regulation of this kind.

In May 1974 importers were required to deposit 50 per cent of the import value in a non-interest-bearing account. This requirement was removed in

March 1975. On 20 January 1976, the authorities made the drastic decision to suspend foreign exchange trading, but not before wasting a very large amount of foreign reserves in an attempt to curb the depreciation of the lira which started again to lose value when trading resumed the following March. In April, foreign exchange violations were brought within the domain of criminal law. In May, the authorities extended the requirement of a non-interest-bearing deposit of 50 per cent to all payments abroad. Banks were also obliged to balance forward transactions with non-residents. In October, all residents had to pay a tax of 10 per cent on purchases of foreign currency. This tax, which was equivalent to a lira devaluation, and the non-interest-bearing deposit were removed in February and April 1977, respectively, when it became clear that the business community had found a way of circumventing the law by leaving the proceeds of exports abroad to pay for imports.[9]

In summary, the monetary authorities' subservience to fiscal authority led to a series of foreign exchange restrictions, which severely limited the freedom of individuals, firms and banks.

Business cycles, the external constraint and monetary policy

Determinants of the current account

Italian economic policy has traditionally responded to developments in the balance of payments; this was especially true in the seventies. In table 8.5 we quantified three factors which affect the current account of the balance of payments. The first is the difference between domestic and foreign economic growth. Given the strong positive relationship between imports and domestic output, an increase in the output growth differential exerts a negative influence on the current-account balance. During the seventies, Italian real gross domestic product grew, on average, at approximately the same rate as other industrialised countries'; the Italian economy grew more rapidly during the years 1973–4 and 1979–80, and less rapidly in 1975 and 1977–8. The data in the table underscore the expected negative correlation between the growth differential and the direction of the current-account balance.

The second factor shown in the table is competitiveness, which is measured by changes in the ratio of Italian export prices to those of other industrialised countries, all expressed in dollars. An alternative measure of competitiveness is given by the real exchange rate, with a positive value denoting a real depreciation of the lira (see the fifth column). The average values of these two measures of competitiveness were 0.53 and –0.52, respectively. This means that, on average, either Italy lost competitiveness or the lira appreciated in real terms. The loss in competitiveness

Table 8.5 *The determinants of the current account, 1970–1980*

Year	Current account (bn lire)	Growth differential (% change)	Competitiveness (% change)	Real exch. rate (% change)	Terms of trade (% change)
1970	476	2.4	−1.0	–	0.5
1971	981	−2.0	0.6	0.5	−0.2
1972	1,169	−2.2	−0.3	0.3	0.3
1973	−1,473	1.0	−2.3	4.6	−12.1
1974	−5,212	3.5	2.4	−10.4	−26.5
1975	−337	−3.2	−0.6	2.4	5.5
1976	−2,343	0.9	−4.0	2.5	−3.3
1977	2,175	−2.0	4.4	−1.5	3.2
1978	5,261	−1.3	−1.3	3.3	2.3
1979	4,553	1.6	4.2	−3.4	−2.2
1980	−8,291	2.6	3.7	−3.4	−7.8

Source: Chapter 1.

strengthened the effect of growth differential during 1972, 1974–5 and 1978–80.

The third factor shown in the table is the change in the terms of trade, defined as the ratio of export to import prices. With Italy being primarily a net importer of raw materials and semi-finished products, which are then used as inputs for exported goods and services, the terms of trade indicate the profitability of the exporting sector and the attractiveness of producing in that sector relative to the non-traded sector of the economy.[10] The two oil shocks of 1973–4 and 1979–80 were disastrous for a transforming and oil-dependent economy like Italy; the terms of trade tumbled, with annual average decline of 3.7 per cent.

In conclusion, at least two of the three factors moved in the expected direction when the current-account balance deteriorated, with the three factors acting in unison during the most acute crises of 1974 and 1980.

Pressures on the lira in the exchange market

Figures 8.1 through 8.3 address three aspects of the exchange market: the lira–dollar spot rate, the three-month forward discount of the lira against the dollar, and the differential between the three-month rate of interest on Eurolira deposits (the off-shore rate) and the yield on the three-month Italian Treasury bills (the on-shore rate). The data are monthly and can capture a great deal of the dynamic information present in the time series.

Figure 8.1 The lira–dollar exchange rate, 1970–1980 (average monthly value)
Source: Weekly Review, Harris Bank.

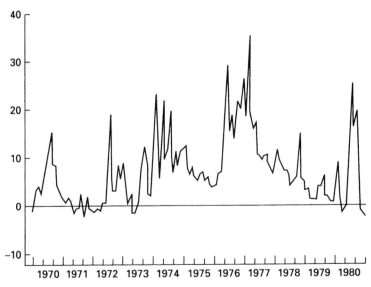

Figure 8.2 Three-month forward discount of the lira relative to the dollar,
1970–1980 (annual percentage changes)
Source: Weekly Review, Harris Bank.

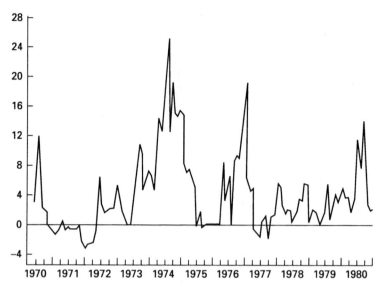

Figure 8.3 Difference between three-month off-shore and on-shore interest rates, 1970–1980
Source: Weekly Review, Harris Bank and Bollettino Statistico della Banca d'Italia.

The lira entered a period of turbulence and depreciation toward the end of 1973. A second phase of sharp depreciation took place at the beginning of 1976, when the rate jumped from about 700 to 900 and then fluctuated between 840 and 900 from 1976 to 1980. The lira was at a forward discount against the dollar for most of the seventies. The discount was particularly high between 1973 and 1975 and, more so, between 1976 and 1978, reflecting brisk speculative activities against the currency. Another peak occurred in the middle of 1980. The difference between off-shore and onshore Italian interest rates was positive from 1973 to the early part of 1975, for most of 1976, and in 1980. These differentials clearly indicated that the Italian financial markets were separated from financial markets abroad.

Monetary and business cycles

The final piece of information of this section pertains to the monetary cycles. In table 8.6 we indicate the turning points of the adjusted monetary base measured in terms of its annual growth rates.

Growth rates at peaks show an upward trend after 1971; by contrast, growth rates at trough display a declining trend. The diverging patterns of high and low growth rates denote a process of money creation which

Table 8.6 *Monetary cycles, 1970–1980*

Turning points	Date:quarter	Annual growth rate Adjusted monetary base
Peak	1971:2	24.1
Trough	1972:4	10.5
Peak	1973:4	18.7
Trough	1975:1	7.2
Peak	1976:1	25.2
Trough	1977:2	7.9
Peak	1978:4	27.9
Trough	1980:4	5.0

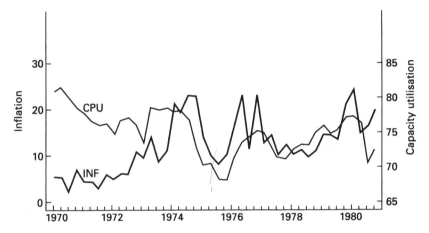

Figure 8.4 Capacity utilisation (CPU) and CPI inflation rate (INF), 1970–1980
Source: OCSE, Main Econmic Indicators, various numbers.

became more volatile over time. In fact, the spread between high and low growth rates of the adjusted monetary base in the fourth monetary cycle was more than twice as large as the spread of the second monetary cycle that coincided with the first oil shock. Figure 8.4 aids us in comparing the monetary cycle with the inflation and the business cycles. The capacity utilisation series shows low points in 1973:1, 1975:4 and 1980:3, and these coincide with the low inflation rate points.

Our interpretation of the relationship between the monetary cycles and the business cycles of the sixties becomes even more relevant in the seventies. Monetary policy in the seventies was very expansive on average, with the justification that it had to stimulate production and investments. It was also very cyclical. Typically, the expansion process would go so far as to precipitate a balance-of-payments crisis. At that point, the need to act expeditiously would prevent the authorities from employing traditional monetary instruments. Instead, they would resort to administrative measures such as quantitative ceilings on bank loans and restrictions on foreign exchange and capital movements. Then, as soon as the crisis would peter out, the authorities would go back to pushing on the monetary accelerator and start a new expansion. In brief, a policy of stop and go was the norm.

In chapter 7 we saw that the 1966–9 interest rate pegging policy contributed to the 1969–70 balance-of-payments crisis. By 1970 a new expansive monetary cycle had already begun. On this aspect, Fazio (1979, p. 288) wrote:

Monetary policy was restrictive during almost the entire first half of 1970 . . . but a clear reversal occurred by the summer, in conjunction with the improvement of the foreign exchange situation and a set-back in output growth.

As usual, the correction of an external deficit and the desire to speed up output growth paved the way for an acceleration of monetary and credit aggregates. A reduction in interest rates also followed. The offshore–onshore differential of interest rates reached 12 per cent in 1970 (figure 8.3). It is difficult to understand why the central bank would want to strive for low interest rates when capital was flowing out of the country on a net basis and the forward discount on the lira exceeded 15 per cent. In 1971, the capital account balance deteriorated by a factor of two. In 1972, the net capital outflow rose to about five times that of 1971 and brought about a negative overall balance-of-payments deficit.

On 24 April 1972 some member countries of the European Community agreed to contain their bilateral exchange-rate fluctuations within a band of 2.25 per cent.[11] But already in June, Italy, pressed by a massive capital outflow, requested an exemption from some clauses of the agreement. The forward discount on the lira rose, while the differential between off-shore and on-shore lira rates returned to positive values. The difference between domestic and foreign long-term interest rates widened as well; in 1973, German rates of interest exceeded the Italian ones by seven percentage points.

The authorities' priority to stimulate domestic production was in direct conflict with exchange-rate stability. As international ties could not be disregarded for long, the authorities resorted to administrative measures. As already indicated, repatriated Italian currency was proclaimed inconvertible between June 1972 and January 1973 and a two-tier foreign exchange market was established. The so-called 'financial' lira had already lost 6 per cent in relation to the 'commercial' lira by the early days of the new regime.

In 1973, a deep domestic recession, low interest rates and expectations of further lira depreciations (which also encouraged inventory hoarding) brought about a sustained demand for imports. The authorities relied on the two-tier foreign exchange system to place a wedge between low domestic interest rates and capital outflows. Later they used portfolio constraints to prevent a collapse of the domestic demand for long-term securities. The two decisions were complementary: the first confined savings to the domestic market, the second channelled these savings towards government securities.

The connection between an expansive monetary policy and the external deficits was never in dispute. Nonetheless, the authorities postponed taking corrective decisions. After conceding that monetary base creation was 'excessive' at the outbreak of the energy crisis, Fazio (1979, p. 295) went on to say that: 'it did not appear to be necessary to drastically modify the course of monetary policy'. The oil crisis came at a time when monetary policy was decidedly expansive. The combined effect of the negative supply shock and monetary largesse triggered a current-account deficit and a sharp rise in domestic prices. Yet once more, BI preferred to stimulate aggregate spending at the expense of an external imbalance.

To regain control of the situation, the authorities obtained a loan from the EC, signed a stand-by agreement with the International Monetary Fund, introduced a non-interest-bearing deposit on imports, and launched a credit squeeze (BI, R.A. 1974, pp. 61–3 and 250–1). The latter turned out to be stronger than what was agreed with the IMF.[12] The partly unexpected credit tightening made the on-going recession of 1975 worse, but improved the external imbalance.

As so often occurred in the past, pressure was exerted on the monetary authorities to stimulate the production process. There was no reason to reflate in light of the large cumulative external deficits Italy had suffered from 1972 to 1974. Furthermore, domestic and international business cycles were not synchronised in 1974. The novelty was that, this time, BI considered it premature to stimulate domestic spending. Government, however, held a different view; in the summer, monetary and fiscal policies became strongly expansionary (Fazio 1984). Regulations on banks' lending activities were revoked and subsidised export credit was introduced, which enabled banks to automatically rediscount 50 per cent of such credit at the central bank. The monetary base creation accelerated and, within a few months, money market interest rates declined from 15 to 8 per cent.[13]

Economic activity recovered at the end of 1975, with a resulting increase in imports. 1976 turned out to be the most chaotic year of the post-war period. The year started with the country holding a stock of international reserves equal to less than two weeks of imports. A political crisis and adverse expectations on the lira were so strong as to compel the authorities to take the drastic decision of suspending foreign exchange trading activities for two months. The monetary authorities were shaken by these events. Their initial reaction was to tighten monetary policy, but they ended up taking half-baked measures. In the words of Governor Baffi (1976):

the appropriateness not to hinder the productive recovery, which was beginning to take place after the 1975 stagnation, led us to mitigate the intensity of the restriction. In the attempt to reconcile two conflicting objectives, monetary policy's sphere of action therefore became severely constrained.

Fazio (1979, p. 306) admits that BI's actions were 'not sufficiently restrictive'.[14]

The real bottleneck was the political crisis which impeded the adoption of stronger measures. In March a new government was formed, whose priority continued to be the promotion of economic activity. The automatic rediscount of export credits at the central bank was discontinued and the discount rate was raised by four additional percentage points. This, however, proved to be a very small increase in relation to the seriousness of the situation. Foreign exchange trading activities were resumed, but the lira lost 5.8 per cent in March and 5.7 per cent in April, despite the fact that the authorities intervened with 1 billion dollars – i.e., the entire proceeds of the EC loan – to support the currency. The lira depreciation was both nominal and real. During the year, the forward discount of the lira with respect to the dollar exceeded 35 per cent on an annual basis. As we discussed earlier, a number of administrative measures were progressively introduced: a travel allowance for Italian tourists going abroad, mandatory-term payments for imports and exports, a requirement to finance in foreign currencies short-term export receivables, compulsory non-interest-bearing deposits, a specific tax on purchases of foreign-currency assets, and the assignment of foreign exchange violations to the jurisdiction of the criminal code. The official discount rate was first increased to 12 per cent and subsequently to 15 per cent, but remained negative in real terms. At the year's end, real income had grown by 5.6 per cent, but the balance-of-payments position remained precarious.

In 1977, three facts stood out. First, pressures from the government induced banks to substantially increase their exposures to foreign lenders. As a result, an inflow of liquid foreign capital enabled the authorities to cover deficits accumulated in the first part of the year. Second, for the first time since 1971 the balance of payments showed a global surplus, thanks to a production slowdown both in absolute terms and in relation to foreign countries, and an improvement in the terms of trade (table 8.4). Third, there was a sizable reduction in the forward discount of the lira with respect to the dollar and a flattening of the interest rate differential (figures 8.2 and 8.3).

The continuation of low rates of economic activity in 1978, coupled with a further improvement in the terms of trade, produced a rise in the current-account balance of approximately 3,000 billion lire. The negative interest rate differential remained small and favoured the realisation of a positive capital-account balance. The overall external position reached the highest value recorded during the seventies.

Starting with 1978, monetary policy turned its attention again to stimulating output. Already in the summer, the differential between international and domestic interest rates began to grow. At the year's end, net capital outflows totalled 2,400 billion lire. Domestic production recovered, much more than in other countries, and the terms of trade deteriorated. It was not a surprise, therefore, that the current account went from a comfortable surplus to the worst deficit of the decade. This imbalance stemmed from the combined effect of the second oil crisis and highly unsynchronised business cycles at home and abroad. In many ways, it was a repetition of 1974 events. At the end of 1980, the current-account deficit was 8,300 billion lire and the overall balance-of-payments deficit 6,300 billion lire. Predictably, monetary policy would soon become restrictive – in the spring of 1981 – in response to the external constraint.

Conclusions

The striking feature of the seventies was the monetary authorities' acquiescence to government deficits, which skyrocketed primarily because of a surge in transfer payments. The authorities could not or did not want to prevent monetisation of a large portion of those deficits. In practice, BI adopted a policy aimed at minimising the political cost of budget deficits.

Monetary policy's acquiescence was formalised by introducing Total Domestic Credit as the primary intermediate target. Within the TDC's framework, public-sector financing requirements were taken as an exogenous variable. Initially, targets could be met by restricting credit to the private sector; later, they simply became impractical to reach.

Credit ceilings, portfolio restrictions and controls on capital movements and foreign exchange transactions were adopted to channel the economy's savings to finance the large and expanding stock of government debt and to prevent capital outflows.

Unfortunately, the goal of minimising the political cost of budget deficits was in itself an incentive to generate a higher growth of government expenditures. This, in turn, was conducive to the instability of monetary aggregates, an inflationary process never before experienced in peacetime, and a rapid succession of massive foreign exchange crises. Finally, this policy lowered the efficiency of the financial sector and heightened Italy's isolation from international financial markets.

9   Italy in the eighties: towards central bank independence

We have seen that the leitmotif of Italian monetary history has been fiscal dominance, that is the supremacy of the Executive in monetary policy matters. The genesis of fiscal dominance goes back to 1 May 1866 when legislation was passed that prevented banks of issue from altering the discount rate without prior government authorisation. The same legislation decided that the Banca Nazionale would grant a loan of Lit 250 million to Treasury, with the amount to be credited to a newly opened Treasury current account (*conto corrente di Tesoreria*). This account eventually evolved into a virtually automatic mechanism through which the Italian government could finance large portions of budget deficits. Fiscal dominance became very acute in the 1970s under the Governorship of Guido Carli (see chapter 8). The appointment of Paolo Baffi in 1975 represented an intellectual turning point in the history of fiscal dominance. But it was up to Carlo Azeglio Ciampi, who succeeded Baffi in 1980, to put into practice many of the ideas cherished by Baffi. Thus, the struggle of BI to acquire monetary policy autonomy is the principal theme of this chapter. The European Monetary System (EMS), which Italy joined under special conditions, and the Maastricht Treaty of 1991 must be seen in the light of this long overdue process of giving the Italian central bank a degree of independence it had never before been granted.

At the time of writing, BI has completed the process of central bank independence, consistent with the provisions of the Maastricht Treaty. Yet, two critical issues need to be resolved. First, how is BI going to use her new independence? Will she pursue price level stability or will she target multiple and conflicting objectives as in the past? The new Governor of BI, Antonio Fazio, has yet to clarify the Bank's objectives. The second issue pertains to the fiscal correction which is now in its infancy. The lessons from the *History* suggest that the quality of monetary policy cannot be divorced from the course of public finance. Price level stability is likely to depend more on the stabilisation of the debt-to-GDP ratio than on central bank independence.

This chapter starts with a brief discussion of the EMS, an 'external' event that promotes a transformation of BI into a more conservative central bank, while at the same time giving impetus to the Italian government to grant BI more autonomy from the Treasury. We then discuss the extent to which BI gained autonomy from the Treasury and became a more conservative central bank. In the subsequent section we quantify the extent of the Italian disinflation relative to six other original EMS signatories. Then we assess the Italian fiscal correction of the late eighties and relate it to those of other EMS countries.

The main conclusions are that the Italian fiscal authorities significantly reduced the primary deficits during the second half of the eighties; that the fiscal correction occurred after BI was granted a larger degree of independence from the Treasury; and that the fiscal correction will have to proceed much farther if Italy is to join the European Monetary Union. Our *History* formally ends with 1991. Several important events occurred between 1991 and the time of this publication to justify a postscript wherein we detail the completion of the process of central bank independence and the reasons underlying the Italian exit from the Exchange Rate Mechanism (ERM) in September 1992. Our conclusion is that this currency crisis is not too different from others that occurred throughout the 131 years. The critical ingredients were an inflation rate stubbornly higher than the core EMS countries, and the market's skepticism about the government's ability to stabilise the debt-to-GDP ratio.

The European Monetary System

The EMS consists of four main institutional elements: (1) a basket currency, the ECU, (2) the ERM, (3) credit provisions among the participating central banks, and (4) the pooling of reserve assets among the members.[1] The cornerstone of the EMS is the agreement to limit bilateral exchange-rate fluctuations within margins of ±2.25 per cent around predetermined central parities.[2] Italy managed to obtain the wider margins of +6 per cent for the lira in 1978; only on 5 January 1990, did the lira enter the narrow band.[3] Baffi (1989) provides an informative account of the hectic negotiations that won Italy the wider margins. In essence, the Italian position, and in particular the Governor's, was that the ±2.25 per cent margins would be too much of a straight jacket, forcing Italy to a real appreciation of the lira and to a deterioration of the trade account. The wider band, it was argued, would make the need for frequent realignments less pressing. Baffi's arguments eventually won and Italy was granted the wider band.[4]

The ERM was not supposed to be a rigid system of fixed exchange rates. There was a common understanding that the central parities would be adjustable to changing economic conditions and the relative performance of the participating economies. Early proponents of the EMS stressed that the frequency of realignments should not be regarded as a criterion of success or failure of the system (Commission of the EC 1979, p. 78; van Ypersele 1979, p. 9). From 1979 to 1990 there were twelve realignments: two in 1979, two in 1981, two in 1982, one in 1983, one in 1985, two in 1986, one in 1987, and the 'technical' adjustment of the Italian lira from the wide to the narrow band in 1990; for details refer to Fratianni and von Hagen (1992, table 2.2). Clearly, the EMS was a much more flexible system in the early period (1979–83) than in the subsequent years (1984–91). With the parity realignment of 1987 the EMS actually became a *de facto* fixed exchange-rate system (Giavazzi and Spaventa 1990).

There is a vast literature on the EMS and its functioning. It is beyond our objective to go into details. For present purposes we have to think of the EMS as a specific form of policy coordination, brought about by participating countries giving up some monetary policy independence. More specifically, if the EMS were to behave like an exchange-rate union among N countries, N-1 central parities would be predetermined, leaving the union with one degree of freedom to choose the union's common monetary policy. This degree of freedom would determine the union's response to factors affecting all members in the short run, but in the long run it would uniquely serve to determine the union's inflation rate.

While there are various ways to implement so constrained a system, it is useful to consider two extreme solutions. The first is that there can be in the union at most one monetary authority who determines its policy independently of the other members. This is the hegemonic solution by which the largest or most important member sets its own money supply growth rate and, thus, the union's inflation rate. The United Kingdom in the classical gold-standard period and the United States in the Bretton Woods system were interpreted as exercising hegemonic power (Kindleberger 1973; Keohane 1984; Eichengreen 1989). Many authors have described the EMS in terms of this solution, assigning to Germany the role of the hegemon (Giavazzi and Giovannini 1989). According to this view, high-inflation countries like Italy have used the EMS to achieve a lower inflation rate under the leadership of the Bundesbank. The latter can set autonomously the money supply, whereas the other members cannot do so. A country like Italy is bound to let its money supply adjust endogenously to the constraint of maintaining a fixed lira/deutsche mark parity.

The other extreme solution to the Nth degree-of-freedom constraint is that members of the union cooperate with one another, thus making monetary policy the outcome of a joint decision-making process. According to this view, coordination determines the level of money stock in the union and the amount each country can create (Fratianni and von Hagen 1992, chapter 6).

The empirical evidence is that the EMS has worked differently for different member countries, that is, asymmetries have been at work. More specifically, there is a core of countries, consisting of Germany, Belgium and the Netherlands, which has acted more homogeneously and more independently than the rest of the EMS. France and Italy, in contrast, have had weak positions in the EMS monetary policy making relative to their size and economic importance. These asymmetries are not the same as the German Bundesbank dominating the EMS (Fratianni and von Hagen 1992, chapter 6).

In sum, Italy's participation in the EMS imposed a new constraint on the ability of the central bank to conduct a monetary policy independently of the other members of the exchange-rate agreement. A completely independent monetary policy is bound to create conflict with the exchange-rate commitment, thus forcing the central bank to choose to either pursue the independent monetary policy and seek a parity realignment, or maintain the existing parities and adjust monetary policy accordingly. Since there were 12 parity realignments, central banks must have pursued combinations of these two options rather than either one in isolation.

From 1979 to 1990 Italy accumulated very large inflation differentials *vis-à-vis* the other six EMS countries that were original signatories of the agreement (Belgium, Denmark, France, Germany, Ireland and the Netherlands). These differentials led to a depreciation of the lira which compensated only in part for the cumulative inflation differential. Consequently, the lira appreciated considerably in real terms with respect to the other EMS participants (table 9.1). For example, over the 12-year period Italy inflated 98 percentage points more than Germany. The nominal depreciation of the lira in relation to the mark was 56 per cent, leaving a real appreciation of 42 per cent terms. This outcome was the result of a policy decision to use real exchange-rate appreciations as a method of squeezing inflation in the country. The natural historical parallel is the 1920s when Mussolini used the exchange rate as a way to bring about an industrial restructuring. In the 1980s, as in the 1920s, the authorities wanted to signal to the export industry not to count on home-currency depreciation to restore margins and profits. The industry had to bite the bullet and implement cost-cutting strategies to remain competitive in international markets.

The loss of competitiveness of Italian industry in the 1980s was considerable, and can be seen from the deterioration in the trade account and the upward shift of non-traded goods prices relative to traded goods prices. During the period 1970–9 the trade account had an average annual deficit of Lit 1,070 billion; in the subsequent 12 years the average trade deficit almost

Table 9.1 *Inflation and real exchange rates*
cumulative bilateral values vis-à-vis *Italy,*
1979–1990 (per cent)

	Inflation	Real appreciation of the lira
Belgium	77.4	48.8
Denmark	53.6	34.8
France	46.8	31.1
Germany	98.2	42.0
Ireland	34.1	18.8
Netherlands	99.5	47.8

Notes:
Inflation is measured by the rate of change of the
consumption deflator; the real exchange-rate change
is the difference between nominal exchange-rate
changes and the inflation differences.
Source: Fratianni and von Hagen (1992, tables 2.3
and 2.4).

quintupled to Lit 5,388 billion.[5] Yet, real income growth differentials
between Italy and the other 6 EMS countries did not change appreciably.[6]
Hence, the real lira appreciation was responsible for much of the increase of
the Italian trade deficit.

The sharp appreciation of the lira was also responsible for a sharp movement in relative prices towards non-traded goods, thus favouring an expansion of this sector at the expense of the traded goods sector. The explanation
goes as follows. The traded goods industry competes at the world level and
cannot raise prices beyond those charged by its trading countries. On the
other hand, the non-traded goods sector (mostly services) is sheltered from
foreign competition. With a fixed exchange-rate commitment, unit labour
cost increases in the traded goods industry in excess of those prevailing
abroad cannot be passed on to higher prices; the domestic export industry
must either reduce costs or accept lower profit margins. The non-traded
goods sector, instead, does not face international competition and can raise
prices if unit labour costs increase in excess of unit labour cost increases in
the traded industry. There are no published data on traded and non-traded
goods price indices, but it is possible to create such indices by identifying
traded goods and non-traded goods sectors. This is what Savona (1993)
does and he concludes that over the 1982–91 period the ratio of non-traded

to traded goods' prices rose by 35 per cent. A change of this size is bound to provide strong incentives to move resources away from the competitive and high-productivity international sector to the protected and low-productivity domestic sector.[7]

In sum, the operation of the EMS meant that Italy could disinflate relative to the other members by letting the real value of the lira appreciate. Given the relative rigidity of domestic wages and prices, the real exchange-rate appreciation implied a deterioration in the international competitiveness of Italian industry and a shift of resources into the low-productivity sheltered sector.

A more independent and conservative Banca d'Italia

We have argued in much of our *History* that the Banca Nazionale first and the Banca d'Italia later often pursued accommodation with respect to the fiscal authorities. During the tenure of Governor Carli the conduct of monetary policy became fully subservient to the objectives of fiscal policy. We labelled that period as one of fiscal dominance. With the advent of Paolo Baffi in 1975 as the successor to Guido Carli, the intellectual climate in BI changed. Baffi, while unable to implement many of the ideas he was professing, represented a breath of fresh air in the strongly Keynesian tradition of BI. To better understand the significance and depth of this philosophical change, it behooves us to dwell on the thinking of Baffi and of Carlo Azeglio Ciampi who succeeded him at the end of 1980.

Paolo Baffi

Baffi's intellectual influence appears from 'his' first BI Annual Report in which the Governor tackles the link between money and economic growth. As if to challenge the fundamental tenets of the dominant school of thought which would like to continue using money as an engine of economic growth, Baffi states that (BI R.A. 1975, p. 426):

the Italian society . . . must confront the problem of increasing the supply side of the economy with tools that prove to be less facile and illusory than the mere expansion of monetary aggregates.

The Governor is openly critical of theories that postulate the existence of a stable trade-off between inflation and unemployment (Baffi 1976) and objects to relying on inflation to redistribute resources against wage earners and creditors and in favour of capital owners and debtors (BI R.A. 1977, pp. 397–9).

Baffi points to the large government deficit as a source of monetary instability and argues that BI should have full autonomy in determining

purchases and sales of government securities (BI R.A. 1976, pp. 410–11).
It is somewhat ironic that the divorce decree of 1981 did not take place
under Baffi's Governorship. But perhaps Baffi was more adept in presenting the arguments than in precipitating institutional solutions. The same
can be said with respect to the plethora of administrative rules that characterise Italian monetary policy in the 1970s. The Governor laments a deterioration in the quality of monetary policy because the Bank, rather than
focusing on the creation of the monetary base, relies on quantitative
constraints, about which he gave the following evaluation (BI R.A. 1976,
pp. 409–10):

The system of constraints allows the achievement of more objectives than it would
be permitted by focusing exclusively on the control of the monetary base. Yet, it
would be imprudent to [overlook] . . . the costs that a such a system has generated. . . .
One such cost is the loss of allocative efficiency . . . suffered by financial intermediaries . . . [Another is] . . . the deterioration of our skills as the constraints persist. . . .
But the highest cost stems from the creation and maintenance of a system whose
ends and means are arbitrary relative to a set-up where financial institutions are free
to make their own decisions.

Monetary policy, according to Baffi, should have a long-term horizon
and should not be subservient to short-run considerations (BI R.A. 1976,
pp. 382–3):

There is a broad consensus on the fact that the uncertainty stemming from frequent
[policy] adjustments and the lags with which these adjustments make their actions
felt on the economy raise rather than reduce the economy's cyclical variability.

In sum, Baffi's ideal programme entails that (a) the ultimate objectives
of the monetary authorities be in line with the power and limits of monetary policy; (b) the monetary authorities acquire a sufficient degree of
independence from the fiscal authorities; and (c) monetary policy strategy
be based on market rather than administrative solutions. It would fall
on his successor, Carlo Azeglio Ciampi, to implement much of this
programme.

The 'divorce'

Carlo Azeglio Ciampi was appointed BI Governor after a disillusioned
Baffi resigned in October 1980. Ciampi's tenure would last until 1993 when
he became Prime Minister. The first year of his administration is considered
a milestone in the history of the BI. Fortune helped the governor. On 12
February 1981, in fact, Ciampi received the following letter from Treasury
Minister, Beniamino Andreatta (1993):

I have long since realised that many of the problems regarding the conduct of monetary policy have been made more acute by an insufficient degree of autonomy of the Banca d'Italia with respect to Treasury financing requirements. . . . It is my intention therefore to re-examine the merit of the 23 January, 1975 deliberation by the Interministerial Committee for Credit and Saving. . . . This re-examination would lead to a system where the intervention of Banca d'Italia in the BOT [Treasury bills] auctions would be left to a free decision of the Bank herself.

The new system, alluded to by the Minister, became operative in July 1981, thus freeing BI from the obligation of acting as a residual buyer in the government securities auctions.[8] The press christened the event a 'divorce', to indicate the formal separation between the world of public finance and the world of money.

The unusual aspect of this event is that it had not been preceded by public discussion; Epstein and Schor (1989, p. 160) note that 'there are virtually no memoranda or internal documents analysing it'. It is true that the Bank had been successful in developing a secondary market for government securities in 1975 and that she had argued the case for monetary autonomy as a prerequisite for monetary stability (e.g., BI R.A. 1980, pp. 180–3), but it is also true that the Treasury's decision came as a surprise.

Epstein and Schor explain the divorce as part of a longer trend to curb the power of labour unions and other strong pressure groups. They note that not one of the parties, including the Italian Communist Party, opposed the decision. It is hard to see why it would be in the best interest of the Italian Communist Party to reduce the power of labour unions. Equally difficult to explain is the advantage the Christian Democrats hoped to gain in immunising the Bank from the pressure of the many clientele that were so powerful in the party.[9] Why would a Treasury Minister and member of the Christian Democratic Party want to sever an important and easy link to monetary financing? Our explanation lies with the role of innovators in history. History provides examples of individuals who saw the importance of making radical changes and made decisions which perhaps appeared inconsistent with their self-interest. Andreatta, a Professor of Economics at the University of Bologna, was such a person. He himself explains (Andreatta 1993) the motivation for the decision:

The propensity of Italians to own financial assets was dropping frighteningly and the value of real estate was rising at a 100 per cent annual rate. . . . It was imperative to change the regime of economic policy and I did not have allies, but colleagues obsessed with the notion of economic growth at any price, sustained by low real interest rates and a weak exchange rate. . . . I wanted to dramatise the separation between the Bank and Treasury to effect a less painful disinflation in terms of employment and output, backed by a more credible central bank once we had freed her from the role of Treasury's banker.

Without diminishing the significance of the event, one should be careful not to jump to the conclusion that 1981 represented a sharp breaking point between the previous regime of fiscal dominance and the new regime of central bank independence. It is better to think of 1981 as the starting point of a long process that would enable the BI to gradually gain monetary policy independence. The compulsory participation at the Treasury auctions was only one of the ways the Treasury had tied the hands of the monetary authorities: the automatic recourse to central bank financing through the Treasury current account, and Treasury's required consent to changes in the discount rate were two other ways to impose fiscal dominance. It was only in the 1990s that BI would be completely freed from these two constraints. Even though it was strictly confining, the divorce decree had the characteristics more of a separation since it specified predetermined percentages of new securities issues BI had to buy at the auctions. In fact, BI participated at the Treasury auctions for quite some time: for example, in the period July 1987–June 1988, the Bank bought 7.5 per cent of all new issues. These purchases were made necessary because bids fell short of supply (Buttiglione and Prati 1990, table 6) and the Treasury was setting a base price or a maximum rate of interest. It was only in July of 1988 that the maximum rate of interest was abolished for the 3-month Treasury bills, and in March 1989 for the 6- and 12-month maturities. Even after March 1989 the Bank remained active at the auctions with the intent of raising the average price of the bids, as well as for its own portfolio needs.[10] In sum, BI interventions at the bi-weekly auctions petered out, but did not vanish altogether. Despite these qualifications, we will treat 1981 as the beginning of a new era in the relationship between Treasury and BI.

Freeing banks from quantitative constraints

The second achievement of the Ciampi's governorship was the dismantling of the three quantitative limitations that had straight jacketed the banking system: portfolio constraints, credit ceilings and controls on exchange rates and capital movements. We recall from chapter 8 that portfolio constraints required that banks purchase a minimum amount of medium- and long-term government securities expressed in terms of a fixed percentage of the new flow of deposits. This fixed percentage was 30 up to 1976, then fell to 6.5 in 1978, was further reduced to 5.5 in 1983, and finally disappeared in April 1987.

Credit ceilings were eliminated in June 1983, reintroduced in January 1986, and finally abolished in March 1988. In conformity with the provisions of the Single European Act, Treasury started dismantling the heavy architecture of controls on exchange rates and capital flows in February

1987. The process was completed by May 1990, long before the deadline imposed by the Single European Act.

A more conservative BI

The third innovation took place towards the end of the 1980s and registered a clear shift towards a higher degree of conservativeness of BI. This shift was undoubtedly influenced by similar changes in attitudes prevailing place in other central banks (Chouraqui and Price 1984; Fratianni 1993a), and reflected the growing importance of the idea that Italy ought to be part of a low-inflation European monetary union. Yet, one ought not to minimise the significance of the cultural transformation that BI underwent:

The experience of the last twenty years as well as the theoretical analysis have rein-forced the conviction that there is no long-run incompatibility between steady econ-omic growth and price stability, but on the contrary these two objectives can be pursued jointly through a firm, credible monetary policy   (BI R.A. 1989, p. 198).

Such a statement brings us back to the intellectual climate of the early 1950s, when Donato Menichella was in charge of BI. Gone are the days of the sixties and seventies when policy activism reigned supreme. A further proof of the regime shift comes from the Final Considerations of the Governor in the 1991 Annual Report. The paragraph is appropriately titled 'The monetary constitution':

Monetary stability is the ultimate objective of the central bank. A healthy currency is the base of a just democracy, [and] a prerequisite of economic development and orderly civil interaction. The depreciation of the monetary unit generates uncer-tainty and distrust, [and] dissolves economic transactions and the very social fabric.
(BI R.A. 1991, p. 340)

Monetary policy strategy

The final innovation under Ciampi's tenure pertains to monetary policy strategy. The changes affected the selection of intermediate targets and instruments of monetary policy. We recall from chapter 8 that the Italian monetary authorities in the seventies were using total domestic credit, or TDC, as the preferred intermediate target of monetary policy. We also recall that TDC is very suitable to a regime of fiscal dominance. There are two temporal phases in the application of TDC. In the first phase, BI adhered to the TDC quantitative targets, letting the private sector take the brunt of the adjustment when the government budget deficits exceeded their targets. Thus, larger budget deficits crowded out private-sector credit. The crowding out occurred only in part through higher interest rates. The authorities were reluctant to let interest rates find their equilibrium value and introduced credit rationing. In the second phase, the authorities failed to control TDC because they did not offset unexpected increases in credit flows to the government sector with equivalent decreases in private-sector credit. Consequently, TDC lost significance in favour of monetary aggregates.

The shift from TDC to an inclusive definition of money stock, M2, took place between 1983 and 1984. Officially, BI held the position that it was following several intermediate targets, but in practice M2 had replaced TDC.[11]

Summary

In the eighties the regime of fiscal dominance – which had been prevalent through much of the *History* and, in particular, during the sixties and seventies – began to break down. The reasons were Italy's participation in the EMS, the decision by an enlightened Treasury minister to free BI from the obligation of being a residual buyer of short-term securities at Treasury auctions, a shift in BI's preferences towards reducing inflation, and a monetary policy strategy more suitable to the aims of a more conservative central bank.

The pendulum swung from fiscal dominance towards monetary independence in the eighties. As of 1991, the end point of our *History*, monetary independence of the type enjoyed by the Bundesbank was in the making, under the thrust of the Maastricht Treaty.

A quantitative glance at the period

In the first two sections we dwelt on the importance of two broad sets of events, the EMS and the internal political climate, both of which permitted BI to deliver a lower inflation rate. Oddly enough, the two events worked in opposite directions in the sense that the EMS reduced BI's degrees of freedom, whereas the internal political climate gave the Bank more independence from the executive branch of government. Had the Bank been more independent and conservative in the 1970s, the EMS would have been much less of a constraint on policy in the 1980s. However, the EMS and the internal political climate reinforced each other in raising the central bank's credibility.

It is now time to look at the key macroeconomic variables that characterise Italian performance in the eighties. We begin with our customary review of the period in the context of the broader historical trend. Period averages indicate that money growth and output growth in the eighties returned to the 131-year trend. Insofar as the equation of exchange is concerned, the significant difference between the eighties and the entire period is velocity growth: in the eighties it is growing at an annual rate of 1.5 per cent, whereas during the entire *History* it is falling at approximately the same rate (table 1.3). The higher average inflation rate of the eighties reflects, consequently, the divergence of velocity growth from long-run trend.

All fiscal variables accelerate. The size of the central government budget deficit, as a proportion of national income, almost doubles in the eighties with respect to the seventies, despite a very drastic rise in the tax burden. The central government tax ratio jumps, in fact, by 16 percentage points from the seventies to the eighties; but the central government expenditure ratio leaps by an astonishing 22 percentage points (table 1.4) The swing towards monetary independence and conservativeness on the part of BI appears in the monetisation ratio that drops to 18 per cent, from 52 per cent in the seventies.

Real interest rates rise substantially in the eighties in absolute terms and in relation to US real rates. The gradual elimination of controls on exchange markets and capital movements, the integration of financial markets around the world, and the inability of the Treasury to rely on the central bank to finance its budget deficits were strong forces underlying the alignment of Italian real rates of interest to levels prevailing abroad.

The key feature of the eighties, as we have seen, is monetary adjustment. Dynamics, rather than averages, can reveal the full extent of this adjustment. Given the significance of the EMS, we thought it appropriate to compare Italy with the other six original 'signatories' of this arrangement. We begin with monetary factors and end with fiscal variables, and argue that in both areas Italy has made an adjustment towards the EC values.

Monetary adjustment

Any cursory examination of the data indicates that Italy disinflated during the 1980s; but so did most industrial countries (Fratianni 1993a). Thus, the relevant question is whether Italy disinflated relative to the EMS countries. Figure 9.1 clearly indicates that Italy did just that, particularly from 1980 to 1987.[12] The relative Italian disinflation was not the outcome of favourable events but the result of a deliberate policy decision. To measure the thrust of monetary policy, we applied McCallum's (1989, chapter 16) stable-price monetary rule

$$\Delta b - (\Delta \bar{y} - \bar{v}), \tag{9.1}$$

where the first term on the right-hand side is the growth rate of the monetary base, the second term the trend growth rate of output, and the last term the three-year moving average of the growth rate of velocity (defined as

nominal GDP divided by the monetary base).[13] The expression in parenthe-
ses defines the value of the growth rate of the monetary base consistent with
a stable price level. The higher the value of (9.1), the more expansionary is
monetary policy. Figure 9.2 indicates that Italian monetary policy became
more restrictive in 1980 and progressively so through most of the period
under consideration. More importantly, the gap between Italian monetary
policy and that of the rest of the EMS narrowed considerably, and by 1991 it
had completely disappeared. In sum, figures 9.1 and 9.2 indicate that Italian
relative disinflation was for the most part engineered by BI policy actions.

An extreme form of monetary disinflation arises when the central bank
has full independence in setting inflation targets. We have seen that beginning with the divorce of 1981 BI gradually acquired the ability to set monetary policy independently of fiscal considerations. What might have
happened if the prevailing regime had been one of monetary dominance,
that is, a regime under which a high-inflation, high-debt country – such as
Italy – joins a fixed exchange-rate arrangement such as the post-1987 EMS?

Fratianni and von Hagen (1993) consider such a scenario and build a
model in which parity realignments are ruled out. Therefore, the expected
change in the exchange rate is zero. Furthermore, the price leadership
exerted by the rest of the EMS implies that Italian monetary policy must
adapt endogenously so as to maintain a fixed exchange rate. Thus, if Italian
debt is growing relative to output, money in Italy must grow less rapidly
than in the rest of the union to prevent a continuous shift into foreign-
denominated assets. The faster debt grows relative to output, the tighter
must the Italian central bank behave to prevent a continuous shift away
from lira-denominated assets. In other words, the monetary authorities
provide an effective counterweight to the profligate behaviour of the fiscal
authorities, with looser fiscal policy being offset by tighter monetary
policy.[14]

The critical implication of full monetary dominance is the inverse relationship between the primary deficit and the domestic interest rate, meaning
that an independent central bank could discipline the fiscal authority to
accept a budget deficit lower than it would be otherwise. Under this scenario, if government were to set expenditures and tax rates at such a level as
to make debt grow faster than real GDP, the central bank would respond by
tightening monetary policy to impede capital from flowing out of the
country. In turn, the ensuing rise in the domestic interest rate would induce
the Treasury to reduce its deficit. In this sense, monetary dominance,
coupled with a risk premium on government debt, would exert discipline on
fiscal policy.

The main message of this exercise is to draw attention to the implications
of an extreme condition under which the monetary authorities not only

ignore altogether the public-sector borrowing requirements but offset them to maintain their commitment to a fixed exchange rate. To be sure, BI is not the 'idealised' independent central bank of the model, nor is the EMS the credible fixed exchange-rate arrangement assumed by the model. However, we have seen in this chapter that in the 1980s BI gained independence and tightened monetary policy relative to the past and relative to monetary policy in the rest of the EMS. We shall see later to what extent, if any, budget deficits in Italy adjusted in accordance with the model's implications.

As Italian inflation fell relative to the rest of the EMS countries, so did market rates of interest; see figure 9.3. The difference between Italian and EMS short-term interest rates rose from 3.4 percentage points in 1979 to 9.5 percentage points in 1983, and then gradually declined. In 1991 the differential had returned to approximately the 1979 level. Since the interest-rate differential is equal to the expected size of the devaluation of the home currency multiplied by the number of devaluations within a given period, it is clear that the EMS was never a credible arrangement in the sense that the market, on average, anticipated a sizable devaluation of the Italian lira (Fratianni and von Hagen 1992, tables 7.7 and 7.9).

Real interest rates, that is, the difference between short-term rates of interest and the one-year inflation rate, rose over the 1980s; see figure 9.4. At the start of the EMS, Italian real rates were sharply negative, but then rose progressively. From 1983 onward Italian real rates of interest were significantly above those of the other six EMS countries: fluctuating from a maximum of 247 basis points in 1986 to a minimum of ten basis points in 1990, and averaging 139 basis points during those years. This upward adjustment in real rates of interest reflected the opening of the Italian financial markets through the progressive dismantling of exchange and capital controls as well as the switch from credit ceilings to real interest-rate policies on the part of BI.

The high levels of Italian interest rates, together with an increasing ratio of government debt to GDP, heightened the concern of investors that Italian government debt would be subject to a risk premium, that is, a risk connected with a sudden fall in the price of Italian government securities. Such a price decline could result from debt repudiation, either partial or full, retroactive taxation of interest and principal payments, or consolidations such as the one that took place in November 1926 (chapter 5). For bearing such a risk, investors would have to be compensated. Giovannini and Piga (1992) look at the issue of an Italian risk premium by comparing the yield on a dollar-denominated bond issued by the Italian government in the Eurodollar market with the yield on a dollar-denominated debt of similar maturity issued by the World Bank for the period May 1991 to May 1992. They conclude that the risk premium on Italian debt fluctuated from

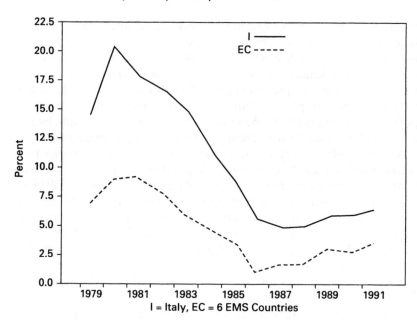

Figure 9.1 Inflation rates in the 1980s

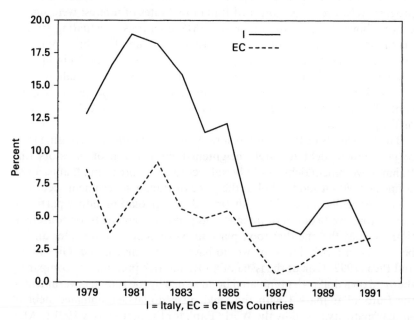

Figure 9.2 Thrust of monetary policy in the 1980s

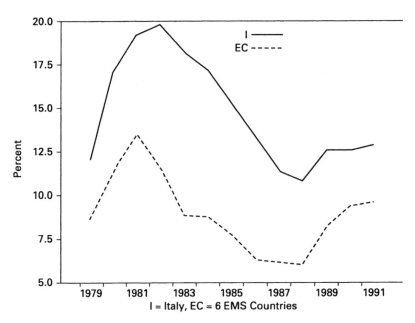

Figure 9.3 Nominal interest rates in the 1980s

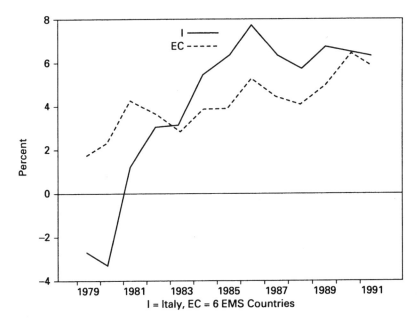

Figure 9.4 Real interest rates in the 1980s

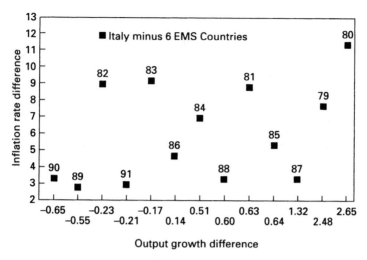

Figure 9.5 Inflation–output trade-off

22 to 42 basis points. That is, the default risk on Italian debt was small (see also Alesina *et al.* 1992). We are left with the conclusion that devaluation risk is the main reason Italian interest rates have remained high relative to those of the other EMS countries in the 1980s.

The trade-off between inflation and output

Did the stronger disinflation in Italy than in the rest of the EMS countries imply that Italy paid a higher cost in terms of growth or unemployment? Figure 9.5 addresses this topic by plotting the difference in the inflation rate between Italy and the six EMS countries against the difference in output growth rates. A Phillips Curve-type trade-off would imply that the points be located on an imaginary line going from south-west to north-east. Such a trade-off appears to exist if one compares the first three years with the last three years of the sample period. At the start of the 1980s, Italy had an inflation rate and output growth way above the average of the other six EMS countries. At the end of the 1980s the relative inflation rate had declined by 6.5 percentage points, whereas relative output growth had declined by more than 2 percentage points.[15] The approximate three to one trade-off is rather stiff.

This trade-off is more favourable, however, if one considers the intermediate period from 1982 to 1987. Giavazzi and Spaventa (1989) have analysed these years and have concluded that Italy was able to improve its inflation-output trade-off *vis-à-vis* other countries (but especially the United

Kingdom), not because of the credibility of the EMS, but because of a supply-side policy. The Italian government absorbed the costs of labour layoffs through a temporary unemployment insurance fund, the *Cassa Integrazione Guadagni*, and made it possible for Italian industry to undertake badly needed restructuring. Without *Cassa Integrazione*, the unions would have opposed layoffs, and higher labour productivity could not have come about. In other words, the government enacted a redistribution of resources in favour of firms' profits, which was responsible for alleviating the Phillips-Curve-like effects of inflation on output growth. In sum, the Italian disinflation of the 1980s, operating through continuous real appreciation of the lira, determined a shift in relative prices towards the low-productivity sheltered sector. By the end of the 1980s this real appreciation had left a depressing effect on the overall performance of the economy in relation to the other six EMS countries.

Fiscal correction

The eighties were years of disinflation; there were also years when BI partially regained independence from the Treasury. An implication of full monetary independence, with the central bank aiming at a low inflation target, is that the 'cost' of budget deficits to the Treasury rises and a fiscal correction becomes more likely. In this section we will to explore the relative magnitude of the Italian budget problem and the adjustment that took place in the 1980s. We will quantify government expenditures, tax revenues and budget deficits not in absolute terms but as a deviations from the weighted averages of the original six EMS countries. The following definition of total budget deficit, *total def*, is adopted

$$total\ def = Gc + Gk + Gtr + Gi - tax, \tag{9.2}$$

where Gc=government consumption expenditure, Gk=government capital expenditure, Gtr=net transfer payments to households and firms, Gi=interest payments on government debt, and Tax=total tax revenues. All of the variables in (9.2) are expressed as a ratio of nominal GDP and represent the difference between the Italian variable and the weighted average of the six EMS countries, with weights determined by ECU shares at the time of the 12 January 1987 realignment. The source of the data is the OECD, *Economic Outlook*. Data and measurement procedures are described in table 9.2.

The data of table 9.2 reveal that the large Italian budget deficit and debt resulted not from an 'excessive' flow of expenditures in Gc, Gk or Gtr, but from a 'scarcity' of tax revenues. The terms 'excessive' and 'scarcity' have no particular economic meaning other than to indicate that Italy was behaving

Table 9.2 Government expenditures, tax returns, deficits and debts: Italy minus weighted average of 6 EMS countries (per cent of GDP)

Year	Consumption expenditures	Capital expenditures	Transfer payments	Interest payments	Total expenditures	Tax revenues	Total deficit	Primary deficit	Net debt
1980	-4.51	-0.24	-4.66	3.13	-6.27	-12.65	-6.14	-3.01	35.04
1981	-3.80	0.46	-4.24	3.34	-4.24	-12.01	-7.58	-4.24	36.13
1982	-3.84	0.95	-4.16	3.93	-3.12	-10.90	-7.09	-3.16	37.99
1983	-3.32	1.47	-3.31	3.85	-1.30	-9.38	-6.77	-2.92	40.28
1984	-3.18	0.87	-3.62	4.12	-1.81	-10.09	-8.33	-4.21	44.58
1985	-2.90	-0.17	-3.20	3.95	-2.23	-9.83	-9.84	-5.89	50.20
1986	-2.72	0.17	-2.42	4.50	-0.47	-8.19	-9.01	-4.51	53.71
1987	-2.26	0.33	-2.89	4.11	-0.71	-8.09	-8.49	-4.38	57.48
1988	-1.69	0.09	-2.73	4.39	0.06	-6.99	-8.43	-4.03	59.58
1989	-1.16	0.35	-1.58	5.29	2.90	-4.95	-8.85	-3.56	62.20
1990	-0.31	-0.06	-2.63	5.94	2.93	-3.28	-8.04	-2.10	63.17
1991	0.02	0.36	-3.23	6.27	3.42	-2.75	-7.07	-0.80	63.29

Notes:
Consumption expenditure is total government consumption, including wages. Capital expenditure is the sum of gross government investment and miscellaneous capital transactions. Transfer payments is the sum of social security benefits and transfers paid by government. Interest payments consist of property income paid by government. Tax revenue is the sum of total direct taxes, social security contributions received by government, other current transfers received by government, property income of government and indirect taxes. Total deficit is the difference between total expenditures and tax revenues. Primary deficit is the difference between total deficit and interest payments. Net debt is government net debt. All variables are expressed as a per cent of nominal GDP.

Source: OECD, Economic Outlook, data diskettes N. 44 and N. 50.

differently than the other six original EMS countries. The same is also true for the 1970s which are not shown (Fratianni 1993b). Consumption expenditures and transfer payments in Italy were consistently below the values of the 6-EMS group, although with a tendency towards convergence. Italian tax revenues in the seventies (again not shown) and in the first half of the eighties were sharply below the 6-EMS group. As a result, total budget deficits in Italy rose sharply to double-digit levels, as did debt. In 1979, for example, Italian total budget deficit was 11.6 per cent of GDP and debt 55.6 per cent of GDP. The rising debt-to-GDP ratio implied rising interest payments. In 1979, *Gi* accounted for half of *total def*. As debt rose relative to the 6-EMS group, so did Gi. By 1991, Gi accounted for virtually the entire value of total def.

We have seen above that fiscal authorities ought to adjust to a regime of monetary independence in an environment of credible fixed exchange rates by reducing the primary deficit. Table 9.2 shows that Italian primary deficits rose relative to the 6-EMS group until 1985 and then declined. By 1991 the gap between Italy and the 6-EMS group had virtually disappeared. The same pattern emerges when one considers only Italian primary deficits: the decline started in 1986 and continued until 1991 when the Treasury finally recorded a small surplus in the primary budget. The fact that Italian primary deficits were closely correlated with deviations of primary deficits indicates that the adjustment had fallen principally on the fiscal side. Higher ratios of tax revenues to GDP, rather than lower ratios of total expenditures of GDP, were the driving force of the Italian fiscal adjustment.

In sum, the pattern of the data is broadly consistent with the Italian fiscal authorities taking some corrective actions, as BI was becoming more independent and the EMS constraint more binding. We cannot prove that monetary dominance was responsible for the partial fiscal correction. The latter could have taken place regardless of the prevailing regime. The sequence of events, however, is consistent with the implication of the model that says that primary budget deficits fell, other things being the same, when monetary authorities did not have to monetise them.

The fact that a fiscal correction was initiated does not imply either that the size of the correction was consistent with Italy remaining in the EMS or that the correction will be ultimately completed. Indeed, the lessons from the *History* make us cautious in concluding that Italy has turned the corner of fiscal profligacy. Our volume concludes with 1991; yet, we feel we owe the reader a postscript that tries to bridge the gap between 1991 and more recent events, especially those concerning the currency crisis of September 1992.

Postscript

In accordance with the provisions of the Maastricht Treaty, the Italian legislator has continued to grant additional autonomy to the central bank. In January 1992 Parliament legislated that BI, and not the Treasury, had the power to change the discount rate. On the other hand, the same legislation called for BI to take into account the desires of the government, a condition that weakens the power of changing the discount rate. On 26 November 1992 Parliament passed a law abolishing the old *conto corrente di tesoreria* that allowed the Treasury to borrow from BI. In its place, there will be a non-interest-bearing account with an initial balance of Lit 31,000 billion funded by a debt issue purchased by BI. The debt accumulated under the old *conto corrente di tesoreria* will be transformed into long-term debt at an interest rate of 1 per cent. The new Treasury account does not allow overdraft (BI, *Bollettino Economico*, February 1994, N. 22, p. 55). The same law gave BI the authority to change reserve requirement ratios. Finally, as of 1 January 1994 BI will no longer be a participant in the Treasury auctions. All in all, the existing legislation would give BI the independence required by the Maastricht Treaty for those countries that intend to join the monetary union. It would also give BI a degree of monetary autonomy from the Treasury that only the Banca Nazionale had before 1866 (see chapter 3).

Central bank independence does not automatically result in the monetary authority pursuing a zero or low-inflation strategy. The critical question is how will BI use her newly gained independence. Antonio Fazio, the new Governor of BI, has yet to state unambiguously that the primary objective of the central bank is to stabilise the price level. The Governor, instead, has spoken often about the cost of high unemployment and the implied role of the central bank in reducing it. In the last two annual reports of the Bank (1992 and 1993), statements about the inverse relationship between inflation and unemployment have re-emerged, indicating that the old philosophical tradition has not disappeared. Furthermore, the reports are much less crisp about the causal relationship between money growth and inflation. Inflation is said to be caused by a variety of factors, including but not primarily monetary policy. Might the Bank have stepped back to the older framework of multiple and conflicting objectives and a very eclectic view of inflation?

The process of fiscal correction continues, and is far from over. The ratio of debt-to-GDP has surpassed unity and interest payments account for the entire deficit. Italian economic policy remains hostage to the fiscal profligacy of the past. Fiscal policy now, as throughout the *History*, remains the Achilles' heel of the country.

On 16 September 1992 the lira left the ERM. The crisis had been brewing

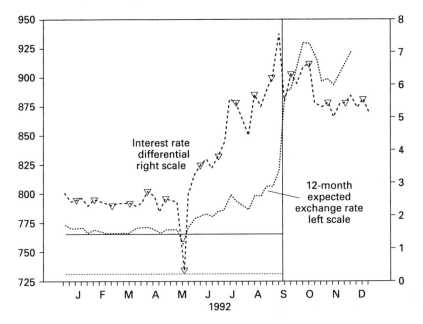

Figure 9.6 Expected exchange rate and interest differential

for quite some time. Figure 9.6 plots weekly movements of two series during 1992. The first series is the expected twelve-month Lira/DM exchange rate computed on the assumption that uncovered interest-rate parity holds.[16] The second series is the difference between the twelve-month Eurolira interest rate and the twelve-month Eurodm interest rate. The data indicate that the markets had little confidence in the parity throughout 1992. In fact, the expected exchange rate was outside the upper limit of the band from January to May, with the interest rate differential averaging 2.5 percentage points. In June 1992 the credibility problem deteriorated, with the interest rate differential rising to 5 percentage points. After an improvement in August, events turned for the worse and exploded in the first half of September. BI intervened in the exchange markets with a net loss of Lit 30,000 billion in foreign reserves and a capital loss on those transactions of Lit 4,394 billion (R.A. 1992, p. 118 and p. 121).

There is ongoing research aimed at understanding the reasons underlying the September 1992 crisis. Eichengreen and Wyplosz (1993) propose four explanations: competitiveness difficulties in high-inflation countries resulting from the fixity of the exchange rate, the consequences of German monetary unification, anticipated policy shifts in response to deteriorating domestic economic conditions, and self-fulfilling speculative crises. The first explanation fits Italy, which had a competitive loss, especially when measured in terms of unit labour costs of approximately 20 per cent from 1988 to September 1992 (Eichengreen and Wyplosz 1993, figure 1).

The competitive loss was caused by an Italian inflation rate which was persistently higher than that of Germany.[17] We noted earlier that a competitive export industry cannot raise prices beyond those charged by its trading partners. Under a fixed exchange rate, increases in unit labour costs in excess of those borne by foreign competition translate into a competitive loss. The sheltered sector, instead, is able to pass on to consumers the higher prices. In fact, the real appreciation of the lira was matched by a relative price shift in favour of the non-traded sector. Using services as a proxy of the sheltered sector, and goods – net of food and energy – as a proxy of the traded sector, there was a 13 percentage point cumulative rise in the price level of the sheltered sector relative to that of the traded sector from 1988 to 1992 (R.A. 1993, appendix, table aB32). In sum, past competitive losses and a redistribution of resources in favour of the low-productivity sheltered sector were of such a magnitude as to justify corrective action. Such an action could have taken place as early as 1991.

The timing of the September 1992 currency crisis is the result of many contributing factors, including the general decline in the commitment to monetary union. For Italy, what turned out to be particularly damaging was the perception that the future promised more of the same. The attention of financial markets was focused on the inability of government to produce a programme aimed at reducing budget deficits. Typical of such a mood was George S. Harjoullis, Executive Director of Morgan Stanley, who on 19 May 1992 wrote in the *Global Bonds–Italy Special* that:

The failure to elect a president or establish any visible means of government is becoming very disconcerting. Italy's ills require immediate and severe treatment and there is precious little evidence of this. Failure to produce some convincing proposals to control the ballooning deficit soon may even lead to the more sanguine investors losing confidence. . . . I am of the opinion that the risk in holding Lire bonds is no longer adequately compensated. It is time to take profits and look elsewhere until the authorities again earn the benefit of the doubt.

For most of 1992 the government budget deficit was substantially higher than the target value of Lit. 127,800 billion. Drastic fiscal measures were postponed until 19 September, that is, until three days after the lira left the ERM.

In sum, the September 1992 events challenged the credibility of the EMS and monetary union. In the EMS Italy stood as the (relatively) high-inflation, high-debt country; that is, as a country at risk. While the timing of the currency crisis is difficult to explain, its occurrence appears to be broadly in line with our explanation of why most currency crises in the *History* occurred: profligate public finance and an accommodative monetary policy.

Conclusions

The leitmotif of this chapter was the ascendancy of BI which gradually regained monetary-policy autonomy during the eighties, and thus reversed a long period of what we have called fiscal dominance. Several factors were responsible for this regime change. To begin with, we need to credit the force of monetarism, which at the end of the seventies left a profound impact on central bankers in North America and Europe. Central banks in the industrialised world became more conservative concerning inflation. The new BI governors, Paolo Baffi first and Carlo Azeglio Ciampi later, were very different from Guido Carli. Carli was steeped in Keynesian doctrine and had a proclivity for activism. Baffi, instead, was a monetary economist in the classical mould and less inclined to adapt monetary policy to short-run objectives. Ciampi, a lesser intellectual than either Carli or Baffi, had the 'savoir faire' of bringing about the reforms that had eluded Baffi. Baffi set the intellectual climate for reform, but Ciampi realised it. Although the renaissance of BI in the eighties owes a great deal to Ciampi, the Governor was aided by the enlightened Treasury Minister, Beniamino Andreatta, who signed the 'divorce' decree of 1981.

The EMS was the external constraint to which the monetary authorities constantly referred in pursuing a gradual disinflation policy. As has been true for much of the *History*, Italian monetary policy tends to be lax when the external constraint is perceived to be loose. BI, however, did not continue the disinflation process to the point of aligning the Italian inflation rate to the German inflation rate. The inability to squeeze out the inflation differential *vis-à-vis* Germany would have had minor consequences if the old EMS had been in place. Instead, the EMS changed character after 1987, moving from flexibility to complete rigidity. The inconsistency of a rigid exchange rate with a permanent inflation differential was bound to emerge. Saddled with large competitive losses and a high level of debt, Italy left the ERM on 16 September 1992.

Monetary policy autonomy facilitated the long overdue correction in fiscal policy. The most recent data indicate that Italy has achieved a primary surplus, that is, a situation in which government revenues exceed expenditures net of interest payments on debt. The fiscal correction is in its infancy and it is too early to proclaim that a decline of the debt-to-GDP ratio is in sight. The 131-year *History* suggests caution when speaking about public finance.

10 Conclusions

In this chapter we intend to draw general conclusions and lessons that emanate from our *History*. Six themes emerge from our work, themes which are not entirely unique to the Italian experience. Space and knowledge prevent us from pointing to similarities and dissimilarities between Italy and other countries. So, as a next best solution, we invite the economic historian and monetary economist of other countries to make the appropriate comparisons.

First theme: What is money?

At the time of political unification, people had a preference for money in the form of gold and silver coins. Paper notes were imperfect substitutes for metal coins. There were historical and political reasons for this relative distrust of paper money. Paper money was a newcomer to the market, making money holders reluctant to use it. The negative 'network' effect was reinforced by a deep suspicion that paper money was more prone to depreciation than gold or silver. Confidence in paper money derives from confidence in those institutions and governments that directly affect the purchasing power of money. The political history of Italy, with its century-old regional turmoil, did not inspire in money holders the trust necessary to make paper notes perfectly equivalent to metal coins.

The several banks of issue did not have a nation-wide branch network; consequently, their liabilities were regarded with some suspicion outside their local markets. It was only after Italy's exit from the gold standard that paper notes, both those issued by the government and those by the banks, gained wider acceptance. Similarly, bank deposits were very undeveloped at the time of political unification. Their acceptance evolved slowly over time. In sum, money was initially held primarily in the form of coins. As the banking industry deepened and widened in the national territory, the composition of money holdings shifted from coins to notes and from coins and notes to bank deposits.

Metal remained important even after Italy left the gold standard for two reasons. First, the quantity of currency outstanding was to a large extent endogenous and demand-driven because the banks of issue, and in particular the Banca Nazionale, had a lira exchange-rate target. Second, the demand for gold stemmed from the fact that it would hold its purchasing power better than paper money.

The behaviour of money velocity, as well as the empirical studies on the demand for money, underscore that money was a luxury good and that Italians were rapidly raising monetary assets relative to income. The deepening of currency and of bank deposits tended to occur simultaneously, except during the banking crises of 1866 and 1893 and the two world wars, when the composition of money shifted sharply away from bank deposits and towards currency (during the Second World War there was a global decrease in money demand as well).

Second theme: Regulation of money and credit

The authorities adjusted to the shift in the composition of money by regulating first the volume of bank notes and later also by controlling the expansion of bank deposits. Regulation of bank notes actually preceded political unification and consisted of setting maximum ratios of bank notes to bank capital and/or metal reserves. The international gold standard automatically enforced an upper limit on the size of bank notes through the convertibility clause. After Italy's exit from the standard in 1866, the legislature became more active in regulating note volume by refusing the charter to new banks of issue and by imposing quantitative limits on bank notes. The limits were first imposed on the largest bank of issue, the Banca Nazionale, in 1868 and then on the other banks of issue in 1874. Overissue was a quite common response to very lenient enforcement. Eventually, government had to resort to direct supervision of note printing.

Control over bank deposit expansion came much later, towards the end of the nineteenth century. The first experiments were limited to the deposit liabilities of banks of issue and left significant gaps in the money stock control procedure which was significantly improved, however, when BI was made the sole bank of issue in 1926 and when reserve requirements were introduced in 1947. These two events not only christened BI as the bank of banks, but gave it full power to regulate money. In 1936 the legislature elevated the concept of money and credit to the equivalent of a public good. The new law formalised the ultimate power of government over banking matters. The central bank and commercial banks assumed the status of public institutions, and bank officials received the status of public servants. The 1936 Banking Law legitimised the supremacy of politics over banking.

It is not surprising that the fascist regime would pass such a legislation. What is surprising is that such a law lasted through almost fifty years of republican life.

With the aforementioned law, banks moved to centre stage and attracted the bulk of the private sector's financial wealth; bonds and equities represented but a small share of portfolios. Business financed projects either through undistributed profits or through bank loans or participations. Before 1936, banks were closer to the model of the modern universal bank. The banking crisis of the thirties – both in Italy and abroad – convinced the legislature to sharply differentiate commercial banks from industrial banks. The key distinction between the two was that the deposit-taking commercial banks were limited to granting short-term loans, whereas the industrial banks could finance long-term projects by tapping the bond market. The separation principle, which is also codified by the Glass–Steagall Act in the United States, aimed at insulating banks from shocks originating in the industrial sector and reassuring deposit holders about the safety of their claims.

Third theme: Causes of inflation

The annual inflation rate during the *History* was, on average, approximately 7 per cent. Inflation, however, was mostly a twentieth-century phenomenon, since the price level fluctuated around the zero growth line from 1861 to 1913. The two world wars were high inflation periods; the inter-war years price stable, encompassing however a phase of actual deflation; and the post-Second World War era, but especially the seventies, were high peace-time inflation years.

Exchange-rate regimes affect the relative performance of Italy. During the years of the gold standard and Bretton Woods, nominal variables behaved roughly in line with those of rest of the world. An Italian diversity or peculiarity emerged in the inter-war years and more so in the seventies and the eighties, when domestic inflation markedly rose, domestic real interest markedly dropped, and the lira appreciated in real terms. The seventies, more than any other historical phase, fits the characterisation of a 'national preference' for (relatively) high inflation, low interest rates and financial market segmentation. In essence, inflation changed from period to period and there is no evidence that the price level was subject to an inevitable secular increase.

Annual money growth exceeded output growth by more than 8 percentage points, that is, one percentage point higher than the average inflation rate. Money growth rates were much higher during war than peace time; and almost three times higher after BI was granted the monopoly of issue than in the pre-monopolist period. On the other hand, money growth was very contained during the gold standard and even more so in the inter-war period. Money growth was historically high during the Bretton Woods years and was associated with an average annual inflation rate of 3.6 per cent and an average output growth of 5.6 per cent. Money growth and inflation rose considerably during the seventies and then slowed down during the eighties.

The monetary base represented the dominant factor underlying money growth. On average, the inclusive monetary base growth accounted for 93 per cent of money growth over the entire period. In turn, the growth of the monetary base was dominated by the growth of the Treasury component, while the foreign component alternated periods of positive growth with periods of negative growth. Changes in the money multiplier influenced the growth of money more in the short than in the long run, a result that is in line with similar findings from other countries. Of the three determinants of the money multiplier, the one which exerted the biggest impact was the ratio of public-held monetary base to bank deposits.

Fiscal impulses, in addition to monetary impulses, explain the bulk of the behaviour of Italian inflation. To be sure, there were periods, such as during the Second World War, when shifts in the aggregate supply of output were a powerful force on the inflation rate, but on the whole aggregate demand shifts dominated aggregate supply shifts. We find, in essence, very little evidence that inflation could be sustained by autonomous increases in input costs – which is not to deny that input prices adjust to inflation – or by inter-group conflicts on income distribution. If anything, the direction of causality seems to go from inflation to social conflict and not vice versa.

Inflation expectations played a critical role in the inflation process. The *History* provides examples of both quick disinflation (e.g., 1926 and 1947) and slow disinflation (part of the seventies and the eighties). The difference lies in the stubbornness of expectations which, in turn, reflect the public's assessment of the monetary authorities' commitment to a disinflationary strategy. When the commitment is perceived to be strong, inflation expectations adjust rapidly and disinflation comes about quickly. When the commitment is perceived to be weak or time dependent, inflation expectations remain stubbornly high and disinflation is a long drawn out process.

Price and exchange controls turned out to be either ineffective or, when these controls altered the relative price structure of the economy, to actually delay the return to monetary stability. In at least one period (at the end of the First World War), direct price controls had such adverse consequences on the government budget deficit as to precipitate near hyperinflation.

Finally, disinflationary programmes were enhanced when the authorities perceived they were under a severe external constraint. The most recent example of such a constraint is the European Monetary System to which the Italian monetary authorities constantly referred in pursuing the gradual disinflation policy of the eighties.

Fourth theme: Trade-offs between inflation and output?

Economic growth was higher in the twentieth century than in the nineteenth century. In addition, it was more volatile in the gold standard and inter-war years than after the Second World War. The largest output drop took place in the Second World War. Of particular importance is the relationship between output growth and inflation. Post-Second World War theories, such as the one underlying the Phillips Curve, have emphasised a trade-off between output growth (or unemployment) and inflation, implying that inflation and economic growth would be positively related unless the economic system were disturbed by negative supply shocks. The Italian data exclude any systematic positive association between output growth and inflation.

This is not to deny the existence of short-run Phillips-Curve effects. Indeed, our *History* has isolated several instances in which policymakers were able to rely on inflation to stimulate growth. These stimulative actions, however, had temporary effects and could not be reproduced year after year.

Fifth theme: Behaviour of the monetary authorities

We have noted that the bulk of money growth in Italy can be traced to the growth of the monetary base, which, in turn, was fuelled by the growth of its domestic source component, in particular the Treasury's. We have also noted that the process of money and credit control evolved in a laborious manner. This process was heavily influenced by the objectives pursued by various institutions, as well as by the interaction among banks and between banks and the political system. What principles or economic factors guided the banks of issue and the political authorities in creating monetary base?

The actions of the monetary authorities during the fixed exchange-rate regimes were guided by the size of the government deficit and the desire to sterilise reserve flows. More than once the legislator defined precise ceilings on paper currency growth, freezing at the same time the levels of interest rates. So banks of issue aimed at controlling both the quantity of money and the levels of interest rates. Often, the interest rate objective was more important than the quantity objective.

The preference for targeting interest rates had less to do with technical issues and more to do with the dominance of politics. Our key theme of the

History, which is summarised below, is the subservience of the banks of issue to political power and hence the endogeneity of monetary policy with respect to fiscal policy. The stock of international reserves was the other key variable influencing the behaviour of the monetary authorities in the early as well as the later days of the *History*. In the early days the profit-seeking banks of issue had a bias for a low discount rate (i.e., high growth of the domestic source component), a policy that often ran into conflict with the maintenance of a stable ratio of specie to currency in circulation. The periodic balance-of-payments crises forced these banks to raise their effective discount rates, often to levels considerably higher than those prevailing in London or Paris. In the Bretton Woods era, decelerations in the domestic component of the monetary base occurred and were justified because they stopped the loss of international reserves. In the seventies, the monetary authorities resorted to a web of exchange and credit controls to prevent capital and reserve outflows.

The importance of the external constraint on monetary policy actions and outcomes emerges from two conflicting forces: the openness of the Italian economy and the desire of policy makers to achieve high growth rates of output and low unemployment rates. This conflict became more pronounced in modern times with the rise of Keynesian economics. Indeed, it is not surprising that the policy of the seventies to decouple Italian financial markets from those abroad through a panoply of exchange control and credit ceiling regulations coincided with the central bank's adoption of a wage-push view of inflation.

Another general aspect of the behaviour of the monetary authorities was their proclivity to accommodate, rather than counteract, the business cycle. Namely, monetary expansion tended to be carried out until a balance-of-payments and/or currency crisis would occur; then the monetary brakes and/or controls would be applied immediately. Once the turnaround was achieved, monetary expansion would resume.

Sixth theme: Fiscal dominance

Fiscal and monetary policies have often been intertwined during the *History*. In the early days, the profit-seeking banks of issues were constrained by the convertibility clause and by a legal ceiling on their outstanding currency. The high probability, if not certainty, that government would legalise the excessive circulation, while maintaining the prices of bank notes unchanged, raised the expected profits of the overissuing bank. Had the latter faced a sharp drop in the price of her notes, its supply behaviour would have been different. The weak link in the system was government, which maintained fixed relative prices among notes without actually controlling the aggregate amount of total currency in circulation. This weakness, in turn, had more of a political than an intellectual root: government borrowings were often the reason for breaking through the note ceiling.

Budget deficits were directly or indirectly responsible for Italy's exit from the gold standard in 1866, the monetary shocks of 1866–7 and 1870–2, the *de facto* suspension of convertibility from the mid-1880s onward, and the monetary deterioration at the beginning of the subsequent decade. Similarly, monetary stability was often the result of the improvement in public finances.

The influence of public finances on monetary policy became even stronger in modern times, with the peak being reached in the seventies. Banca d'Italia was too dependent on government to assert an autonomous policy; often she accommodated the objective of government by financing large budget deficits at low rates of interest, that is by excessive monetary base creation. A relentless growth of government spending, rather than sluggish tax revenues, were responsible for the budget deficits. Transfer payments were the least controllable expenditure category, especially after the Second World War.

The central bank gradually regained monetary policy autonomy during the eighties. The reason for this long and overdue process was partly due to the intellectual force of monetarism, partly to the role played by Governors Paolo Baffi and Carlo Azeglio Ciampi and Treasury Minister Beniamino Andreatta, and partly to the long wave of monetary integration in the European Union.

While the high inflation rates of the seventies and early eighties appear as a distant memory, the currently high debt-to-GDP ratio casts a long shadow on the completion of monetary correction in Italy.

Notes

1 Structure, main themes and data of the monetary history

1 Space limitations prevent us from printing the other time series we have used in the *History*. These data can be obtained by writing to either one of the authors and enclosing a 3.5-inch diskette with a self-addressed, self-stamped envelope.

2 Strictly speaking this is not correct because the Treasury issues coins.

3 Cf. the Glass–Steagall Act of 1933 in the United States.

4 UIC succeeded the Istituto Nazionale per i Cambi con l'Estero created in 1917.

5 The exclusive definition is used also in Fratianni and Spinelli (1984).

6 We shall abbreviate BI's *Relazioni Annuali* or Annual Reports by R.A.

7 Repaci (1962), however, reports budget figures on the basis of the fiscal year ending 30 June. The fiscal-year flows were transformed into calendar-year flows according to $y(t) = 0.5x(t) + 0.5x(t+1)$ where $y(t)$ is calendar-year data in year t, $x(t)$ is fiscal-year data ending in 30 June of year t, $x(t+1)$ is fiscal-year data ending in 30 June of year $t+1$.

8 See Formentini (1986). Actually the variable *MBTR* was computed in an indirect way. To the stock of domestically held debt, defined as the sum of *debiti patrimoniali* and *debiti fluttuanti*, we added the liabilities of the Treasury *vis-à-vis* the banks of issue (De Mattia 1967, p. 187 line 1E up to 1935 and BI afterwards) and the stock of postal deposits held by the public and then subtracted $S(d)$. From 1884 to 1927 $S(d)$, as well as MBTR, were valued as of 30 June rather than at the end of the year. To obtain the year-end observation we used the same transformation made for budget data.

9 Our series of $eS(f)$ starts in 1917 and consists of Treasury bills sold abroad and loans from the United States and the United Kingdom. Foreign debt represents a large share of total debt. In 1919 it is equal to approximately 33 per cent of domestically owned debt. In 1926 the foreign loans of the United States and the United Kingdom disappear from the government books; an amortisation fund is created to repay the interest and principal of the loans with the proceeds of the war payments made by Austria. Payments on foreign debt are suspended from 1936 to the end of the Second World War. The government books do not acknowledge the existence of foreign debt which reappears in 1946 when much of the debt is renegotiated. Finally, it should be noted that there are discrepancies in the data as reported by domestic sources and by US Congress–Senate Commission of Gold and Silver Inquiry (1925).

10 Since many other factors intervened after 1926, one cannot strictly infer from this observation than an issue monopolist inflates more than competing banks of issue.

11 We are excluding war years which reinforce the Italian peculiarity, except for the real depreciation of the lira in the First World War.

12 The interested reader may want to consult Klein (1978) and the studies in Bordo and Schwartz (1984) on the general properties of nominal variables under the gold standard.

2 Money growth and its determinants

1 From chapter 1 our rest-of-world real income is U.K. real income from 1861 to 1945 and US real income from 1946 to 1991. For prices, interest rates and exchange rates we use French data from 1861 to 1913, UK data from 1914 to 1945 and US data from 1946 to 1991.

2 The monetary slowdown is not a phenomenon unique to Italy. Other countries, inside and outside the EMS, experienced a monetary disinflation (Fratianni and von Hagen 1992, chapter 2).

3 For the inclusive definition the range goes from a minimum of 73 per cent in the gold standard period to a maximum of 111 per cent during the 1980s. For the exclusive (of time deposits) definition the range is even wider, from a minimum of –18 per cent in the inter-war period to a maximum of 123 per cent in the 1938–49 years.

4 Table 2.2 shows that both MBTR and MBOT reinforce each other from 1921 to 1937. However, these results are very hard to interpret in light of the very large interactive term.

5 The empirical literature on the money multiplier has followed either a disaggregated or 'component' approach (Rasche and Johannes 1987) or an aggregative approach (Bomhoff 1977; Fratianni and Nabli 1979; Hafer and Hein 1984).

6 The standard reference on transfer functions is Box and Jenkins (1971, part III). Cf. also Fratianni and Nabli (1979) for an application of one-input transfer functions to the money multiplier.

7 The standard reference on the monetary theory of the balance of payments is the volume edited by Frenkel and Johnson (1976). Also useful is the survey by Kreinin and Officer (1978).

8 The instrumental variables were a trend, the exogenous variables, the two endogenous variables lagged one period and changes in the foreign nominal income (see chapter 1 for the definition and measurement of these variables). The pattern of the estimated residuals from the estimated regressions suggested significant heteroskedasticity. Consequently, the variables were re-weighted and the system estimated using the White (1980) adjustment method.

9 Seigniorage is usually defined as government's revenues accruing from the creation of money. Empirically, seigniorage tends to be measured by the change in the monetary base deflated by the price level. Our measure of seigniorage is more restrictive in the sense that we consider the flows of the Treasury component of

the monetary base rather than the entire monetary base. The reason for this choice has to do with the ease with which government can 'borrow' from the central bank. This distinction is rather important because in principle it is possible for an independent central bank to extract a great deal of seigniorage and yet not influence the growth of the money supply. On this point see Klein and Neumann (1989).

10 Our measure of seigniorage is equal to the flow of MBTR divided by the price level, all as a fraction of real national income.

11 We exclude the two world wars because we consider them legitimate examples of monetary financing.

3 From political unification to 1913

1 Garelli 1879; Supino 1895; Monzilli 1896; Canovai 1912; Cornaro 1931; Di Nardi 1953; De Mattia 1959; and Da Pozzo and Felloni 1964.

2 It is interesting to note that this active process of exchanges was also recorded in a historical review undertaken by the Banca d'Italia itself, which is the direct successor of these two banks (De Mattia 1991, pp. 476 and 1049).

3 According to the new statute, the bank was allowed to carry out the following transactions: (i) discount of bills of exchange issued to order with a maturity not exceeding three months and bearing three signatures; (ii) advances on precious metals, coupons of specified government securities, silk and bills of exchange payable abroad; (iii) deposit-taking in non-interest-bearing current accounts; (iv) acceptance of other deposits; (v) investment of its reserve funds in government securities, up to one-fifth of its capital; and (vi) issuance of notes.

4 Some official documents, referred to by De Cecco (1990), fully confirmed that the bank had no intention to adjust the rates, even when foreign banks raised them. By the same token, the way in which the bank managed its own government securities portfolio was not consistent with the full use of the interest rate mechanism. In fact, from time to time, what prevailed was either mere profit maximisation through arbitrage operations between domestic and international prices, and between existing and new securities, or the desire to 'assist' the Treasury through massive purchases of securities. At the time of the country's political unification, the second alternative seemed to prevail. In fact, the bank held a government securities portfolio at the maximum level permitted by its statute.

5 One Tuscan lira was equivalent to approximately 0.8 lire of the Kingdom of Sardinia or Italian lire.

6 The bank was going through a process of restructuring when the Roman revolution took place. The resulting Republic authorised the bank to issue a large quantity of new notes, but at the same time proclaimed notes no longer convertible.

7 The scudo was equivalent to approximately 5 lire.

8 In effect, loan facilities extended to the Vatican state never exceeded 6 per cent of the bank's total assets.

9 In accordance with its statute, and unlike other banks of issue, the bank could accept interest-bearing deposits.

10 One ducato was equivalent to approximately 4 lire.

11 One fiorino was equivalent to approximately 2.5 lire.

12 Therefore, this was not a bank of issue of a former state. Nonetheless, we mention it to provide a complete picture of all banks of issue existing during the first years of the unified state.

13 See, for instance, Ferrara (1868). Garelli, another important authority with regard to money matters, supported the same school of thought, while Busacca was not completely against the idea of a 'super' bank (Garelli 1879; Busacca 1870). In an interesting article, Cardarelli (1990, p. 173) first indicated that Banca Nazionale convinced both Canovai and Boccardo (initially an advocate of liberal theories) to intervene in favour of monopoly and then added: 'only seldom was their participation in the debate objective and unbiased. Generally speaking, their positions were dictated or instigated by the banks themselves. . . . The 1893 House enquiry . . . in fact, brought clearly to light that the banks of issue sponsored various magazines for the purpose of protecting their own interests, and there were also instances of subsidies for the publication of brochures and essays.'

14 Sannucci (1990, p. 184) went so far as to suggest that Banca Nazionale was the most suitable to perform the function of the leading bank in Italy for the reason that, on two previous occasions, it already operated under a regime of inconvertible paper currency.

15 Readers interested in learning more about this may refer to the excellent work of De Mattia (1959).

16 Laidler (1991) has an excellent survey on developments of the international monetary theory of the period 1870–1914.

17 Starting in 1848 and following the gold discoveries in Russia, Australia and California, the value of this metal declined.

18 We underline the 'partial and short-lived' nature of the solution, pending enactment of permanent legislation on the monetary system. In fact, in these circumstances, economic agents in the north found it advantageous to exchange gold against silver at the official price, and then to transfer the silver to the south to be converted again into gold, but at a market price.

19 In fact, foreign silver coins, with a fineness of 900/1,000, had to be transferred to Italy to be smelted and, at the same time, foreign exporters did not accept Italian silver coins with a fineness lower than that of their coins.

20 In effect, until 1848 France was unable to curb the outflow of gold, as its market price was higher than its official exchange rate. In practice, there was then a silver-based monometallism. Subsequently, due to a sudden and significant drop in the gold price on the free market, the situation was reversed and the French monetary system became a monometallism based on gold. Particulars of the 1803 French monetary system can be found in Lesourd and Gerard (1978). On the recurring problems brought about by Gresham law, see Commission on the Role of Gold in the Domestic and International Monetary System (1982).

21 And of the non-negligible fact that metal money had an intrinsic value.

22 Judging from the works of Willis (1901) and Gille (1968), these reasons undoubtedly played a significant role.

23 See Yeager (1976). Hawtrey (1927, p. 81) argued that the French view might be correct. In fact, countries such as Spain, Serbia, Bulgaria and Romania had already implemented bimetallism and Austria and Finland adopted this system from time to time; see Muhleman (1896). The future of silver was decided only after 1870.

24 Without that coordination, differences in prices and interest rates generated not only flows of reserves, but also of small coins.

25 However, it is worth noting that the mistake of insisting on the role of silver was made by many countries. In fact, between 1867 and 1871, Romania, Greece, Spain, Austria, Chile, Colombia and Venezuela also tried to promote the role of silver (Martello 1883, pp. 6–7). In 1870, a change of preference in favour of gold began. In the meantime, silver production doubled owing to the discovery of mines in Nevada. In 1876, the ratio between gold and silver prices was 1:18. Other countries ended up overvaluing silver. As these were less developed countries, such as Russia and the Austrian-Hungarian empire, the excess of silver flowed towards the wealthy countries of the Latin Monetary Union (Muhleman 1896; Cornaro 1931; Yaeger 1976; De Cecco 1979).

26 As an example, the minting of five franc silver coins was first restricted and then discontinued altogether. Another example was the decision of the central banks in Belgium, Switzerland and Italy to hold most of their own reserves in gold. There are no doubts as to the reasons why Italy, pursuing the objective of a monometallism based on gold, did not break away from the Union. As years went by and Italian coins were gradually transferred abroad, the theoretical reasons which at first prompted Italy to join the Union were superseded by more practical ones: the country had no interest in leaving the Union as it would otherwise be obliged to withdraw all coins from foreign countries and to convert them into gold at their nominal value. See Muhleman (1896), Corbino (1933, p. 410) and Ferraris (1879).

27 De Mattia (1967, table 20) has very detailed statistics on discount rates in Italy. On the 1863–4 international financial crisis, see Supino (1929, p. 15), Cornaro (1931, p. 18) and Di Nardi (1953, pp. 75–7).

28 See Di Nardi (1953, p. 65). It is also interesting to note Castronuovo's remarks (1975, p. 9): 'Certain modern forms of circulating wealth did not seem to have made much progress from the time when, in 1837, Cattaneo wrote: "paper money is the bogey we see regularly when we deal with a contract or other similar instrument. In all clauses, the notary public always includes three great enemies: death, disagreement and paper money, and the good gold and silver coins remain in our notarial archives as the only symbol of public and private faith".'

29 The recognition of the role played by fiscal and monetary policies in the decision to abandon the gold standard enables us also to realise how excessive is the importance attributed by some historians to other factors. In particular, it does

not appear reasonable to insist on the manufacturers' and farmers' claim that the lira should be depreciated in order to improve the competitiveness of their products in international markets. Apart from the fact that this argument would be valid only if expressed in terms of real depreciation, to improve competitiveness one could also resort to protective measures. Another aspect to consider is that the Italian crisis was almost concurrent with a banking panic in the United Kingdom in 1866; see Gilbert and Wood (1986). What was the impact of the British crisis? It played a part in sparking internal conflicts in Italian economic policy. These conflicts were the true underlying reason behind the government's decision to go off gold.

30 The term 'riscontrata' indicates the obligation on the part of a bank of issue to withdraw its notes from other banks against delivery of an equivalent value of those banks' notes.

31 We already mentioned that, until 1913, due to the closer commercial and financial relationship with France, it was helpful to look at the exchange rate between the Italian lira and the French franc. This opinion was shared by Jannaccone (1918) and Borgatta (1933).

32 The strong reaction of the lira exchange rate was already highlighted by Romanelli in a 1875 essay (De Cecco 1990, p. 624).

33 We agree with the view that, *vis-à-vis* France, the gold points were approximately 100.50 and 99.50 or 0.50 per cent above and below the gold parity. See, for instance, the report on the Miceli–Giolitti Bill of 30 December 1889, BI R.A. (1913), Borgatta (1933), Morgenstern (1959) and Einaudi (1960a).

34 As a result of this legislation, the currency limit relating to notes 'on behalf of the government' was changed to one billion lire. We arrive at this figure by adding loans authorised between 1870 and 1872, the 250 million lire loan of May 1866 and the additional one of 28 million of 5 October 1866.

35 We say six because, in 1870, Rome also was annexed and therefore Banca Romana operated within the Kingdom of Italy.

36 See Viner (1937, p. 134). Jannaccone (1918) wrote that changes in the lira exchange rate usually preceded those regarding the paper currency stock, thanks to the anticipation of this event. Spinelli (1989c) demonstrated that only by accident did Jannaccone not realise how much this was also true for the decline of the lira exchange rate from 1880 to 1881.

37 On the difficulties surrounding this transaction, see especially Rozenraad (1899). The official documents were reported by De Cecco (1990, p. 361). The issue was launched at 88.25, including the commission of 1 per cent in favour of the banks. In effect, the Italian government received 644 million lire in metal, as the commission was also paid in Rendita Italiana bonds.

38 For others, 17 years of inconvertibility were sufficient to convince the business community of the superiority of notes compared with metal currency; hence, their propensity not to demand conversion of notes into metal; see Kindleberger (1984a, p. 140). The increasing acceptance of notes was well described by De Mattia (1991, p. 609).

39 It is appropriate to recall that the 1874 law imposed on banks of issue the payment

of a currency tax on notes not covered by metal reserves, which were two thirds of all notes in circulation. As the currency supplement now permitted was fully covered by reserves, on this the banks did not pay any taxes. This means that banks were encouraged to issue the full value of additional notes permitted by law.

40 Pantaleoni 1895; De Rosa 1963, 1964a, 1964b, 1965; Vitale 1972; Confalonieri 1974, 1975; Negri 1990; Spinelli 1989b.

41 On the gradual departure from the liberal policy with regard to international commercial relations and on the trade war with France during the years 1888–92, see De Rosa (1982) and, above all, the five volumes by Vitale (1979).

42 In 1887, some banks became insolvent and there were initiatives aimed at rescuing the Esquilino firm and, indirectly, Banca di Torino which had financed it. Later, failures and rescue operations became more and more recurrent. According to Confalonieri (1974, p. 188), BN played along in the rescue operations as, in so doing, it hoped to accelerate the process of getting the monopoly in issuing notes.

43 Di Nardi 1953; De Rosa 1963, 1964a, 1964b, 1965; Confalonieri 1974.

44 See Negri (1990) on events analysed in this section.

45 In this, Italy was not different from other countries. A universal movement was taking place, away from the gold standard and towards the gold exchange standard; see Bloomfield (1959).

46 This rule was introduced to avoid the banks of issue finding themselves in a situation where the currency stock was at its maximum and depositors would withdraw their funds.

47 It is interesting to compare the uncertain effects brought about by the establishment of Banca d'Italia with those more positive effects associated with the creation of the Federal Reserve System; see Mankiw, Miron and Weil (1987).

48 In confirmation of the fact that the law was viewed negatively in international financial markets, we quote an excerpt from a letter of the Prime Minister, dated July 1893: 'Questioned on the new bank act Hambro replied: "its base is not solid. Too many non-performing assets"' (see also De Cecco 1990).

49 There was an increase in prices also at the international level. Between 1897 and 1913, the Sauerbeck price index increased by 33 per cent. Within the same period of time, Italian wholesale prices increased by 24 per cent, and the income deflator by 21 per cent. Furthermore, between 1873 and 1896, Italian prices moved in concert with world prices. These three price indexes dropped by 60, 30 and 21 per cent, respectively. In summary, the cycle of Italian prices appeared to be synchronised with that of the rest of the world, but moved within a narrower band.

50 At the beginning, in order to maximise profits, BI considered it necessary to ask for an extension of the period required by law to place its financial affairs in order. An agreement with the government signed in October 1894 recognised this need and extended the term from ten to twenty years. In the Banca d'Italia's R.A. (1895, p. 27) we read: 'Since we began to study the most appropriate way of conveniently solving the problem of liquidating illegal transactions, we realised that the Bank would have required a certain freedom in dealing with such a large portion of its assets, without being pressed by the urgency to act, without being

constrained by the too narrow terms imposed by the law passed on 10 August 1893. The agreement of 30 October 1894 came timely to our rescue, as it extended the period of time set for the liquidation of those transactions from ten to twenty years, and . . . provided the Bank with the tools to cope with eventual losses . . . and to rightly and legally distribute a part of the profits to its share-holders'. *Ex–post*, the extension of such period turned out to be extremely posi-tive, both for the banks' income statements and for strengthening the country's financial structure. In fact, it became much easier and less onerous for the banks of issue to liquidate non-performing assets, considering the acceleration of the process of economic development, the reduction of nominal and real interest rates, and the subsequent increase in the prices of private and public securities as well as real estate assets. See Confalonieri (1975, p. 103).

51 These facts are consistent with Triffin's thesis (1964).

4 The First World War: inflation and stabilisation

1 Griziotti (1926, pp. 18–19), Einaudi (1933, p. 41), Trupiano (1982, pp. 238 and 252).

2 It is appropriate to recall that Alberti (1931, p. 107) expressed the following com-ments on the financial aspects of the war in Libya, which preceded the world war by a very few years: 'Circumstances did not appear to be such as to allow com-plete transparence in accounting records, and therefore the government chose not to disclose the cost of war to the Italian people.'

3 Einaudi himself stated (p. 52) that already at the time of the Libyan war the motto was 'not a cent of new taxes'. He also mentioned 'the hard work necessary to extract only two additional cents [of taxes] from parliament at the time of the Messina and Reggio Calabria earthquake', which also preceded the world war by a very short time.

4 With interest deducted from their nominal price at the outset.

5 The rigidity of nominal interest rates, and hence the fall of real interest rates, was also emphasised by Modigliani and Jappelli (1986). These authors attributed it to the fact that, until the 1960s, inflation followed a white noise process and, therefore, was not a good proxy of anticipated inflation from which to compute real rates of interest. On our part, we are inclined to impute the fall in real rates to rate controls. Furthermore, inflation was not white noise during the war.

6 This is from Bachi who wrote for the US Congress (1925).

7 This enabled the Bank of England to always maintain the discount rate at a level lower than that for other countries (Lindert 1969).

8 In a June 1916 letter, reported by Toniolo (1989), the BI's manager proposed to the Treasury Minister to purchase government securities, which would have recorded as a bill of exchange discount transaction.

9 In another letter, also reported by Toniolo (1989, p. 107), the same BI's manager admitted that, in order to stimulate securities underwriting, the banks of issue would have to grant bigger loans backed by securities advances at interest rates lower than the yields on the same securities.

10 While the Banca Commerciale Italiana, Credito Italiano and Banco di Roma managed to overcome these difficulties, the fourth largest bank, the Banca Italiana di Sconto, had to close its branches at the end of 1921. Then, BI had no choice but to lend the necessary funds to the bank's liquidators (Sraffa 1922; Rossi 1950; Guarnieri 1953).

11 Cassel (1922, p. 38), Heilperin (1968, p. 111), Bresciani Turroni (1931) and Friedman and Schwartz (1963, p. 267).

12 The decline in the demand for base money at the end of the First World War was rather general (Bresciani Turroni 1931; and Lehefeld 1923). This was obviously the time when economic agents were investing the excess liquidity accumulated during the war. These episodes were also reported by Keynes (1923, pp. 42–3), who, however, did not seem to grasp the real nature of the phenomenon. In fact, he maintained that, in agricultural countries, people saved money in the first phase of the inflationary process, because they were unable to distinguish between nominal and real income. We move two objections to this story: first, the increase in note demand is also typical of industrialised countries and, second, it is not appropriate to speak of money illusion.

13 Einaudi claimed that, even when the authorities were successful in controlling the prices of some goods, the business community reacted by raising the price of analogous goods not subject to controls, more than would otherwise have been warranted.

14 Basically, this was the predecessor of the existing Ufficio Italiano Cambi (Italian Foreign Exchange Institute).

15 This aspect was also noted with concern by the BI's manager; see his letter of 20 November 1918 reported by Toniolo (1989, p. 306).

16 It is worth recalling that the drop in prices after the end of the war was also an international phenomenon (League of Nations 1922; Einzig 1935; Yeager 1981).

17 It is not appropriate to refer to industrial production data since they were largely influenced by peculiar events, such as labour unrests in 1920–1.

18 At the same time, we cannot disregard the positive impact on production and domestic prices, which stemmed from the concurrent recovery of world demand and decline in import prices.

19 The official resolution of the 1920 Brussels International Monetary Conference stated that, where there was an excess quantity of money, there was also 'a perverse spiral between price and salary growth, with a resulting disruption in productive processes, trade . . . and social conflict'. On the subject of the direction of causality between inflation and social conflict, see the exchange between Capie (1986) and Fratianni (1986). To avoid misunderstandings, we wish to emphasise that we are well aware of the mere political developments which may have contributed to spark social conflicts during the period in question.

5 The 1920s and 1930s: foreign exchange policy and industrial and financial restructuring

1 Even though the National Bureau of Economic Research places the beginning of the US recession in August 1929, we have maintained a uniform period

classification to facilitate comparisons. For an international analysis of the recession, also see Saint-Etienne (1984). The magnitude of the US production collapse is well documented in the literature. The reasons behind the collapse remain somewhat controversial: see for instance Friedman and Schwartz (1963), Brunner (1981) and Saint-Etienne (1984). In any event, our table 5.1 indicates that the US monetary squeeze was the tightest from 1927 to 1933, whereas UK money growth rose sharply relative to the first sub-period.

2 For the United States and the United Kingdom, annual growth rates of both the monetary base and the multiplier were:

	United States			United Kingdom		
	M	MB	V	M	MB	V
average 1921–6	3.8	–0.4	4.2	–2.0	–2.9	0.9
average 1927–33	–4.3	1.8	–6.1	1.6	0.2	1.4
average 1934–7	8.7	12.5	–3.8	3.6	4.2	–0.6

Both countries restrained their monetary base in the first sub-period, relaxed it in the second, and speeded up its growth in the third. The multiplier played a decisive role in the United States (Friedman and Schwartz 1963, pp. 332–3). The closest correlation in the three countries' monetary variables was reached in the third sub-period, when the monetary base grew significantly everywhere.

3 The decision to look also at the dollar was prompted by the fact that, in those years, the US dollar emerged as the leading currency in international financial markets and also became the main point of reference for the Italian monetary authorities. For example, in a letter of May 1917, BI's manager stated that: 'The war brought about structural changes in Italy's trade relations with the rest of the world. The United States has assumed a predominant position' (Toniolo 1989, p. 250).

4 From data provided by Friedman and Schwartz (1982), we note that the British income deflator (1929 = 100) dropped from 154 to 106 between 1920 and 1923 and then remained stable. The US income deflator (1929 = 100) fell from 121 to 99 between 1920 and 1922 and maintained the same level afterward. Sauerbeck prices (1867–77 = 100) decreased from 251 to 131 between 1920 and 1922, and reached the 139 mark in 1924.

5 To have a better idea of the amounts involved, it suffices to recall that, at the end of 1926, outstanding Treasury bills amounted to 15.5 billion lire against a total value of paper currency held by the public of 18.9 billion lire.

6 Short-term Treasury bills, as well as the five and seven-year bonds with maturities commencing on 11 November 1926 became non-redeemable. For each 100 lire worth of old securities, one obtained a nominal value from 112 to 116.5 of new perpetual securities. The conversion of nine-year bonds, 5 and 4.75 per cent coupons, was left to the holders' option. For each 100 lire of these securities, the government offered new perpetual securities with a nominal value of 107.5 and 102 lire, respectively. New debt was also offered to the public at the issue price of 87.5 lire.

7 The conversion decree itself stated that, up to 31 December 1927, BI's paper currency in circulation was allowed to exceed the limit of 7 billion lire, without incurring a penalty at the discount rate plus one third. The rationale of this provision was to mitigate the negative effects on the economy arising from the inability of the public to convert debt into paper currency.

8 See our data of chapter 1 or those of Bachi published in US Congress (1925).

9 Retail prices were much more sluggish than wholesale prices (Del Vecchio 1928; Molinari 1928; Supino 1929). This feature was so pronounced that the *Economist* of 11 December 1926 reported that public opinion was 'rather frustrated by what appears to be an unjustified resistance by retailers to reduce prices'.

10 Gualerni (1982, p. 49) argues that the industrial and financial restructuring processes implemented in Italy, as well as the target rate of '90' with the pound, mitigated the effects of the crisis on Italian output levels in the Great Depression.

11 Bank for International Settlements (1947, p. 50), Rey (1978, p. 291), Paradisi (1976, pp. 296–7).

12 Alberti (1931), Miller (1940), Paradisi (1976), Tattara and Toniolo (1976), Rey (1978), Gualerni (1976, 1982).

13 BI (R.A. 1929, pp. 23–4, R.A. 1933, p. 21); Tattara and Toniolo (1976, p. 130); Cohen (1972, p. 653).

14 The war in Ethiopia accelerated protectionism and made it justifiable to both the domestic and international public opinions. In fact, the massive purchases of war equipment abroad and the military traffic through the Suez Canal required large quantities of foreign currencies, which had to be diverted from the private sector. Furthermore, the United Kingdom requested that the League of Nations embargo Italian exports. At the same time, all foreign loan facilities to Italy were cancelled and all her purchases abroad had to be settled fully in cash.

15 Two decrees were passed on 7 September and 6 November 1926 to protect depositors. The legislation provided that all financial institutions: a) were required to obtain a license at the time of incorporation and prior to subsequent expansions; b) were subject to the control of a regulator, who reviewed their annual reports and periodical financial information; c) had to set aside part of their profits in a reserve fund; and d) were obliged to abide by limits set for their total deposit base and overall exposure to a single customer. With the new rules, the business of banking moved from the private to the public domain.

6 The Second World War and the 1947 stabilisation

1 The reader may want to consult De Vita (1947), BI (1947), Bank for International Settlements (1947, 1950), Foa (1949), Corbino (1962), Gualerni (1980, 1982) and Rasi (1982c).

2 BI R.A. (1942, p. 126), Azzolini (1943, p. 59), Mancini (1947, pp. 4–5), Bank for International Settlements (1947, p. 30), Baffi (1965, pp. 138–9, 229).

3 De Vita (1949, p. 55) reported that the rate on normal savings accounts, set at 2

per cent on 1 April 1934, was reduced first to 1.5 on 1 October 1944, then to 1 per cent on 16 February 1945. Similarly, the three-month term deposit rate was reduced from 2.5 to 2 and later to 1.5 per cent.

4 With regard to the process of monetary base creation, the landing of allied armies in Sicily and Italy's division into two areas created a very peculiar situation. Allied military authorities issued the AM lira, which was used to pay troops' salaries, as well as all other war expenditures in the country. The printing of AM lire stopped on 15 March 1946, when BI regained the exclusive control of issuing notes. From that date onward, BI provided the necessary Italian lire to the Allies. Obviously, the Italian government received its notes from BI. In the north, BI supplied banknotes to the Social Republic and German military authorities. On this subject, see BI (R.A. 1945, p. 74) and Bank for International Settlements (1947, p. 29): 'Between September 1943 and April 1945, the Allied military authorities issued 32 per cent of total new notes, the Italian government 3 per cent, and the Social Republic and the Germans 65 per cent.'

5 The *Economist* of 5 February 1944 and Corbino (1962) blamed that decision for contributing to the inflation explosion through the printing of large quantities of lire by the Allies, the AM lire. Baffi (1965) argues that this criticism was overdone.

6 When the loan was launched, similar securities in the market yielded 4.5 to 5 per cent. At the beginning, the loan produced interest at 3.5 per cent, but contained an exemption clause relative to a future extraordinary tax that was under discussion and was also expected to be levied on securities. In the spring of 1947, it was decided that the tax was not applicable to income from securities. Consequently, the interest rate on this loan was formally increased to 5 per cent.

7 The two-tier foreign exchange system was criticised by the Bank for International Settlements (1947, p. 67) and Baffi (1965, p. 191). On the other hand, Baffi (1965, pp. 260–1) justified such a system if accompanied by a similar duality in the price system.

8 We were unable to find monthly data for bank credit. We therefore decided to resort to data obtained through the following accounting equations. Apart from the net worth, a bank's balance sheet may be expressed as follows:
  (i) reserves + bank credit = deposits
By adding publicly held cash to both sides of the balance sheet, we obtain:
  (ii) monetary base + bank credit = money
As money (M) is given by the product of the money multiplier (m) and the monetary base (BM), we can rewrite (ii) as
  (iii) bank credit = $(m-1)$ x BM
where $(m-1) = a$ is the credit multiplier.
On the basis of (iii), it is possible to derive monthly series of bank credit from monthly data, relative to the money multiplier and monetary base.

9 The two–tier foreign exchange system was therefore discontinued.

10 The elasticity of the bank credit multiplier (a) with respect to the mandatory reserve coefficient (rr) is equal to $(da/drr)/(rr/a)$. While $(da/drr) = (dm/drr)$, the

ratio rr/a is higher than rr/m. Hence, it follows that the absolute value of the elasticity of the credit multiplier is higher than that of the money multiplier.

11 The Final Remarks ('Considerazioni Finali') closely reflect the thinking of the governor who reads aloud during the Annual Meeting of BI.

12 As reported in chapter 8, a similar strategy was followed by Governor Carli in the 1970s, when he stated in the Final Remarks that a decline in credit assistance to the government would be regarded as a rebellious act against the state (BI R.A. 1973, p. 418).

13 On 2 October 1946, the governors of the International Monetary Fund and the World Bank accepted Italy's membership in the two associations.

14 The Italian share for participating in the International Monetary Fund and the World Bank was 180 million dollars in each case.

15 A charming account of the US visit can be found in Carli (1993, pp. 53–5).

16 There was also a tendency toward an increasingly sustained credit growth in the last quarter of 1947. In fact, while credit petered out by 149 per cent in October, it grew by 11 and 47 per cent in November and December, respectively.

17 BI (R.A. 1947, p. 107), Lanzarone (1948, p. 5), Bresciani Turroni (1950, p. 278), Bank for International Settlements (1950, p. 183), BI (R.A. 1959, p. 352), Gangemi (1961, p. 411), Hirschman (1968, p. 603) and Masera (1983, p. 34) all concur with the announcement hypothesis.

18 De Cecco (1968, p. 132) was of the opposite view when he wrote: 'The route chosen by the Italian government in September 1947 cannot be rationalised . . . in economic terms. The freezing of bank deposits at the Treasury and the Central Bank, reached through the introduction of mandatory minimum reserves . . . can only have a political motivation. . . . The 1948 elections are getting closer and the governing parties appear to prefer the support of the middle class and the farmers. The latter would not be affected by deflation . . . dependent as they are on agricultural sustenance. The former . . . would regain their confidence in the government only if the continuing increase in prices could be suddenly stopped.' Our view is that the measures were prompted primarily by economic requirements, as recognised by De Cecco himself in other parts of his book (for instance, see p. 126).

19 This aspect also explains why 1947 was not a replica of 1926 in bringing about a real appreciation of the Italian lira.

20 See BI (R.A. 1947, p. 233, 1950, p. 261, 1956, p. 356), Bresciani Turroni (1950), V. Lutz (1950), Bank for International Settlements (1950, p. 50).

21 We shall see how in the 1970s this mechanism became ineffective when the Treasury succeeded in reinstating its dominance over an accommodating (BI) governor.

7 The fifties and sixties

1 The behaviour of those variables which are either intermediate targets or ultimate targets of monetary policy – monetary base, money stock, prices, exchange-rates, interest rates and seigniorage – suggests a change in regime

between the end of the sixties and the beginning of the seventies. Thus, we decided to separate the fifties and sixties from the seventies. Actually, Italian monetary policy lost its bearings much earlier, in 1960 when Guido Carli replaced Donato Menichella as BI governor.

2 Also in this case, the process of theoretical revision preceded the actual turn of events. In fact, crucial developments such as the separation of BI from the Treasury, the rise in real interest rates, the reduction in inflation and a reluctance to continuosly depreciate the lira were the concrete result of a change in attitudes. Such a change can be traced back to the time when Paolo Baffi replaced Guido Carli as BI governor in 1975. In sum, there are two turning points, one around the sixties, when Carli replaced Menichella, and the other towards the end of the seventies, when Baffi succeeded Carli.

3 In this case, the maximum value is already recorded in 1975, not in 1978 when the monetary base showed its highest level.

4 There are other considerations that prompted us to end the first sub-period in 1969. First, there was a change from fixed to floating exchange rates. For a relatively small open economy such as Italy, where the authorities consider international reserves to be the only true constraint on their behaviour, a change in the international monetary system is bound to have important repercussions, both at the level of monetary policy formulation and implementation. Second, Italy suffered a deterioration in its terms of trade following the oil shock. Finally, Italy experienced the so-called 'hot autumn', whose effects drastically and permanently changed the domestic labour market.

5 In October 1959, the Italian contribution to the International Monetary Fund increased from 180 to 270 million dollars. It also doubled its contribution to the International Bank for Reconstruction and Development to 360 million.

6 Similar problems were experienced by Germany in 1931 and 1959, and by the United Kingdom in 1947 and 1957.

7 Inter-bank agreements on interest rates paid by banks on deposits or interest rates charged to customers were not only an accepted practice, but received the official approval of the monetary authorities.

8 A country can borrow in foreign currency and thus enable BF to become negative only in the short run.

9 On top of the 3.5 per cent, banks would be subject to a graduated scale, starting from a minimum of 4 per cent and rising according to the size, duration and frequency of the loan.

10 Definition (7.4) is similar to what is commonly known as the balance on official settlement basis, the difference between the two being the change in the banks' net foreign asset position.

11 See Fratianni (1971), Tullio (1977, 1981) and Bini-Smaghi and Tardini (1983).

12 The authorities will later acknowledge that a large portion of capital outflows was botivated by tax considerations (BI R.A. 1966, p. 176), The regulation in question was removed in 1964 and then reintroduced in 1967; see Mesalles (1968), Onida (1974, p. 85) and Basevi et al. (1978, p. 157).

13 Until this time, there was an unlimited commitment to purchase and sell short-term Treasury bills (BOTs) at the official discount rate.

14 The authorities' intention to put an end to the rate stabilisation policy is revealed by Fazio (1979, p. 284): 'we hope that the market may find a new equilibrium, where yields are half or, at maximum, 1 percentage point higher than previous levels'. With this hope, the official discount rate was raised from 3.5 to 4 per cent in August.

8 The seventies

1 The measurement is based on the national income deflator. De Grauwe and Fratianni (1985) calculated that, in the sixties and seventies, the differential between Italian consumer price inflation and average inflation in the G7 countries was 0.2 and 4.5 percentage points, respectively.

2 The growth accounting literature demonstrates that the slowdown in economic growth is a generalised phenomenon and certainly not isolated to Italy; read Stern (1967), Graziani (1969), Modigliani and Tarantelli (1973), Rosa (1975, 1982), Valli (1976), Basevi *et al.* (1978), Denison (1979), Kendrick (1981), Maddison (1982), Swoboda (1983), Saidi and Huber (1983) and Lindbeck (1983).

3 As of 1993 the European Community, EC, has become European Union, EU. Since our *History* stops in 1991 we shall use the historically correct label of EC.

4 In support of this hypothesis, we note that criteria for qualifying for a disability pension were made so as to maximise the power of discretion. Furthermore, disability pensions were much more concentrated in high-unemployment areas (e.g., the south) than in low-unemployment areas (e.g., the north).

5 Non-residents also held domestic debt, but it was a very negligible amount during the seventies and is therefore ignored.

6 Caranza and Fazio (1984), perhaps alluding to the monetary approach of the balance of payments, explained that, in 1974, the decision to exclude foreign debt from TDC stemmed from the need to encourage the inflow of foreign currency necessary to cover that part of the budget deficit caused by the increase in oil prices. There were other alternatives for attracting foreign currencies (for instance, by controlling the money stock and domestic credit expansion). Above all, the problem of controlling the domestic economy and the need to acquire foreign capital did not take place at exactly the same time.

7 For a detailed account of *massimali* and portfolio constraints read Spinelli and Fratianni (1991, pp. 548–50).

8 From 1972 to 1979, the Italian real *ex-post* short-term interest rate was, on average, lower than the German one by 3.68 percentage points; the long-term rate was lower by 5.23 percentage points. See Fratianni (1987, p. 270).

9 According to BI's estimates, the outflow of capital hidden under the entry 'tourism' was 560 billion lire in 1974 and 535 in 1975 (see 1976 Annual Report, p. 163). It was not until 1977 that the illegal capital outflow came to an end. During that year, the discount of Italian banknotes circulating abroad also disappeared.

10 Grilli, Kregel and Savona (1982) emphasise the role of the terms of trade to explain the Italian business cycles.

11 This arrangement was known as the European 'snake' or the 'snake in the tunnel'. It ended in March, 1973. For more details on the objectives and mechanics of this arrangement read BI (R.A. 1972, pp. 67–74).

12 TDC grew by about 2,000 billion lire less than the amount Italy and the IMF had stipulated (Bini-Smaghi and Tardini 1983).

13 In addition, credit institutions were allowed to revalue their assets, so that the effective required reserve ratio dropped from 15 to 8 per cent.

14 The discount rate was raised from 6 to 8 per cent and required reserves were increased.

9 Italy in the eighties: towards central bank independence

1 See Commission of the European Communities (1979, 1982) for detailed descriptions.

2 More precisely, the upper part of the band is 2.275 per cent above the central parity, whereas the lower part of the band is 2.225 per cent below the central parity.

3 Spain joined the ERM on 19 June 1989, and the United Kingdom on 8 October 1990 at the wider band of ±6 per cent. The Portuguese escudo would join later, while the Greek drachma never joined. It falls outside our objective to give a precise account of the events of the EMS. For more information the reader can refer to Fratianni and von Hagen (1992, chapter 2).

4 Incidentally, Baffi argues that the wider band would have also served the United Kingdom well, for which he cites the article by Samuel Brittan in the *Financial Times* 16 November 1978, titled 'The case for the Italian band'.

5 The source of the data is BI, *Bollettino economico*, table 'bilancia dei pagamenti economica'.

6 Italy grew 39 basis points per annum more rapidly that the 6 EMS countries in the 1971–8 period and 54 basis points in the 1979–91 period. The 6 EMS countries are aggregated using fixed ECU weights.

7 It is interesting to note that Minford (1994) argues that this mechanism facilitates an increase in government subsidies to the traded goods sector and makes the EMS an inferior alternative to a regime of independent central banks operating in an environment of flexible exchange rates.

8 Treasury auctions for short-term bills, the so-called 'buoni ordinari del Tesoro'. had been deeply modified in 1975. The changes went in the direction of making the auctioning process more sensitive to market conditions.

9 Goodman (1991) cannot explain the divorce by reference to Italy's political structure. He also seems to give weight to the role of the politician innovator.

10 Over the period March 1989–February 1990, the Bank bought 3 per cent of auctioned bills (Buttiglione and Prati, table 6).

11 The ambiguity of the official position is well reflected in this statement by Ciampi: 'In her actions the Central Bank has a plurality of reference points:

among these are particularly important credit to the economy, money (M2), real interest rates, the exchange rate. None of these variables is to be identified as the primary reference in an absolute sense' (Ciampi 1983, testimony to both chambers of Parliament).

12 The curve EC in figure 9.1 as in the subsequent figures refers to the weighted average of the six original EMS countries, the weights being the ECU weights.

13 The data come from Fratianni and von Hagen (1992): the source for output and price data is the OECD, the source of the monetary base is the IMF. For comparability purposes we did not use our measure of monetary base.

14 The Delors Report of 1989 was very skeptical about the efficacy of markets to discipline fiscal authorities. On this point, see Fratianni and von Hagen (1990, pp. 396–7).

15 We measure the difference between the average values of the 1989–91 period and the average values of the 1979–81 period.

16 The expected twelve-month exchange rate is the ratio of one plus the twelve-month Eurolira interest rate to the corresponding Eurodm interest rate multiplied by the spot exchange rate lira/DM.

17 For example, the cumulative inflation difference from 1988 to 1992 between Italy and Germany, measured in terms of the consumer price index, was 15.2 percentage points.

Bibliography

Abrate, M. 1978. Moneta e risparmio in Italia negli anni della grande crisi. In *Industria e banca nella grande crisi 1929–1934*, G. Toniolo (ed.). Milan: Etas-Libri.

Ackley, G. 1972. Lo sviluppo economico italiano del dopoguerra e gli insegnamenti che è possibile trarne per la politica economica degli Stati Uniti. In *L'economia italiana: 1945–1970*, A. Graziani (ed.). Bologna: Il Mulino.

Alberti, M. 1931. La vicenda economico monetaria dell'Italia dal 1913 al 1929. In *Banche di emissione, moneta e politica monetaria in Italia dal 1848 al 1929*, M. Alberti and V. Cornaro (eds.). Milan: GUF.

Alesina, A., de Broeck, M., Prati, A. and Tabellini, G. 1992. Default Risk on Government Debt in OECD Countries. Manuscript, May.

Alesina, A. and Summers, L. 1993. Central Bank Dependence and Macroeconomics Performance: Some Comparative Evidence, *Journal of Money, Credit and Banking*, 25, 2: 151–62.

Amantia, A. 1933. *La difesa della lira*. Catania: Studio Editoriale Moderno.

Andreatta, B. 1993. Il divorzio dieci anni dopo. *Il Sole–24 Ore*, 26 July.

Azzolini, R. and Marani, U. (eds.). 1982. *Politica monetaria e debito pubblico*. Milan: Angeli. 1984

Azzolini, V. 1943. I riflessi della guerra sui fenomeni della moneta e del credito. *Rivista Bancaria*, 24 (February 28): 532–65.

Bachi, R. 1922. Italy. In *The Recommendations and Their Applications. A Review of Two Years, Vol. II, Italy*, League of Nations (ed.). Geneve: Kundig.

1926. *L'alimentazione e la politica annonaria in Italia*. Bari: Laterza.

Baffi, P. 1965. *Studi sulla moneta*. Milan: Giuffrè.

1973. *Nuovi studi sulla moneta*. Milan: Giuffrè.

1976. Il governo della moneta nel nostro tempo. *Bancaria*, 32 (January): 7–13.

1989. Il Negoziato sullo SME. *Bancaria*, 45 (January): 67–70.

Bagehot, W. 1873. *Lombard Street*. London: Henry S. King.

Banca d'Italia. various years. *Relazione annuale [R.A.]*. Roma: Banca d'Italia. (The year refers to the year of the Report and not to the year of publication.)

various issues. *Bollettino statistico*. Rome: Banca d'Italia.

1994. *Bollettino economico* (February), 22. Rome: Banca d'Italia.

1986. *Donato Menichella: Scritti e discorsi scelti, 1936–1966*. Rome: Banca d'Italia.

Bank for International Settlements. 1947. Italy's Economic Financial Position in the Summer of 1947. Basle: Bank for International Settlements.

    1950. *Twentieth Annual Report* (June). Basle: Bank for International Settlements.

Barberi, B. 1947. La lira italiana dal 1913 al 1946. *Congiuntura Economica*, 2, 15 (May): 4–8.

Barro, R.J. 1989. *Macroeconomics* (2nd edition). New York: Wiley and Sons.

Basevi, G. *et al.* 1978. *La bilancia dei pagamenti italiana*. Bologna: Il Mulino.

Benini, R. 1894. L'azione dello Stato sui mercati dei cambi ed i criteri dell'amministrazione italiana. *Giornale degli economisti* (April): 299–322.

Bini-Smaghi, L. and Tardini, P. 1983. The Effectiveness of Monetary Policy, an Empirical Investigation for Italy (1966–1981). *Giornale degli economisti e Annali di Economia* (September–October): 679–90.

Bloomfield, A. 1959. *Monetary Policy under the International Gold Standard: 1880–1914*. New York: Federal Reserve Bank.

Bomhoff, E.J. 1977. Predicting the Money Multiplier, a Case Study for the US and the Netherlands. *Journal of Monetary Economics*, 3: 325–45.

Bonelli, F. 1991. *La Banca d'Italia dal 1894 al 1913. Momenti della formazione di una banca centrale*. Bari: Laterza.

Borgatta, G. 1933. *Bilancia dei pagamenti*. Milan: Giuffrè.

Bordo, M. and Schwartz, A.J. (eds.). 1984. *A Retrospective on the Classical Gold Standard, 1821–1931*. Chicago: University of Chicago Press.

Box, G.E.P. and Jenkins. G.M. 1970. *Time Series Analysis, Forecasting and Control*. San Francisco: Holden Day.

Bresciani Turroni, C. 1931. Le vicende del marco tedesco. *Annali di economia*, 7, 1–2. Milan: Università Bocconi Editrice.

    1950. Due giudizi contrastanti sulla politica economica dell'Italia. *Moneta e Credito*, 3 (September): 277–82.

Brittan, S. 1978. The Case for the Italian Band. *Financial Times* (November 16).

Bruins, G.M. 1920. *Memorandum Prepared for the International Financial Conference at Bruxelles*. London: Harrison and Sons (for the League of Nations).

Brunner, K. (ed.). 1981. *The Great Depression Revisited*. Boston: Martinus Nijhoff Publishing.

Brunner, K. and Meltzer, A.H. 1964. Some Further Investigation of Demand and Supply Function of Money. *Journal of Finance* (May): 240–83.

    1968. Liquidity Traps for Money, Credit and Interest Rates. *Journal of Political Economy*, 76 (January–February): 1–37.

    1989. Money Supply. In *Survey of Monetary Economics*, B. Friedman and F. Hahn (eds.). Amsterdam: North-Holland.

Bruno, M. and Sachs, J. 1985. *Economics of Worldwide Stagflation*. Cambridge, MA: Harvard University Press.

Burger, A.E. 1971. *The Money Supply Process*. Belmont, CA: Wadsworth Publishing Co.

Busacca, R. 1870. *Studio sul caso forzoso dei biglietti di banca in Italia*. Firenze: Tipografia della Banca d'Italia.

Buttiglione, L. and Prati, A. 1990. La scelta del meccanismo di collocamento dei titoli di Stato: analisi teorica e valutazione dell'esperienza italiana. *Contributi all'analisi economica del Servizio Studi*, 6 (December). Rome: Banca d'Italia.

Cagan, P. 1965. *Determinants and Effects of Changes in the Stock of Money, 1875–1960*. New York: Columbia University Press.

Calliari, S., Spinelli, F. and Verga, G. 1984. Money Demand in Italy: A Few More Results. *The Manchester School of Economic and Social Studies*, 2: 141–59.

Canovai, T. 1912. *Le banche di emissione in Italia*. Rome: Casa Editrice Italiana.

Capie, F. 1986. Conditions in Which Very Rapid Inflation has Appeared. In *The National Bureau Method, International Capital Mobility and Other Essays*, K. Brunner and A.H. Meltzer (eds.). Carnegie-Rochester Conference Series on Public Policy, Vol. XXIV. Amsterdam: North-Holland.

Caranza, C. and Fazio, A. 1984. The Evolution of the Methods of Monetary Control in Italy: 1974–1983. Paper presented at the Conference on Money, Credit and Economic Activity in Italy, Oxford.

Cardarelli, S. 1990. La questione bancaria in Italia dal 1860 al 1982. In *Ricerche per la storia dlela Banca d'Italia*, Vol. I. Bari: Laterza.

Carli, G. 1993. *Cinquant'anni di vita italiana*. Rome: Laterza.

Cassel, G. 1920. *Memorandum on the World's Monetary Problems*. London: Harrison and Sons (for the League of Nations).

1922. *Money and Foreign Exchange after 1914*. London: Constable.

1928. *Post-war Monetary Stabilization*. New York: Columbia University Press.

Castronuovo, V. 1975. La storia economica. *Storia d'Italia, dall'unità ad oggi*, 4, 1. Torino: Einaudi.

Catalano, F. 1975. *L'Italia dalla dittatura alla democrazia 1919–1948*. Milan: Feltrinelli.

Chouraqui, J.C. and Price, R.W.R. 1984. Medium-term Financial Strategy: The Co-ordination of Fiscal and Monetary Policies. *OECD Economic Studies*, 2: 7–49.

Ciampi, C.A. 1983. Funzioni della banca centrale nell'economia di oggi. In *La moneta e l'economia: il ruolo delle banche centrali*, P. Ciocca (ed.). Bologna: Il Mulino.

Cianci, E. 1933. *Dinamica dei prezzi delle merci in Italia dal 1870 al 1929*. Annali di statistica, series VI, 20. Rome: Istat.

Ciocca, P. 1976. L'economia italiana nel contesto internazionale. In *L'economia italiana nel periodo fascista*, P. Ciocca and G. Toniolo (eds.). Bologna: Il Mulino.

Ciocca, P. and Toniolo, G. (eds.). 1976. *L'economia italiana nel periodo fascista*. Bologna: Il Mulino.

Cohen, J.S. 1972. The 1927 Revaluation of the Lira: A Study in Political Economy. *The Economic History Review*, 4: 642–54.

Commission of the European Communities. 1979. The European Monetary System. *European Economy*, 3 (July): 65–111.

1982. The European Monetary System. *European Economy*, 12 (July): 13–128.

1984. *European Economy*.

Commission on the Role of Gold in the Domestic and International Monetary System. 1982. *Report*. Washington, DC: Government Printing Office.

Confalonieri, A. 1974. *Banca e industria in Italia 1894–1906. Vol. I: Le premesse: dall'abolizione del corso forzoso alla caduta del Credito Mobiliare.* Milan: Banca Commerciale Italiana.

1975. *Banca e industria in Italia 1894–1906. Vol. II: Il sistema bancario tra due crisi.* Milan: Banca Commerciale Italiana.

1982a. *Banca e industria in Italia dalla crisi del 1907 all'agosto del 1914. Vol. I: Il sistema bancario di un'economia in transizione.* Milan: Banca Commerciale Italiana.

1982b. *Banca e industria in Italia dalla crisi del 1907 all'agosto del 1914. Vol. II: Crisi e sviluppo nell'industria italiana.* Milan: Banca Commerciale Italiana.

Coppola d'Anna, F. 1946a. Il reddito nazionale italiano nel 1945. *Congiuntura Economica*, 9: 4–8.

1946b. *Esperienze monetarie di questo dopoguerra.* Milan: Istituto Editoriale Galileo.

Corbino, E. 1931. *Annali dell'economia italiana. Vol. 1: 1861–1870.* Città di Castello: Leonardo da Vinci.

1933. *Annali dell'economia italiana. Vol. III: 1881–1890.* Città di Castello: Leonardo da Vinci.

1938. *Annali dell'economia italiana. Vol. V: 1901–1914.* Città di Castello: Leonardo da Vinci.

1962. *L'economia italiana dal 1860 al 1960.* Bologna: Zanichelli.

Cornaro, V. 1931. Le vicende economico monetarie dell'Italia dal 1849 al 1913. In *Banche di emissione, moneta e politica monetaria in Italia dal 1849 al 1929*, M. Alberti and V. Cornaro (eds.). Milan: GUF.

Cotula, F., Masera, R. and Morcaldo, G. 1979. Bilancio pubblico a prezzi correnti e a prezzi costanti in Italia: alcuni aspetti poco noti del 'crowding out' reale. Manuscript.

Cotula, F. and Micossi, S. 1977. Riflessioni sulla scelta degli obiettivi intermedi della politica monetaria nella esperienza italiana. *Contributi alla ricerca economica.* Rome: Banca d'Italia.

Da Pozzo. M. and Felloni, G. 1984. *La borsa valori di Genova nel secolo XIX.* Archivo Economico dell'Unificazione Italiana, series II, X. Torino: ILTE.

D'Adda, C. 1976. Le relazioni monetarie ed il costo delle deflazioni. *Un modello per l'economia italiana. Il modello econometrico dell'università di Bologna: struttura e simulazioni*, C. D'Adda *et al.* (eds.). Bologna: Il Mulino.

De Angelis, G. 1982a. La politica monetaria e creditizia ed i rapporti con l'estero. *Annali dell'economia italiana, vol. 6, tomo 1: 1923–1929.* Milan: IPSOA.

1982b. La politica monetaria e creditizia ed i rapporti con l'estero. *Annali dell'economia italiana, vol 7, tomo 1: 1923–1929.* Milan: IPSOA.

1982c. La politica monetaria e creditizia ed i rapporti con l'estero. *Annali dell'economia italiana, vol. 11, tomo 1: 1953–1958.* Milan: IPSOA.

De Cecco, M. 1968. *Saggi di politica monetaria.* Milan: Giuffre'.

1976. Banca d'Italia e conquista politica del sistema del credito. Tecnocrazia e politica nel governo della moneta tra gli anni '50 e '70. In *Il governo democratico dell'economia.* Bari: De Donato.

1979. *Moneta e impero. Il sistema finanziario internazionale dal 1880 al 1914.* Torino: Einaudi.

1990. *L'Italia e il sistema finanziario internazionale 1861–1913.* Bari: Laterza.

De Felice, R. 1968. *Mussolini il fascista.* Vol. II: *L'organizzazione dello Stato fascista 1925–1929.* Torino: Einaudi.

De Grauwe, P. and Fratianni, M. 1985. Interdependence, Macroeconomics and All That. *The World Economy*, 8, 1 (March): 63–80.

De Johannis, A.J. 1904. *La conversione della rendita.* Firenze: Barbera.

De Maria, G. 1928. I saggi di riporto e deporto della lira italiana dal 1921 al 1928. *Rivista internazionale di scienze sociali*, 32, 3: 22–51, 133–84.

De Mattia, R. 1959. *L'unificazione monetaria italiana.* Archivio economico dell'unificazione italiana, series III, vol. II. Torino: ILTE.

1967. *I bilanci degli istituti di emissione italiani dal 1845 al 1936, altre serie storiche di interesse monetario e fonti.* Rome: Banca d'Italia.

1969. *I bilanci degli instituti di emissione italiana.* Torino: ILTE.

1977. *Storia del capitale della Banca d'Italia e degli instituti predecessori.* Rome: Banca d'Italia.

1978. *Storia del capitale della Banca d'Italia e degli istituti predecessori.* Rome: Banca d'Italia.

1990. *Gli istituti di emissione in Italia. I tentativi di unificazione (1843–1892).* Bari: Laterza.

1991. *Storia delle operazioni degli istituti di emissione italiani dal 1845 al 1936 attraverso i dati dei loro bilanci.* Rome: Banca d'Italia.

De Rosa, L. 1963. Il Banco di Napoli e la crisi economica del 1888–1894. Part I. *Rassegna economica*, 27, 2 (May–August): 349–431.

1964a. Il Banco di Napoli e la crisi economica del 1888–1894. Part II. *Rassegna economica*, 28, 1 (January–April): 19–111.

1964b. Il Banco di Napoli e la crisi economica del 1888–1894. Part III. *Rassegna economica*, 28, 2 (May–August): 352–430.

1965. Il Banco di Napoli e la crisi economica del 1888–1894. Part IV. *Rassegna economica*, 29, 1 (January–April): 88–146.

1982. Economics and Nationalism in Italy (1961–1914), *The Journal of European Economic History*, 11, 3: 4–11.

De Vita, A. 1947. Le variazioni del potere d'acquisto della lira. *Congiuntura Economica*, 2, 16 (June): 4–11.

De Vita, A. (ed.). 1949. *Annuario della congiuntura economica italiana 1938–1947.* Firenze: Vallecchi.

Del Vecchio, G. 1928. Considerazioni tecniche sopra il ritorno al biglietto convertibile. *Giornale degli economisti*, serie IV, XLIII, LXVIII (April): 270–88.

1932. *Cronache della lira in pace e guerra.* Milan: Treves.

Del Vecchio, E. 1979. La via italiana al protezionismo. Le relazioni economiche internazionali dell'Italia 1878–1888 (5 volumes). Roma: Archivio storico della Camera dei Deputati.

Dell'Amore, G. 1961. Il processo di costituzione della banca centrale in Italia. *Economia e storia*, 6.

Denison, E.F. 1979. *Accounting for Slower Economic Growth: the United States in the 1970s*. Washington, DC: The Brookings Institution.

Di Nardi, G. 1953. *Le banche di emissione in Italia nel secolo XIX*. Torino: UTET.

Dornbush. R. 1980. *Open Economy Macroeconomics*. New York: Basic Books.

Economic Report of the President. 1982. Washington, DC: US Government Printing Office.

Eichengreen, B. 1989. Hegemonic Stability Theories of the International Monetary System. In *Can Nations Agree?*, R. N. Cooper, B. Eichengreen, C. R. Henning, G. Holtham and R. D. Putnam (eds.). Washington, DC: Brookings Institution.

Eichengreen, B. and Wyplosz, C. 1993. The Unstable EMS. *Brookings Papers on Economic Activity*, 1: 51–124.

Einaudi, L. 1947. Discorso all'Assemblea Costituente del 18 giugno. *Interventi e relazioni parlamentari*, Vol. II. Torino: Einaudi.

    1960a. *Cronache economiche e politiche di un trentennio (1893–1925). Vol. I: 1893–1902*. Torino: Einaudi.

    1960b. *Cronache economiche e politiche di un trentennio (1893–1925). Vol. III: 1910–1914*. Torino: Einaudi.

Einzig, M. 1935. *World Finance 1914–1935*. New York: MacMillan.

Epstein, G. and Schor, J.B. 1989. The Divorce of the Banca d'Italia and the Italian Treasury: a Case Study of Central Bank Dependence. *State, Market, and Social Regulation: New Perspectives on Italy*. In P. Lange and M. Regini (eds.). Cambridge: Cambridge University Press.

Fazio, A. 1969. Monetary Base and the Control of Credit in Italy. Banca Nazionale del Lavoro. *Quarterly Review*, 89 (June): 146–69.

    1979. La politica monetaria in Italia dal 1947 al 1978. *Moneta e Credito*, 32, 127: 269–320.

    1984. Evoluzione dei metodi di controllo monetario. *Banche e Banchieri*, 11, 9–10: 703–14.

Ferrara, F. 1868. Del corso forzoso e della maniera di abolirlo. *Nuova Antologia*, 1: 503–25.

    1879. *La convenzione monetaria 5 novembre 1878 ed il corso forzoso*. Milan: Hoepli.

Ferraris, C.F. 1879. *La convenzione monetaria 5 Novembre 1878 ed il corso forzoso*. Milan: Hoepli.

Filosa, R., Rey, G.M. and Sitzia, B. 1976. Uno schema di analisi quantitativa dell'economia italiana durante il fascismo. In *L'economia italiana nel periodo fascista*, P. Ciocca and G. Toniolo (eds.). Bologna: Il Mulino.

Foa, B. 1949. *Monetary Reconstruction in Italy*. New York: King's Crown Press.

Formentini, S. 1986. *Livello e occupazione del debito pubblico interno dall?unità ad oggi*. Tesi di laurea. Milan: Università Cattolica del Sacro Cuore.

Fratianni, M. 1971. Bank Credit, Money Supply Processes, and Monetary and Fiscal Policies in an Open Economy: The Italian Experience, 1958–1969, Ph.D dissertation, Ohio State University.

    1972. Bank Credit and Money Supply Processes in an Open Economy: A Model Applicable to Italy. *Metroeconomica*, 24 (January–April): 24–69.

1976. On the Effectiveness of Monetary Policy under Fixed Rates of Exchange. *Journal of Monetary Economics*, 2, 1: 63–79.

1986. Conditions in Which Very Rapid Inflation Has Appeared: A Comment. In *The National Bureau Method, International Capital Mobility and Other Essays*, K. Brunner and A.H. Meltzer (eds.). Carnegie-Rochester Conference Series on Public Policy, Vol. 24. Amsterdam: North-Holland.

1987. Italy in the Eighties: Opportunities and Prospects. *Review of Economic Conditions in Italy*, 2: 253–77.

1988. Money Growth in Italy: The Long Record, Paper presented at the XIX Konstanzer Seminar on Monetary Theory and Monetary Policy. Konstanz, Germany.

1993a. Attitudes Toward Inflation and the Viability of Fixed Exchange Rates: Evidence from the EMS-Comment. In *A Retrospective on the Bretton Woods System*, M. Bordo and B. Eichengreen (eds.). Chicago: The University of Chicago Press.

1993b. Le Implicazioni Fiscali di Maastricht per l'Italia. *Sviluppo economico*, 1, 2: 139–59.

Fratianni, M. and Huang, H. 1995. Central Bank Reputation and Optimal Conservativeness, LSE Financial Market Group Discussion Paper no. 216. London: London School of Economics.

Fratianni, M. and Nabli, M..1979. Money Stock Control in the EEC Countries. *Weltwirtschaftliches Archiv*, 115, 3: 401–23.

Fratianni, M. and Ranuzzi de Bianchi, P. 1971. La moneta potenziale e la base monetaria aggiustata in Italia dal 1958 al 1969. *Bancaria*, 27, 3: 361–7.

Fratianni, M. and Spinelli, F. 1982. The Growth of Government in Italy: Evidence from 1861 to 1979. *Public Choice*, 39, 2: 221–43.

1984. Italy in the Gold Standard Period, 1861–1914. *A Retrospective on the Classical Gold Standard, 1821–1931*, M. Bordo and A.J. Schwartz (eds.). Chicago: University of Chicago Press.

1985. Currency Competition, Fiscal Policy and the Money Supply Process in Italy from Unification to World War I. *Journal of European Economic History*, 14 (Winter): 473–99.

Fratianni, M. and von Hagen, J. 1990. Public Choice Aspects of European Monetary Unification. *The Cato Journal*, 10: 389–411.

1992. *The European Monetary System and European Monetary Union*. Boulder and London: Westview.

1993. European Monetary Union and Central Bank Dependence. *Regional Science and Urban Economics*, 23: 401–25.

Frenkel, J. A. and Johnson, H.G. (eds.). 1976. *The Monetary Approach to the Balance of Payments*. London: George Allen and Unwin.

Friedman, M. and Schwartz, A.J. 1963. *A Monetary History of the United States, 1867–1960*. Princeton: Princeton University Press.

1982. *Monetary Trends in the United States and the United Kingdom. Their Relation to Income, Prices, and Interest Rates, 1867–1975*. Chicago: Chicago University Press (for the NBER).

Gangemi, L. 1961. Due processi di difesa della lira nel quadro delle vicende monetarie italiane dal 1918 al 1959. In *Studi in onore di Epicarmo Corbino*, D. de Marco (ed.). Milan: Giuffrè.

Garelli, A. 1879. *Le banche*. Biblioteca dell'economista, Serie III, Vol. VI. Torino: UTET.

Giavazzi, F. and Giovannini, A. 1989. *Limiting Exchange Rate Flexibility: The European Monetary System*. Cambridge, MA: MIT Press.

Giavazzi, F. and Spaventa, A. 1990. The New EMS. In *The European Monetary System in the 1990s*, P. de Grauwe and L. Papademos (eds.). London: Longman.

Gilbert, R.A. and Wood, G.E. 1986. Coping with Bank Failures: Some Lessons from the United States and the United Kingdom. Federal Reserve Bank of St. Louis. *Review* 68, 10 (December): 5–14.

Gille, B. 1968. *Les investissements francais en Italie (1815–1914)*. Archivio storico dell'unificazione italiana, serie II, vol. XVI. Torino: ILTE.

Giovannini, A. and Piga, G. 1992. Understanding the High Interest Rates of Italian Government Securities. Typescript, May.

Goodman, J. 1991. The Politics of Central Bank Dependence. *Comparative Politics*, 23, 3: 329–50

Graziani, A. 1969. *Lo sviluppo dell'economia italiana come sviluppo di una economia aperta*. Torino: Einaudi.

Grifone, P. 1971. *Il capitale finanziario in Italia*. Torino: Einaudi.

Grilli, E., Kregel, J.A. and Savona, P. 1982. Terms of Trade and Italian Economic Growth: Accounting for Miracles. Banca Nazionale del Lavoro *Quarterly Review*, 143, 4: 395–416.

Griziotti, B. 1926. *La politica finanziaria italiana. Studi sui problemi monetari e finanziari*. Milan: Istituto Editoriale Scientifico.

Gualerni, G. 1976. *dustria e fascismo*. Milan: Vita e Pensiero.

   1980. *Ricostruzione e industria. Per una interpretazione della politica industriale nel secondo dopoguerra 1943–1951*. Milan: Vita e Pensiero.

   1982. *Lo stato industriale in Italia 1890–1940*. Milan: Etas Libri.

Guarnieri, F. 1953. *Battaglie economiche tra le due grandi guerre*. Milan: Garzanti.

Hafer, R.W. and Hein, S.E. 1984. Predicting the Money Multiplier: Forecasts from Component and Aggregate Models. *Journal of Monetary Economics*, 14, 3: 375–84.

Harjoullis, G.S. 1992. *Global Bonds – Italy Special* (May 19). New York: Morgan Stanley.

Hawtrey, R.G. 1927. *The Gold Standard in Theory and Practice*. London: Longmans.

Heilperin, M.A. 1968. *Aspects of the Pathology of Money*. London: Joseph.

Hildebrand, G.H. 1965. *Growth and Structure in the Economy of Modern Italy*. Cambridge, MA: Harvard University Press.

Hirschman, A.O. 1948. Inflation and Deflation in Italy. *American Economic Review*, 38, 4: 598–606.

Holbrick, K. 1959. *Italy in International Cooperation*. Padova: Cedam.

Il Sole-24 Ore. 1991. Il Divorzio (July 26). Milan: Il Sole-24 Ore.

International Monetary Fund. various issues. *International Financial Statistics*. Washington, DC: International Monetary Fund.

Isco. various issues. *Quadri della contabilità nazionale*. Rome: Isco.

Istat. various years. *Annuario statistico italiano*. Rome: Istat.

　1957. *Indagine statistica sullo sviluppo del reddito nazionale dell'Italia dal 1861 al 1956*. Annali di Statistica, serie VIII, vol. IX. Rome: Istat.

　1976. *Sommario di statistiche storiche dell'Italia 1861–1975*. Rome: Istat.

Jannaccone, P. 1918. Relazioni fra commercio internazionale, cambi esteri e circolazione monetaria in Italia nel quarantennio 1871–1913. *Riforma Sociale* XXV, XXIX, XI–XII (November-December). Reprinted in: *Prezzi e mercati*. Torino: Einaudi, 1951.

Kendrick, J.W. 1981. International Comparisons of Recent Productivity Trends. *Contemporary Economic Problems*, W. Fellner (ed.). Washington, DC: American Enterprise Institute.

Keohane, R.O. 1984. *After Hegemony: Cooperation and Discord in the World Political Economy*. Princeton, NJ: Princeton University Press.

Keynes, J.M. 1923. *A Tract on Monetary Reform*. London: Macmillan.

Kindleberger, C.P. 1973. *The World in Depression, 1929–1939*. Berkeley and Los Angeles: University of California Press.

　1984. *A Financial History of Western Europe*. London: Allen and Unwin.

Klein, B. 1978. The Measurement of Long and Short Term Price Uncertainty: A Moving Regression Time Series Analysis. *Journal of Monetary Economics*, 16 (July): 438–53.

Klein, M. and Neumann, M.J.M. 1989. Seigniorage: What is it and Who Gets it? Projektbereich B, Discussion Paper N. B-124, University of Bonn.

Kreinin, M.E. and Officer, L.H. 1978. *The Monetary Approach to the Balance of Payments: A Survey*. Princeton Studies in International Finance, no. 43. Princeton: Princeton University Press.

Laidler, D. 1991. *The Golden Age of the Quantity Theory*. Hemel Hempstead, Hertfordshire: Philip Allan.

Lanzarone, G. 1948. La politica del credito e dei mercati finanziari in Italia. *Congiuntura Economica*, 3, 28–9 (July–August): 4–7.

League of Nations. 1922. *The Recommendations and Their Applications. A Review of Two Years. vol. II, Italy*. Geneve: Kundig.

Lehefeld, R.A. 1923. *Restoration of the World's Currencies*. London: Kings.

Lesourd, J.A. and Gerard, C. 1978. *Storia economica dell'Ottocento e del Novecento*. Milan: Isedi.

Lindbeck, A. 1983. The Recent Slowdown of Productivity Growth. *Economic Journal*, 93: 13–34.

Lindert, P.H. 1969. *Key Currencies and Gold 1900–1913*. Princeton Studies in International Finance, no. 24. Princeton: Princeton University Press.

Lutz, F.A. and Lutz, V. 1950. *Monetary and Foreign Exchange Policy in Italy*. Princeton Studies in International Finance, no. 1. Princeton: Princeton University Press.

Lutz, V. 1950. Italy: Economic Recovery and Development. *The Economics of*

Freedom: The Progress and Future of Aid Europe. H.S. Ellis (ed.). New York: Harper and Brothers.

Maddison, A. 1982. *Phases of Capitalist Development.* Oxford: Oxford University Press.

Majorana, G. 1893. *I dati statistici nella questione bancaria.* Rome: Loescher.

Mancini, M. 1947. Aspetti dell'andamento dei depositi bancari e postali rispetto alla circolazione in periodo bellico. *Congiuntura Economica*, 11, 12 (February): 4–9.

Mankiw, J.A., Miron, J.A. and Weil, D.J. 1987. The Adjustment of Expectations to a Change in Regime: A Study of the Founding of the Federal Reserve. *American Economic Review*, 77, 3 (June): 358–74.

Marcoaldi, F. (ed.). 1986. *Vent'anni di economia e politica. Le carte De' Stefani (1922–1941).* Milan: Angeli.

Marconi, M. 1979. Lineamenti di un trentennio di politica monetaria. *Capitale industriale e capitale finanziario: il caso italiano*, F. Vicarelli (ed.). Bologna: Il Mulino.

Martello, T. 1883. *La moneta e gli errori che corrono attorno ad essa.* Firenze: Le Monnier.

Masera, R.S. 1983. Inflation, Stabilization and Economic Recovery in Italy After the War: Vera Lutz's Assessment. Banca Nazionale del Lavoro, *Quarterly Review*, 144 (March): 29–50.

McCallum, B. 1989. *Monetary Economics: Theory and Policy.* New York: MacMillan Publishing.

Mengarelli, G. (ed.). 1976. *Toria monetaria e struttura finanziaria in Italia.* Venezia: Marsilio.

Menichella, D. 1956. The Contribution of the Banking System to Monetary Equilibrium and Economic Stability: the Italian Experience. Banca Nazionale del Lavoro. *Quarterly Review*, 9, 36–7 (January–June): 5–21.

Mesalles, V. 1968. Banknote Remittances: Italy's Recent Experience. Banca Nazionale del Lavoro. *Quarterly Review*, 84 (March): 87–99.

Meyer, P. A. and Neri, J. A. 1975. A Keynes–Friedman Money Demand Function. *American Economic Review*, 65, 4: 610–25.

Meyer, R.H. 1970. *Banker's Diplomacy. Monetary Stabilization in the Twenties.* New York: Columbia University Press.

Michaely, M. 1968. *Balance-of-Payment Adjustment Policies.* New York: National Bureau of Economic Research.

Migone, G. 1971. *Problemi di storia nei rapporti tra Italia e Stati Uniti.* Torino: Rosenberg and Sellier.

Miller, H.S. 1940. Italian Monetary and Exchange Policies under Fascism. *American Economic Review*, 30, 3: 554–60.

Minervini, G. 1987. Tre controlli sul pubblico risparmio, ma chi li coordina? *Corriere della Sera* (1 August).

Minford, P. 1994. The Political Economy of the Exchange Rate Mechanism, *Open Economies Review*, 5: 235–47.

Mitchell, B.R. 1962. *Abstract of British Historical Statistics.* Cambridge: Cambridge University Press.

1978. *European Historical Statistics*. New York: Columbia University Press.

Mochi, C. 1982. Commercio e turismo. *Annali dell'economia italiana, vol. 8, tomo 2: 1930–1938*. Milan: IPSOA.

Modigliani, F. and Jappelli, T. 1986. Politica fiscale e risparmio in Italia a partire dal 1860. *Rivista Milanese di Economia*, 18 (April–June): 41–78.

Modigliani, F. and Tarantelli, E. 1973. A Generalization of the Phillips Curve for a Developing Country. *Review of Economic Studies*, 40, 2 (April): 203–23.

1977. Market Forces, Trade Union Action, and the Phillips Curve in Italy. Banca Nazionale del Lavoro. *Quarterly Review*, 120, 1: 3–36.

Molinari, A. 1928. La rivalutazione della lira, i prezzi al minuto ed i salari. *Giornale degli economisti*, serie IV, XLIII, 67 (April): 334–9.

Monzilli, A. 1896. *Note e documenti per la storia delle banche di emissione in Italia*. Citta' di Castello: LAPI.

Moreau, E. 1986. *Memorie di un governatore della Banca di Francia*. Bari: Cariplo-Laterza.

Morgenstern, O. 1959. *International Financial Transactions and Business Cycles*. Princeton: Princeton University Press.

Muhleman, M. 1896. *Monetary Historical Statistics*. New York: Columbia University Press.

Muscatelli, V. A. and Spinelli, F. 1993. An Econometric and Historical Perspective on the Long-run Stability of the Demand for Money: The Case of Italy. Typescript.

Negri, G. 1990. *Giolitti e la nascita della Banca d'Italia nel 1893*. Bari: Laterza.

Nurkse, R. 1944. *International Currency Experience: Lessons of the Inter-war Period*. Princeton: Princeton University Press.

OECD. 1973. *Monetary Policy in Italy*. Paris: OECD.

Various issues. *Economic Outlook*. Paris: OECD.

Onida, F. 1974. *La bilancia dei pagamenti come vincolo alla politica economica*. Milan: Angeli.

Pantaleoni, M. 1895. La caduta della Societa' Generale di Credito Mobiliare Italiano. *Giornale degli Economisti* (April, May and November). Reprinted in *Studi storici*. Bologna: Zanichelli, 1936.

Paradisi, M. 1976. Il commercio con l'estero e la struttura industriale. In *L'economia italiana nel periodo fascista*, P. Ciocca and G. Toniolo (eds.). Bologna: Il Mulino.

Parlato, G. 1982. La politica sociale e sindacale. *Annali dell'economia italiana, vol. 6, tomo 1: 1915–1922*. Milan: IPSOA.

Penati, A. and Tullio, G. 1983. Total Domestic Credit as an Intermediate Target of Monetary Policy in Italy. In *Monetary Policy, Fiscal Policy and Economic Activity. The Italian Experience*, F. Spinelli and G. Tullio (eds.). Aldershot: Gower.

Putnam, R. D. 1993. *Making Democracy Work: Civic Traditions in Modern Italy*. Princeton, NJ: Princeton University Press.

Rasche, R. and Johannes, J. 1987. *Controlling the Growth of Monetary Aggregates*. Boston: Kluwer Academic Publishers.

Rasi, G. 1982a. La politica economica ed i conti della nazione. *Annali dell'economia italiana, vol. 6, tomo 1: 1915–1922*. Milan: IPSOA.

1982b. La politica economica ed i conti della nazione. *Annali dell'economia italiana, vol. 9, tomo 1: 1939–1945*. Milan: IPSOA.

1982c. La politica economica ed i conti della nazione. *Annali dell'economia italiana, vol. 10, tomo 1: 1946–1952*. Milan: IPSOA.

Repaci, F.A. 1962. *La finanza pubblica italiana nel secolo 1861–1960*. Bologna: Zanichelli.

Rey, G.M. 1978. Una sintesi dell'economia italiana durante il fascismo. In *L'econmia italiana 1861–1940*, G. Toniolo (ed.). Bari: Laterza.

Ripa di Meana, A. and Sarcinelli, M. 1990. Unione monetaria, competizione valutaria e controllo dlela moneta: è d'aiuto la storia italiana? Ministero del Tesoro, *L'unione economica e monetaria: problemi e strategie*. Rome: Istituto Poligrafico e Zecca dello Stato.

Robbins, L. 1935. *Di chi la colpa della grande crisi?* Torino: Einaudi.

Rolnick, A.J. and Weber, W.E. 1986. Gresham's Law or Gresham's Fallacy? Federal Reserve Bank of Minneapolis. *Quarterly Review*, 10, 1 (Winter): 17–24.

Rosa, G. 1975. *Aspetti quantitativi dello sviluppo industriale italiano*. Rome: S.I.P.I.

1982. *L'aggiustamento dell'industria italiana: aspetti settoriali, dimensionali e territoriali*. Rome: S.I.P.I.

Rossi, C. 1950. *L'assalto alla Banca di sconto*. Milan: Ceschina.

Rossi, L. 1954. Economia e buon senso. *Rivista di politica economica*, 44, 6 (June): 644–51.

Rozenraad, C. 1899. Il prestito italiano per l'abolizione del corso forzoso. *Biblioteca dell? Economista*, Appendix to Goshen, *La teoria dei cambi esteri*, serie 4, vol. II, parte II.

Saidi, N. and Huber, G. 1983. Postwar Business Cycles and Exchange Rate Regimes: Issues and Evidence. Paper presented at the Konstanz Seminar on Monetary Theory and Monetary Policy (June), Konstanz.

Saint-Etienne, C. 1984. *The Great Depression, 1929–1938: Lessons for the 1980s*. Stanford: Hoover Institution Press.

Sannucci, V. 1990. Molteplicità delle banche di emissione: ragioni economiche ed effetti sull'efficacia del controllo monetario (1860–1890). *Ricerche per la storia della Banca d'Italia*, Vol I. Bari: Laterza.

Sarcinelli, M. 1965. La creazione di liquidità e la politica della banca centrale in Italia dal 1958 al 1964. In *Letture di politica economica e finanziaria*, a cura di Banca Popolare di Milano. Milan: Banca Popolare di Milan.

Savona, P. 1993. Sviluppo, profitti e finanza in Italia. *Sviluppo Economico*, 1, 1: 29–58.

Simpson, E.S. 1949–50. Inflation, Deflation and Employment in Italy. *The Review of Economic Studies*. 17, 3: 203–25.

Smid, A. 1948. Un indice del corso delle azioni alla borsa di Milano. In *Congiuntura Economica*, 28–29 (July–August), pp. 8–14.

Southard, F.A. 1946. *The Finances of European Liberation with Special Reference to Italy*. New York: King's Crown.

Spinelli, F. 1980. The Demand for Money in the Italian Economy: 1867–1965. *Journal of Monetary Economics*, 6, 1: 83–104.

1989. *Per la storia monetaria dell'Italia*, Vol. I. Torino: Giappichelli.

1990. *Per la storia monetaria dell'Italia*, Vol. II. Torino: Giappichelli.

1991. *Per la storia monetaria dell'Italia*, Vol III. Torino: Giappichelli.

Spinelli, F. and Fratianni, M. 1991. *La storia monetaria d'Italia*. Milan: Mondadori.

Spinelli, F. and Toso, L. 1990. Il tasso di cambio settimanale a breve della lira nelle rilevazioni de Il Sole 24 Ore: 1865–1985. In F. Spinelli, *Per la storia monetaria dell'Italia*, vol. II. Torino: Giappichelli.

Spinelli, F. and Vismara, D. 1990. Quali garanzie per i sottoscrittori dei titoli di stato? Una rilettura del rapporto della Commissione Economica dell'Assemblea Costituente. In *Per la storia monetaria dell'Italia*, Vol. II, F. Spinelli (ed.). Torino: Giappichelli.

Sraffa, P. 1922. The Bank Crisis in Italy. *Economic Journal* (June). Reprinted in F. Cesarini and M. Onado (eds.). 1979. *Struttura e stabilità del sisterna finanziario*. Bologna: Il Mulino.

Stern, R.M. 1967. *Foreign Trade and Economic Growth in Italy*. New York: Praeger.

Stringher, B. 1926. Unificazione dell'emissione e deflazione cartacea. *Nuova Antologia*, fasc. 1311 (1 November): 64–83.

Supino, C. 1895. *Storia della circolazione bancaria in Italia dal 1860 al 1894*. Torino: Bocca.

1929. *Storia della circolazione cartacea in Italia dal 1860 al 1928*. Milan: Società Editorale Libraria.

Swoboda, A.K. 1983. Exchange Rate Regimes and U.S. European Policy Interdependence. *International Monetary Fund Staff Papers* 30, 1: 75–108.

Tabellini, G. 1988. Monetary and Fiscal Policy Coordination with a High Public Debt. In *High Public Debt: The Italian Experience*, F. Giavazzi and L. Spaventa (eds.). Cambridge: Cambridge University Press.

Tagliacarne, G. 1928. Prezzi all'ingrosso e rivalutazione della lira. *Giornale degli Economisti*, serie IV, 43 (67): 329–33.

Tasca, A. 1927. La rivalutazione della lira e i prestiti americani. *Lo stato operaio* (March–April): 278–86.

Tattara, G., and Toniolo, G. 1976. L'industria manifatturiera: cicli, politiche e mutamenti di struttura (1921–37). In *L'economia italiana nel periodo fascista*, P. Ciocca and Toniolo, G. (eds.). Bologna: Il Mulino.

Thaon di Revel, P. 1942. La finanza di guerra. *Rivista ternazionale di Scienze Economiche*, 14,3: 203–38.

Toniolo, G. 1989. *La Banca d'Italia e l'economia di guerra 1914–1919*. Bari: Laterza.

Triffin, R. 1964. *The Evolution of the International Monetary System: Historical Reappraisal and Future Perspective*. Princeton Studies in International Finance, n. 12. Princeton: Princeton University Press.

Trupiano, G. 1982. La politica fiscale e la finanza pubblica. In *Annali dell'economia italiana*, vol. VI, tomo 1, *1915–1922*, a cura di IPSOA. Milan: IPSOA.

Tullio, G. 1977. 'Monetary Equilibrium and Balance of Payments Adjustment:

Empirical Tests of the U.S. and Italian Balance of Payments'. Ph.D. dissertation. University of Chicago.

Tullio, G. 1981. Demand Management and Exchange Rate Policy: The Italian Experience. International Monetary Fund, *Staff Papers,* 28 (March): 80–117.

United Nations Economic Commission. 1950. *Economic Survey of Europe in 1949.* Geneva.

US Congress-Senate Commission of Gold and Silver Inquiry. 1925. *European Currency and Finance.* Washington, DC: US Government Printing Office.

Valli, V. 1976. *L'economia e la politica economica italiana (1945–1975).* Milan: Etas Libri.

van Ypersele, J. 1979. Operating Principles and Procedures of the EMS. In *The EMS: Its Promise and Prospects*, P. H. Trezise (ed.). Washington, DC: Brookings Institution.

Viner, J. 1937. *Studies in the theories of in International trade.* New York: Harper and Brother.

Vitale, E. 1972. *La riforma degli istituti di emissione e gli scandali bancari in Italia, 1892–1896.* Roma: Archivio Storico della Camera dei Deputati.

Volpi, G. 1928. La riforma monetaria illustrata dal ministro delle Finanze (speech at the Senate on February 17, 1928). *Giornale degli economisti*, Serie IV, XLIII, LXVII: 247–68.

White, H. 1980. A Heteroskedasticity-consistent Co-variance Matrix Estimator and Direct Test for Heteroskedasticity. *Econometrica*, 48: 817–38

Willis, H. 1901. *A History of the Latin Monetary Union.* Chicago: University of Chicago Press.

Yeager, L.B. 1976. *International Monetary Relations: Theory, History and Policy.* New York: Harper and Row.

1981. *Experiences with Stopping Inflation.* Washington, DC: American Enterprise Institute.

Zamagni, V. 1976. La dinamica dei salari nel settore industriale. In *L'economia italiana nel periodo fascista*, P. Ciocca and G. Toniolo (eds.). Bologna: Il Mulino.

Index of authors

Ackley, G. 196
Alesina, A. 5, 46, 250
Alberti, M. 2, 114n, 118–19, 137–8, 149, 151n
Amantia, A. 108, 120, 130
Andreatta, B. 241
Azzolini, V. 165, 165n, 221

Bachi, R. 125–6
Baffi, P. 149, 161, 165n, 166, 167n, 168–70, 170n, 171, 179, 181, 183–4, 196–7, 231, 235, 235n
Bagehot, W. 103
Barberi, B. 166
Basevi, G. 208n, 214n
Benini, R. 87, 90
Bini-Smaghi, L. 204n, 231n
Bloomfield, A. 40, 93n
Bomhoff, E.J. 37n
Bonelli, F. 99–100, 102
Bordo, M. 20n
Borgatta, G. 76n, 83
Box, G.E.P. 38n
Bresciani Turroni, C. 118, 120n, 181n, 185n
Bruins, G.M. 114
Brunner, K. 30, 37–8, 133n, 207
Bruno, M. 22
Burger, A.E. 27
Busacca, R. 63n
Buttiglione, L. 242, 242n

Cagan, P. 30
Calliari, S. 17
Canovai, T. 55n, 63, 83
Capie, F. 125n
Caranza, C. 218n, 219
Cardarelli, S. 63n
Carli, G. 178, 196, 198
Cassel, G. 114, 120n, 121, 124, 149
Castronuovo, V. 104, 169, 180
Chouraqui, J.C. 243

Ciampi, C.A. 188, 244n
Cianci, E. 96, 121, 124, 126
Ciocca, P. 141–3
Cohen, J.S. 151n
Confalonieri, A. 82, 87–9n, 94, 97, 99, 99n, 104–5
Coppola d'Anna, F. 161–2, 166
Corbino, E. 2, 56, 68n, 73, 75, 84, 121, 161n, 167n, 179
Cornaro, V. 2, 55n, 68n, 70n, 73–4
Cotula, F. 216, 220

Da Pozzo, M. 55n, 70, 73, 79, 94
De Angelis, G. 114, 138, 198
De Cecco, M. 47, 57n, 65, 68n, 76n, 84n, 94n, 100, 171, 175, 182, 182n, 187
De Felice, R. 139
De Grauwe, P. 214n
De Maria, G. 139, 147
De Mattia, R. 8, 11n, 12, 55n, 63–4, 64n, 69, 70n, 72, 76, 79, 85n, 102, 110, 127–8, 140, 166
De Rosa, L. 82, 87n, 89n
De Vita, A. 161n, 164, 165n, 169
Del Vecchio, G. 84, 118–19, 137, 145, 147, 149, 149n
Dell'Amore, G. 63
Denison, E.F. 214n
Di Nardi, G. 2, 55n, 57, 70n, 72, 72n, 87, 89, 89n, 90, 105
Dornbush, R. 40

Eichengreen, B. 236, 256
Einaudi, L. 76n, 102, 113, 114n, 118–19, 120–1, 171, 175, 177
Einzig, M. 123n, 124, 127, 131
Epstein, G. 241

Fazio, A. 209–10, 211n, 218n, 219–20, 229–32
Felloni, G. 55n, 70, 72, 79, 94

296

Ferrara, F. 63n, 74, 76
Ferraris, C.F. 68n, 76–7
Filosa, R. 138–9, 141, 143
Foa, B. 161, 161n, 162, 168–9, 176, 181
Formentini, S. 11n
Fratianni, M. 3, 9, 9n, 24, 34n, 37, 37n, 38,
  38n, 39, 46, 48, 117, 121, 124, 125n, 166,
  181, 200, 204n, 214n, 216, 222–3n, 235n,
  236–8, 243, 246, 246n, 247, 253
Frenkel, J.A. 40n
Friedman, M. 12, 17, 27, 30, 76, 120n,
  132–3, 133–4n, 137n

Gangemi, L. 169, 181n
Garelli, A. 55n, 56, 63, 63n
Gerard, C. 66n
Giavazzi, F. 236, 251
Gilbert, R.A. 75n
Giovannini, A. 236, 247
Gille, B. 67n, 73, 84, 88
Goodman, J. 241n
Graziani, A. 214n
Grifone, P. 142
Grilli, E. 226n
Griziotti, B. 114n
Gualerni, G. 141–2, 149n, 151, 151n, 161n,
  184
Guarnieri, F. 119n, 151

Hafer, R.W. 37n
Hawtrey, R.G. 66, 67n
Heilperin, M.A. 113, 120n
Hein, S.E. 37n
Hildebrand, G.H. 181, 183, 185
Hirschman, A.O. 171, 181n, 182–3
Holbrick, K. 198
Huang, H. 46
Huber, G. 214n

Jannaccone, P. 76n, 83n
Jappelli, T. 117n
Jenkins, G.M. 38n
Johannes, J. 37n
Johnson, H.G. 40n

Kendrick, J.W. 214n
Keohane, R.O. 236
Keynes, J.M. 120n, 131
Kindleberger, C.P. 74, 85n, 236
Klein, B. 20n
Klein, M. 42n
Kregel, J.A. 226n
Kreinin, M.E. 40n

Laidler, D. 65n
Lanzarone, G. 181n

Lehefeld, R.A. 120n
Lesourd, J.A. 66n
Lindbeck, A. 214n
Lindert, P.H. 72, 118n
Lutz, F.A. 171, 181–2, 184, 186
Lutz, V. 161, 171, 179, 181–2, 184, 185n,
  186

Maddison, A. 214n
Majorana, G. 73–4
Mancini, M. 164, 165n
Mankiw, J.A. 94n
Marani, U. 221
Marcoaldi, F. 141
Marconi, M. 187
Martello, T. 68n
Masera, R.S. 181n
Meltzer, A.H. 30, 37–8
Mengarelli, G. 220
Menichella, D. 138, 197
Mesalles, V. 208n
Meyer, R.H. 143
Michaely, M. 40
Micossi, S. 220
Migone, G. 141–3
Miller, H.S. 151n
Minervini, G. 187
Minford, P. 239n
Miron, J.A. 94n
Mitchell, B.R. 12, 148
Mochi, C. 151
Modigliani, F. 117n, 214n
Molinari, A. 149n
Monzilli, A. 55n
Moreau, E. 139, 143
Morgenstern, O. 76n
Muhleman, M. 67–8n
Muscatelli, V.A. 105

Nabli, N. 37–8n
Negri, G. 87n, 92n
Neumann, M.J.M. 42n
Nurkse, R. 40, 149

Officer, L.H. 40n
Onida, F. 208n

Pantaleoni, M. 87n
Paradisi, M. 142, 150–1n
Parlato, G. 114
Penati, A. 217, 220
Piga, G. 247
Prati, A. 242, 242n
Price, R.W.R. 243
Putnam, R.D. 216

Subject Index

Aggregate supply
  shifts in, 161
Allied military lira, 276
Allied Military Relief Programme, 180
Allies, 165–6
Andreatta, Beniamino, 240, 256, 264
Ansaldo, 138
Association of Italian Industries, 142
Australia, 268
Austria, 265, 269
Austria–Hungary, 114, 117, 269
Authorities' credibility, 139, 181, 256

Bagehot, Walter, 102
Balance-of-payments
  capital account, 202
  crisis, 184, 223, 229
  current account, 202, 208
  surplus, 202
  turnaround, 209
Banca Commerciale Italiana, 4, 104, 272
Banca Generale, 95
Banca d'Italia (BI), 13, 28–9, 46, 53, 64, 87, 92, 234
  Annual Reports of, 3, 9, 109, 127–8
  Article 81 of Republican Constitution and, 188
  Bollettino Statistico, 8
  competent senior management and, 189
  conservative, 239, 243
  dependence on government, 156
  divorce, 2, 24, 240
  domestic variables, 99
  Federal Reserve System and, 271
  government securities
    secondary market, 241
  governors
    appointment, 186
    Baffi, 3, 222, 234, 238–42, 256, 264, 278
    Carli, 3, 47, 208, 234, 239, 256, 278
    Ciampi, 3, 234, 239–40, 242–3, 256, 264, 280

  Einaudi, 158, 175, 177–9, 189
  Fazio, 209, 234
  Menichella, 3, 158, 169, 174, 182, 185, 189, 199, 243, 278
  independence, 1, 5, 13, 22, 239, 242, 244, 254
  international reserves, 99, 117
    accumulation in, 151
    excessive?, 185
    loss in the 1930s, 150
  management, 127
  monetary constitution, 243
  moral suasion, 224
  open market operations, 217
  political leverage of, 189
  politics and, 186–9
  profit maximisations, 99, 271
  public-interest institution, 156
  rediscounting of agricultural bills, 177
  shareholders, 99, 272
  sterilisation instruments, 197
  Treasury
    auctions, 241
    conto corrente di tesoreria, 254
    dependence on, 188
    loans to, 154, 188, 220
    relations with, 156
    reserve requirement, 254
  UIC and, 178
Banca di Roma, 4, 13, 138, 272
Banca Italiana di Sconto, 119, 138, 272
Banca Nazionale, 268
Banca Nazionale del Lavoro, 4
Bank credit, 171, 276
  interest rate and, 220
  money and, 181
  money multiplier and, 171
  multiplier, 171, 276
  squeeze, 182
Bank deposits, 174
  transaction value, 38
Bank of England, 118, 272

Bank of France, 67
Banking crisis, 87–9, 260
Banking laws
  1862, of, 66
  1866, of, 53, 77
  1868, of, 53
  1870, of, 78
  1874, of, 53, 79–81, 86
  1880, of, 53
  1883, of, 86
  1884, of, 86
  1893, of, 92
  1895, of, 100
  1897, of, 100
  1926, of, 13, 144, 170
  1927, of, 146
  1928, of, 146–7
  1936, of, 4, 13, 47, 153–6, 174, 187, 259
Banks
  agricultural sector, and, 87
  banks of issue (see below)
  borrowings
    from BI, 201–3
    from rest of the world, 201–3
  ceilings, 279
  credit allocations, 221–2
  degree of specialisation, 87
  depository, 4
  dismantling constraints, 242
  financing farm land regulations, 93
  government strategic planning, subject to, 187
  industry, and, 87
  international financial markets, 88
  lack of confidence in, 120
  loan ceilings, 221–2
  merchant, 154
  net foreign position, 208, 210, 232, 278
    BI regulations, 201
  non-performing assets, 87
  ordinary credit institutions, 4
  portfolio constraints, 221–2, 279
  rescue operations, 88, 155
  real estate, and, 87
  separations between, 155
  short- and long-term financing, 155
  special credit institutions, 4
  subjugation to politics, 156
  supervision, 155
Banks of issue, 3
  Banca degli Stati Parmensi, 60–1
  Banca delle Quattro Legazioni, 59, 61
  Banca di Genova, 55
  Banca di Sconto di Firenze, 57
  Banca di Sconto di Livorno, 57
  Banca di Torino, 55, 271

Banca Nazionale degli Stati Sardi, 46, 55–6, 58, 64, 70
Banca Nazionale nel Regno d'Italia (BN), 5, 13, 46, 57, 61, 63–5, 70, 72–5, 78, 80, 88, 90, 92
Banca Nazionale Toscana, 5, 58, 64, 70, 80
Banca Romana (Banca dello Stato Pontificio), 5, 58–9, 80, 82, 90–2, 97
Banca Toscana di Credito per le Industrie e il Commercio d'Italia, 5, 60, 80
Banco delle Due Sicilie, 59–60
Banco di Napoli, 5, 13, 59, 80, 92, 95, 97
Banco di Sicilia, 5, 13, 80, 92, 95, 97
  before unification, 53–62
  competition among, 3, 97
  issue monopolist, 3, 44, 61–2
  Stabilimento Mercatile di Venezia, 60–1
  supervision, 79, 87
Barberi, 161, 166
Belgium, 66–7, 143, 153, 237, 269
Berlin, 70
bf ratio, 201–3, 213
bh ratio, 201–3, 213
Bimetallism, 65–8
  gold-silver exchange rate, 66–7
  silver, 269
Boccardo, 168
Bologna, 125, 241
Bread price, 126–7
Bretton Woods, 13–14, 17, 31, 34, 188, 193, 260, 263
Brussels International Monetary Conference of 1920, 273
Budget deficits, 22–4, 88, 213
Bulgaria, 269
Bundesbank, 5, 237, 244

California, 268
Canovai, 268
Capital circuit
  direct, 163–4
  indirect, 164
Capital movements
  controls on, 19, 47, 208, 222–4, 229
  free, reservations about 199
  illegal, 208, 224, 279
  interest rates and, 222
  tax-induced arbitrage, 208, 278
Caporetto, 109
Carli, Guido, 195, 277
Cassa del Mezzogiorno, 11
Cassa Depositi e Prestiti, 5–6, 25–8
Cassa Integrazione Guadagni, 251
Cavour, 46, 56–7, 63
Competitiveness, 225–6